Applications of Computational Intelligence, Volume 2

Applications of Computational Intelligence, Volume 2

Guest Editors

Yue Wu
Kai Qin
Maoguo Gong
Qiguang Miao

Basel • Beijing • Wuhan • Barcelona • Belgrade • Novi Sad • Cluj • Manchester

Guest Editors

Yue Wu
School of Computer Science
and Technology
Xidian University
Xian
China

Kai Qin
Department of Computer
Science and Software
Engineering
Swinburne University
of Technology
Victoria
Australia

Maoguo Gong
School of Electronic
Engineering
Xidian University
Xian
China

Qiguang Miao
School of Computer Science
and Technology
Xidian University
Xian
China

Editorial Office
MDPI AG
Grosspeteranlage 5
4052 Basel, Switzerland

This is a reprint of articles from the Special Issue published online in the open access journal *Electronics* (ISSN 2079-9292) (available at: www.mdpi.com/journal/electronics/special_issues/L1W153433S).

For citation purposes, cite each article independently as indicated on the article page online and using the guide below:

Lastname, A.A.; Lastname, B.B. Article Title. *Journal Name* **Year**, *Volume Number*, Page Range.

ISBN 978-3-7258-1912-6 (Hbk)
ISBN 978-3-7258-1911-9 (PDF)
https://doi.org/10.3390/books978-3-7258-1911-9

© 2024 by the authors. Articles in this book are Open Access and distributed under the Creative Commons Attribution (CC BY) license. The book as a whole is distributed by MDPI under the terms and conditions of the Creative Commons Attribution-NonCommercial-NoDerivs (CC BY-NC-ND) license (https://creativecommons.org/licenses/by-nc-nd/4.0/).

Contents

Ying Li, Ning Wang, Wei Zhang, Qing Liu and Feng Liu
Discrete Artificial Fish Swarm Algorithm-Based One-Off Optimization Method for Multiple Co-Existing Application Layer Multicast Routing Trees
Reprinted from: *Electronics* **2024**, *13*, 894, doi:10.3390/electronics13050894 . . . . **1**

Chenhuzhe Shao, Yue Liu, Zhedian Zhang, Fulin Lei and Jinglun Fu
Fast Prediction Method of Combustion Chamber Parameters Based on Artificial Neural Network
Reprinted from: *Electronics* **2023**, *12*, 4774, doi:10.3390/electronics12234774 . . . . **23**

Xianhe Wang, Mu Qiao, Ying Li, Adriano Tavares, Qian Qiao and Yanchun Liang
Deep-Learning-Based Water Quality Monitoring and Early Warning Methods: A Case Study of Ammonia Nitrogen Prediction in Rivers
Reprinted from: *Electronics* **2023**, *12*, 4645, doi:10.3390/electronics12224645 . . . . **42**

Lei Lu, Tongfei Liu, Fenlong Jiang, Bei Han, Peng Zhao and Guoqiang Wang
DFANet: Denoising Frequency Attention Network for Building Footprint Extraction in Very-High-Resolution Remote Sensing Images
Reprinted from: *Electronics* **2023**, *12*, 4592, doi:10.3390/electronics12224592 . . . . **60**

Jun Yang, Zilu Wu and Renbiao Wu
Micro-Expression Spotting Based on VoVNet, Driven by Multi-Scale Features
Reprinted from: *Electronics* **2023**, *12*, 4459, doi:10.3390/electronics12214459 . . . . **78**

Tao Wu, Shuo Xiong, Hui Liu, Yangyang Zhao, Haoran Tuo, Jiaxin Zhang and Huaizheng Liu
PSRGAN: Perception-Design-Oriented Image Super Resolution Generative Adversarial Network
Reprinted from: *Electronics* **2023**, *12*, 4420, doi:10.3390/electronics12214420 . . . . **92**

Bing Li and Qi Liu
Optimal Scheduling of Emergency Materials Based on Gray Prediction Model under Uncertain Demand
Reprinted from: *Electronics* **2023**, *12*, 4337, doi:10.3390/electronics12204337 . . . . **110**

Junkai Yi and Lin Guo
AHP-Based Network Security Situation Assessment for Industrial Internet of Things
Reprinted from: *Electronics* **2023**, *12*, 3458, doi:10.3390/electronics12163458 . . . . **132**

Fangchun Dong, Jingbing Li, Uzair Aslam Bhatti, Jing Liu, Yen-Wei Chen and Dekai Li
Robust Zero Watermarking Algorithm for Medical Images Based on Improved NasNet-Mobile and DCT
Reprinted from: *Electronics* **2023**, *12*, 3444, doi:10.3390/electronics12163444 . . . . **152**

Dekai Li, Jingbing Li, Uzair Aslam Bhatti, Saqib Ali Nawaz, Jing Liu, Yen-Wei Chen and Lei Cao
Hybrid Encrypted Watermarking Algorithm for Medical Images Based on DCT and Improved DarkNet53
Reprinted from: *Electronics* **2023**, *12*, 1554, doi:10.3390/electronics12071554 . . . . **169**

Chao Xiang, Cong Fu, Deng Cai and Xiaofei He
Modeling Noncommutative Composition of Relations for Knowledge Graph Embedding
Reprinted from: *Electronics* **2023**, *12*, 1348, doi:10.3390/electronics12061348 . . . . **186**

Article

Discrete Artificial Fish Swarm Algorithm-Based One-Off Optimization Method for Multiple Co-Existing Application Layer Multicast Routing Trees

Ying Li [1,2], Ning Wang [1,2], Wei Zhang [3], Qing Liu [4] and Feng Liu [1,2,*]

1. School of Computer Science, Xi'an Polytechnic University, Xi'an 710048, China; 20190503@xpu.edu.cn (Y.L.); wangning@stu.xpu.edu.cn (N.W.)
2. Shaanxi Key Laboratory of Clothing Intelligence, Xi'an Polytechnic University, Xi'an 710048, China
3. China Mobile System Integration Co., Ltd., Xi'an 710077, China; zhangwei1@cmict.chinamobile.com
4. Department of Information and Control, Xi'an University of Technology, Xi'an 710018, China; liuqing@xaut.edu.cn
* Correspondence: liufeng@xpu.edu.cn

Abstract: As an effective multicast application mechanism, the application layer multicast (ALM) determines the path of data transmission through a routing tree. In practical applications, multiple multicast sessions often occur simultaneously; however, few studies have considered this situation. A feasible solution is to sequentially optimize each co-existing ALM routing tree. However, this approach can lead to node congestion, and, even if the node out-degree reservation strategy is adopted, an optimal solution may not be obtained. In this study, to solve the problem of routing tree construction for multiple co-existing application layer multicast sessions, an optimization model that minimizes the overall delay and instability is constructed, and a one-off optimization method based on the discrete artificial fish swarm algorithm (DAFSA) is proposed. First, Steiner node sets corresponding to the multicast sessions are selected. Then, the routing trees for each multicast session are obtained through the improved spanning tree algorithm based on the complete graph composed of Steiner node sets. The experimental results show that the proposed method can simultaneously obtain multiple co-existing ALM routing trees with a low total delay and low instability. Even if the input is a single multicast session, it can lead to ALM routing trees with a lower delay and less instability than other algorithms, and the introduction of a penalty function can effectively avoid the problem of excessive replication and forwarding loads on some end-hosts. In addition, the proposed algorithm is insensitive to parameter changes and exhibits good stability and convergence properties for networks of different sizes.

Keywords: multiple co-existing ALM routing trees; node congestion; one-off optimization; DAFSA

Citation: Li, Y.; Wang, N.; Zhang, W.; Liu, Q.; Liu, F. Discrete Artificial Fish Swarm Algorithm-Based One-Off Optimization Method for Multiple Co-Existing Application Layer Multicast Routing Trees. *Electronics* **2024**, *13*, 894. https://doi.org/10.3390/electronics13050894

Academic Editor: Christos J. Bouras

Received: 4 February 2024
Revised: 21 February 2024
Accepted: 23 February 2024
Published: 26 February 2024

Copyright: © 2024 by the authors. Licensee MDPI, Basel, Switzerland. This article is an open access article distributed under the terms and conditions of the Creative Commons Attribution (CC BY) license (https://creativecommons.org/licenses/by/4.0/).

1. Introduction

With the increasing number of Internet users and the constantly updating and evolving forms of Internet, the proportion of real-time multimedia transmission application scenarios has increased significantly, leading to higher requirements for information transmission. Under the current application requirements, IP multicast technology has developed rapidly. As a one-to-many communication mode, IP multicast technology can effectively save network bandwidth and reduce the network load. It is suitable for applications that are centralized in time and distributed in space, such as video conferencing, streaming media, and so on. However, due to the charging mechanisms and technical limitations of Internet service providers (ISPs), the popularity of IP multicasting [1,2] on the Internet is restricted. In contrast, the application layer multicast (ALM) [3] migrates multicast data transmission from the IP layer to the application layer; data are replicated and forwarded through end-hosts. Furthermore, such approaches have the advantages of being easy to deploy and economical, as communication between the underlying layers of ALM sessions is still based on the very widespread unicast technology.

The key in application layer multicast communication is the construction of an ALM routing tree, which is mainly used to determine the tree structure in which data are delivered from the sender to all the receivers in the group. ALM routing trees are composed of user nodes, which may exit or fail. This uncontrollability can lead to instability in the ALM routing tree, thus affecting the ability of users to receive multicast data [4]. Many researchers have attempted to reduce the instability caused by user nodes' behavior by optimizing the topology of ALM routing trees [5]. End-hosts with high stability are more easily used as core nodes to transmit the data based on the behavior and attributes of the user nodes. To optimize the ALM routing tree topology, Cao et al. have established an instantaneous stability model for the application layer multicast [6] and successfully addressed the bounded-delay and high-stability model challenges [7]. In application layer multicast optimization, the delay is also an important optimization objective. Huo et al. proposed an algorithm based on the stability probability and contribution link of nodes (CL-S) [8]. This approach incorporates considerations for node out-degree and edge delay. Mercan et al. proposed the virtual direction multicast (VDM) [9] and noted that, as long as the virtual distance is based on the delay and the stability, the VDM can construct a stable ALM routing tree with a low transmission delay. Li et al. have noted that in the coverage network, apart from the link delay, the replication delay of user nodes in processing messages should also be considered [10]. Liao et al. have proposed an ALM model based on the node potential (NP) and a topological index (TI), which is suitable for applications in large-scale, real-time multimedia environments [11]. Li et al. have proposed a class of algorithms that create a greedy multicast tree based on the ratio of fan-out to delay (RFD) and the probability of terminal stability to obtain a high performance in multicast sessions [12]. This problem belongs to the class of combinatorial optimization problems, which is characterized by a high degree of complexity and computational difficulty. However, intelligent algorithms have some significant advantages in this regard. Some scholars have utilized neural networks to solve similar problems [13,14]. Some scholars have used evolutionary algorithms to solve it. For example, Pan et al. have designed a genetic algorithm to minimize the end-to-end delay under the out-degree constraint [15]. In addition to the delay, Ma et al. have considered the average path stretch and used the artificial fish swarm algorithm to solve the problem [16]. Based on previous research, Liu et al. have further considered the instability index of an ALM routing tree and designed an encoding-free non-dominated sorting genetic algorithm to simultaneously optimize the total delay and instability of the ALM routing tree [5].

The above algorithms mainly optimize the delay and stability of ALM routing trees; however, several problems remain to be solved. The existing research has been optimized under a single conversation scenario. However, multiple multicast sessions existing simultaneously is fairly common. At present, studies on the simultaneous optimization of multiple co-existing ALM routing trees are rare. One feasible method for achieving this is to use a single ALM routing tree construction method multiple times; that is, the algorithms are used sequentially to construct each ALM routing tree. It is worth noting that, to improve the stability of data transmission, when constructing the ALM routing tree, the user nodes with a higher stability are preferentially selected as the core nodes for data forwarding. However, if these user nodes appear in multiple co-existing ALM routing trees at the same time, these user nodes' out-degree (the number of times end-hosts copy and forward the data) significantly increases. Due to the limitations in the ability of end-hosts to copy and forward data, when the out-degree of user nodes is too large, node congestion will occur. This is especially relevant for forwarding nodes that are close to the source and may experience massive stress issues [17], further affecting the stability of the ALM routing tree. Therefore, when multiple ALM routing trees are optimized at the same time, the out-degree of the user nodes in each ALM routing tree needs to be reasonably distributed to ensure that the total out-degree of each end-host does not exceed their capability.

This study aims to obtain multiple co-existing ALM routing trees based on multiple co-existing multicast sessions while striking a balance between minimizing the total delay and instability of these ALM routing trees. We introduce the node out-degree as a constraint to prevent the instability of multicast sessions caused by node congestion. First, a low delay and low instability model of multiple co-existing ALM routing trees is established. To achieve the optimization goal, a one-off solution method is proposed in this study. In this method, the encoding of the DAFSA represents the selection scheme of Steiner node sets for multiple multicast sessions, and then multiple ALM routing trees are obtained from the complete graph corresponding to the multiple Steiner node sets through the use of the spanning tree algorithm. The fitness function in the DAFSA is used to evaluate the generated ALM routing tree, which is iterated continuously to find the optimal ALM routing tree. Node congestion analysis is performed on the designed algorithm to verify the effectiveness of the algorithm in dealing with the node out-degree constraints, and the performance of the algorithm is verified through detailed simulation experiments. Due to the large difference in the importance of the two objective functions—namely, the delay and the instability—a weight selection method is used to assist in decision making.

The rest of this paper is organized as follows. In Section 2, the constructed application layer multicast stability model is introduced. In Section 3, the idea to solve the model of the problem is introduced, which is divided into two parts: selecting the Steiner point sets and improving the spanning tree algorithm. In Section 4, the design of the DAFSA and the improvement of Prim's spanning tree algorithm are described in detail. In Section 5, exhaustive simulation experiments are shown, and the obtained results are analyzed. In Section 6, the experimental results and the design approach of this paper are discussed. In Section 7, a summary is given.

2. Optimization Model for Multiple Co-Existing ALM Routing Trees

The application layer network can be expressed as $G = (V, E)$, consisting of a vertex set V and an edge set E. $v \in V$ represents a user node and $e \in E$ represents the communication channel between two user nodes. For a communication channel e, the transmission delay is denoted as $d(e)$, and the delay caused by message processing in the user node is denoted as $d(v)$. The user node v has a probability $p(v)$ of leaving from graph G. For a user node v, the out-degree is denoted as Od_v (which cannot exceed D_v), and the number of its descendants is denoted as Nd_v. In this paper, we mainly optimize the delay and instability of ALM routing trees. The routing tree for a single multicast session, including one source and multiple destinations, can be denoted as $T_k = \{V^{T_k}, E^{T_k}\}$. The optimization model for multiple co-existing ALM routing trees needs to be based on K groups as the source and M destinations, generating K ALM routing trees, which are denoted as $T_1, T_2, \cdots T_k, \cdots T_K$. The out-degree of user node $v_i^{T_k}$ in ALM routing tree T_k is denoted as $Od_{v_i^{T_k}}$.

2.1. Delay

Delay refers to the time required for data to travel from a source node to a destination node. In an application layer multicast session, the intermediate nodes that forward data are the end-hosts. The equipment of the end-hosts has a limited forwarding capability, so the processing delay cannot be ignored. Therefore, the delay in this paper includes two parts: the transmission delay and the processing delay in end-hosts. The delay of the ALM routing tree T_k is denoted as $f_1(T_k)$, and the total delay is calculated as shown in Equation (1).

$$\min \sum_{k=1}^{K} f_1(T_k) = \sum_{k=1}^{K} \left(\sum_{e_i^{T_k} \in E^{T_k}} d(e_i^{T_k}) + \sum_{v_i^{T_k} \in V^{T_k}} d(v_i^{T_k}) Od_{v_i^{T_k}} \right) \qquad (1)$$

2.2. Instability

Instability mainly focuses on the exit and failure of user nodes. Node exiting means that a user node voluntarily leaves the application layer multicast session, while user node failure means that a user node leaves the application layer multicast session without notifying any other user nodes. In the ALM routing tree, the exit and failure behaviors of non-leaf nodes cause their descendant nodes to lose connectivity with the root node of the multicast tree.

2.2.1. Reducing the Impact of User Nodes' Exiting Behavior

User nodes exiting is a spontaneous behavior. As the distribution of the online times for the end-hosts in multicast sessions shows a heavy-tailed phenomenon [7,18], this study pays more attention to the probability of user nodes exiting and uses the average number of descendant user nodes affected by the exit of the user nodes to measure the instability of ALM routing trees. The instability of ALM routing tree T_k is denoted as $f_2(T_k)$, and the total instability is calculated as shown in Equation (2).

$$\min \sum_{k=1}^{K} f_2(T_k) = \sum_{k=1}^{K} \left(\frac{1}{1 + Nd_{source^{T_k}}} \sum_{v_i^{T_k} \in V^{T_k}} p(v_i^{T_k}) Nd_{v_i^{T_k}} \right) \quad (2)$$

2.2.2. Reducing the Risk of User Nodes' Failure

User node failure is a passive behavior, which usually occurs as user nodes lose the ability to forward data due to experiencing a heavy load. Therefore, in this study, the out-degree of a node is limited to reduce the load on the end-host. Equation (3) is the constraint.

$$s.t. \sum_{k=1}^{K} Od_{v_i^{T_k}} \leq D_v \quad (3)$$

In this study, the delay and instability are considered as the optimization objectives. However, these two objective functions may be in conflict. To find an appropriate trade-off in the multi-objective problem, weights for the objective functions are introduced to convert the multi-objective problem into a single-objective problem. Equation (4) is the specific formula.

$$\min \quad w_1 \sum_{k=1}^{K} f_1(T_k) + w_2 \sum_{k=1}^{K} f_2(T_k) \quad (4)$$

3. One-Off Optimization

The problem of ALM routing tree construction is essentially the Steiner tree problem in graph theory [19,20]. This problem requires finding the optimal tree that contains specified terminal nodes. However, solving this problem is very complicated: it has been proven to be NP-complete [21], which means that there is no effective algorithm for solving it in polynomial time, and the solution space can be searched only with methods of exponential or even factorial complexity.

In the construction of multiple co-existing ALM routing trees, multiple co-existing application layer multicast sessions correspond to multiple Steiner trees. This further escalates the difficulty of solving the problem, as different multicast sessions may share nodes, and the out-degree of a node needs to be guaranteed not to exceed the performance limit of the node.

Although the co-existing Steiner tree optimization problem is difficult to solve, the spanning tree problem is relatively simple, which involves finding a single tree that contains all the vertices. This has been studied in depth and includes the minimum spanning tree problem [22,23], the degree-constrained minimum spanning tree problem [24], the multi-objective spanning tree problem [25], and so on.

In addition, it is very difficult to rationally allocate the out-degree of nodes between multiple co-existing ALM routing trees, which often results in an inability to obtain a feasible solution. However, the good adaptability and global search ability of the DAFSA enable it to perform well when dealing with problems involving complex constraints [26]. At present, the processing methods for infeasible solutions include the use of penalty functions, repair methods, and so on.

In this study, the problem is decomposed into the following two parts.

3.1. Evolution: Using the DAFSA, Based on the Actual Source Nodes and the Destination Nodes, an Appropriate Set of Steiner Nodes Is Selected through a Population Iteration

The key to solving the considered problem is selecting the other user nodes that are not the source and the destinations (Steiner nodes) instead of user nodes. These nodes serve as the core nodes that connect the destination nodes. The positions and numbers of these nodes usually vary, according to the nature of the problem and the optimization goal. A trade-off needs to be struck between low node instability and a low delay between the source and the destinations while also considering the out-degree constraints of the user nodes to rationally distribute the Steiner nodes in each tree. These nodes, the source nodes, and the destination nodes are combined into a complete subgraph.

The discrete artificial fish swarm algorithm is a swarm intelligence algorithm. The basic idea of this algorithm is to simulate the behavior of individual fish in a fish swarm, such that the whole swarm can cooperatively find an optimal solution in the solution space. Each artificial fish represents a candidate solution in the solution space, and they exchange information and adjust their positions to find an optimal solution. Owing to a number of salient properties, which include flexibility, a fast convergence, and insensitivity to the initial parameter settings, the AFSA family has emerged as an effective swarm intelligence (SI) methodology that has been widely applied to solving real-world optimization problems [27]. One of its main advantages is the ability to perform a global search in the search space and avoid becoming trapped in local optimal solutions.

The algorithm contains a series of behavior rules, such as foraging, following, randomly moving, and so on. These rules simulate the behavior of individual artificial fish when searching for food and avoiding danger:

(1) Randomly moving behavior: The individual randomly moves in various directions within its *step* limit.

(2) Foraging behavior: The individual randomly explores a new position within its *visual* limit. If the new position has a better fitness, it moves toward this position within its *step* limit; otherwise, if a position with a better fitness cannot be found within a limited number of *try_number* times, it will move randomly.

(3) Following behavior: The individual perceives the optimal individual within its *visual* limit and moves toward that individual if the surrounding area is not crowded; otherwise, the individual performs foraging.

In this study, the artificial fish school behavior strategy designed by Ma et al. [16] was used. First, whether the artificial fish (AF) are crowded or not is determined. If not, the fish perform the following behavior and the algorithm ends. Otherwise, the individual enters into foraging behavior.

3.2. Evaluation: Based on the Spanning Tree Algorithm, the Complete Subgraph Is Converted into an ALM Routing Tree, and the Fitness Value Is Calculated

For this part, an ALM routing tree must be constructed based on the obtained complete subgraph; that is, all of the terminal nodes are connected using Steiner nodes, ensuring that the objective function is optimized. This problem is similar to the minimum spanning tree problem.

Prim's algorithm [22] has the advantages of simplicity and efficiency in processing the minimum spanning tree problem, the basic idea of which is to start from an initial node and gradually select the shortest edge connected to the current spanning tree until all the nodes are covered. According to the objective function defined above, this study improves Prim's algorithm to heuristically construct an ALM routing tree with a low delay and better stability.

4. One-Off Optimization Method for Multiple Co-Existing Application Layer Multicast Trees

In this study, the DAFSA is used as the core method for the optimization of multiple co-existing ALM routing trees. First, based on the input multicast session, multiple sets of suitable Steiner node sets are selected to form a complete subgraph, as shown in Figure 1. Then, multiple subgraphs are converted into ALM routing trees using the improved spanning tree algorithm. Subsequently, evaluation and updating of the bulletin board (used to store the set of optimal routing trees) was performed. The optimal ALM routing trees were ultimately obtained through continuous iteration. It is worth noting that the improved spanning tree algorithm is a deterministic algorithm, and the selected Steiner node set directly affects the fitness function used to evaluate the ALM routing tree.

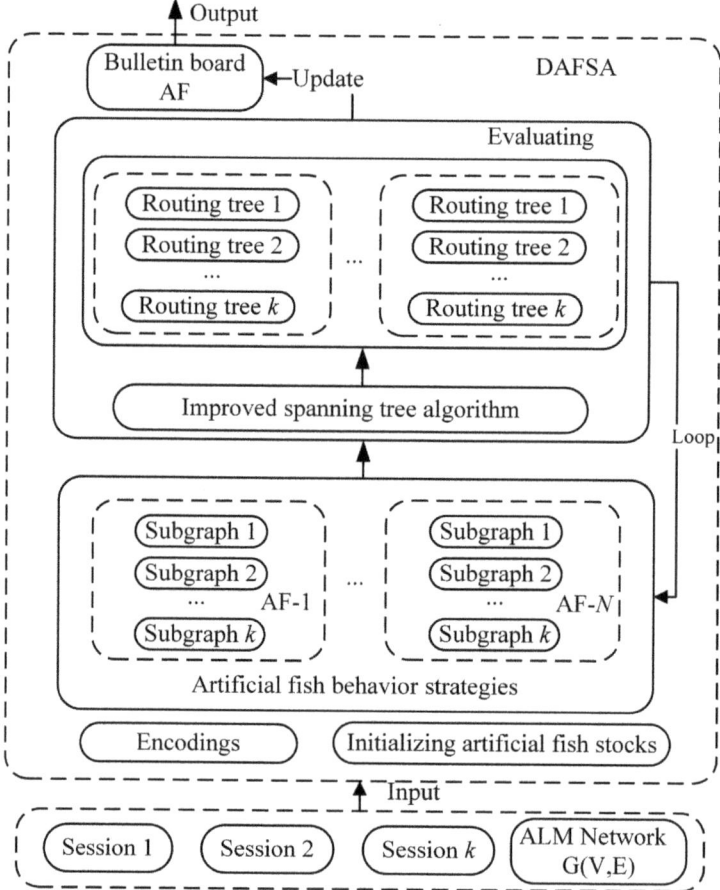

Figure 1. Optimization framework for multiple co-existing ALM routing trees.

4.1. Application of DAFSA in Multiple Co-Existing ALM Routing Trees

4.1.1. Encoding

The genotypes of the artificial fish are represented using matrix coding, where each row represents a Steiner node selection scheme for a multicast session, and this set of nodes forms a complete subgraph $subG_j$. Equation (5) represents the code for artificial fish X (AF-X).

$$X = \begin{bmatrix} subG_1 \\ \cdots \\ subG_j \\ \cdots \\ subG_K \end{bmatrix} = \begin{bmatrix} x_{1,1} \cdots x_{1,i} \cdots x_{1,|V|} \\ \cdots \\ x_{j,1} \cdots x_{j,i} \cdots x_{j,|V|} \\ \cdots \\ x_{K,1} \cdots x_{K,i} \cdots x_{K,|V|} \end{bmatrix} \quad (5)$$

where each row has $|V|$ elements and each element can only be 0 or 1. If the complete subgraph $subG_j$ contains vertex i, then $x_{j,i} = 1$; otherwise, $x_{j,i} = 0$. All the elements in any $subG_j$ corresponding to the source and destinations should always be 1, as all potential complete subgraphs must contain the source and destinations.

4.1.2. Fitness Function

The fitness function is used to evaluate the quality of the artificial fish. To address the artificial fish that do not satisfy the constraints, a penalty value is introduced into the fitness function. The artificial fish that do not meet the constraints are eliminated in the iterative process when the fitness function takes a large value. This strategy helps to emphasize the importance of satisfying the constraint conditions and guides the algorithm to find suitable solutions in the search space. The formula for the *Fitness* is as follows:

$$Fitness = w_1 \sum_{k=1}^{K} f_1(T_k) + w_2 \sum_{k=1}^{K} f_2(T_k) + p \cdot \sum_{v_i \in V} Q(v_i) \quad (6)$$

$$Q(v_i) = \begin{cases} \sum_{k=1}^{K} Od_{v_i^{T_k}} - D_v, & \sum_{k=1}^{K} Od_{v_i^{T_k}} > D_v \\ 0, & \sum_{k=1}^{K} Od_{v_i^{T_k}} < D_v \end{cases} \quad (7)$$

where p in Equation (6) is the penalty factor and $Q(v_i)$ in Equation (7) represents the number of out-degree of node v_i that exceeds the degree constraint.

4.1.3. Behavior of Artificial Fish

The artificial fishes cooperatively search the solution space through the execution of behaviors. Specifically, optimal behavior is realized through a change in spatial position. As the solution space is discrete, the Hamming distance [28] is used to measure the distance between two artificial fishes. In this study, the behaviors used in the DAFSA were designed as follows:

(1) Randomly moving behavior

The encoding method used in this study is binary encoding. To implement this behavior, we only need to randomly flip the elements that do not correspond to the source and destinations used in the encoding matrix of AF-X, in the manner of $x_{j,i} = 1 - x_{j,i}$.

(2) Foraging behavior

Suppose the current position of an AF is X. Then, the AF randomly moves to a new position X'. If the foraging behavior is successful (i.e., $Fitness(X') < Fitness(X)$), then the AF will randomly select $r(r \in [1, step])$ different elements between X and X' in X to cover the corresponding elements in X'; otherwise, the AF will perform random movement.

(3) Following behavior

Following (or tail-chasing) is a behavior that imitates other AFs, especially those that perform well. Suppose that, within the visual range of AF-X, there are n AFs and X_p is the solution with the optimal fitness. Assume that the Hamming distance between X and X_p is equal to N_d, which means there are N_d elements in the encoding matrix of X that differ from the corresponding ones in X_p. The fitness function is satisfied if and only if $Fitness(X) > Fitness(X_p)$ and $n < N \times \delta$, in which case the following behavior will be executed. The specific way in which this is executed is to randomly select $r(r \in [1, min(step, N_d)])$ elements from the above N_d elements in X_p to cover the corresponding elements in the AF, such that the distance between the two AFs will decrease and the similarity will increase.

4.2. Improved Spanning Tree Algorithm

During the decoding of an individual artificial fish, a tree that connects all the nodes needs to be obtained based on a complete graph. To make the constructed tree more stable with less delay under the condition that the out-degree constraint of the user node is satisfied, this study improves Prim's algorithm by comprehensively considering the delay and the instability, instead of using the edge weights, to weigh the order of joining in the minimum spanning tree. We used the contributions of the delay and the instability (DIC), calculated as follows:

$$DIC = min\{w_1(d(e_{v_i}) + d(v_i)) + w_2 \cdot l_{v_i} \cdot p(v_i)\} \qquad (8)$$

In Equation (8), l_{v_i} represents the corresponding depth when node v_i joins the tree, $d(e_{v_i})$ represents the corresponding edge delay after node v_i is added to the tree, $d(v_i)$ represents the replication delay of node v_i, and $p(v_i)$ represents the probability of node v_i leaving a multicast session.

The node depth refers to the number of nodes that pass from the source node to a given node. The greater the depth of a node, the more unstable the data transmission path is, as the departure of any of the node's ancestor nodes will cause it to receive no data. Therefore, to increase the stability of the entire tree, the depth of each node should be kept as small as possible.

When the delays of the end-hosts are the same, the preference is to choose the end-hosts with a low leaving rate, as the nodes that are preferentially added to the tree are more likely to serve as transit nodes for data forwarding. In this way, the overall stability of the multicast tree can be increased. Similarly, when nodes have the same probability of leaving, the node with the shortest delay is selected first, which can reduce the overall delay. Smaller *DIC* nodes should be at the upper level of the multicast tree, in order to take full advantage of their low delay and low instability, thus improving the two target values of the ALM routing tree.

By borrowing ideas from Prim's algorithm, a preliminary ALM routing tree can be obtained that connects all the nodes in the complete graph. However, in the process of generating the tree, the phenomenon of node redundancy may occur due to improper selection of the Steiner node set; that is, non-destination nodes may appear at leaf nodes and are only involved in receiving data, not in forwarding it. The data transmission corresponding to this part has no practical significance and will only increase the delay and instability. These redundant branches need to be pruned, in order to ensure that the leaf nodes only contain the destination nodes of the session.

The improved spanning tree algorithm based on Prim's algorithm is constructed in Algorithm 1.

Algorithm 1: *DIC*-based tree generation algorithm

Data: Complete subgraph $subG(V, E)$
Result: ALM routing tree
Initialize an empty tree T, add the source node to T;
while $|T| \, != |V|$ **do**
  Generate alternative edges sets according to node in T;
  Calculate *DIC* of nodes in $\overline{T}$ and sort the them;
  Choose the *DIC* smallest node v_i in $\overline{T}$, add it and its corresponding edge e_{v_i} to T;
  The available out-degree of node v_i minus one;
  Update the collection T, $\overline{T}$;
Prune the tree T.

4.3. Algorithm Process

(1) The application layer network $G = (V, E)$ is input, and the relevant sources and destinations in K co-existing multicast sessions are specified;

(2) The algorithm-related parameters, such as the *popsize*, *visual*, *step*, *try_number*, δ, and p are set;

(3) Individual artificial fish execute the behavior strategy and obtain multiple Steiner node sets;

(4) The improved spanning tree algorithm is used to obtain the co-existing ALM routing trees corresponding to the multiple Steiner node sets obtained for the AF;

(5) The fitness of the AF individuals are evaluated by calculating the delay and instability of multiple co-existing ALM routing trees. The current best AF individual is compared with those recorded on the bulletin board, and if its fitness is better, the bulletin is updated;

(6) It is determined whether the algorithm termination condition has been met. If not, steps (3)–(6) are repeated; otherwise, the ALM routing tree corresponding to the multicast sessions is output.

5. Simulation Experiment Analysis

The DAFSA approach designed in this paper was written and tested in C++. The simulations were run on a computer (AMD Ryzen 7 5700U) with an 1.80 GHz Radeon GPU, 16.00 GB of RAM, and the Windows 7 (x64) operating system. The parameter settings were as follows: $popsize = 20$, $visual = 20$, $step = 6$, $try_number = 100$, $\delta = 0.5$, $p = 1$, $iteration = 200$, $D_v = 5$, $w_1 = 1$, and $w_2 = 0.0001$. These parameters are chosen experimentally. The detailed discussion on parameter settings will be given in Sections 5.4 and 5.5.

Figure 2 shows the IP network diagram. The circles in the diagram represent the user nodes, and the squares represent the router nodes. Each user node has two transmission parameters: the node replication delay and the departure probability. The weights between nodes represent the data transfer delays. Although the application layer multicast approach uses user nodes to transmit data, the underlying layer was still propagated through a routing node unicast approach. The edge delay between each pair of user nodes was obtained using the Dijkstra shortest path algorithm.

The session results for the optimization of four co-existing multicast sessions, each with one source node and eight destination nodes, are shown in Table 1, and the ALM routing trees obtained using the proposed algorithm are shown in Figure 3. For each ALM multicast tree corresponding to a multicast session, the out-degrees of all the nodes in Figure 3 satisfied the constraint. The out-degrees of nodes 8, 30, 38, and 24 were all 5, as the instability probabilities of nodes 8, 30, and 38 were very low (i.e., two orders of magnitude lower than those of the other nodes). Therefore, when constructing the ALM routing tree, these three nodes were preferentially selected as the transfer nodes for data transmission. The out-degree of node 24 was also 5, as the out-degrees of nodes 8, 30, and 38 were allocated and because the data could only be forwarded through other nodes. However, the other nodes had a high probability of instability and, thus, were not suitable as transfer nodes. Therefore, the root node was directly used to transmit data to reduce the depth of the entire tree, thereby reducing the instability of the ALM routing tree.

Table 2 lists the delay and instability of the ALM routing tree for the four multicast sessions. As analyzed above, ALM trees a, b, and c used nodes 8, 30, and 38 as the transit nodes, respectively, which effectively reduced the instability. However, to satisfy the node out-degree constraint, the algorithm eventually selected some transit nodes (i.e., non-source and non-destination Steiner nodes), resulting in an increase in the link delay. In contrast, although ALM tree d (corresponding to multicast session 4) achieved a lower delay, it paid a higher price with its instability, which further illustrates that the algorithm made a certain trade-off between delay and stability.

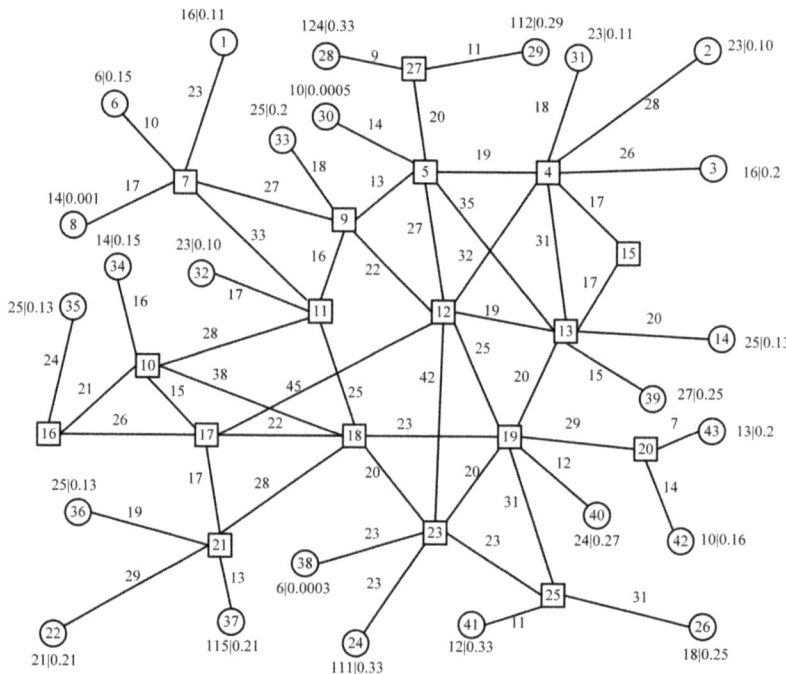

Figure 2. IP network instance.

Table 1. Multicast session information.

Multicast Session	Source	Destination
1	8	2, 14, 22, 24, 26, 28, 29, 31
2	2	1, 29, 31, 32, 41, 37, 36, 42
3	14	2, 6, 21, 31, 33, 35, 36, 40
4	24	28, 29, 32, 34, 36, 39, 40, 41

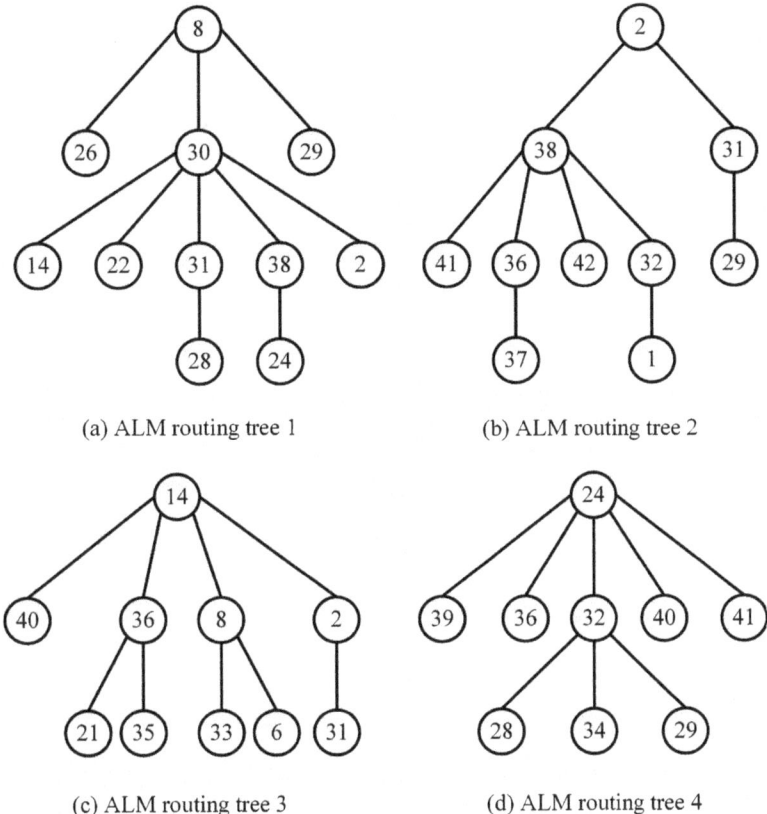

Figure 3. Obtained ALM routing trees.

Table 2. ALM routing tree information.

Multicast Session	Replication Delay (ms)	Link Delay (ms)	Instability	Total Delay (ms)
1	121	832	0.010	953
2	141	659	0.124	800
3	201	586	0.153	787
4	124	578	0.326	702
Total	587	2655	0.614	3242

In fact, the routing tree obtained with the algorithm was based on the application layer, and the actual data forwarding process used by the routing nodes to forward the data was in the form of an IP unicast. Taking ALM tree b from session 2 as an example, the actual data transmission process is shown in Figure 4. The transmission path between each pair of nodes was the transmission path with the lowest delay.

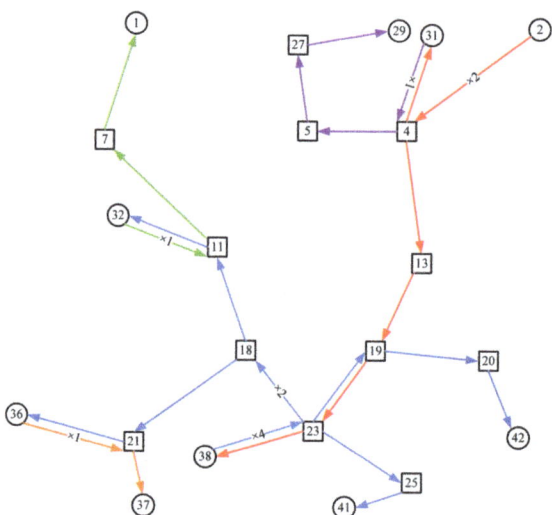

Figure 4. Actual data transmission path in multicast session 2. The red arrow indicates a path for the user node 2 to transmit data, the blue arrow indicates a path for the user node 38 to transmit data, the orange arrow indicates a path for the user node 36 to transmit data, and the green arrow indicates a path for the user node 32 to transmit data.

5.1. Comparison Between One-Off Optimization and Sequential Optimization

5.1.1. Comparison of Sequential Optimization That Does Not Consider the Out-Degree Constraint

In sequential optimization without considering the out-degree constraint, only one multicast session is optimized at a time, and the out-degree constraint on nodes is not considered. In one-off optimization, multiple multicast sessions are considered simultaneously to yield all multicast session transmission schemes. Different numbers of multicast sessions and destination nodes in each multicast session were set, and the node congestion under the two approaches described above was analyzed.

Figure 5 shows the fitting curves under sequential optimization and one-off optimization. The black dots indicate the out-degree violations under the two algorithms. The fitting surface shows that the node out-degree violation under sequential optimization increased exponentially with the number of multicast sessions and destination nodes, while one-off optimization presented no node constraint violations.

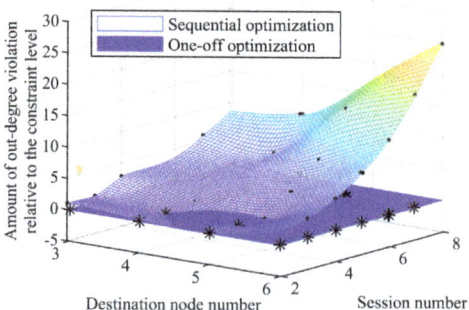

Figure 5. Violation of the out-degree constraint fitting surface under one-off optimization and sequential optimization approaches. The color represents the value that is out of bounds, the lighter the color the more out of bounds it is.

From the above analysis, as nodes 8, 30, and 38 were suitable transit nodes for forwarding data, their out-degree easily exceeded the constraint. For further analysis, we designed each session to contain five destination nodes and tested the out-degree of these three nodes under different numbers of multicast sessions.

Figure 6 shows that, in sequential optimization, when the number of multicast sessions was greater than four, the out-degree of node 30 exceeded the constraint, and when the number of multicast sessions was greater than six, the out-degree of node 38 exceeded the constraint; meanwhile, for node 8, the out-degree was basically maintained at 3 and was within the constraint. With an increase in the number of sessions, the out-degree of nodes 30 and 38 increased significantly. In addition, we found that the sum of the out-degree violation levels for nodes 30 and 38 and of all the nodes was equal, indicating that, under the considered experimental conditions, these two nodes caused the ALM routing tree to fail to satisfy the constraints.

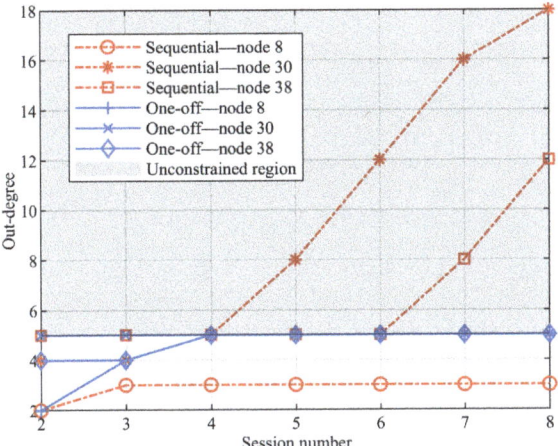

Figure 6. The out-degree in multiple multicast sessions with five destination nodes.

In contrast, in one-off optimization, when the number of sessions reached four, the out-degrees of nodes 8, 30, and 38 were all 5, equal to the critical constraint value. However, as the number of multicast sessions increased, the out-degree of these three nodes did not exceed the constraint. This indicates that the one-off optimization method can make full use of the out-degree of core nodes and obtain an optimal solution under the constraint conditions.

5.1.2. Comparison with Sequential Optimization While Considering the Out-Degree Constraint

The above experiments provided in-depth information on the impact of not introducing constraint processing technology in sequential optimization. Notably, sequential optimization can also consider the out-degree of a node as a constraint condition. We adopted the node out-degree reservation strategy; that is, each time the optimization of an ALM routing tree is completed, the out-degree of the corresponding node is purposefully reduced. In the next optimization of the ALM routing tree, we can choose only those nodes that still have a valid out-degree. However, this strategy may trap the entire ALM routing tree in a local optimal solution.

This occurs because, during the construction of the ALM routing tree, better nodes are initially selected. As the out-degree of such core nodes is exhausted, the subsequent ALM routing tree can use only other nodes with a greater delay and a greater instability, resulting in a sharp increase in the instability and delay of the whole tree.

Table 3 shows the optimization results obtained for four multicast sessions. The number of destination nodes for each session was five, and the out-degree of each node was two. Although the one-off optimization method was not as good as the sequential optimization method in the construction of the first ALM routing tree, the results of the one-off optimization method showed a lower delay and instability when constructing the third and fourth ALM routing trees. When considering multiple co-existing ALM routing trees, the overall delay and stability were significantly better than those of the trees constructed using the sequential optimization method.

Table 3. Comparison of the one-off optimization and sequential optimization results.

Sessions	Sequentially Optimizing		One-Off Optimizing	
	Delay (ms)	Instability	Delay (ms)	Instability
1	671	0.0167	732	0.0514
2	501	0.135	501	0.135
3	588	0.235	494	0.17
4	580	0.376	555	0.326
total	2340	0.762	2282	0.682

As can be seen from Figure 7, in the first ALM routing tree, nodes 8, 30, and 38 were used, which decreased the delay and instability. However, in the third and fourth ALM routing trees, as the out-degrees of the selected core nodes 8, 30, and 38 had been used up, the other nodes were selected only to transmit data, resulting in significant increases in delay and instability in the two routing trees.

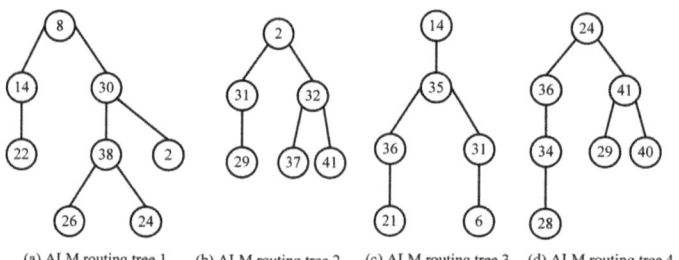

(a) ALM routing tree 1   (b) ALM routing tree 2   (c) ALM routing tree 3   (d) ALM routing tree 4

Figure 7. Routing trees obtained through sequential optimization.

In contrast, Figure 8 shows the results of one-off optimization. Through the rational distribution of nodes—for example, by using the out-degree of nodes 14 and 38 in ALM routing trees 3 and 4—the delay and instability of ALM routing trees 3 and 4 were reduced. Although this optimized allocation slightly increased the delay and instability of the first routing tree, it reduced the delay and instability of the multiple ALM routing trees as a whole. This result further clarifies the limitations of independently optimizing the ALM routing tree for each session. In contrast, the one-off optimization method used in this paper can more effectively optimize the overall performance.

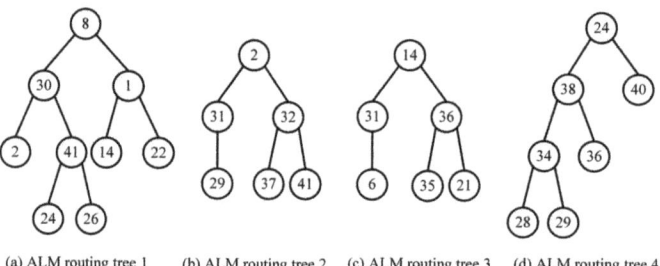

(a) ALM routing tree 1   (b) ALM routing tree 2   (c) ALM routing tree 3   (d) ALM routing tree 4

Figure 8. Routing trees obtained through one-off optimization.

5.2. Validation of the Penalty Function Mechanism

For the optimization of multiple co-existing ALM multicast routing trees, violating the out-degree constraint of nodes may cause failure of data transmission. Therefore, determining how to guide individual artificial fish to search in the feasible solution domain is highly important. In this study, a penalty mechanism was introduced to eliminate solutions that do not satisfy the constraints. In Figure 9, we compare the effect of the algorithm with and without the use of the penalty mechanism regarding the out-degree violation of nodes.

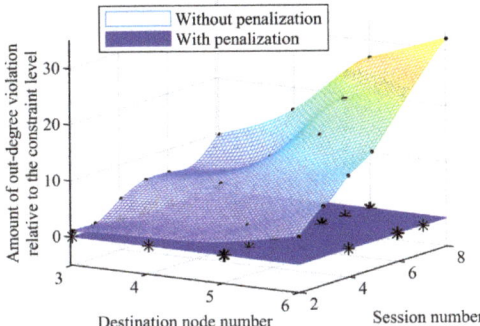

Figure 9. Fitted surfaces with and without penalty function for out-degree violations. The color represents the value that is out of bounds, the lighter the color the more out of bounds it is.

As the scale of the multicast sessions increased, among the results obtained with the algorithm without a penalty mechanism, a greater node out-degree violation indicated that a very large number of destination nodes needed to copy and forward the data in large quantities. When the performance limit of a node is exceeded, the end-host will be down, which will cause the session to fail. On the other hand, when the penalty mechanism was used, the results obtained with the algorithm did not include nodes exceeding the degree constraint. This demonstrates that the penalty mechanism can effectively solve the out-degree constraint problem. In particular, when the scale of multicast sessions increases, the algorithm with the penalty mechanism performed better in terms of reducing the out-degree violations of nodes.

5.3. Algorithm Convergence Analysis

The execution of various behaviors enables the artificial fish swarm to perform more flexible and diverse searches in the solution space. However, under some circumstances—especially when the problem is complex and the solution space is large—these behavior modes may cause the algorithm to converge slowly, and the algorithm may be prone to becoming trapped in local optimal solutions. To verify the convergence and accuracy of the algorithm for the optimization problem in this paper, we conducted an analysis of scenarios using networks containing 25, 50, and 75 randomly distributed user nodes. In these networks, four multicast sessions were input, where each multicast session contained one source node and eight destination nodes.

The randomness of the artificial fish swarm algorithm may make the algorithm unstable. To reduce the impact of randomness on the algorithm results, multicast optimization was performed for each network 50 times, and a box plot was generated to show the locations of the distribution centers of these results and the distribution range. As shown in Figure 10, for the networks with 25 and 50 user nodes, the box plot appears as a straight line; as such, the maximum and minimum values are the same, and there are no outlier values. When the network size increased to 75, the convergence stability of the algorithm decreased slightly, with a maximum value of 0.74014 and a minimum value of 0.73346, comprising a difference of only 0.9%. This indicates that the algorithm had relatively good stability under different network sizes.

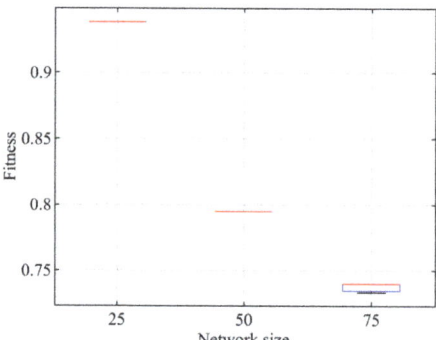

Figure 10. Fitness box plots under different network sizes. Black indicates the edge, red the upper quartile, and blue the lower quartile.

To further verify the convergence ability of the algorithm, the fitness values of the 50 results were summed and averaged, and the obtained iteration diagram is shown in Figure 11a. With network sizes of 25, 50, and 75 user nodes, the fitness value decreased rapidly at the beginning of the iteration, as the algorithm eliminated infeasible solutions. When the number of iterations reached approximately 10, the increase in the fitness value slowed down, as the solutions listed in the bulletin board already satisfied the constraints and its fitness function was low. Subsequently, as shown in Figure 11a–c, the algorithm approached the optimal solution as it iterated and converged at 81, 98, and 191 iterations, respectively.

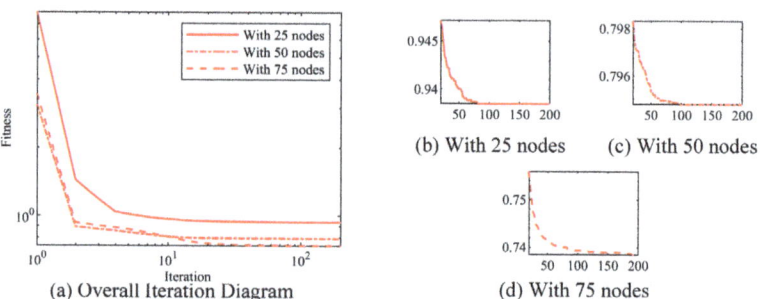

Figure 11. Algorithm evolution diagrams under different network sizes.

5.4. Parameter Sensitivity Analysis

Swarm intelligence algorithms usually exhibit good adaptability. However, setting reasonable parameters is still a key task when using optimization algorithms. The appropriate selection of parameters can significantly improve the performance of the algorithm. The main parameters of the artificial fish swarm algorithm include the population size *popsize*, the field of view *visual*, the step size *step*, the number of attempts *try_number*, and the degree of congestion δ. Figure 12 shows the results of the algorithm from 20 to 200 iterations under different parameter settings.

Regarding the effect of the population size on the algorithm, as shown in Figure 12a, when the population size increased, the number of iterations needed for the algorithm to converge decreased. However, in each iteration, the number of AFs participating in the optimization search increased. Therefore, this parameter had no significant impact on the overall convergence time. As can be seen from Figure 12b–e, setting different values for the other parameters affected only the iterative process of the algorithm and had a relatively insignificant impact on the final convergence result, which indicates that the algorithm is insensitive to parameter changes and has good robustness.

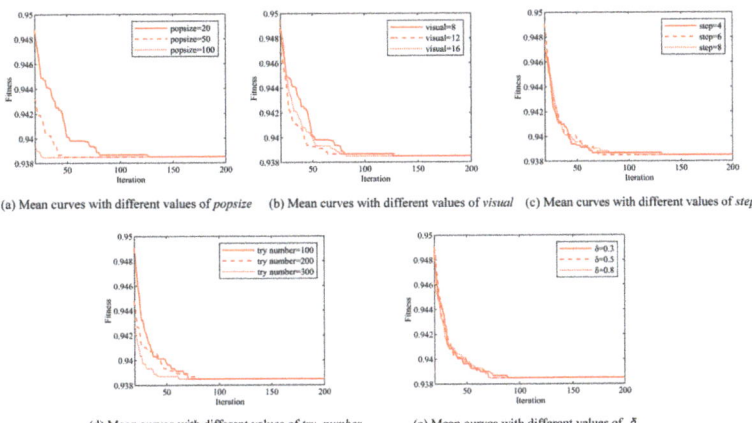

Figure 12. Comparison of the effect of each parameter on the performance of the algorithm.

5.5. Selection of Weights

In this study, the optimization of the ALM routing tree involves two objectives, namely, the delay and the instability, with corresponding weights w_1 and w_2, respectively. The selection of these weights directly affects the performance of the algorithm and search results. In the experiments, the magnitude of the observed delay was much greater than that of the instability. This may have caused the delay to be too significant in the overall optimization process, leading to the contribution of instability being ignored. By adjusting the weights, the influence of the different objectives during the optimization process can be controlled.

The weights w_1 and w_2 can be determined in a number of ways. For example, the subjective judgment method [29], statistical method [30], and sensitivity analysis [31] can be used. However, neither of the first two methods is applicable; the subjective judgment method requires an expert's deep understanding of the problem and an accurate estimation of the contribution of each objective. Statistical methods require a large amount of supporting data; however, the resulting data of this problem are related to the number of source nodes, the destination nodes, the number of multicast sessions, and the network distribution and size, making this method costly. In contrast, sensitivity analysis, which directly assesses the impact of input parameters on the model output, is a simple and intuitive approach that requires less data and is easy to understand and implement.

Therefore, we used sensitivity analysis, and different weight combinations were used to cover the possible weight value ranges. The influences of these weights on the final optimization result were investigated, as shown in Figure 13. In general, there was an increase in the weight ratio (w_2/w_1) as the instability of the ALM routing tree gradually increased, while the total delay continuously decreased. This is due to the increase in the value of the weight w_1; that is, the contribution of the delay increased.

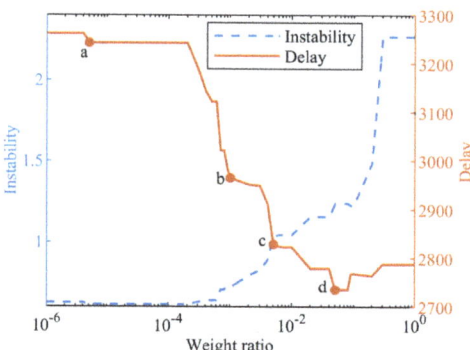

Figure 13. Comparison of results obtained under different weights.

In the process of gradually increasing the weight ratio, several inflection points appeared, indicated by the red points (a, b, c, and d) in the figure. These points are the turning points where the rate of decrease in the delay became slower, the rate of increase in the instability became greater, or both. Table 4 lists the results under the weight ratios corresponding to these points. By analyzing these points, we could obtain a locally optimal weight ratio; that is, a significant reduction in the instability or delay can be obtained without a significant increase in the delay or instability, respectively.

Table 4. Comparison of optimization results with different weights.

	Weight	Total Delay (ms)	Instability
	0:1	3633	0.567
a	0.00005:1	3242	0.614
b	0.001:1	2965	0.720
c	0.005:1	2823	1.019
d	0.05:1	2735	1.239
	1:0	2788	2.266

For example, consider the process from point a to point b: the delay was sharply reduced, while the instability increased slightly. Therefore, choosing point a will be less unstable than choosing any point between a and b, and the delay will not increase much as the delay does not change sharply. Meanwhile, the delay is lower when point b is selected, and the increase in instability is not significant.

When only the instability was optimized, the instability value reached 0.567. Meanwhile, when only the total delay was optimized, the total delay reached 2788 ms. These results provide a reference for weight selection under different optimization objectives, such that the algorithm can be flexibly adapted to the specific needs of a given application. Decision makers can consider the importance of each objective to the overall goal and determine the optimal combination of weights by considering the practicality, expertise, and relevant interests.

5.6. Analysis of Solution to the Routing Tree Problem for a Single Multicast Session

Although this study is optimizing the multiple co-existence application layer multicast routing tree structure problem, the method is equivalent to optimizing a single multicast session when we set the input to only one multicast session. To evaluate the performance of the proposed algorithm regarding the optimization of a single multicast session, a multicast session in which the number of source nodes was 8 and the numbers of destination nodes were 2, 3, 14, 26, 24, 37, 22, 35, 28, 29, and 31 was set up. The algorithm in this paper was compared with three single multicast session multi-objective optimization algorithms, namely, Cao's algorithm [7], the CL-S [8], and the VDM [9]; all three algorithms are for single multicast sessions. Because of the differences between their optimization models and the one we formulated, we set the end-to-end latency constraint and the degree constraint in Cao's algorithm to 300 and 5 and made the CL-S take the form of transmission delay in our formulated optimization model and constructed the virtual distance for the VDM based on our objective. Such a modification ensures comparability but will not alter the performance. Table 5 shows that the proposed algorithm was superior to the three algorithms used for comparison, in terms of its total delay and instability.

Table 5. Comparison of ALM routing tree optimization results.

Algorithm	Total Delay (ms)	Instability
CL-S	1346	0.070
VDM	1359	0.073
CAO	1411	0.042
DAFSA	1075	0.016

6. Discussion

We investigate a key limitation of existing application layer multicast (ALM) routing optimization algorithms, namely, that these algorithms mainly focus on the optimization of individual multicast routing trees, whereas sequential one-by-one optimization is usually required when dealing with multiple co-existing multicast sessions. However, as the experimental results show, this sequential optimization approach can very easily lead to an excessive out-degree of user nodes suitable for forwarding data, triggering node congestion. And this phenomenon will be more serious with increases in the multicast session size, which will lead to a failure of data transmission in the session. Moreover, it is also difficult to make reasonable use of the node out-degree if we want to take into account the node out-degree constraints in the sequential optimization. The node out-degree reservation strategy mentioned in the previous section is a simple method of out-degree allocation, but it only ensures that all nodes can satisfy the constraints, which can easily lead to falling into a local optimum. Specifically, the routing tree optimized first performs well, while the performance of the routing tree optimized later gets worse. For multiple co-existing multicast sessions, such an allocation appears to be extremely unfair, and the performance of all multicast sessions cannot be optimized.

The discrete artificial fish swarming algorithm we designed takes multiple co-existing multicast sessions as a whole and achieves the optimization of the objective function values of multiple co-existing application layer multicast routing trees by continuously evolving artificial fish with higher fitness functions. Due to the introduction of a penalty function mechanism, this approach helps the algorithm filter the solutions that do not satisfy the node out-degree constraints and avoids session instability caused by node congestion. Experimental results show that the algorithm achieves satisfactory results, with trade-offs in node allocation across multicast sessions and a reduced overall delay and reduced instability. In addition, we note that our proposed algorithm is also effective in optimizing individual multicast sessions. Steiner nodes, selected by the DAFSA, have been proven to be very suitable as intermediate nodes for forwarding data, thus guaranteeing the performance of individual multicast sessions.

However, the present algorithm also has limitations. First, in setting the weights, when the network structure changes significantly, such as when the number of multiple co-existing application layer multicast sessions increases or the nodes of each session become complex, we are unable to find the optimal weighting parameter through multiple experiments because of the huge cost involved. This is mainly due to the fact that single-objective weighting methods are very sensitive to the choice of weights and are usually difficult to adapt to new contexts or changes in objectives. To overcome these problems, we propose to consider using a multi-objective decision-making approach [32] to optimize the relationship between multiple objectives more comprehensively. Further, this study deals with node out-degree constraints using a penalty function, but the effect of the penalty function is highly dependent on the chosen penalty parameter, which adds to the complexity of the problem [33]. In solving these problems, an improved spanning tree algorithm ensures that the nodes in the current multicast session do not exceed the constraints. But how to consider multiple co-existing complete graphs and generate application layer multicast routing trees that satisfy the constraints to avoid the use of the penalty function remains a problem that requires in-depth research.

Moreover, the application layer multicast routing tree construction problem is usually dynamic in nature. That is, the network topology, multicast session members, etc., may change over time. The swarm intelligence algorithm has difficulty in dealing with dynamically changing problems at the time of application, and as the problems become more complex, its search space becomes larger, which can easily lead to a decreased search efficiency. In contrast, trained neural networks have the ability to generalize to unseen situations and can adapt to the complexity of the problem by learning patterns and features of the data without the need for explicit rules [34]. Therefore, we will include neural network methods in our future research.

7. Conclusions

In this paper, a one-off optimization method based on the discrete artificial fish swarm algorithm was proposed, which optimizes multiple co-existing application layer multicast sessions simultaneously, rather than optimizing them sequentially and independently. The contributions of this paper can be summarized as follows:

(1) The use of the DAFSA was proposed for the determination of multiple co-existing ALM routing trees. Compared with the sequential optimization algorithm, the multiple ALM routing trees obtained presented a better performance in terms of delays and stability. For the optimization of a single ALM routing tree, the proposed algorithm also outperformed other existing algorithms.

(2) In terms of degree constraint processing, a penalty function was used to ensure that the out-degree of nodes in the entire ALM routing tree did not exceed the constraint limit, effectively preventing the algorithm from obtaining infeasible solutions.

(3) In the evaluation section, we improved Prim's algorithm such that an ALM routing tree with a low delay and a low stability could be obtained from the subgraph. This process can be understood as the decoding process of the DAFSA such that this algorithm can be applied to the considered problem; in this way, a better ALM routing tree scheme can be iteratively generated.

(4) When processing application layer networks of various scales, the system quickly and reliably reached the optimal solution or a state close to the optimal solution. This stable convergence helps to improve the applicability and effectiveness of the algorithm in various network scenarios.

(5) Even under different parameter settings, the proposed method still reached a stable convergence state after a relatively short number of iterations, which helps to improve the reliability and applicability of the algorithm in practical problems.

(6) We have provided a variety of applicable weight determinations that can help provide more practically applicable decision support.

However, there are still some directions worthy of further exploration and improvement:

(1) When converting a multi-objective problem into a single-objective problem, we faced problems such as weight selection and information loss. To better retain the trade-off relationships between the objectives, a multi-objective optimization algorithm, such as the multi-objective genetic algorithm, can be introduced. Directly addressing multi-objective problems is a direction worth exploring.

(2) When dealing with constrained problems, a penalty function-based algorithm is often used. However, the introduction of a penalty function may complicate the calculation of the evaluation process, and determining the penalty factor is difficult.

For this problem, the use of an adaptive penalty function or other advanced constraint-processing techniques can be considered, in order to more effectively address the constraint conditions and reduce the complexity of the search space.

Author Contributions: Conceptualization, Y.L., N.W. and Q.L.; data curation, Y.L., N.W. and W.Z.; methodology. Y.L., N.W. and F.L.; validation, F.L., W.Z. and N.W.; investigation, N.W., Y.L. and W.Z.; writing—original draft preparation, N.W.; writing—review and editing, Y.L., N.W., Q.L. and F.L.; visualization, W.Z., N.W. and Q.L. All authors have read and agreed to the published version of the manuscript.

Funding: This research received no external funding.

Data Availability Statement: The code for the DAFSA can be provided upon request from the corresponding author, Feng Liu.

Conflicts of Interest: Author Wei Zhang was employed by the company China Mobile System Integration Co., Ltd. The remaining authors declare that the research was conducted in the absence of any commercial or financial relationships that could be construed as a potential conflict of interest.

References

1. Deering, S.E. Multicast routing in internetworks and extended LANs. In Proceedings of the Symposium Proceedings on Communications Architectures and Protocols, Stanford, CA, USA, 16–18 August 1988; pp. 55–64.
2. Deering, S.E. *Host Extensions for IP Multicasting*; Stanford University: Stanford, CA, USA, 1988.
3. Chu, Y.h.; Rao, S.G.; Seshan, S.; Zhang, H. A case for end system multicast. *IEEE J. Sel. Areas Commun.* **2002**, *20*, 1456–1471. [CrossRef]
4. Su, J.; Cao, J.; Zhang, B. A survey of the research on ALM stability enhancement. *Chin. J Comput.* **2009**, *32*, 576–590.
5. Liu, Q.; Tang, R.; Ren, H.; Pei, Y. Optimizing multicast routing tree on application layer via an encoding-free non-dominated sorting genetic algorithm. *Appl. Intell.* **2020**, *50*, 759–777. [CrossRef]
6. Cao, J.; Su, J.; Wu, C. Modeling and analyzing the instantaneous stability for application layer multicast. In Proceedings of the 2008 IEEE Asia-Pacific Services Computing Conference, IEEE, Yilan, Taiwan, 9–12 December 2008; pp. 217–224.
7. Cao, J.; Su, J. Delay-bounded and high stability spanning tree algorithm for application layer multicast. *J. Softw.* **2010**, *21*, 3151–3164. [CrossRef]
8. Lin Hou, D.L.a.T. Algorithms of Spanning Tree Based on the Stability Probability and Contribution Link of Nodes for Application Layer Multicast. *J. Comput. Res. Dev.* **2012**, *49*, 2559–2567.
9. Mercan, S.; Yuksel, M. Virtual direction multicast: An efficient overlay tree construction algorithm. *J. Commun. Netw.* **2016**, *18*, 446–459. [CrossRef]
10. Lin, H.C.; Lin, T.M.; Wu, C.F. Constructing application-layer multicast trees for minimum-delay message distribution. *Inf. Sci.* **2014**, *279*, 433–445. [CrossRef]
11. Xiaofei, L.; Yiliang, X.; Xuance, S.; Demin, L. Application Layer Multicast Model with Low Delay and High Stability. *J. Donghua Univ.* **2023**, *40*, 74.
12. Li, D.; Wang, Z.; Wei, Y.; Yao, J.; Tan, Y.; Yang, Q.; Wang, Z.; Cao, X. Generation of Low-Delay and High-Stability Multicast Tree. *Comput. Mater. Contin.* **2023**, *76*, 561–572. [CrossRef]
13. Chen, H.; Wang, S.; Li, J.; Li, Y. A hybrid of artificial fish swarm algorithm and particle swarm optimization for feedforward neural network training. In Proceedings of the International Conference on Intelligent Systems and Knowledge Engineering 2007, Chengdu, China, 15–16 October 2007; Atlantis Press: Amstelkade, The Netherlands, 2007; pp. 1025–1028.
14. Sheverdin, A.; Monticone, F.; Valagiannopoulos, C. Photonic inverse design with neural networks: The case of invisibility in the visible. *Phys. Rev. Appl.* **2020**, *14*, 024054. [CrossRef]
15. Pan, Y.; Yu, Z.; Wang, L. Genetic Algorithm for Solving Application Level Multicast Routing Problems. *Mini-Micro Syst.* **2009**, *26*, 55–58.
16. Ma, X.; Tang, R.; Kang, J.; Liu, Q. Optimizing application layer multicast routing via artificial fish swarm algorithm. In Proceedings of the 2016 12th International Conference on Natural Computation, Fuzzy Systems and Knowledge Discovery (ICNC-FSKD), IEEE, Changsha, China, 13–15 August 2016; pp. 115–120.
17. Vik, K.H.; Halvorsen, P.; Griwodz, C. Evaluating Steiner-tree heuristics and diameter variations for application layer multicast. *Comput. Netw.* **2008**, *52*, 2872–2893. [CrossRef]
18. Popescu, A.; Constantinescu, D.; Erman, D.; Ilie, D. *A Survey of Reliable Multicast Communication*; IEEE: Piscataway, NJ, USA, 2007.
19. Ljubić, I. Solving Steiner trees: Recent advances, challenges, and perspectives. *Networks* **2021**, *77*, 177–204. [CrossRef]
20. Dreyfus, S.E.; Wagner, R.A. The Steiner problem in graphs. *Networks* **1971**, *1*, 195–207. [CrossRef]
21. Garey, M.R. Computers and intractability: A guide to the theory of np-completeness, freeman. *Fundamental* **1997**, 498–500.
22. Prim, R.C. Shortest connection networks and some generalizations. *Bell Syst. Tech. J.* **1957**, *36*, 1389–1401. [CrossRef]
23. Jnr, J.K. On the shortest spanning subtree and the traveling salesman problem. *Proc. Am. Math. Soc.* **1956**, *7*, 48–50.

24. Singh, K.; Sundar, S. A hybrid genetic algorithm for the degree-constrained minimum spanning tree problem. *Soft Comput.* **2020**, *24*, 2169–2186. [CrossRef]
25. Majumder, S.; Barma, P.S.; Biswas, A.; Banerjee, P.; Mandal, B.K.; Kar, S.; Ziemba, P. On multi-objective minimum spanning tree problem under uncertain paradigm. *Symmetry* **2022**, *14*, 106. [CrossRef]
26. Yang, X.S. Nature-inspired optimization algorithms: Challenges and open problems. *J. Comput. Sci.* **2020**, *46*, 101104. [CrossRef]
27. Pourpanah, F.; Wang, R.; Lim, C.P.; Wang, X.Z.; Yazdani, D. A review of artificial fish swarm algorithms: Recent advances and applications. *Artif. Intell. Rev.* **2023**, *56*, 1867–1903. [CrossRef]
28. Norouzi, M.; Fleet, D.J.; Salakhutdinov, R.R. Hamming distance metric learning. *Adv. Neural Inf. Process. Syst.* **2012**, 1–9.
29. Paramanik, A.R.; Sarkar, S.; Sarkar, B. OSWMI: An objective-subjective weighted method for minimizing inconsistency in multi-criteria decision making. *Comput. Ind. Eng.* **2022**, *169*, 108138. [CrossRef]
30. Zheng, J.; Du, Z.; Zou, J.; Yang, S. A weight vector generation method based on normal distribution for preference-based multi-objective optimization. *Swarm Evol. Comput.* **2023**, *77*, 101250. [CrossRef]
31. Goodridge, W.S. Sensitivity analysis using simple additive weighting method. *Int. J. Intell. Syst. Appl.* **2016**, *8*, 27. [CrossRef]
32. Jiang, S.; Zou, J.; Yang, S.; Yao, X. Evolutionary dynamic multi-objective optimisation: A survey. *ACM Comput. Surv.* **2022**, *55*, 76. [CrossRef]
33. Liang, J.; Ban, X.; Yu, K.; Qu, B.; Qiao, K.; Yue, C.; Chen, K.; Tan, K.C. A survey on evolutionary constrained multiobjective optimization. *IEEE Trans. Evol. Comput.* **2022**, *27*, 201–221. [CrossRef]
34. Schuetz, M.J.; Brubaker, J.K.; Katzgraber, H.G. Combinatorial optimization with physics-inspired graph neural networks. *Nat. Mach. Intell.* **2022**, *4*, 367–377. [CrossRef]

Disclaimer/Publisher's Note: The statements, opinions and data contained in all publications are solely those of the individual author(s) and contributor(s) and not of MDPI and/or the editor(s). MDPI and/or the editor(s) disclaim responsibility for any injury to people or property resulting from any ideas, methods, instructions or products referred to in the content.

Article

Fast Prediction Method of Combustion Chamber Parameters Based on Artificial Neural Network

Chenhuzhe Shao [1,2], Yue Liu [1,2,*], Zhedian Zhang [1,2], Fulin Lei [1,2] and Jinglun Fu [1,3]

1. University of Chinese Academy of Sciences, Beijing 100190, China; shaochenhuzhe@iet.cn (C.S.)
2. Key Laboratory of Advanced Energy and Power, Institute of Engineering Thermophysics, Chinese Academy of Sciences, Beijing 100045, China
3. Advanced Gas Turbine Laboratory, Institute of Engineering Thermophysics, Chinese Academy of Sciences, Beijing 100045, China
* Correspondence: liuyue16@iet.cn

Abstract: Gas turbines are widely used in industry, and the combustion chamber, compressor, and turbine are known as their three important components. In the design process of the combustion chamber, computational fluid dynamics simulation takes up a lot of time. In order to accelerate the design speed of the combustion chamber, this article proposes a combustion chamber design method that combines an artificial neural network (ANN) and computational fluid dynamics (CFD). CFD results are used as raw data to establish a fast prediction model using ANN and eXtreme Gradient Boosting (XGBoost). The results show that the mean squared error (MSE) of the ANN is 0.0019, and the MSE of XGBoost is 0.0021, so the ANN's prediction performance is slightly better. This fast prediction method combines CFD and the ANN, which can greatly shorten CFD calculation time, improve the efficiency of gas turbine combustion chamber design, and provide the possibility of achieving digital twins of gas turbine combustion chambers.

Keywords: gas turbine; combustion chamber; artificial neural network

1. Introduction

The gas turbine is a complex multidisciplinary coupling device that transforms the energy of fuel into useful work by using a continuous flow of gas as the working mass to drive the impeller to rotate at high speed. It is known as the jewel in the crown of the equipment manufacturing industry. Gas turbines are used in a wide range of applications, including ship power, aviation power, energy generation, and many other fields. Due to its low pollution, high efficiency, and reliability, the advanced gas turbine is the most competitive way to provide clean, environmentally friendly, high-quality, and efficient power generation and combined heat and power generation, and it has become the core of industrial technology in the 21st century. Since the world's first gas turbine was built in Switzerland in 1939, there have been more than 21,000 gas turbines for power generation of more than 1 MW worldwide, with a total capacity of more than 1000 GW, and gas turbines account for 1/5 of the world's total power generation [1].

The combustion chamber is the heart of the gas turbine, which needs to maintain a stable working state for a long time under the harsh conditions of high temperature and high pressure. However, the combustion chamber of an aeroengine faces the problem of rapidly variable and dynamic characteristics [2]. Furthermore, the development process of the combustion chamber has the characteristics of great difficulty, a long cycle, and high cost. Plus, in order to meet the increasing requirements and technical indicators of the engine, the complexity of the engine system has increased significantly, and the combustion chamber design is also facing the challenge of leapfrog development [3].

The combustion chamber design system mainly consists of one- or two-dimensional thermal design and three-dimensional combustion simulation. Combustion is a complex combination of chemical reaction and turbulent flow, and the combustion chamber needs to rely on a large number of tests for continuous iterative design. The main goal of gas turbine combustion chamber design is to achieve low emission, as well as transient and highly stable combustion under high-temperature and -pressure conditions, while having the ability to burn multiple fuels, including low-calorific-value fuels such as blast furnace gas with hydrogen doping, especially pure hydrogen fuel with zero carbon emissions. Computational fluid dynamics (CFD) is an important simulation design tool, the difficulties of which lie in thermoacoustic oscillations and fluid–thermal coupling. Three-dimensional design simulation has been more widely used, and full four-dimensional non-constant design simulation is in the development and research stage. As numerical simulation tests use a number of assumptions and fixed boundary conditions, which cannot map all the characteristics of the physical object, a wise and prudent use of numerical simulation tests, combined with physical test verification, can effectively avoid the risk of misdirection brought about by numerical tests. At the same time, the increasing number of meshes in CFD simulation calculations makes it difficult to reduce the combustion chamber design cycle further. Intelligent algorithms such as machine learning can instead be used to mine big simulation data, not only to share some of the computational tasks to speed up the simulation calculation process but also to perform well in predicting non-constant phenomena in flow and heat transfer [4].

Machine learning methods can be divided into two aspects: traditional machine learning and deep learning. In the early stages of applying machine learning to scientific discoveries, scientists generally used traditional machine learning methods due to limitations in data volume and computational power. Based on the classic model, appropriate adjustments are made to the input, hyperparameters, structure, etc., of the model according to specific problems, in order to achieve the best results in classification and regression tasks [5,6]. Naive Bayes, logistic regression, K-nearest neighbors, and decision trees are relatively simple methods that have the characteristics of being intuitive and easy to implement [7–9].

Deep learning methods directly mine raw data and are adept at exploring the hidden structures and correlations of high-dimensional data. They can learn complex features and patterns that cannot be clearly extracted at the moment, break through the limitations of manual feature extraction, avoid deviations, and reduce the time required to calculate features. Compared to traditional machine learning methods, they have achieved better results. However, due to the complex structure and lack of interpretability of deep learning models, their application is to some extent limited [10,11]. Therefore, deep learning methods are suitable for scenarios with sufficient computing and data resources, complex problems, and poor performance in manually extracting features. Among them, common convolutional neural network structures include LeNet [12], AlexNet [13], ResNet [14], etc.; common recurrent neural network structures include LSTM [15] and GRU [16]; and common deep generation models include the variational autoencoder (VAE) [17] and generative adversarial network (GAN) [18].

The use of a neural network approach to build a fast prediction model for combustion chamber parameters can shorten the combustion chamber design cycle by omitting complex physical relationship calculations as it is fully data-driven. In addition, with sufficient data, it is possible to predict the state of a gas turbine combustion chamber entity using a fast prediction model of the combustion chamber. Therefore, the application of neural network methods to the field of combustion chamber design is very practical and has great potential.

Zhao Gang [19] of Zhengzhou Gas Power Generation Co., Ltd. used a single-hidden-layer artificial neural network to build a NOx emission prediction model and trained the model using gas turbine plant operating data to achieve prediction of four operating parameters, namely unit power, NOx concentration, combustion chamber vibration acceleration, and combustion chamber pressure pulsation. Warren G. Lamont [20] performed artificial neural network (ANN) modeling of a gas turbine combustion unit to predict gas turbine exhaust gas emissions and combustion chamber outlet temperature. Qian Wang [21] realized the regression model of unsteady flow through proper orthogonal decomposition (POD) and a feedforward neural network (NN). Gianmarco Aversano [22] combined principal component analysis (PCA) with Kriging's method to determine accurate low-order models. In this approach, PCA is used to identify and separate the invariants of the system, and then the Kriging method is used to find a response surface for these coefficients, thus generating a proxy model that allows parametric operations to be performed at a lower computational cost. Woojin Lee [23] used the proper orthogonal decomposition (POD) as well as the Kriging method and radial-basis-function neural network (RBFN) to perform a regression model, in which 500 MWe tangentially fired pulverized coal boilers were regressed and a reduced order model (ROM) was constructed. Wu Yifan et al. [24] combined the elementary cascade method and random forest method to achieve the prediction of compressor outlet temperature and pressure. Part of the feature data was collected using the primitive cascade method, and historical data were inputted into a model based on the random forest method to train and output the compressor outlet temperature and pressure. The average relative errors of the total pressure ratio and variable efficiency calculated by the model were −0.13% and 0.04%, respectively. The maximum relative errors were 2.11% and 1.90%, respectively. Gu X [25] and others used performance deviation models and extreme value function theory to monitor turbine exhaust temperature, mainly including backpropagation neural network (BPNN) models and performance deviation models. By training the BPNN model to output the performance deviation between the predicted and measured values of the turbine exhaust temperature, the normal or abnormal state can be determined. This method has an accuracy of up to 99.85%. The RBF neural network prediction model for combustion chamber emissions established by Sun Jihao [26] can accurately and quickly predict combustion chamber outlet emissions under different structural parameters. The maximum error in predicting NOx is 12.28%, and the average error is 4.58%. The maximum error in predicting CO is 2.75%, and the average error is 0.97%. Fentaye A D [27] combined the artificial neural network (ANN) and SVM to achieve multi-component fouling and erosion gas path fault diagnosis for compressors, power turbines, and gas generators. After inputting data into ANN for sample classification, the SVM model is used for diagnosis. Compared with multilayer perception (MLP), the classification accuracy of this method is more than 10% higher, and the classification accuracy for three component faults is 99.4%. Montazeri Gh M et al. [28] combined a growth neural network (GNN) and residual compensation limit learning machine (RCELM) to learn the fault characteristic map (FCM) of components to diagnose fouling and erosion faults in compressors, gas generators, and power turbines. The user inputs known measurement parameters into an extreme learning machine (ELM) to train and output health status bias. After modeling and compensating for the residual, the robust signal is input into the GNN network for detection, isolation, and recognition. The accuracies of fault detection and isolation are 99.97% and 97.74%, respectively.

At present, most scholars apply machine learning methods to two aspects of the gas turbine field, namely gas turbine outlet parameter prediction and gas turbine fault detection. There are relatively few cases where machine learning methods are applied to predict the internal flow field of gas turbines. Therefore, based on existing research, this article studies the application of ANN in predicting the internal flow field of gas turbine combustion chambers, and it proposes a rapid design method combining ANN and CFD for gas turbine combustion chambers.

2. ANN and XGBoost
2.1. ANN

Figure 1 shows a schematic diagram of a single-hidden-layer ANN.

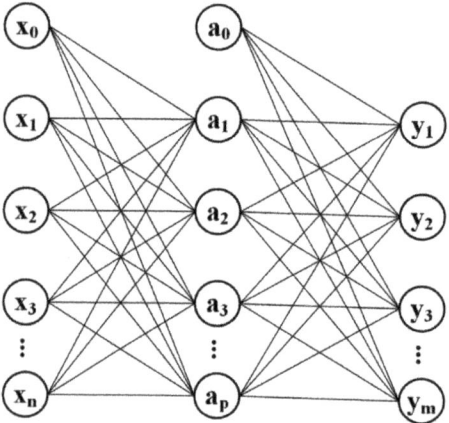

Figure 1. Single-hidden-layer artificial neural network.

The input layer has n neurons from x_1 to x_n, representing each of the n input variables in the dataset. The output layer has m neurons from y_1 to y_m, representing each of the m output variables in the dataset. The hidden layer has p neurons from a_1 to a_p, and passes the data into the output layer after activation by the activation function $tanh(x)$.

$$tanh(x) = \frac{e^x - e^{-x}}{e^x + e^{-x}} \quad (1)$$

From the input layer to the hidden layer, the i-th neuron input to the hidden layer is a_i:

$$a_i = \sum_{k=0}^{n} w_{ik} x_k \quad (2)$$

In the above equation, w_{ik} is the weight of the k-th neuron in the input layer to the i-th neuron in the hidden layer.

The output of the i-th neuron of the hidden layer is z_i:

$$z_i = g(a_i) \quad (3)$$

From the hidden layer to the output layer, the j-th neuron input to the output layer is b_j:

$$b_j = \sum_{i=0}^{p} w_{ji} z_i \quad (4)$$

In the above equation, w_{ji} is the weight of the i-th neuron in the hidden layer to the j-th neuron in the output layer.

The output layer activation function is the Leaky ReLU function $f(x)$:

$$f(x) = \begin{cases} \lambda x, & x < 0 \\ x, & x \geq 0 \end{cases} \quad (5)$$

The output of the j-th neuron of the output layer is y_j:

$$y_j = r(b_j) \quad (6)$$

According to the above algorithm, the neural network propagates forward from the input layer to the output layer, and the value of the output layer can be calculated from the original input data of the dataset and the weights between neurons. The value calculated by the output layer is compared with the value in the dataset, and the neural network node connection weights are continuously updated by using the error backpropagation method (BP algorithm), so as to continuously reduce the error between the model output and the dataset output and optimize the fitting effect. The final output model includes the structure of the neural network, the selection of the neuron activation function, and the connection weight between neurons.

2.2. XGBoost

XGBoost [29] is an efficient gradient boosting decision tree algorithm. It has been improved on the basis of the original GBDT (gradient boosting decision tree), greatly raising the model performance. As a forward addition model, its core is to adopt the integration idea of boosting, which integrates multiple weak learners into a strong learner through certain methods. Multiple trees are used to make joint decisions, and the results of each tree are the difference between the target value and the predicted results of all previous trees. By accumulating all the results, the final result is obtained, thereby improving the overall model performance.

XGBoost is composed of multiple CARTs (classification and regression trees), so it can handle problems such as classification and regression.

The prediction model for XGBoost is

$$\hat{y}_i = \sum_{k=1}^{K} f_k(x_i) \tag{7}$$

In Equation (7), K represents the number of decision trees, f_k represents the k-th decision tree, and $\hat{y}_i$ represents the prediction result of x_i.

Initialization (there is no decision tree in the model, and its prediction result is 0):

$$\hat{y}_i^{(0)} = 0 \tag{8}$$

Add the first decision tree to the model:

$$\hat{y}_i^{(1)} = f_1(x_i) = \hat{y}_i^{(0)} + f_1(x_i) \tag{9}$$

Add the second decision tree to the model:

$$\hat{y}_i^{(2)} = f_1(x_i) + f_2(x_i) = \hat{y}_i^{(1)} + f_2(x_i) \tag{10}$$

Add the t-th decision tree to the model:

$$\hat{y}_i^{(t)} = \sum_{k=1}^{t} f_k(x_i) = \hat{y}_i^{(t-1)} + f_t(x_i) \tag{11}$$

The loss function of XGBoost consists of two parts, namely the training error represented by l and the regularization item represented by Ω:

$$Obj = \sum_{i=1}^{n} l(y_i, \hat{y}_i) + \sum_{k=1}^{K} \Omega(f_k) \tag{12}$$

Every time a decision tree is added to the model, the loss function changes. When the t-th decision tree is added, the previous $t-1$ decision trees have completed training, and the training error and regularization item of the previous $t-1$ decision trees have become constants. Therefore, the loss function can also be written as

$$Obj = \sum_{i=1}^{n} l\left(y_i, \hat{y}_i^{(t-1)} + f_t(x_i)\right) + \Omega(f_t) + C \tag{13}$$

The regularization item can be rewritten as

$$\Omega(f_t) = \gamma T + \frac{1}{2}\lambda \sum_{j=1}^{T} w_j^2 \tag{14}$$

In the above equation, T is the number of leaf nodes, and w is the score of the leaf nodes. Substituting Equation (14) into Equation (13) yields

$$Obj = \sum_{i=1}^{n} l\left(y_i, \hat{y}_i^{(t-1)} + f_t(x_i)\right) + \gamma T + \frac{1}{2}\lambda \sum_{j=1}^{T} w_j^2 + C \tag{15}$$

Perform second-order Taylor expansion on Equation (15), and make the following assumptions:

$$g_i = \partial_{\hat{y}^{(t-1)}} l\left(y_i, \hat{y}^{(t-1)}\right) \tag{16}$$

$$h_i = \partial^2_{\hat{y}^{(t-1)}} l\left(y_i, \hat{y}^{(t-1)}\right) \tag{17}$$

$$G_j = \sum_{i \in I_j} g_i \tag{18}$$

$$H_j = \sum_{i \in I_j} h_i \tag{19}$$

The I_j in Equations (18) and (19) represents the sample on the j-th leaf node. The loss function can be written as

$$Obj = \sum_{j=1}^{T} \left[G_j w_j + \frac{1}{2}(H_j + \lambda) w_j^2 \right] + \gamma T \tag{20}$$

As shown in Equation (20), the loss function can be seen as a quadratic function about w_j, where there exists a w_j that minimizes the loss function:

$$w_j^* = -\frac{G_j}{H_j + \lambda} \tag{21}$$

3. Prediction of Combustion Chamber Parameters

3.1. CFD Calculation

The data used in this paper are from CFD simulations of a single-tube micro-hybrid combustion chamber. The geometry of the single-tube combustion chamber is well defined and the internal flow state is relatively simple, making it suitable for prediction of its internal parameters by artificial neural networks. The development of micro-mix combustion, a combustion technology proposed in recent years for hydrogen-rich fuel combustion, has resulted in smaller gas turbines and more efficient mixing. The principle is to reduce the mixing time by reducing the mixing scale through several simplified micro-nozzles instead of the traditional large-diameter nozzle structure [30].

The structure of the combustion chamber is shown in Figure 2. The main body length of the combustion chamber is 300 mm, the cross-section of the chamber is square, and the side length is 40 mm. The combustion chamber consists of four cylindrical nozzles with a diameter of 12 mm and a length of 64 mm.

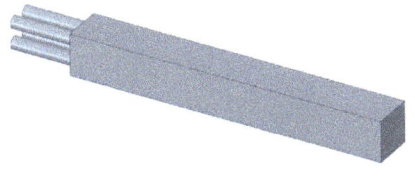

Figure 2. Combustion chamber structure.

The combustion chamber grid is shown in Figure 3.

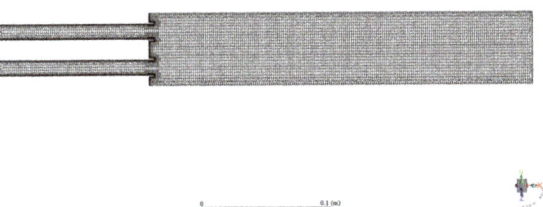

Figure 3. Cross-section grid of combustion chamber.

Using Ansys Fluent 2022R1 for CFD calculation and Reynolds averaged Navier–Stokes (RANS) simulation for combustion chamber flow field, the control equation system cannot be closed due to the introduction of additional stress. Therefore, the Realizable $k-\varepsilon$ model widely used in the field of micro mixed combustion is used. The combustion model adopts Flamelet Generated Manifold (FGM). The continuity equation, momentum equation, and energy equation in the RANS simulation control equation are as follows:

$$\frac{\partial \rho \overline{u}_i}{\partial x_i} + \frac{\partial \rho}{\partial t} = 0 \tag{22}$$

$$\frac{\partial \rho \overline{u}_i}{\partial t} + \frac{\partial \rho \overline{u}_i \overline{u}_j}{\partial x_j} = -\frac{\partial \overline{p}}{\partial x_i} + \frac{\partial \sigma_{ij}}{\partial x_j} + \frac{\partial \left(-\rho \overline{u'_i u'_j}\right)}{\partial x_j} \tag{23}$$

$$\frac{\partial}{\partial t}(\rho \overline{E}) + \frac{\partial}{\partial x_j}\left(u_j(\rho \overline{E} + \overline{p})\right) = \frac{\partial}{\partial x_j}\left(k \frac{\partial \overline{\overline{T}}}{\partial x_j} - \rho c_p \overline{u'_j T'}\right) + S \tag{24}$$

In the above equations, $\overline{u}_i$ represents Reynolds average velocity, σ_{ij} represents stress tensor, $-\rho \overline{u'_i u'_j}$ represents Reynolds stress, k represents turbulent kinetic energy, and u'_i represents pulsating velocity.

The mole fractions of fuel and oxidant, as well as the boundary conditions for CFD solution, are shown in Tables 1 and 2:

Table 1. Mole fraction of fuel and oxidant.

Species	Fuel	Oxid
O_2	0	0.21
CH_4	0.9623	0
CO_2	0.0047	0
C_2H_6	0.0233	0
N_2	0.0097	0.79

Table 2. Boundary conditions in Ansys Fluent 2022R1.

Boundary Condition	Option
Inlet Mass Flow Rate [kg/s]	0.07286
Inlet Turbulent Intensity [%]	20
Inlet Hydraulic Diameter [m]	0.012
Outlet Backflow Turbulent Intensity [%]	5
Outlet Backflow Turbulent Viscosity Ratio	10
Wall Motion	Stationary Wall
Shear Condition	No Slip
Wall Roughness Model	Standard
Ignition Temperature [K]	2000

3.2. Dataset Preprocessing

The raw dataset contains 42 physical parameters on 941,774 grid points in the combustion chamber, containing pressure, density, x-axis direction velocity, temperature, oxygen molar fraction, nitrogen molar fraction, and nitrogen oxide molar fraction. In order to simplify the calculation, the 3D coordinates of the 941,774 grid points of the combustion chamber are chosen as the input X to the artificial neural network in this paper:

$$X = \begin{bmatrix} c_x^1 & \cdots & c_x^{941,774} \\ c_y^1 & \cdots & c_y^{941,774} \\ c_z^1 & \cdots & c_z^{941,774} \end{bmatrix} \quad (25)$$

In the above equation, c_x^1 to $c_x^{941,774}$ are the x-axis coordinates on all grid points; c_y^1 to $c_y^{941,774}$ are the y-axis coordinates on all grid points; c_z^1 to $c_z^{941,774}$ are the z-axis coordinates on all grid points.

The five parameters corresponding to pressure, density, velocity in the x-axis direction, temperature, and molar fraction of oxygen are chosen as the outputs of the artificial neural network Y:

$$Y = \begin{bmatrix} p^1 & \cdots & p^{941,774} \\ d^1 & \cdots & d^{941,774} \\ v_x^1 & \cdots & v_x^{941,774} \\ t^1 & \cdots & t^{941,774} \\ o_2^1 & \cdots & o_2^{941,774} \end{bmatrix} \quad (26)$$

In the above equation, p^1 to $p^{941,774}$ are the pressure values on all grid points; d^1 to $d^{941,774}$ are the density values on all grid points; v_x^1 to $v_x^{941,774}$ are the velocity values in the x-axis direction on all grid points; t^1 to $t^{941,774}$ are the temperature values on all grid points; and o_2^1 to $o_2^{941,774}$ are the oxygen molar fractions on all grid points.

Data preprocessing consists of two main aspects: outlier processing and normalization. The dataset is scanned for outliers using the box line diagram method. As shown in Figure 4, data that are not determined to be outliers are not processed and data that are determined to be outliers are replaced with an upper limit if it is greater than the upper limit of the box plot method and a lower limit if it is less than the lower limit of the box plot method. The first quartile (Q1), also known as the 'lower quartile' or 'lower quartile', is equal to the 25th percentile of all values in the sample in descending order. The second quartile (Q2), also known as the 'median', is equal to the 50th percentile of all values in the sample from the smallest to the largest. The third quartile (Q3), also known as the 'greater quartile' or 'upper quartile', is equal to the 75th percentile of all the values in the sample from the smallest to the largest. Data less than the lower quartile Q1−1.5 × IQR or greater than the upper quartile Q3+1.5 × IQR are considered outliers and are replaced by the lower and upper quartiles, respectively, with the remaining normal values being left untreated.

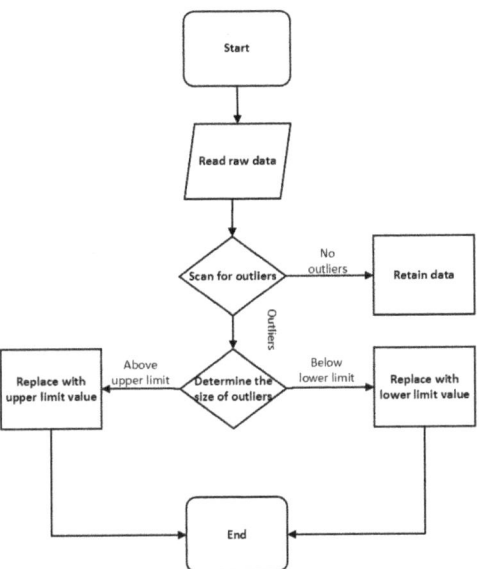

Figure 4. Outlier preprocessing flow chart.

The input and output data have different scale units with large differences in order of magnitude, which is neither conducive to the convergence of the neural network nor to the evaluation of errors in the subsequent process. The dataset is linearly normalized by scaling the input data to $[-1, 1]$ and the output data to $[0, 1]$, as shown in Equations (27) and (28):

$$x' = \frac{x - mean(x)}{max(x) - min(x)} \tag{27}$$

$$y' = \frac{y - min(y)}{max(y) - min(y)} \tag{28}$$

The training set is used to update the weights to fit the network and to continuously improve the accuracy. The validation and test sets are used to check how well the model matches the data not involved in the training, i.e., to check the generalization ability of the model trained from the training set. Due to the large amount of raw data, the partition ratio of the training set, validation set, and testing set is 98:1:1.

3.3. Training of ANN

Firstly, the network structure of the neural network is determined, which mainly includes the number of hidden layers, the number of hidden-layer neurons, the training algorithm, and the activation function of each layer. Theoretically, the structure of multiple hidden layers has a better fitting effect on multivariate non-linear mapping relationships. The number of neurons in the hidden layer is similar to the number of layers in the hidden layer. Increasing the number of neurons can better fit the non-linear relationship, but at the same time increases the possibility of overfitting and time cost, so the number of nodes should be reduced as much as possible while considering the number of input and output features and ensuring the accuracy of the fit. The optimization algorithm is an algorithm that adjusts the connection weights of the neural network nodes according to the error, and the Adam algorithm is chosen. By adjusting its initial learning rate, it can ensure that the update step size is limited to an approximate range, and at the same time can achieve automatic adjustment of the learning rate, which is very suitable for the application scenarios of large-scale data in this paper. The tanh (1) is chosen for the hidden layer, which has a strong learning capability and is a good fit for multivariate non-linear problems with output values in (0, 1). The Leaky ReLU (5) is chosen for the output layer, which can further accelerate the convergence speed.

The mean square error (MSE) was chosen as the loss function, and the ANN model with different numbers of hidden layers, different numbers of neurons, and different initial learning rates was trained 20 times, each time with 2000 epochs. The lowest value of the MSE was taken for comparison to select the artificial neural network model with the best prediction effect. The code for the ANN was written in Python3.9 and PyCharm Community Edition 2023.2.1.

3.4. Training of XGBoost

To simplify the model, only manual adjustments were made to the hyperparameters of learning rate and number of decision trees. The range of learning rate values was 0.01 to 0.2, and the adjustment range for the number of decision trees was 100 to 500. In theory, a small learning rate and a small number of decision trees can lead to poor model accuracy, while large ones carry a greater risk of overfitting. During the hyperparameter adjustment process, if the MSE of the test set no longer decreases as the learning rate and number of decision trees increase, it indicates that the optimal hyperparameter combination has been found.

4. Results Analysis

4.1. Number of ANN Hidden-Layer Neurons and Learning Rate

Theoretically, as the number of hidden layers and neurons increases, artificial neural networks become more capable of extracting the non-linear mapping relationship between input and output. However, in practice, too many layers of hidden layers or the number of neurons can also bring about overfitting problems. In order to obtain the optimal artificial neural network structure, this section explores the effect of different numbers of hidden layers and different numbers of neurons in each hidden layer on the error. As shown in Figure 5, the MSE of the validation set tends to decrease and then increase as the number of neurons increases when only a single hidden layer is used. When 30 neurons are included, the MSE is the smallest, at 0.0108.

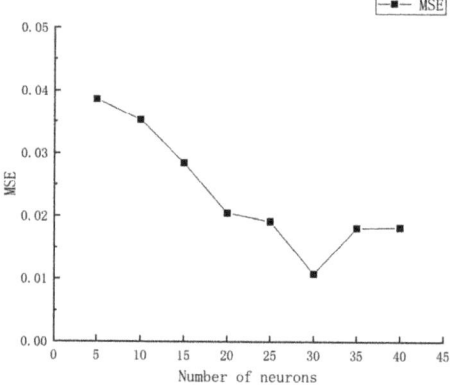

Figure 5. Relationship between number of neurons in single hidden layer and MSE.

As shown in Figure 6, with the use of double hidden layers, the MSE of the validation set is significantly larger when the first hidden layer has 5 and 10 neurons. When the first hidden layer has 15, 20, 25, and 30 neurons, the MSE is relatively well distributed between 0.01 and 0.002. In particular, when the first hidden layer contains 20 neurons and the second hidden layer contains 10 neurons, the mean squared error is the smallest at 0.0019.

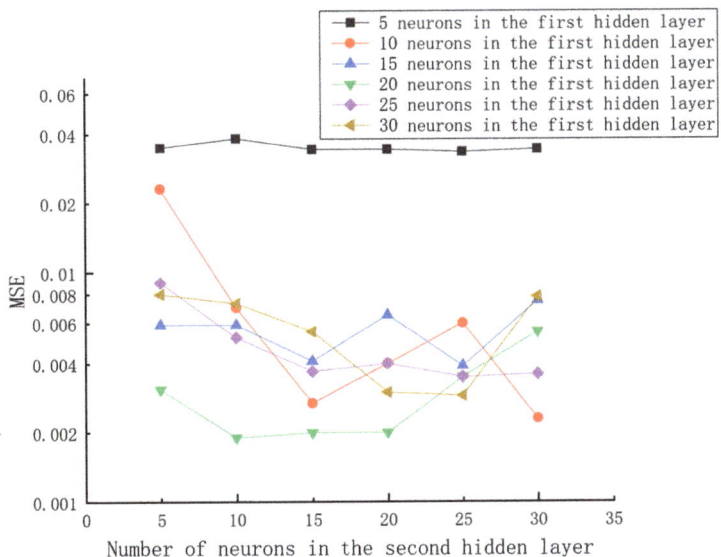

Figure 6. Relationship between the number of double-hidden-layer neurons and MSE.

As shown in Figure 7, 5*10 in the legend represents that the first hidden layer contains 5 neurons and the second hidden layer contains 10 neurons. In the case of using three hidden layers, when the numbers of neurons in the first hidden layer and the second hidden layer are both 5, and when the first hidden layer and the second hidden layer contain 5 and 10 neurons, respectively, the MSE of the validation set is greater than 0.025, which is significantly larger. When the first hidden layer contains 10 neurons, the second hidden layer contains 5 neurons, and the third hidden layer contains 15 neurons, the MSE is the smallest, reaching 0.0035.

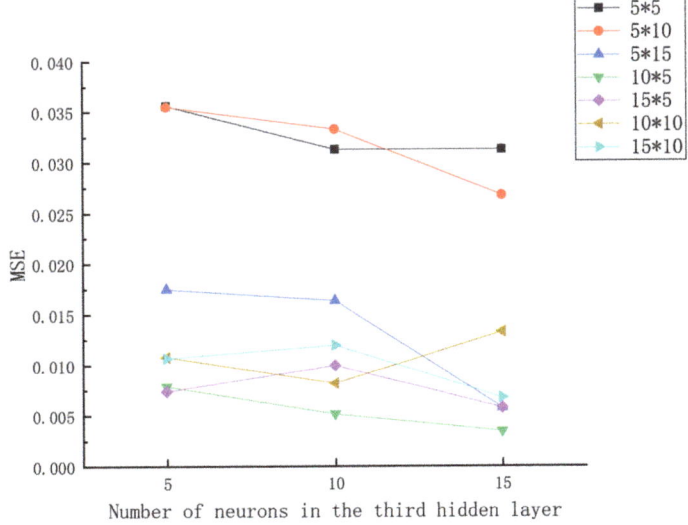

Figure 7. Relationship between number of neurons in three hidden layers and MSE.

In summary, the minimum MSE in learning 2000 epochs is 0.0108 for the single-hidden-layer structure and 0.0019 for the double-hidden-layer structure. The minimum MSE for the triple-hidden-layer structure is 0.0035. Therefore, the optimal structure is the double-hidden-layer structure, where the first hidden layer contains 20 neurons and the second hidden layer contains 10 neurons.

The learning rate affects the speed of convergence of the error. The larger the learning rate, the faster the error decreases, but it may oscillate back and forth around the minimum or even fail to converge. In order to arrive at the most appropriate initial learning rate for the optimal ANN structure explored in the previous section, this paper goes on to compare the effect of different initial learning rates on the error.

As shown in Figure 8, when the initial learning rate is 0.05, 0.01, or 0.005, the mean squared error of the validation set drops to less than 0.01 at 500 epochs of training, and the convergence rate is relatively fast. When the initial learning rate is 0.01, the validation set MSE is the smallest, and the error value is 0.0019 when trained to 2000 epochs.

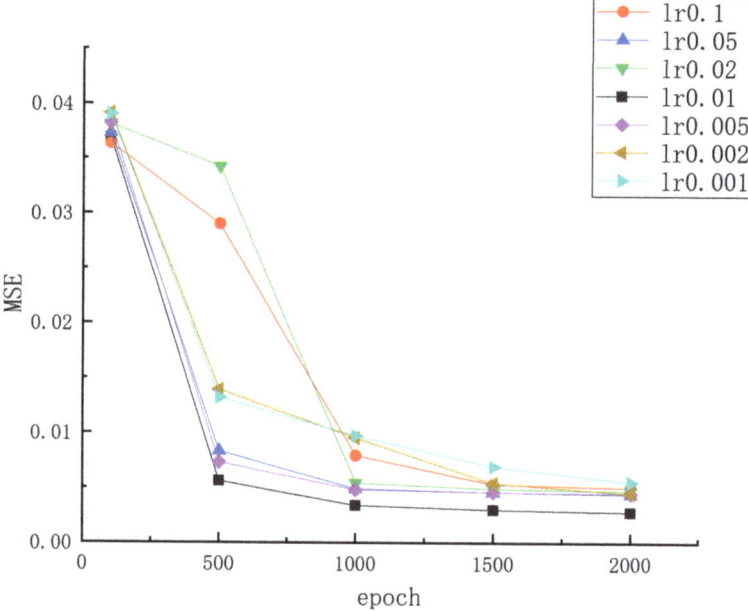

Figure 8. MSE decline process with different initial learning rates.

4.2. XGBoost

The hyperparameters of learning rate and number of decision trees have a significant impact on the error of XGBoost regression. The higher the learning rate, the higher the model accuracy but the greater the tendency for overfitting; the smaller the learning rate, the lower the overfitting tendency of the model, but the lower the accuracy. The more decision trees there are, the more complex the model becomes and the more prone it is to overfitting. As shown in Figure 9, as the learning rate and number of decision trees continue to increase, the MSE of XGBoost on the test set shows a decreasing trend. When the learning rate is 0.2, XGBoost regression has the best effect, but when the number of decision trees exceeds 200, the downward trend of MSE is no longer significant and ultimately reaches 0.0021.

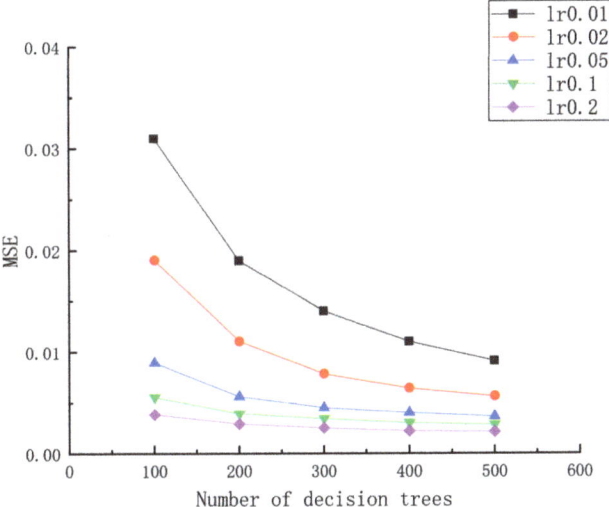

Figure 9. MSE decline process with different initial learning rates and numbers of decision trees.

4.3. Visualization

Predictions of the combustion chamber parameters were made using artificial neural networks based on the studies in the previous two sections. Fourteen groups of CFD raw data and predicted values in the test set were randomly intercepted and compared, as shown in Figures 10–14. Overall, the artificial neural network predictions for the five parameters of pressure, density, x-axis direction velocity, temperature, and oxygen molar fraction are relatively close to the CFD raw data, indicating that the prediction of the combustion chamber parameters using artificial neural networks is feasible.

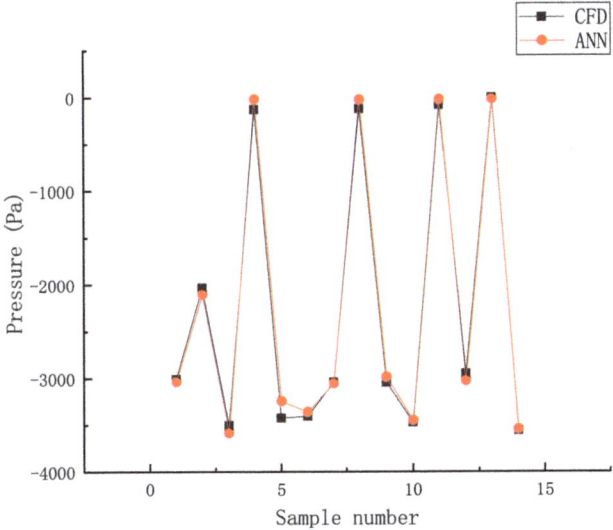

Figure 10. Comparison of raw pressure data and predicted pressure.

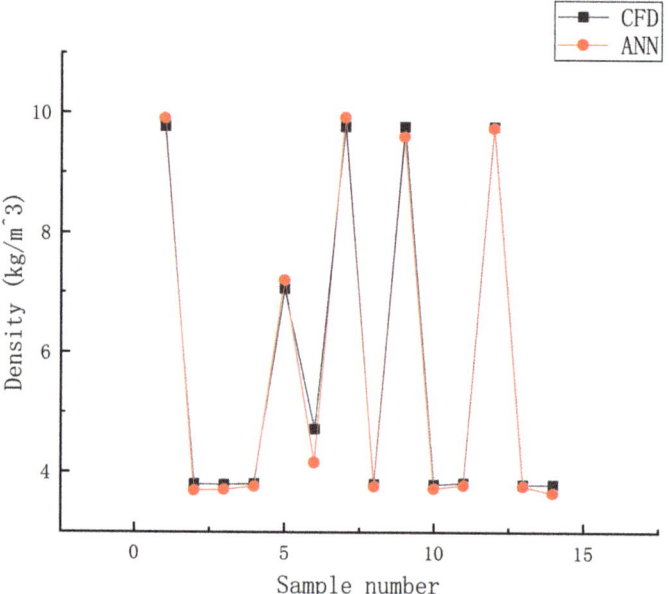

Figure 11. Comparison of raw density data and predicted value.

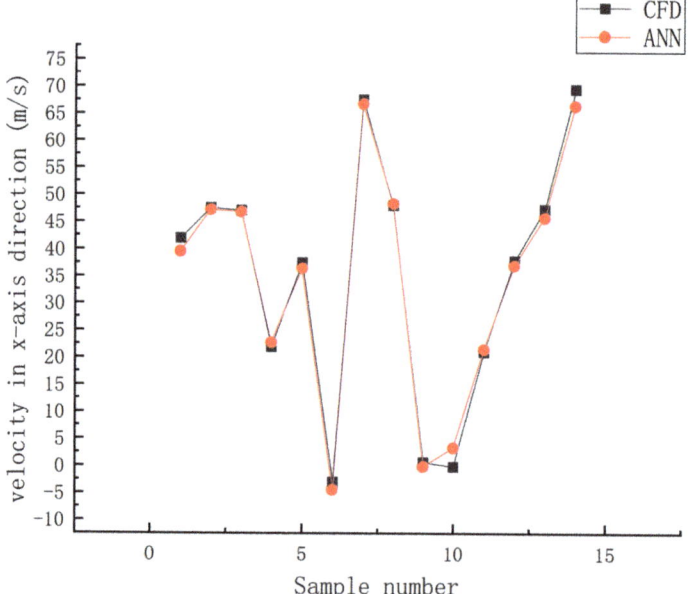

Figure 12. Comparison of raw data and predicted value of velocity in x-axis direction.

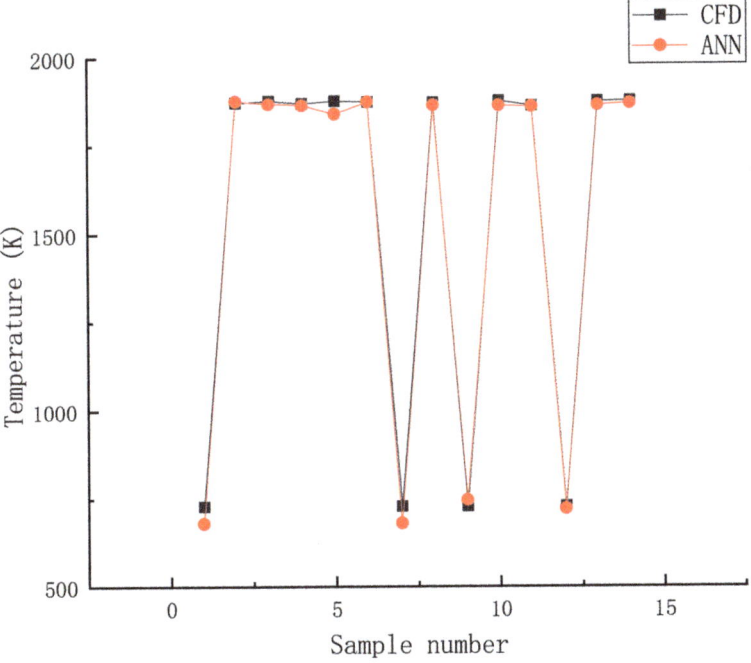

Figure 13. Comparison of raw temperature data and predicted value.

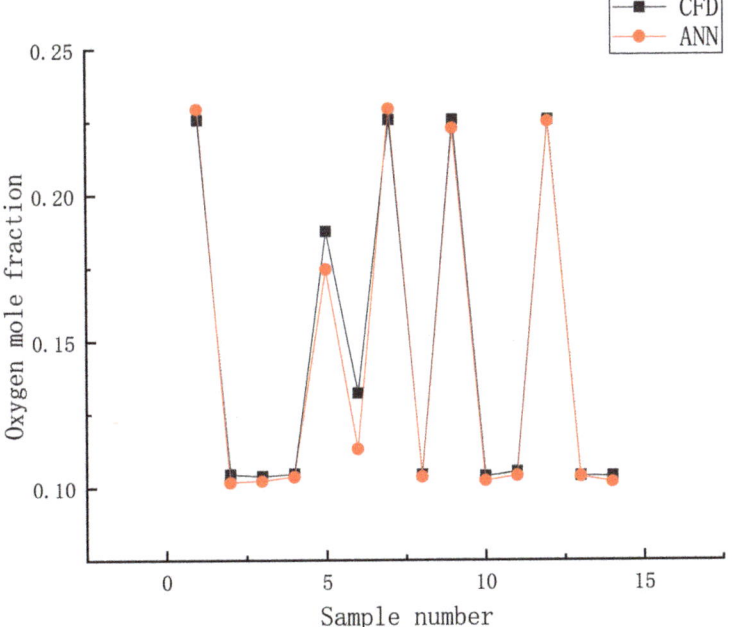

Figure 14. Comparison of raw data and predicted values of oxygen mole fraction.

As shown in Figure 10, except for how the predicted value of the 5th group of pressure is slightly higher than the original data, the other 13 groups of data are very close. In Figure 11, the density prediction value of group 6 is slightly higher than the original data. In Figure 12, the predicted value of the 10th group of x-axis speed is slightly higher than the original data. As shown in Figure 13, the 14 groups of predicted temperature values are close to the original data. In Figure 14, the predicted oxygen mole fraction values of groups 5 and 6 are slightly less than those in the original data.

In order to explore the reasons for the deviation between the above individual predicted values and the original data, the training epoch of the neural network was increased from 2000 to 5000, but there was no change in the experimental results, indicating that the training epoch of the neural network was independent of the deviation. Further conjecture is that there are individual outliers in the original data, and the impact of this aspect needs to be further studied.

For a more intuitive comparison of the prediction accuracies of artificial neural networks, as shown in Figures 15–19, we plotted the original data and predicted values of the test set into point cloud maps. From the results, it can be seen that there are outliers in the point clouds of the raw data of each parameter that differ significantly from the values of nearby grid points, while there are basically no outliers in the predicted point clouds. Overall, the CFD raw data are highly consistent with the ANN predicted values, indicating that outliers in the raw data have a small impact on the ANN predicted results, and the ANN predicted results are in line with expectations.

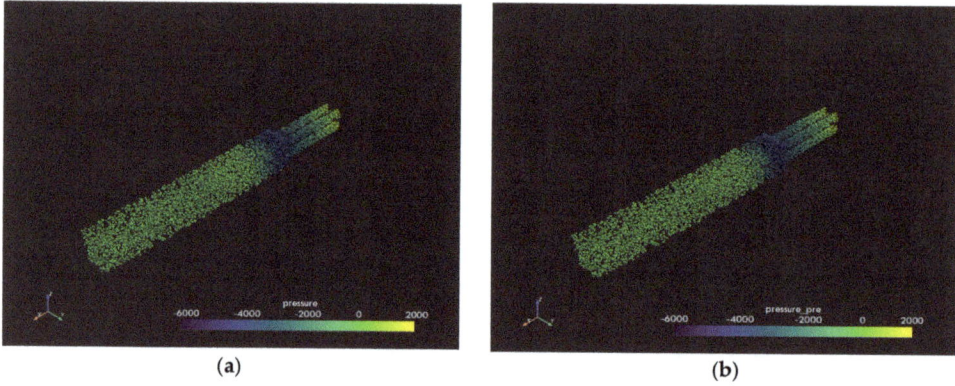

Figure 15. Pressure point cloud: (**a**) original data; (**b**) predicted values.

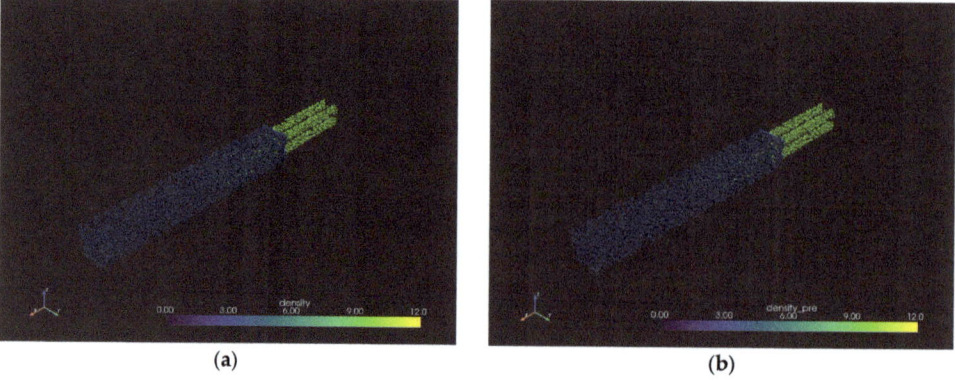

Figure 16. Density point cloud: (**a**) original data; (**b**) predicted values.

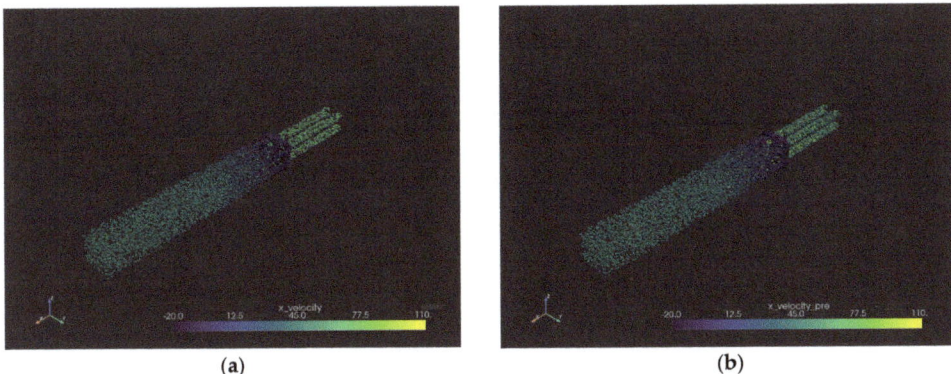

Figure 17. Velocity point cloud in x-axis direction: (**a**) original data; (**b**) predicted values.

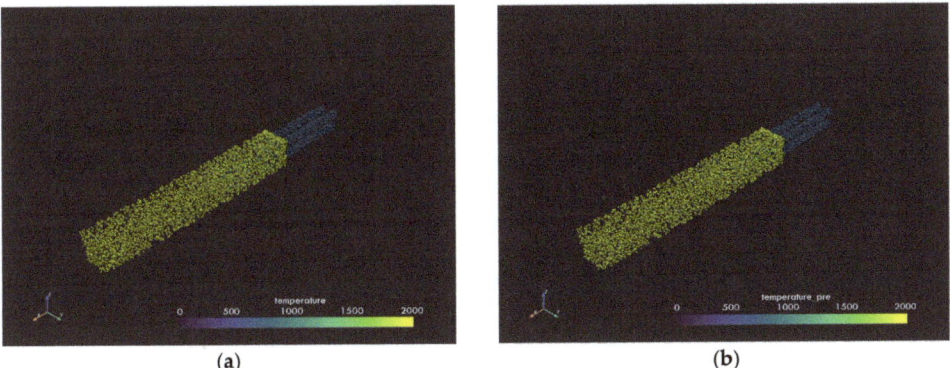

Figure 18. Temperature point cloud: (**a**) original data; (**b**) predicted values.

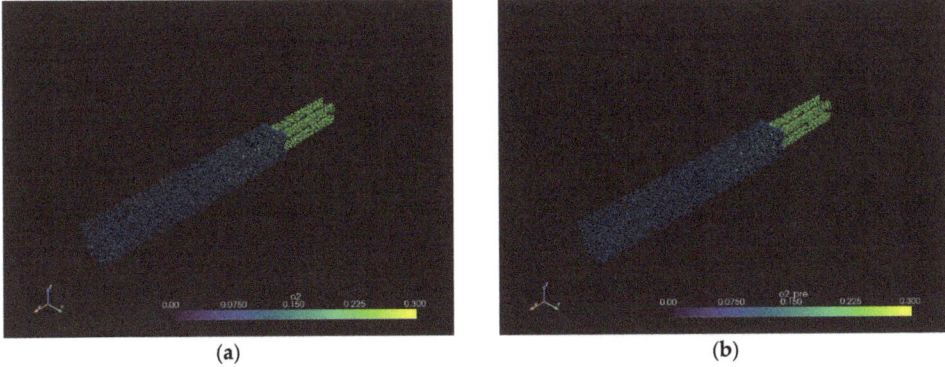

Figure 19. Oxygen mole fraction point cloud: (**a**) original data; (**b**) predicted values.

5. Conclusions

This article applies the CFD calculation results to the training of the ANN and XGBoost for a single-tube micro mixed combustion chamber model. By inputting three-dimensional positional coordinates, we predict the distribution of five parameters in the combustion chamber: pressure, density, x-axis velocity, temperature, and oxygen mole fraction. This article investigates the effects of the number of hidden layers and neurons, as well as the number of decision trees, on two fast prediction models based on the ANN and XGBoost. Research has shown that compared with the CFD calculation results, the MSE of the ANN predicted value is 0.0019, which is better than XGBoost, and the outliers in the predicted value are significantly less than the CFD calculation results. Moreover, the training duration of the ANN is only 6 min, which is much shorter than the calculation duration of CFD, which often takes several hours. Therefore, the fast prediction method of combustion chamber parameters based on artificial neural networks can assist in CFD calculation during the combustion chamber design process, greatly accelerating the calculation speed while ensuring accuracy.

The current research is a preliminary exploration of digital twins in gas turbine components. The research can be extended to the prediction of multiple operating conditions in the combustion chamber, and the fast prediction model can be connected in series with the combustion chamber control system to achieve true digital twins at the component level or even the entire machine level.

Author Contributions: Conceptualization, C.S. and Y.L.; methodology, C.S., Y.L. and Z.Z.; software, C.S. and F.L.; validation, C.S.; formal analysis, C.S.; investigation, J.F.; resources, Y.L. and F.L.; data curation, C.S. and F.L.; writing—original draft preparation, C.S.; writing—review and editing, C.S. and Y.L.; visualization, C.S.; supervision, Y.L. and J.F.; project administration, Y.L.; funding acquisition, Y.L. All authors have read and agreed to the published version of the manuscript.

Funding: This research received no external funding.

Data Availability Statement: The data presented in this study and the code are available on request from the corresponding author.

Acknowledgments: The authors wish to acknowledge the energy and power research center of the Institute of Engineering Thermophysics, Chinese Academy of Sciences for its assistance in the CFD calculation of combustion chamber data.

Conflicts of Interest: The authors declare no conflict of interest.

References

1. Jiang, H. Promote Heavy Duty Gas Turbine Core Technology Development and Industrial Application in China. *J. Chin. Soc. Power Eng.* **2011**, *31*, 563–566.
2. Suo, J.; Feng, X.; Liang, H. Numerical Simulation for Research and Development of Aero Engine Combustor. *Aerosp. Power* **2021**, *2*, 61–65.
3. Cao, J. Status Challenges and Perspectives of Aero-Engine Simulation Technology. *J. Propuls. Technol.* **2018**, *39*, 961–970.
4. National Academies of Sciences, Engineering, and Medicine. *Advanced Technologies for Gas Turbines*; National Academies Press: Washington, DC, USA, 2020.
5. Zhou, Z. *Machine Learning*; Tsinghua University Press: Beijing, China, 2016.
6. Li, H. *Statistical Learning Methods*, 2nd ed.; Tsinghua University Press: Beijing, China, 2019.
7. Raccuglia, P.; Elbert, K.; Adler, P.; Falk, C.; Wenny, M.B.; Mollo, A.; Zeller, M.; Friedler, S.A.; Schrier, J.; Norquist, A.J. Machine-learning-assisted materials discovery using failed experiments. *Nature* **2016**, *533*, 73–76. [CrossRef] [PubMed]
8. Shandiz, M.; Gauvin, R. Application of machine learning methods for the prediction of crystal system of cathode materials in lithium-ion batteries. *Comput. Mater. Sci.* **2016**, *117*, 270–278. [CrossRef]
9. Sendek, A.; Yang, Q.; Cubuk, E.; Duerloo, K.-A.N.; Cui, Y.; Reed, E.J. Holistic computational structure screening of more than 12000 candidates for solid lithium-ion conductor materials. *Energy Environ. Sci.* **2017**, *10*, 306–320. [CrossRef]
10. Tao, Y.; Cui, C.; Zhang, Y.; Xu, Y.; Fan, W.; Han, X.; Han, J.; Li, C.; He, B.; Li, S.; et al. The Application and Improvement of Deep Learning in Astronomy. *Prog. Astron.* **2020**, *38*, 168–188.
11. Chen, Y.; Zou, B.; Zhang, M.; Liao, W.; Huang, J.; Zhu, C. A review on deep learning interpretability in medical image processing. *J. Zhejiang Univ. (Sci. Ed.)* **2021**, *48*, 18–29.
12. LeCun, Y.; Bottou, L.; Bengio, Y.; Haffner, P. Gradient-based learning applied to document recognition. *Proc. IEEE* **1998**, *86*, 2278–2324. [CrossRef]
13. Krizhevsky, A.; Sutskever, I.; Hinton, G. ImageNet classification with deep convolutional neural networks. *Commun. ACM* **2017**, *60*, 84–90. [CrossRef]
14. He, K.; Zhang, X.; Ren, S.; Sun, J. Deep residual learning for image recognition. In Proceedings of the IEEE Conference on Computer Vision and Pattern Recognition, Las Vegas, NV, USA, 27–30 June 2016; pp. 770–778.

15. Hochreiter, S.; Schmidhuber, J. Long short-term memory. *Neural Comput.* **1997**, *9*, 1735–1780. [CrossRef]
16. Cho, K.; Van Merriënboer, M.; Bahdanau, D.; Bengio, Y. On the properties of neural machine translation: Encoder-decoder approaches. *arXiv* **2014**, arXiv:1409.1259.
17. Kingma, D.; Welling, M. Auto-encoding variational bayes. *arXiv* **2013**, arXiv:1312.6114.
18. Goodfellow, I.; Pouget-Abadie, J.; Mirza, M.; Xu, B.; Warde-Farley, D.; Ozair, S.; Bengio, Y. Generative adversarial nets. *Adv. Neural Inf. Process. Syst.* **2014**, *27*, 2672–2680.
19. Zhao, G.; Zhu, H.; Li, S.; Min, Z.; Xiaofeng, W. NOx Emission Prediction and Optimization for Gas Turbines Based on Data and Neural Network. *J. Chin. Soc. Power Eng.* **2021**, *41*, 22–27.
20. Lamont, W.; Roa, M.; Lucht, R. Application of artificial neural networks for the prediction of pollutant emissions and outlet temperature in a fuel-staged gas turbine combustion rig. Turbo Expo: Power for Land, Sea, and Air. In Proceedings of the American Society of Mechanical Engineers 2014, Düsseldorf, Germany, 16–20 June 2014.
21. Wang, Q.; Hesthaven, J.; Ray, D. Non-intrusive reduced order modeling of unsteady flows using artificial neural networks with application to a combustion problem. *J. Comput. Phys.* **2019**, *384*, 289–307. [CrossRef]
22. Aversano, G.; Bellemans, A.; Li, Z.; Coussement, A.; Gicquel, O.; Parente, A. Application of reduced-order models based on PCA & Kriging for the development of digital twins of reacting flow applications. *Comput. Chem. Eng.* **2019**, *121*, 422–441.
23. Lee, W.; Jang, K.; Han, W.; Huh, K.Y. Model order reduction by proper orthogonal decomposition for a 500 MWe tangentially fired pulverized coal boiler. *Case Stud. Therm. Eng.* **2021**, *28*, 101414. [CrossRef]
24. Wu, Y.; Wu, X.; Rui, X.; Tian, R.; Qiu, L.; Yan, J. Study on Characteristics Analysis of Heavy-Duty Gas Turbine Axial Compressor Under off-Design Condition. *Gas Turbine Technol.* **2019**, *32*, 12–15+67.
25. Gu, X.; Yang, S.; Sui, Y.; Papatheou, E.; Ball, A.D.; Gu, F. Real-time novelty detection of an industrial gas turbine using performance deviation model and extreme function theory. *Measurement* **2021**, *178*, 109339. [CrossRef]
26. Sun, J.; Song, Y.; Shi, Y.; Zhao, N.; Zheng, H. Prediction of the pollutant generation of a natural gas-powered coaxial staged combustor. *J. Tsinghua Univ. (Sci. Technol.)* **2023**, *63*, 649–659.
27. Fentaye, A.; Ul-Haq Gilani, S.; Baheta, A.; Li, Y.-G. Performance-based fault diagnosis of a gas turbine engine using an integrated support vector machine and artificial neural network method. *Proc. Inst. Mech. Eng. Part A J. Power Energy* **2019**, *233*, 786–802. [CrossRef]
28. Montazeri-Gh, M.; Nekoonam, A.; Yazdani, S. A novel approach to gas turbine fault diagnosis based on learning of fault characteristic maps using hybrid residual compensation extreme learning machine-growing neural gas model. *J. Braz. Soc. Mech. Sci. Eng.* **2021**, *43*, 430. [CrossRef]
29. Chen, T.; Guestrin, C. Xgboost: A scalable tree boosting system. In Proceedings of the 22nd ACM SIGKDD International Conference on Knowledge Discovery and Data Mining, New York, NY, USA, 13–17 August 2016; pp. 785–794.
30. Yunoki, K.; Murota, T.; Asai, T.; Okazaki, T. Large Eddy Simulation of a Multiple-Injection Dry Low NOx Combustor for Hydrogen-Rich Syngas Fuel at High Pressure. In Proceedings of the ASME Turbo Expo 2016: Turbomachinery Technical Conference and Exposition, Seoul, Republic of Korea, 13–17 June 2016.

Disclaimer/Publisher's Note: The statements, opinions and data contained in all publications are solely those of the individual author(s) and contributor(s) and not of MDPI and/or the editor(s). MDPI and/or the editor(s) disclaim responsibility for any injury to people or property resulting from any ideas, methods, instructions or products referred to in the content.

Article

Deep-Learning-Based Water Quality Monitoring and Early Warning Methods: A Case Study of Ammonia Nitrogen Prediction in Rivers

Xianhe Wang [1,2], Mu Qiao [2], Ying Li [1,2], Adriano Tavares [2], Qian Qiao [1] and Yanchun Liang [3,4,*]

1 School of Applied Chemistry and Materials, Zhuhai College of Science and Technology, Zhuhai 519041, China; wxh@zcst.edu.cn (X.W.)
2 Department of Industrial Electronics, School of Engineering, University of Minho, 4704-553 Braga, Portugal
3 School of Computer Science, Zhuhai College of Science and Technology, Zhuhai 519041, China
4 Key Laboratory of Symbol Computation and Knowledge Engineering of the Ministry of Education, College of Computer Science and Technology, Jilin University, 2699 Qianjin Street, Changchun 130012, China
* Correspondence: ycliang@jlu.edu.cn

Citation: Wang, X.; Qiao, M.; Li, Y.; Tavares, A.; Qiao, Q.; Liang, Y. Deep-Learning-Based Water Quality Monitoring and Early Warning Methods: A Case Study of Ammonia Nitrogen Prediction in Rivers. *Electronics* **2023**, *12*, 4645. https://doi.org/10.3390/electronics12224645

Academic Editor: Ping-Feng Pai

Received: 16 October 2023
Revised: 10 November 2023
Accepted: 12 November 2023
Published: 14 November 2023

Copyright: © 2023 by the authors. Licensee MDPI, Basel, Switzerland. This article is an open access article distributed under the terms and conditions of the Creative Commons Attribution (CC BY) license (https://creativecommons.org/licenses/by/4.0/).

Abstract: In line with rapid economic development and accelerated urbanization, the increasing discharge of wastewater and agricultural fertilizer usage has led to a gradual rise in ammonia nitrogen levels in rivers. High concentrations of ammonia nitrogen pose a significant challenge, causing eutrophication and adversely affecting the aquatic ecosystems and sustainable utilization of water resources. Traditional ammonia nitrogen detection methods suffer from limitations such as cumbersome sample handling and analysis, low sensitivity, and lack of real-time and dynamic feedback. In contrast, automated monitoring and ammonia nitrogen prediction technologies offer more efficient methods and accurate solutions. However, existing approaches still have some shortcomings, including sample processing complexity, interference issues, and the absence of real-time and dynamic information feedback. Consequently, deep learning techniques have emerged as promising methods to address these challenges. In this paper, we propose the application of a neural network model based on Long Short-Term Memory (LSTM) to analyze and model ammonia nitrogen monitoring data, enabling high-precision prediction of ammonia nitrogen indicators. Moreover, through correlation analysis between water quality parameters and ammonia nitrogen indicators, we identify a set of key feature indicators to enhance prediction efficiency and reduce costs. Experimental validation demonstrates the potential of our proposed approach to improve the accuracy, timeliness, and precision of ammonia nitrogen monitoring and prediction, which could provide support for environmental management and water resource governance.

Keywords: artificial intelligence; LSTM model; neural networks; deep learning; applications of computational intelligence

1. Introduction

In recent years, rapid economic development and accelerated urbanization have led to improvements in industrial and agricultural production, as well as the living standards of urban residents. However, this progress has resulted in increased wastewater discharge and agricultural fertilizer usage, leading to a gradual rise in the concentration of ammonia nitrogen in rivers [1]. While ammonia nitrogen is an essential nutrient in river water, excessive levels can cause environmental issues, with water eutrophication being one of the most serious problems [2]. Eutrophication refers to the excessive nutrient content in river water, which triggers a rapid increase in biomass and fundamental changes in the aquatic ecosystem [3]. High concentrations of ammonia nitrogen promote the growth of algae and other aquatic plants, leading to an abundance of algae and phytoplankton discoloration, and the emergence of harmful algae such as "Blue-Green Algae". The proliferation and death of these organisms result in a sharp decline in dissolved oxygen, deteriorating water quality and creating "Dead Zones". These not only affect the river's aquatic ecosystem but also have significant negative consequences for water resource utilization and ecological conservation. Moreover, excessive ammonia nitrogen levels pose risks to other organisms, including fish and invertebrates, affecting their respiratory and reproductive systems, and potentially causing respiratory difficulties, toxin accumulation, and even death. Additionally, ammonia nitrogen can react with other substances in water to form compounds such as nitrites and nitrates, which can harm human and animal health [4–6].

As a result, monitoring ammonia nitrogen concentrations in rivers has become a crucial task for environmental management. By monitoring ammonia nitrogen levels, pollution in river water can be promptly detected, enabling appropriate measures to be taken to prevent water eutrophication and other environmental problems. Furthermore, monitoring ammonia nitrogen levels provides scientific evidence for environmental management and protection, serving as a basis for formulating environmental protection policies and supporting sustainable water resource utilization [7–9].

To address water quality concerns, various water quality monitoring technologies, including ammonia nitrogen detection and early warning techniques, have been developed [10–12]. Traditional methods for ammonia nitrogen detection, such as the Nessler method, evaporation determination method, indicator method, and fluorescence method, have limitations in terms of cumbersome operations, low sensitivity, and limited accuracy. In recent years, automated monitoring technologies such as chromatography, electrochemical methods, optical methods, and biosensors have been widely adopted for ammonia nitrogen detection [13,14]. These methods offer advantages such as simplified operations, high efficiency, and improved accuracy, some of which enable real-time monitoring of water quality. Additionally, current ammonia nitrogen early warning technologies utilize a combination of monitoring instruments and information systems to achieve real-time monitoring and early warning of water quality conditions through data collection, transmission, processing, and analysis. Despite the numerous studies conducted on surface water ammonia nitrogen monitoring and early warning, practical applications still face limitations. Traditional chemical analysis methods involve laborious sample handling and analysis procedures, leading to potential errors. Novel techniques such as biosensors exhibit high sensitivity but encounter interference issues in complex environments. Furthermore, conventional monitoring methods often provide static data information and lack real-time and dynamic information feedback [15]. Therefore, improving the accuracy, timeliness, and precision of ammonia nitrogen monitoring and early warning in surface water remains an important research direction [16–18].

With the rapid development of artificial intelligence, machine learning has emerged as a popular technology in environmental and water resource management. Traditional machine learning methods have many advantages, such as ease of understanding and interpretation, visual analysis, and easy extraction of rules. In a relatively short period of time, these methods can produce feasible and effective results on large data sources and can handle both categorical and numerical data. They are suitable for handling missing samples and have a fast running speed when testing the dataset. However, there are also obvious disadvantages to machine learning, such as difficulties in handling missing data, the tendency to overfit, and ignoring the correlation between attributes in the dataset. Practical applications have shown that deep learning outperforms traditional machine learning and statistical methods in many tasks [19]. For example, deep learning models can learn and capture complex features of data, including nonlinear relationships and high-order interactions, which provides deep learning with greater flexibility and an advantage in dealing with complex, dynamic, and unknown data. It has strong representational power, and is able to handle data with high-dimensional features, nonlinear relationships, and complex patterns. It also has a high tolerance for noise and outliers, better adaptability to real-world applications, and improved robustness and generalization capabilities. As the amount of data increases, traditional machine learning methods may encounter problems such as the curse of dimensionality. However, deep learning models have excellent scalability and can easily handle large-scale datasets, allowing them to learn more complex patterns from a large amount of data. It has strong memory capabilities, and is able to store and recall a large amount of information. This provides deep learning with a great advantage in application scenarios that require long-term memory and historical information. Finally, in many application scenarios, deep learning can achieve higher prediction accuracy than traditional machine learning methods; in particular, in the field of water quality prediction, deep learning algorithms perform significantly better than traditional machine learning algorithms [20]. In this study, a deep learning model called Long Short-Term Memory (LSTM) was employed to process water quality monitoring data and achieved high-precision prediction of ammonia nitrogen indicators through data analysis and modeling [21–23]. LSTM is a recursive neural network (RNN) that solves the problem of gradient disappearance or explosion that exists in traditional RNNs when dealing with long-sequence data by introducing memory units, allowing better capture of the time-series characteristics of the data when dealing with long-sequence data. At the same time, the gate control mechanism in the LSTM model can effectively control the flow of information, avoiding gradient disappearance or explosion problems. Therefore, when dealing with water quality data, LSTM can better capture the long-term dependence relationship between water quality indicators and improve predictive performance through forward and reverse information flow, thus more accurately predicting water quality data [24–26]. Furthermore, correlation analysis between different water quality indicators and ammonia nitrogen indicators helps in the identification of key feature indicators for model input, enhancing prediction efficiency and reducing costs [12,22]. To achieve these objectives, a series of experiments were conducted using historical monitoring data from the Qianshan River in Zhuhai City.

2. Materials and Methods

2.1. Study Area and Data Collection

The Qianshan River waterway plays a vital role as a major inland transportation route in Zhuhai City, China. It is located at 21°48′~22°27′ north latitude and 113°03′~114°19′ east longitude, in the south of Guangdong Province, on the west bank of the Pearl River estuary. Its source can be traced back to Lianshiwan in Tantou Town, Zhongshan City, where water is introduced from the Madaomen waterway and flows eastward, passing through Tantou Town and Qianshan Street in Zhuhai City, until it merges into the Pearl River Estuary at Wanzai Shikaoju lock. With a total length of approximately 23 km, the river encompasses a stretch of about 15 km in Tantou Town, Zhongshan, and varies in width from 58 to 220 m. In Zhuhai, the river extends for about 8 km with a width ranging from 200 to 300 m. The Qianshan River basin covers a watershed area of around 338 km^2, experiencing an annual runoff volume of 1.54 billion cubic meters, an average annual runoff depth of 1100 mm, and an average runoff coefficient of 0.58. The river basin predominantly consists of sedimentary plain landforms, sloping from the northeast to the southwest.

Since 2015, the Qianshan River basin has experienced a total of 107 industrial pollution sources. Out of these, 20 are located in Sanxiang Town, Zhongshan City, representing 18.7% of the total sources, while 45 are situated in Tantou Town, accounting for 42.1%. Additionally, the Zhuhai area hosts 42 industrial pollution sources, making up 39.3% of the overall count. Urban domestic pollution primarily consists of sewage from urban villages and scattered old villages along the river. Figure 1 shows the specific locations of monitoring areas and monitoring stations.

For the purpose of this study, water quality data was collected from the Shijiaoju monitoring point within the Qianshan Street waterway network. The dataset spans from 8 November 2020 to 28 February 2023, providing historical water quality data at four-hour intervals. The dataset comprises a total of 5058 samples, encompassing nine water quality parameters: ammonia nitrogen (NH_3-N), water temperature (Temp), potential of hydrogen (pH), dissolved oxygen (DO), potassium permanganate index (KMnO$_4$), total phosphorus (TP), total nitrogen (TN), conductivity (Cond), and turbidity (Turb).

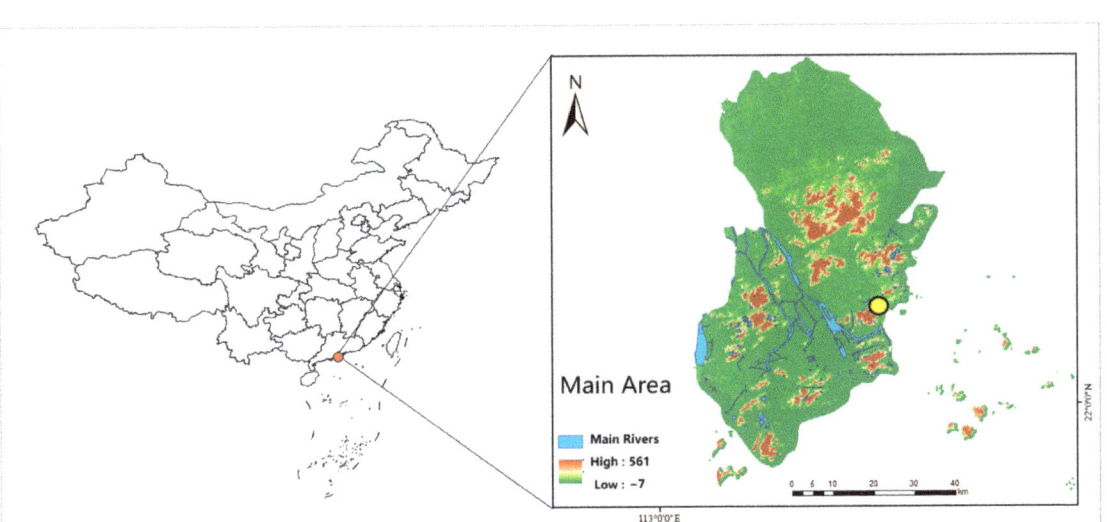

Figure 1. Spatial distribution of monitoring points within the study area.

2.2. Data Preprocessing

During the operation of automated water quality monitoring stations, various factors, including sensor malfunctions, network failures, and unexpected events such as pollutant leaks or extreme weather conditions, can lead to data loss and anomalies. The objective of data preprocessing is to cleanse the raw data by eliminating outliers, noise, and missing values, thereby improving the performance and reliability of water quality prediction models. Thorough data preprocessing ensures that the models are built upon high-quality data, enhancing prediction accuracy and providing a more dependable scientific foundation for water quality monitoring and management decisions [27–29].

In the context of handling missing values, two primary approaches, namely single imputation (SI) and multiple imputation (MI), are commonly used. While MI is more complex in operation and relatively costly, this study, considering the nature of the Qianshan River water quality data, adopts linear interpolation as the method for filling missing values. Linear interpolation, widely employed for filling missing values, is particularly suitable for data with a time dimension, such as time series data. Its fundamental concept involves estimating the missing values by performing linear interpolation between the preceding and subsequent observed values [30,31].

To implement linear interpolation, the positions of the missing values within the time series, referred to as interpolation positions, must be determined. Subsequently, the interpolation values are calculated by applying linear interpolation based on the available observed values, thereby obtaining estimates for the missing values [26,27]. Finally, it is essential to verify the interpolation results by ensuring that the post-interpolation data align with the actual situation, adhere to data distribution characteristics, and maintain consistency with other variables.

Let (X_1, Y_1) represent the preceding observed value of the missing value, (X_2, Y_2) represent the subsequent observed value, and X_0 represent the position of the missing value. The estimated missing value Y_0 can be calculated using the following formula:

$$Y_0 = Y_1 + (X_0 - X_1) \times (Y_2 - Y_1)/(X_2 - X_1) \tag{1}$$

Here, Y_1 and Y_2 represent the values of the observed values preceding and following the missing value, respectively, while X_1 and X_2 represent the corresponding time or position information. X_0 represents the position of the missing value [32]. Figure 2 and Table 1 show the basic situation of the water quality data.

Figure 2. Temporal variation curves of water quality parameters.

Table 1. Summary statistics of water quality parameters.

Variables	Units	Max	Min	Mean	Std
NH_3-N	mg/L	3.095	0.025	0.462	0.462
Temp	°C	32.630	13.400	24.617	4.754
pH	-	9.445	6.406	7.610	0.572
DO	mg/L	28.241	1.010	8.254	3.889
$KMnO_4$	mg/L	10.470	1.120	3.781	1.626
TP	mg/L	0.319	0.031	0.111	0.050
TN	mg/L	5.755	1.945	3.276	0.685
Cond	μs/cm	2988.800	214.301	1261.352	977.574
Turb	NTU	268.377	5.302	53.190	34.524

2.3. Feature Dataset

The dataset was thoroughly analyzed prior to model construction to gain insights into the relationships among variables, particularly focusing on the correlations between the input variables and the output variable [33]. Strong correlations between input and output variables indicate that the input values can effectively predict the output values, enabling the model to utilize this information during the modeling process [34]. Consequently, the model is expected to exhibit superior predictive performance by accurately capturing the relationships between inputs and outputs [22]. Conversely, weak correlations between input and output variables imply limited predictive capability of the input variables for the output variables [35]. In such cases, the model may struggle to capture these relationships, resulting in restricted predictive performance as it fails to extract sufficient information from the input variables to accurately predict the output variables.

In this paper, the Pearson correlation coefficient, a widely used measure for assessing linear correlations between random variables, was employed to analyze the correlations among input variables and between input variables and the output variables. By calculating the Pearson correlation coefficient, we were able to evaluate the strength of correlations among input variables and the association between the input variables and the output variable [36]. This data analysis facilitated the identification of strong correlations among input variables, addressing the issue of redundant information and enhancing the model's efficiency [23]. Table 2 shows the calculation results of Pearson correlation coefficient.

Table 2. Pearson correlation coefficient table.

Variables	NH_3-N	Temp	pH	DO	$KMnO_4$	TP	TN	Cond	Turb
NH_3-N	1								
Temp	0.026	1							
pH	−0.420	−0.331	1						
DO	−0.394	−0.568	0.790	1					
$KMnO_4$	0.209	−0.326	0.527	0.511	1				
TP	0.613	0.426	−0.409	−0.485	0.140	1			
TN	0.447	−0.199	0.199	0.057	0.547	0.466	1		
Cond	−0.038	−0.617	0.627	0.628	0.760	−0.243	0.420	1	
Turb	−0.022	0.362	−0.345	−0.354	−0.203	0.333	−0.149	−0.418	1

The Table 2 analysis revealed significant correlations between NH_3-N and six parameters, namely pH, DO, $KMnO_4$, TP, TN, and Cond. Specifically, the correlation coefficient between NH_3-N and pH was −0.420, demonstrating a significant negative correlation ($p < 0.01$) between NH_3-N and pH. Similarly, NH_3-N and DO exhibited a correlation coefficient of −0.394, indicating a significant negative correlation ($p < 0.01$) between NH_3-N and DO. In contrast, NH_3-N and $KMnO_4$ showed a correlation coefficient of 0.209, suggesting a significant positive correlation ($p < 0.01$) between NH_3-N and $KMnO_4$. The correlation coefficient between NH_3-N and TP was 0.613, indicating a significant positive correlation ($p < 0.01$) between NH_3-N and TP. Moreover, NH_3-N and TN had a correlation coefficient of 0.447, signifying a significant positive correlation ($p < 0.01$) between NH_3-N and TN. Lastly, NH_3-N and Cond exhibited a correlation coefficient of −0.038, indicating a significant negative correlation ($p < 0.01$) between NH_3-N and Cond.

Conversely, no significant correlations ($p > 0.05$) were observed between NH_3-N and Temp or Turb, suggesting no significant relationship between NH_3-N and these two parameters.

Based on the results of the correlation analysis, each parameter was ranked according to the magnitude of their correlation coefficients. The parameters were then divided into nine groups, with increasing correlation coefficient values, as visually depicted in Figure 3. This grouping allows for a better understanding of the relationships between NH_3-N and other parameters, with parameters exhibiting higher correlation coefficients being considered more strongly associated with NH_3-N levels.

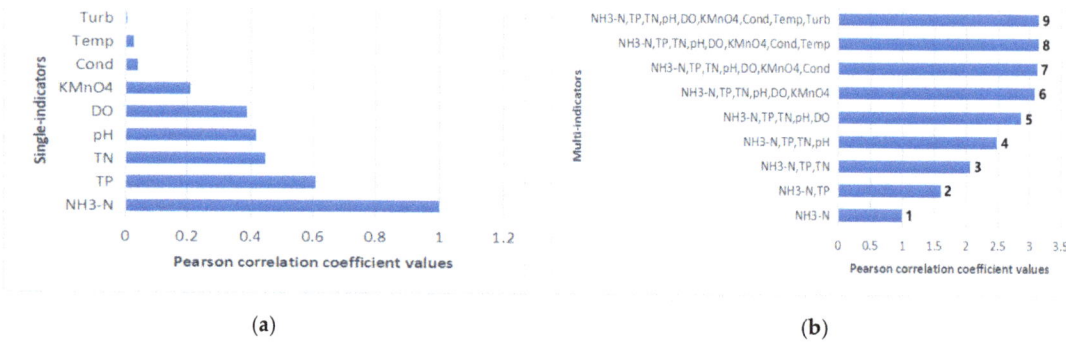

Figure 3. (a) Pearson correlation coefficient between each indicator and ammonia nitrogen; (b) a multiple indicator dataset with progressive accumulation of Pearson correlation coefficient values.

2.4. LSTM Model

2.4.1. Model Construction and Training

The design and training stages of deep learning models are pivotal in water quality modeling and prediction. Given the multifaceted influences and the temporal-spatial patterns inherent in NH_3-N concentrations in surface water, the adoption of the Long Short-Term Memory (LSTM) model, a prominent type of recurrent neural network (RNN), is judicious. Notably, LSTM boasts memory prowess, facilitating adept capture of long-term dependencies inherent in time series data [37]. Especially in the field of water quality prediction, the LSTM algorithm represents a significant improvement compared to traditional machine learning algorithms [38].

During the model training phase, historical NH_3-N monitoring data necessitate partitioning into training, validation, and testing sets, designated for model training, validation, and testing, respectively. This partitioning can be realized through either time-series-based or random division, ensuring that the data in these subsets remain representative both temporally and spatially. In this work, the validation set encompassed 10% of the dataset, totaling 506 samples, while the testing set comprised 5% of the dataset, amounting to 253 samples. The remaining samples were allocated for model training.

For model construction, training, and optimization, renowned deep learning frameworks such as TensorFlow and Keras come to the fore, streamlining efficient model design and training. Techniques including grid search and cross-validation prove instrumental in hyperparameter tuning. Grid search entails training and validating the model with assorted hyperparameter combinations within specified ranges, culminating in the selection of the optimal combination via validation set performance. In contrast, cross-validation involves segmenting the training set into multiple folds, training the model on each fold, validating on the remaining folds, and averaging performance metrics to temper evaluation randomness and bolster generalization proficiency. It is prudent to acknowledge that grid search may dictate considerable computational resources and time, mandating judicious hyperparameter range selection and prudent resource allocation to streamline effective hyperparameter tuning [22,23].

LSTM models typically encompass input layers, LSTM layers, and output layers, among other constituents. Model structure can be tailored to data attributes by adjusting parameters such as the number of LSTM neurons and activation functions. During the model training process, setting appropriate hyperparameters—such as learning rate and batch size—assumes significance. Learning rate governs the magnitude of weight updates per iteration, with extremes preventing convergence or inducing local optima. Batch size dictates the number of samples per parameter update, with excessively large batches causing aggressive updates, while overly small batches yield unstable adjustments. Pragmatic experimentation and optimization are indispensable to ascertain suitable hyperparameter values, fostering superior model performance.

In this work, an LSTM model was crafted within the TensorFlow-GPU 2.9 framework. This model comprises three layers: an input layer, an LSTM layer with 50 neurons; a subsequent LSTM layer with 80 neurons; and the ultimate output layer, featuring a single fully connected neuron for prediction output. Sample data from the past 30 time periods are used to predict data for the next 1 time period. A dropout layer, characterized by a dropout rate of 0.2, intervenes between the second and third layers, systematically discarding a fraction of neuron outputs during model training, thus tempering overfitting risks.

2.4.2. Model Evaluation

The assessment of a model's predictive performance holds paramount importance in affirming its efficacy. Appropriate evaluation metrics must be used to quantitatively gauge the model's predicted outcomes. In this study, the mean square error (MSE) and coefficient of determination (R^2) emerge as primary indices to scrutinize the predictive prowess of the model [39]. Furthermore, the average absolute error (MAE) and root mean square error (RMSE) are also invoked, furnishing a holistic comprehension of the model's predictive capacity pertaining to ammonia nitrogen concentration [40–42].

These four evaluation methods are briefly introduced as follows:

1. Mean square error (MSE): MSE encapsulates the average of squared differences between predicted values and actual values. It provides a measure of prediction accuracy, with lower MSE values denoting enhanced precision in the model's predictions.
2. Coefficient of determination (R^2): R^2 quantifies the proportion of the variability in the dependent variable that can be explicated by the model. It ranges from 0 to 1, with higher R^2 values indicating stronger model performance in explaining the variance in the data.
3. Average absolute error (MAE): MAE computes the average absolute differences between predicted values and actual values. MAE offers insights into the average prediction error magnitude, with lower MAE values reflecting superior prediction accuracy.
4. Root mean square error (RMSE): RMSE calculates the square root of the average of squared prediction errors. It provides an estimation of the model's predictive error spread, with smaller RMSE values signifying improved prediction precision.

By leveraging these evaluation metrics, the model's performance in forecasting ammonia nitrogen concentration can be rigorously assessed, affording a comprehensive understanding of its predictive capabilities.

2.4.3. Model Optimization

In the realm of model optimization, the consideration of model interpretability assumes significance. Deep learning models are often perceived as "black-box" entities, challenging the explanation of the rationale behind their predictions. To address this challenge, visualization techniques and feature importance analysis can be harnessed to unveil the model's prediction process. This augments model interpretability, streamlining model application and refinement. It is imperative to recognize that model evaluation and optimization represent iterative processes. Depending on the context, multiple cycles of evaluation and optimization may be warranted, entailing continuous adjustments to model design and parameters until the desired performance benchmarks are met.

In this study, optimization efforts entailed the utilization of grid search and cross-validation methodologies. The model was encapsulated as a regressor via KerasRegressor, thereby enabling its seamless integration with scikit-learn. A GridSearchCV object was instantiated to orchestrate grid search and cross-validation within the designated parameter space. This parameter space encompassed batch size, epochs, and the optimizer. The "cv" parameter dictated the number of folds for cross-validation, set to 2 in this instance, indicating deployment of 2-fold cross-validation [43–45]. After rigorous experimental comparisons, the following hyperparameters were judiciously selected: a batch size of 32, 50 epochs, and a RMSprop optimizer (root mean square propagation).

RMSprop serves as an optimization algorithm for training neural network models. Operating as an adaptive learning rate technique rooted in the gradient descent algorithm, RMSprop leverages exponentially weighted moving averages of gradients to dynamically adjust the learning rate. In contrast to conventional gradient descent approaches, RMSprop employs the moving average of squared gradients to modulate the learning rate. The central steps of RMSprop entail:

1. Parameter initialization: Weights of the model and exponentially weighted moving average of squared gradients are initialized.
2. Iterative training:
   - Gradients of the model's loss function concerning the weights are computed.
   - The exponentially weighted moving average of squared gradients is updated.
   - Adjustment value for the learning rate is computed based on the moving average.
   - Weights are updated based on the learning rate adjustment value and gradients.
   - The above steps are reiterated until a termination criterion is satisfied, such as reaching the maximum number of iterations or convergence of the loss function.

RMSprop brings forth several merits, including:

1. Adaptive learning rate: RMSprop dynamically tunes the learning rate in response to gradient changes. Large gradients prompt diminished learning rates, curbing parameter updates, while smaller gradients engender augmented learning rates, hastening parameter updates.
2. Applicability to non-stationary data: RMSprop excels in scenarios with non-stationary gradients, augmenting model training stability and convergence pace.
3. Ameliorating gradient explosion and vanishing: Through the utilization of exponentially weighted moving averages of gradients, RMSprop mitigates the adverse effects of gradient explosion and vanishing, thereby amplifying model training effectiveness.

It remains pivotal to acknowledge that RMSprop mandates manual hyperparameter configuration, including of the initial learning rate and decay coefficient. Additionally, RMSprop may not universally serve as the optimal optimization algorithm, and alternatives such as Adam or Adagrad could outperform RMSprop for specific problems [46–48].

3. Results

3.1. Analysis of Spatiotemporal Variation in NH_3-N Content in River Water Quality

Figure 4 illustrates the fluctuations in NH_3-N concentrations within the Qianshan River. The average NH_3-N concentration follows a discernible diurnal rhythm, culminating in the early morning hours (4:00–08:00) and ebbing during the afternoon (16:00–20:00). This diurnal oscillation can be attributed to the urban lifestyle rhythm. The morning surge in NH_3-N concentration arises from activities such as waking and personal hygiene, which augment the discharge of organic wastewater, subsequently elevating NH_3-N levels. Conversely, afternoon hours, dedicated to work and studies, witness a reduction in organic wastewater discharge, thereby leading to a decline in NH_3-N concentration. Temperature variations between these periods may further contribute. Nighttime features lower water temperatures, which retard microbial metabolic activities, facilitating NH_3-N accumulation. Daytime warmth, in contrast, accelerates microbial metabolism, promoting NH_3-N consumption.

Furthermore, the sway of photosynthesis emerges as a potential influence on NH_3-N fluctuations. Aquatic phytoplankton, through photosynthesis, convert carbon dioxide and water into organic matter and oxygen. This process necessitates NH_3-N and other inorganic nitrogen compounds, thereby ushering a dip in NH_3-N concentration during robust photosynthetic phases in daylight. Subsequently, the absence of photosynthesis during nighttime leads to increased NH_3-N concentration.

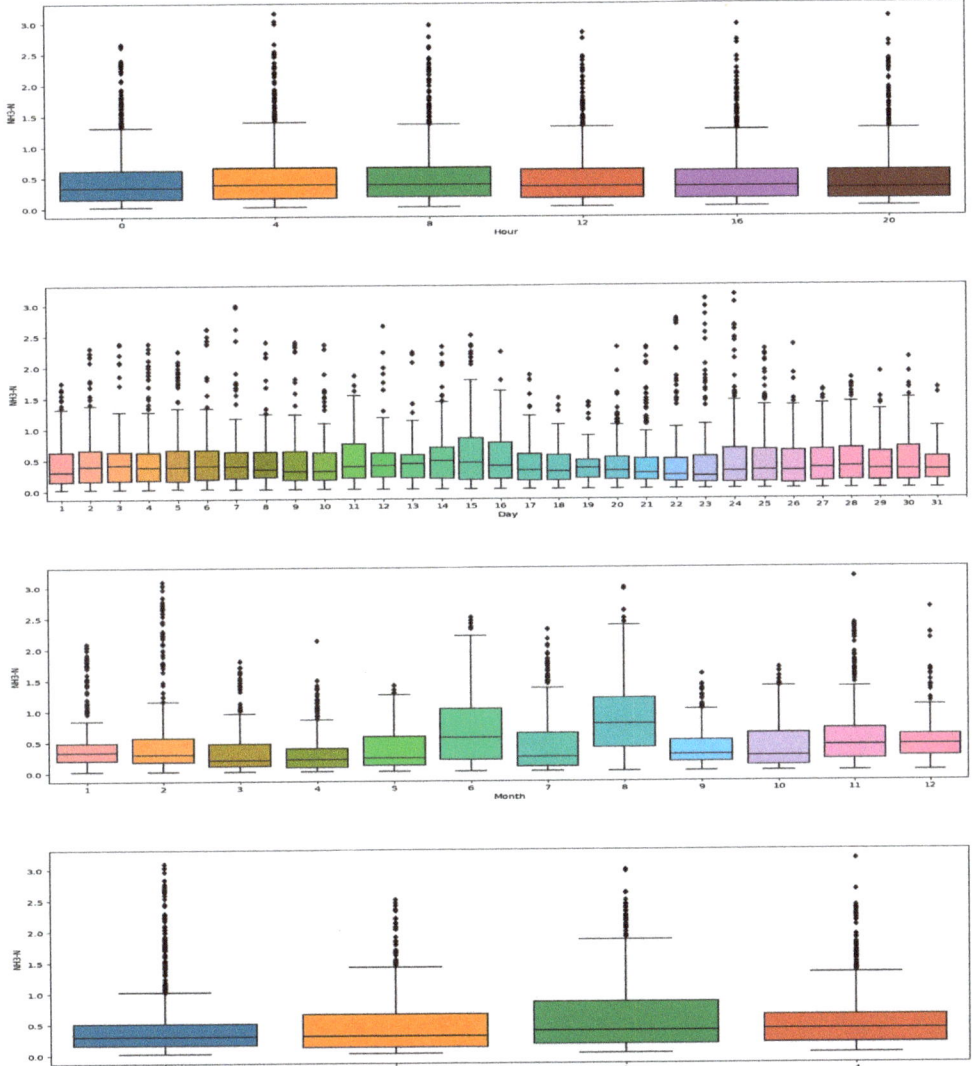

Figure 4. Temporal variations of NH_3-N within the study area at different time scales.

The daily average NH_3-N concentration typically registers an elevation during the middle and upper segments of each month, peaking around the 14th and 15th, while receding during the middle and lower segments, hitting lows around the 18th and 19th. This pattern is intricately intertwined with pollutant emissions and environmental elements. These segments mark peaks for domestic and industrial water usage, leading to wastewater discharge bearing higher NH_3-N content and correspondingly elevated NH_3-N concentration. Towards the end of the month, as environmental factors and pollutant sources dwindle, NH_3-N concentration also gradually diminishes.

Monthly NH_3-N concentration averages tend to surge in August and dip in April. This phenomenon likely stems from temperature and climatic alterations. Summer temperatures expedite water chemical reactions, spur bacterial proliferation, and yield additional NH_3-N through organic matter decomposition, culminating in heightened NH_3-N concentration.

Conversely, spring's cooler temperatures deter chemical reactions and bacterial growth, translating to decreased NH_3-N concentration. Further factors such as increased summer temperatures, reduced rainfall, and slower water flow fostering biological growth and heightened microbial metabolic activity play a role in augmenting NH_3-N concentration. Spring's lower temperatures, amplified rainfall, and swifter water flow, conversely, engender a decline in NH_3-N concentration.

The distinct NH_3-N concentration trends across varied time spans underscore its cyclic variations in the Qianshan River. The multifaceted factors influencing NH_3-N concentration warrant comprehensive consideration for the formulation of effective management strategies against NH_3-N pollution. Moreover, these analytical insights provide pivotal reference points, guiding the development, forecasting, and refinement of subsequent deep learning models.

3.2. Evaluation of NH_3-N Prediction Performance Based on the LSTM Model

The effectiveness of the developed NH_3-N concentration model was rigorously evaluated through the application of key metrics, namely R^2, MSE, and MAE, which were all applied to the validation dataset. The outcomes of this evaluation validate the proficiency of the LSTM model within the research domain, as depicted in Figure 5.

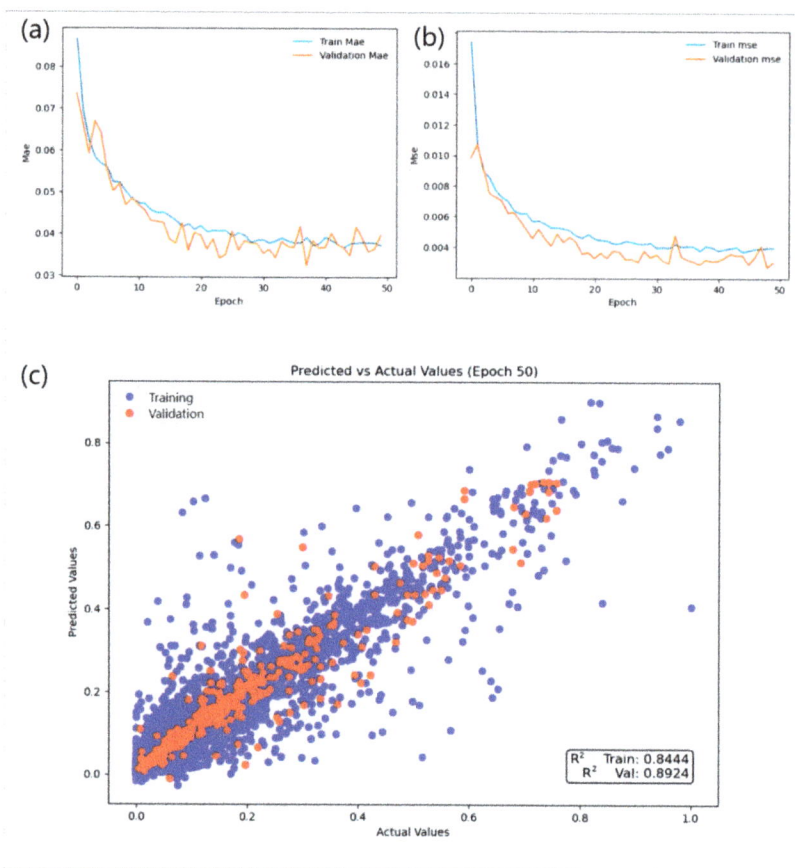

Figure 5. Learning curves and prediction results of the LSTM model on the validation dataset, along with the corresponding R^2 values: (**a**) learning curve (MAE); (**b**) learning curve (MSE); (**c**) observed and predicted NH_3-N concentrations, along with the corresponding R^2 value.

The model's trajectory of convergence and stability was observed within a span of 50 iterations. This achievement was coupled with an impressively low MAE that remained below 0.045, accompanied by a MSE that maintained itself below 0.004. This portrayal in Figure 5 succinctly underscores the model's efficacy in predicting ammonia nitrogen concentrations. The proximity of these metrics to their respective minima enforces the LSTM model's competence in forecasting ammonia nitrogen concentration.

Furthermore, the predictive outcomes gleaned from the model, as aptly showcased in Figure 5c, manifest a remarkable alignment with the actual measured values. This agreement is further underscored by the calculated R^2 value of 0.89. In totality, the LSTM model deftly captures the nuanced concentration variations of NH_3-N coursing through the Qianshan River, thus emerging as a robust and adept predictive model.

3.3. Comparison of NH_3-N Prediction Performance Based on Different Feature Sets

In order to identify the key input variables combinations that influence the prediction results of ammonia nitrogen concentrations, the LSTM model was utilized with different combinations of the nine input variables to predict ammonia nitrogen levels on the test dataset. Based on the strength of the correlation between the input variables and the target output, the nine input variables were sorted in descending order of their correlation coefficient values with the target output. The input feature combinations were gradually formed by cumulatively adding the correlation coefficient values, as shown in Figure 3.

In the sphere of evaluation metrics, the R-squared (R^2) value emerged as a cardinal yardstick, affording substantive insights into the model's capacity to explain the target variable. Spanning the continuum from 0 to 1, an R^2 value approaching unity connoted heightened explanatory efficacy of the model relative to the target variable. Our meticulous scrutiny of R^2 values unveiled the preeminence of feature combination 6, a composition encompassing six variables, which secured the acme R^2 value of 0.82. This pronounced R^2 value underscored the compelling explanatory prowess wielded by feature combination 6 over the target variable.

Furthermore, our scrutiny extended to mean squared error (MSE) and root mean squared error (RMSE), metrics poised to gauge the dissonance between the model's prognostications and the empirical observations. Remarkably, feature combination 6 evidenced commendable proficiency, yielding nominal error values of 0.0047 and 0.0655 for MSE and RMSE, respectively, thereby accentuating the model's prowess in delivering refined predictive accuracy.

Concomitantly, the focus converged on mean absolute error (MAE), a barometer of the average absolute divergence between the model's prognoses and the actual observations. In this purview, feature combination 6 preserved its ascendancy, manifesting a modest absolute error value of 0.0460, an indication of its robust capacity to attenuate prediction bias.

A comprehensive synthesis of Figure 6 and Table 3 unveils compelling revelations. Feature combination 1, characterized by a single indicator, boasted an elevated R^2 value of 0.79, alongside mitigated MSE, RMSE, and MAE values. This configuration accentuated the salience of a single feature's explanatory potential with regard to the target variable, indicating a heightened predictive accuracy. In contrast, feature combinations 2, 3, 4, and 7 followed a trajectory marked by diminished R^2 values and accentuated MSE, RMSE, and MAE values—reflective of dwindling explanatory efficacy and curtailed predictive precision. Feature combinations 5, 8, and 9 presented consistent performance, exhibiting amplified R^2 values juxtaposed against marginally inflated MSE, RMSE, and MAE values with regard to feature combination 6. This nuanced differentiation intimates a marginal reduction in predictive accuracy for these configurations.

A holistic assimilation of the aforesaid analysis unequivocally elevates feature combination 6—a composite of six variables—as an exemplar of superlative performance, as evidenced across a spectrum of evaluation metrics. Supported by an improved R^2 value, reduced MSE, RMSE, and MAE values, as well as enhanced predictive precision, feature combination 6 emerges as a compelling set of input variables, deserving of thorough investigation in future research initiatives and practical implementations.

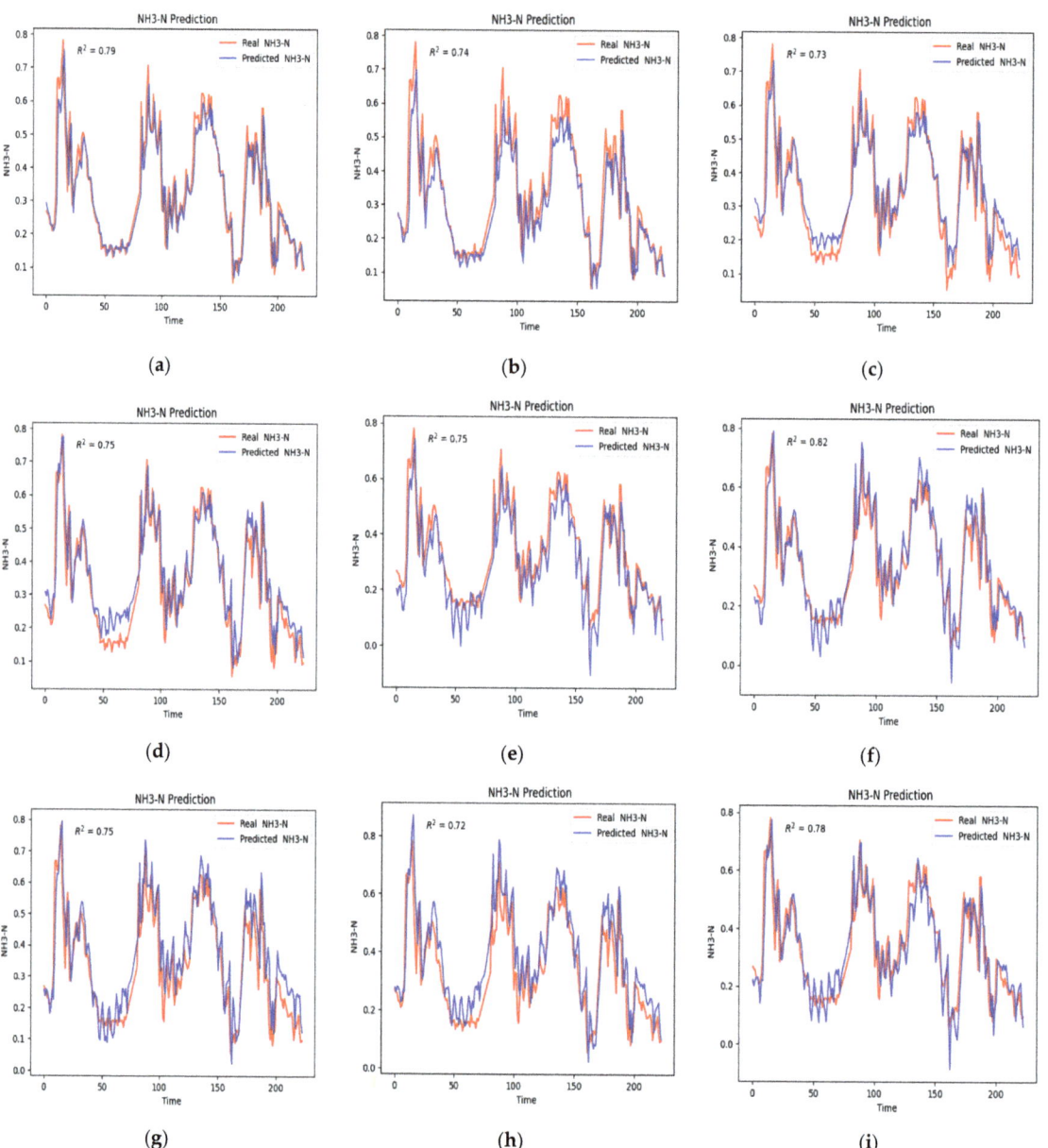

Figure 6. Comparison of observed and predicted NH_3-N concentrations on different feature sets on the test dataset, along with the corresponding R^2 values: (**a**) prediction results of combination 1; (**b**) prediction results of combination 2; (**c**) prediction results of combination 3; (**d**) prediction results of combination 4; (**e**) prediction results of combination 5; (**f**) prediction results of combination 6; (**g**) prediction results of combination 7; (**h**) prediction results of combination 8; (**i**) prediction results of combination 9.

Table 3. Summary statistics of feature sets and their corresponding evaluation metric values.

Indicator Combination	R^2	MSE	RMSE	MAE
Combination 1	0.79	0.0045	0.0674	0.0453
Combination 2	0.74	0.0053	0.0730	0.0503
Combination 3	0.73	0.0048	0.0695	0.0518
Combination 4	0.75	0.0052	0.0722	0.0543
Combination 5	0.75	0.0067	0.0816	0.0629
Combination 6	0.82	0.0047	0.0655	0.0460
Combination 7	0.75	0.0066	0.0814	0.0630
Combination 8	0.72	0.0081	0.0900	0.0695
Combination 9	0.78	0.0057	0.0752	0.0576

4. Discussion

4.1. Feasibility of Using the LSTM Model with Easily Measurable Water Quality Data to Predict Ammonia Nitrogen Concentrations in Water Quality

The LSTM model developed in this study has effectively established a nonlinear mapping relationship between readily measurable water quality parameters (NH_3-N, Temp, pH, DO, $KMnO_4$, TP, TN, Cond, and Turb) and the target variable (NH_3-N). This achievement helps to accurately predict the concentration of ammonia nitrogen in river systems. The model's predicted NH_3-N concentrations closely align with observed values acquired from real-time data collected at river water monitoring sites, attaining an average R^2 value of 0.82. This reflects the strong ability of the model to predict the peak concentration of NH_3-N, which can provide reliable early warnings to mitigate the impact of elevated NH_3-N levels on water quality. This ability is of great significance for intelligent monitoring and management of aquatic environments.

It is worth noting that, unlike the accuracy of predicting concentration peaks, the model exhibits a slight decrease in its effectiveness in predicting NH3-N concentration valleys within specific time intervals, as shown in Figure 6c–i. The model did not fully learn the complexity of data attributes during the training phase NH3-N concentration trough, making it impossible to accurately predict the trough value. Moreover, the limited NH_3-N concentrations within water quality samples during valley periods, coupled with potential measurement deviations in Internet of Things (IoT) real-time monitoring devices, may engender diminished accuracy in raw data. These exceptional circumstances inevitably contribute to the attenuation of training data accuracy, consequently influencing the model's predictive performance. Hence, the acquisition of high-fidelity training data assumes critical importance to reinforce prognostic precision. Furthermore, predicated upon the findings presented in Figure 6, the incorporation of supplementary input variables that wield substantive influence over the output variable could potentially ameliorate model prediction accuracy. Thus, delving into additional potential indicators that affect NH_3-N concentrations within river water quality can serve to augment the model's efficacy, presenting a meaningful avenue for enhancing predictive capabilities.

4.2. Potential for Reducing Model Prediction Costs

In contrast to conventional mechanistic models, the data-driven prediction methodologies surmount the temporal limitations associated with sample procurement, analysis, and detection, concurrently reducing the demand for substantial human, financial, and material resources. However, when scrutinizing indicators that are measurable within brief timeframes of minutes to a day, the adoption of sensors having high temporal resolution might entail elevated costs, notably in terms of instrument probe maintenance. Thus, it is imperative to identify pivotal variables for model training that exhibit a minimal compromise on prediction performance. This understanding may significantly improve the operational efficiency of the model, thereby reducing computational energy consumption and prediction expenses. Empirical findings indicate that using a separate input–output paradigm in the prediction model to achieve accurate NH3-N prediction is not sufficient. Additionally, the iterative approach of progressively augmenting input variables to discern the optimal input combination yielding superior NH_3-N prediction accuracy entails notable temporal and operational investments. Conversely, the methodological application of Pearson correlation coefficient analysis effectively identifies a subset of input variables characterized by robust interactions that materially contribute to the model's output. Notably, the current study demonstrates the relevance of NH_3-N, pH, DO, $KMnO_4$, TP, and TN (as delineated in Figure 3). Therefore, the composition of input variables is amenable to adjustment contingent upon the ordering of their correlations, thereby engendering the identification of an optimal input indicator combination predicated upon prediction performance.

5. Conclusions

In this investigation, a data-driven Long Short-Term Memory (LSTM) model was designed to predict NH_3-N concentrations in river water networks. This model shows good accuracy in predicting NH_3-N concentration. Primarily, an exploratory examination was undertaken to assess the aptitude of deep learning methodologies in NH_3-N prediction. The outcomes manifestly underscored the data-driven NH_3-N prediction model's robust generalization potential, led by an impressive R^2 value of 0.82 for the optimal input indicator amalgamation. Furthermore, the model's performance was amenable to enhancement through judiciously modulating the number of layers and neurons within the LSTM framework. Equally noteworthy, the employment of Pearson correlation coefficient analysis expeditiously illuminated and quantified the multi-faceted contributions of diverse input variables to the model's predictive outcomes. This analytical framework significantly enriched our comprehension of deep learning results and facilitated model optimization. Overall, the proposed LSTM-based NH_3-N prediction model effectively overcomes the limitations of traditional monitoring methods in terms of time and economic costs and enables fast modeling at low costs. This provides a feasible solution for early warning of high NH_3-N concentrations in river water, enabling water environmental management departments to develop inspection plans and reduce incidents of water quality hazards caused by excessive NH3-N concentrations.

However, the proposed model has some limitations. Rooted in the underpinnings of the deep learning algorithm, modeling efficacy hinges upon the interplay between input and output variables. This study predominantly accentuated the correlation existing between input and output variables, thereby inadvertently disregarding the latent interplay amongst the input variables themselves. This analytical disposition could potentially lead to the inadvertent omission of pivotal variables, given the plausible existence of inherent correlations amongst the input variables. It is plausible that certain features might furnish supplementary insights that underpin enhanced predictive capabilities. The inadvertent oversight of internal feature correlations could yield the exclusion of such salient features, impinging upon the model's precision and performance. Additionally, the introduction of redundant features—features with a high degree of correlation—might entail unwarranted complexities, hampering model training and generalization proficiencies. In scenarios wherein inter-feature correlations exist, the model may inadvertently assign disproportionate weights to features exhibiting elevated correlations, inadvertently sidelining features characterized by lower correlations. This asymmetry in feature weighting can engender biased feature attributions and potentially compromise the model's adeptness in harnessing the complete spectrum of available information. Neglecting the intrinsic feature correlations further augments the model's tendency to disproportionately depend on specific features during the training phase, thereby amplifying the risk of overfitting. Consequently, in the realm of feature engineering, a judicious consideration of both the correlation between input–output variables and the internal inter-feature correlations is indispensable, potentially culminating in more exhaustive and precise predictive models.

In summary, the future research should focus on improving model performance, expanding application domains, streamlining workflows, and further enhancing model interpretability to better support various aspects of water quality environmental management and governance. To better understand the model's performance variations at different times, we plan to incorporate seasonality and other temporal patterns as input features. This step will enable us to more accurately capture the seasonal variations in water quality, providing precise data support for water quality management. Furthermore, we will actively investigate various data processing and feature selection methods, such as principal component analysis and causal analysis, to gain a deeper understanding of the reasons behind performance differences. By continually optimizing the model, enhancing its generalization capabilities and robustness, we will ensure that the model performs excellently under diverse conditions [49]. Simultaneously, we will compare the performance of different deep learning models, streamline model algorithms, and improve model interpretability. By quantifying model costs, we will maintain efficient workflows while enhancing performance. This approach will better serve the needs of water quality prediction and water quality environmental management.

Author Contributions: Conceptualization, X.W., Y.L. (Yanchun Liang) and A.T.; methodology, M.Q.; software, X.W. and Y.L. (Ying Li); validation, A.T., X.W. and M.Q.; formal analysis, X.W. and A.T.; investigation, X.W.; resources, M.Q. and Q.Q.; data curation, X.W. and Y.L. (Ying Li); writing—original draft preparation, X.W.; writing—review and editing, Q.Q., A.T. and Y.L. (Yanchun Liang); visualization, X.W.; supervision, Y.L. (Yanchun Liang); project administration, Y.L. (Ying Li). All authors have read and agreed to the published version of the manuscript.

Funding: This research was funded in part by the NSFC (62372494, 61972174), the Guangdong Universities' Innovation Team (2021KCXTD015), the Key Disciplines Projects (2021ZDJS138), and the Guangdong Provincial Junior Innovative Talents Project for Ordinary Universities (2022KQNCX146).

Data Availability Statement: Data shall be provided by the first and corresponding authors upon special request.

Acknowledgments: Thanks to Qingyue Data (data.epmap.org) for support of environmental data.

Conflicts of Interest: The authors declare no conflict of interest.

References

1. Mohapatra, J.B.; Jha, P.; Jha, M.K.; Biswal, S. Efficacy of Machine Learning Techniques in Predicting Groundwater Fluctuations in Agro-Ecological Zones of India. *Sci. Total Environ.* **2021**, *785*, 147319. [CrossRef]
2. Wang, S.; Peng, H.; Liang, S. Prediction of Estuarine Water Quality Using Interpretable Machine Learning Approach. *J. Hydrol.* **2022**, *605*, 127320. [CrossRef]
3. Rostam, N.A.P.; Malim, N.H.A.H.; Abdullah, R.; Ahmad, A.L.; Ooi, B.S.; Chan, D.J.C. A Complete Proposed Framework for Coastal Water Quality Monitoring System with Algae Predictive Model. *IEEE Access* **2021**, *9*, 108249–108265. [CrossRef]
4. Ransom, K.M.; Nolan, B.T.; Traum, J.A.; Faunt, C.C.; Bell, A.M.; Gronberg, J.A.M.; Wheeler, D.C.; Rosecrans, C.Z.; Jurgens, B.; Schwarz, G.E.; et al. A Hybrid Machine Learning Model to Predict and Visualize Nitrate Concentration throughout the Central Valley Aquifer, California, USA. *Sci. Total Environ.* **2017**, *601–602*, 1160–1172. [CrossRef]
5. Mejía, L.; Barrios, M. Identifying Watershed Predictors of Surface Water Quality through Iterative Input Selection. *Int. J. Environ. Sci. Technol.* **2022**, *20*, 7201–7216. [CrossRef]
6. Azrour, M.; Mabrouki, J.; Fattah, G.; Guezzaz, A.; Aziz, F. Machine Learning Algorithms for Efficient Water Quality Prediction. *Model. Earth Syst. Environ.* **2022**, *8*, 2793–2801. [CrossRef]
7. Lin, K.; Zhu, Y.; Zhang, Y.; Lin, H. Determination of Ammonia Nitrogen in Natural Waters: Recent Advances and Applications. *Trends Environ. Anal. Chem.* **2019**, *24*, e00073. [CrossRef]
8. Li, D.; Xu, X.; Li, Z.; Wang, T.; Wang, C. Detection Methods of Ammonia Nitrogen in Water: A Review. *TrAC Trends Anal. Chem.* **2020**, *127*, 115890. [CrossRef]
9. Insausti, M.; Timmis, R.; Kinnersley, R.; Rufino, M.C. Advances in Sensing Ammonia from Agricultural Sources. *Sci. Total Environ.* **2020**, *706*, 135124. [CrossRef]
10. Wan, H.; Xu, R.; Zhang, M.; Cai, Y.; Li, J.; Shen, X. A Novel Model for Water Quality Prediction Caused by Non-Point Sources Pollution Based on Deep Learning and Feature Extraction Methods. *J. Hydrol.* **2022**, *612*, 128081. [CrossRef]
11. Du, Z.; Qi, J.; Wu, S.; Zhang, F.; Liu, R. A Spatially Weighted Neural Network Based Water Quality Assessment Method for Large-Scale Coastal Areas. *Environ. Sci. Technol.* **2021**, *55*, 2553–2563. [CrossRef] [PubMed]
12. Hu, Z.; Zhang, Y.; Zhao, Y.; Xie, M.; Zhong, J.; Tu, Z.; Liu, J. A Water Quality Prediction Method Based on the Deep LSTM Network Considering Correlation in Smart Mariculture. *Sensors* **2019**, *19*, 1420. [CrossRef]
13. Akbar, M.A.; Selvaganapathy, P.R.; Kruse, P. Nanocarbon Based Chemiresistive Detection of Monochloramine in Water. *ECS Meet. Abstr.* **2022**, *MA2022-01*, 2137. [CrossRef]

14. Kruse, P.; Akbar, M.A.; Sharif, O.; Selvaganapathy, P.R. Single-Walled Carbon Nanotube Chemiresistive Sensors for the Identification and Quantification of Disinfectants. In *Proceedings of the ECS Meeting Abstracts*; The Electrochemical Society, Inc.: Pennington, NJ, USA, 2021; Volume 2021, p. 1613.
15. Wei, L.; Zhang, Y.; Han, Y.; Zheng, J.; Xu, X.; Zhu, L. Effective Abatement of Ammonium and Nitrate Release from Sediments by Biochar Coverage. *Sci. Total Environ.* **2023**, *899*, 165710. [CrossRef]
16. Yu, H.; Yang, L.; Li, D.; Chen, Y. A Hybrid Intelligent Soft Computing Method for Ammonia Nitrogen Prediction in Aquaculture. *Inf. Process. Agric.* **2021**, *8*, 64–74. [CrossRef]
17. Jiang, Y.; Dong, X.; Li, Y.; Li, Y.; Liang, Y.; Zhang, M. An Environmentally-Benign Flow-Batch System for Headspace Single-Drop Microextraction and on-Drop Conductometric Detecting Ammonium. *Talanta* **2021**, *224*, 121849. [CrossRef] [PubMed]
18. Zhao, Y.; Shi, R.; Bian, X.; Zhou, C.; Zhao, Y.; Zhang, S.; Wu, F.; Waterhouse, G.I.; Wu, L.-Z.; Tung, C.-H.; et al. Ammonia Detection Methods in Photocatalytic and Electrocatalytic Experiments: How to Improve the Reliability of NH_3 Production Rates? *Adv. Sci.* **2019**, *6*, 1802109. [CrossRef] [PubMed]
19. Zhang, S.-Z.; Chen, S.; Jiang, H. A Back Propagation Neural Network Model for Accurately Predicting the Removal Efficiency of Ammonia Nitrogen in Wastewater Treatment Plants Using Different Biological Processes. *Water Res.* **2022**, *222*, 118908. [CrossRef]
20. Wang, X.; Li, Y.; Qiao, Q.; Tavares, A.; Liang, Y. Water Quality Prediction Based on Machine Learning and Comprehensive Weighting Methods. *Entropy* **2023**, *25*, 1186. [CrossRef]
21. Yu, X.; Cui, T.; Sreekanth, J.; Mangeon, S.; Doble, R.; Xin, P.; Rassam, D.; Gilfedder, M. Deep Learning Emulators for Groundwater Contaminant Transport Modelling. *J. Hydrol.* **2020**, *590*, 125351. [CrossRef]
22. Jiang, Y.; Li, C.; Song, H.; Wang, W. Deep Learning Model Based on Urban Multi-Source Data for Predicting Heavy Metals (Cu, Zn, Ni, Cr) in Industrial Sewer Networks. *J. Hazard. Mater.* **2022**, *432*, 128732. [CrossRef]
23. Jiang, Y.; Li, C.; Zhang, Y.; Zhao, R.; Yan, K.; Wang, W. Data-Driven Method Based on Deep Learning Algorithm for Detecting Fat, Oil, and Grease (FOG) of Sewer Networks in Urban Commercial Areas. *Water Res.* **2021**, *207*, 117797. [CrossRef] [PubMed]
24. Kumar, L.; Afzal, M.S.; Ahmad, A. Prediction of Water Turbidity in a Marine Environment Using Machine Learning: A Case Study of Hong Kong. *Reg. Stud. Mar. Sci.* **2022**, *52*, 102260. [CrossRef]
25. Wang, K.; Band, S.S.; Ameri, R.; Biyari, M.; Hai, T.; Hsu, C.-C.; Hadjouni, M.; Elmannai, H.; Chau, K.-W.; Mosavi, A. Performance Improvement of Machine Learning Models via Wavelet Theory in Estimating Monthly River Streamflow. *Eng. Appl. Comput. Fluid Mech.* **2022**, *16*, 1833–1848. [CrossRef]
26. Zhi, W.; Feng, D.; Tsai, W.-P.; Sterle, G.; Harpold, A.; Shen, C.; Li, L. From Hydrometeorology to River Water Quality: Can a Deep Learning Model Predict Dissolved Oxygen at the Continental Scale? *Environ. Sci. Technol.* **2021**, *55*, 2357–2368. [CrossRef] [PubMed]
27. Tung, T.M.; Yaseen, Z.M. A Survey on River Water Quality Modelling Using Artificial Intelligence Models: 2000–2020. *J. Hydrol.* **2020**, *585*, 124670.
28. Diez-Gonzalez, J.; Alvarez, R.; Prieto-Fernandez, N.; Perez, H. Local Wireless Sensor Networks Positioning Reliability under Sensor Failure. *Sensors* **2020**, *20*, 1426. [CrossRef]
29. Gaddam, A.; Wilkin, T.; Angelova, M.; Gaddam, J. Detecting Sensor Faults, Anomalies and Outliers in the Internet of Things: A Survey on the Challenges and Solutions. *Electronics* **2020**, *9*, 511. [CrossRef]
30. Huang, G. Missing Data Filling Method Based on Linear Interpolation and Lightgbm. In *Proceedings of the Journal of Physics: Conference Series*; IOP Publishing: Bristol, UK, 2021; Volume 1754, p. 012187.
31. Park, I.; Kim, H.S.; Lee, J.; Kim, J.H.; Song, C.H.; Kim, H.K. Temperature Prediction Using the Missing Data Refinement Model Based on a Long Short-Term Memory Neural Network. *Atmosphere* **2019**, *10*, 718. [CrossRef]
32. Li, Y.; Kong, B.; Yu, W.; Zhu, X. An Attention-Based CNN-LSTM Method for Effluent Wastewater Quality Prediction. *Appl. Sci.* **2023**, *13*, 7011. [CrossRef]
33. Kayhomayoon, Z.; Arya Azar, N.; Ghordoyee Milan, S.; Kardan Moghaddam, H.; Berndtsson, R. Novel Approach for Predicting Groundwater Storage Loss Using Machine Learning. *J. Environ. Manag.* **2021**, *296*, 113237. [CrossRef] [PubMed]
34. Zavareh, M.; Maggioni, V. Application of Rough Set Theory to Water Quality Analysis: A Case Study. *Data* **2018**, *3*, 50. [CrossRef]
35. Li, Q.; Yang, Y.; Yang, L.; Wang, Y. Comparative Analysis of Water Quality Prediction Performance Based on LSTM in the Haihe River Basin, China. *Environ. Sci. Pollut. Res.* **2022**, *30*, 7498–7509. [CrossRef] [PubMed]
36. Barzegar, R.; Razzagh, S.; Quilty, J.; Adamowski, J.; Pour, H.K.; Booij, M.J. Improving GALDIT-Based Groundwater Vulnerability Predictive Mapping Using Coupled Resampling Algorithms and Machine Learning Models. *J. Hydrol.* **2021**, *598*, 126370. [CrossRef]
37. Zhang, Y.; Li, C.; Jiang, Y.; Sun, L.; Zhao, R.; Yan, K.; Wang, W. Accurate Prediction of Water Quality in Urban Drainage Network with Integrated EMD-LSTM Model. *J. Clean. Prod.* **2022**, *354*, 131724. [CrossRef]
38. Yu, Q. Enhancing Streamflow Simulation Using Hybridized Machine Learning Models in a Semi-Arid Basin of the Chinese Loess Plateau. *J. Hydrol.* **2023**, *617*, 129115. [CrossRef]
39. Zhao, Z.; Wang, Z.; Yuan, J.; Ma, J.; He, Z.; Xu, Y.; Shen, X.; Zhu, L. Development of a Novel Feedforward Neural Network Model Based on Controllable Parameters for Predicting Effluent Total Nitrogen. *Engineering* **2021**, *7*, 195–202. [CrossRef]
40. Deng, T.; Chau, K.-W.; Duan, H.-F. Machine Learning Based Marine Water Quality Prediction for Coastal Hydro-Environment Management. *J. Environ. Manag.* **2021**, *284*, 112051. [CrossRef]

41. Li, H.; Zhang, G.; Zhu, Y.; Kaufmann, H.; Xu, G. Inversion and Driving Force Analysis of Nutrient Concentrations in the Ecosystem of the Shenzhen-Hong Kong Bay Area. *Remote Sens.* **2022**, *14*, 3694. [CrossRef]
42. Hadjisolomou, E.; Stefanidis, K.; Herodotou, H.; Michaelides, M.; Papatheodorou, G.; Papastergiadou, E. Modelling Freshwater Eutrophication with Limited Limnological Data Using Artificial Neural Networks. *Water* **2021**, *13*, 1590. [CrossRef]
43. Ranjan, G.; Verma, A.K.; Radhika, S. K-Nearest Neighbors and Grid Search Cv Based Real Time Fault Monitoring System for Industries. In Proceedings of the 2019 IEEE 5th International Conference for Convergence in Technology (I2CT), Bombay, India, 29–31 March 2019; IEEE: Piscataway, NJ, USA, 2019; pp. 1–5.
44. Ahmad, G.N.; Fatima, H.; Ullah, S.; Saidi, A.S. Efficient Medical Diagnosis of Human Heart Diseases Using Machine Learning Techniques with and without GridSearchCV. *IEEE Access* **2022**, *10*, 80151–80173. [CrossRef]
45. Alhakeem, Z.M.; Jebur, Y.M.; Henedy, S.N.; Imran, H.; Bernardo, L.F.; Hussein, H.M. Prediction of Ecofriendly Concrete Compressive Strength Using Gradient Boosting Regression Tree Combined with GridSearchCV Hyperparameter-Optimization Techniques. *Materials* **2022**, *15*, 7432. [CrossRef]
46. Xu, D.; Zhang, S.; Zhang, H.; Mandic, D.P. Convergence of the RMSProp Deep Learning Method with Penalty for Nonconvex Optimization. *Neural Netw.* **2021**, *139*, 17–23. [CrossRef] [PubMed]
47. Kumar, A.; Sarkar, S.; Pradhan, C. Malaria Disease Detection Using Cnn Technique with Sgd, Rmsprop and Adam Optimizers. In *Deep Learning Techniques for Biomedical and Health Informatics*; Springer: Cham, Switzerland, 2020; pp. 211–230. [CrossRef]
48. Shi, N.; Li, D.; Hong, M.; Sun, R. RMSprop Converges with Proper Hyper-Parameter. In Proceedings of the International Conference on Learning Representations, Addis Ababa, Ethiopia, 26–30 April 2020.
49. Zavareh, M.; Maggioni, V.; Sokolov, V. Investigating Water Quality Data Using Principal Component Analysis and Granger Causality. *Water* **2021**, *13*, 343. [CrossRef]

Disclaimer/Publisher's Note: The statements, opinions and data contained in all publications are solely those of the individual author(s) and contributor(s) and not of MDPI and/or the editor(s). MDPI and/or the editor(s) disclaim responsibility for any injury to people or property resulting from any ideas, methods, instructions or products referred to in the content.

Article

DFANet: Denoising Frequency Attention Network for Building Footprint Extraction in Very-High-Resolution Remote Sensing Images

Lei Lu [1,*], Tongfei Liu [2,*], Fenlong Jiang [3], Bei Han [1], Peng Zhao [1] and Guoqiang Wang [1]

[1] School of Information Engineering, Yulin University, Yulin 719000, China; hanbei@yulinu.edu.cn (B.H.); zhao_peng@yulinu.edu.cn (P.Z.); 2312710107@yulinu.edu.cn (G.W.)
[2] Shaanxi Joint Laboratory of Artificial Intelligence, Shaanxi University of Science and Technology, Xi'an 710021, China
[3] Key Laboratory of Collaborative Intelligence Systems, School of Computer Science and Technology, Ministry of Education, Xidian University, Xi'an 710071, China; fljiang@xidian.edu.cn
* Correspondence: lulei@yulinu.edu.cn (L.L.); liutongfei@sust.edu.cn (T.L.)

Abstract: With the rapid development of very-high-resolution (VHR) remote-sensing technology, automatic identification and extraction of building footprints are significant for tracking urban development and evolution. Nevertheless, while VHR can more accurately characterize the details of buildings, it also inevitably enhances the background interference and noise information, which degrades the fine-grained detection of building footprints. In order to tackle the above issues, the attention mechanism is intensively exploited to provide a feasible solution. The attention mechanism is a computational intelligence technique inspired by the biological vision system capable of rapidly and automatically catching critical information. On the basis of the a priori frequency difference of different ground objects, we propose the denoising frequency attention network (DFANet) for building footprint extraction in VHR images. Specifically, we design the denoising frequency attention module and pyramid pooling module, which are embedded into the encoder–decoder network architecture. The denoising frequency attention module enables efficient filtering of high-frequency noises in the feature maps and enhancement of the frequency information related to buildings. In addition, the pyramid pooling module is leveraged to strengthen the adaptability and robustness of buildings at different scales. Experimental results of two commonly used real datasets demonstrate the effectiveness and superiority of the proposed method; the visualization and analysis also prove the critical role of the proposal.

Keywords: computational intelligence; neural networks; building footprint extraction; attention mechanism; remote-sensing images

Citation: Lu, L.; Liu, T.; Jiang, F.; Han, B.; Zhao, P.; Wang, G. DFANet: Denoising Frequency Attention Network for Building Footprint Extraction in Very-High-Resolution Remote Sensing Images. *Electronics* 2023, *12*, 4592. https://doi.org/10.3390/electronics12224592

Academic Editors: Yue Wu, Gerardo Di Martino, Kai Qin, Maoguo Gong and Qiguang Miao

Received: 16 October 2023
Revised: 3 November 2023
Accepted: 8 November 2023
Published: 10 November 2023

Copyright: © 2023 by the authors. Licensee MDPI, Basel, Switzerland. This article is an open access article distributed under the terms and conditions of the Creative Commons Attribution (CC BY) license (https://creativecommons.org/licenses/by/4.0/).

1. Introduction

With the rapid development of satellite, aircraft, and UAV technology, it has become easier to obtain high-resolution and very-high-resolution (VHR) remote-sensing images [1]. Based on these high-quality remote-sensing images, the detailed information of ground objects can be clearly depicted, which facilitates many remote-sensing tasks, including but not limited to land-cover classification [2], object detection [3], change detection [4], etc. Among the ground objects covered by VHR images, buildings, as the carrier of human production and living activities, are of vital significance to the human living environment, and are good indicators of population aggregation, energy consumption intensity, and regional development [5]. Therefore, the accurate extraction of buildings from remote-sensing images is conducive to the study of urban dynamic expansion and population distribution patterns, promoting the digital construction and management of cities, and enhancing the sustainable development of cities [6].

Although some research progress has been made in building footprint extraction in recent years, the diversity of remote-sensing image sources and the complexity of the environment still bring many challenges to this task, mainly including:

(a) In optical remote-sensing images, buildings have small inter-class variance and large intra-class variance [7]. For example, non-buildings such as roads, playgrounds, and parking lots have similar characteristics (such as spectrum, shape, size, structure, etc.), which are easy to confuse the extraction method [8].

(b) Due to the different imaging angles of sensors, high-rise buildings often produce different degrees of geometric distortion, which increases the difficulty of algorithm recognition [9].

(c) Due to the difference in the sun's altitude angle when shooting, buildings tend to produce shadow areas at different angles, which not only interferes with the coverage area of the building itself, but also easily conceals the characteristics of other buildings covered by shadows [10].

In recent years, deep learning methods represented by the convolutional neural network (CNN) have shown great potential in the fields of computer vision [11,12] and remote-sensing image interpretation [13,14]. With the powerful ability to extract high-level features, CNN-based building footprint extraction methods alleviate the above-mentioned problems to a certain extent. Most of these methods adopt the fully convolutional architecture of the encoder–decoder. For example, Ji et al. proposed a Siamese U-shaped network named SiU-Net for building extraction, which enhances the robustness of buildings of different scales by simultaneously processing original images and downsampled low-resolution images [15]. The method proposed by Sun et al. improves the detection accuracy of building edge by combining CNN with active contour model [16]. Yuan et al. designed a CNN with a simple structure, which integrates pixel-level prediction activated by multiple layers and introduces a symbolic distance function to establish boundaries to represent the output, which has a stronger representation ability [17,18]. In addition, BRRNet proposed by Shao et al. introduced the atrous convolution of different dilation rates to extract more global features by gradually increasing the receiving field in the feature extraction process and the residual refinement module to further refine the residual between the result of the prediction module and the real result [19]. However, existing approaches still suffer from challenges and limitations. Most of the methods above are an extension of the general end-to-end semantic segmentation method, do not carry out targeted analysis of the characteristics of the building itself, and do not filter the noise effectively.

Inspired by the human visual attention mechanism and the frequency characteristics of different ground objects, in this paper, we propose a denoising frequency attention network (DFANet) for building footprint extraction in VHR images. The whole network still adopts the fully convolutional architecture of encoder–decoder, but introduces two designed modules, namely the denoising frequency attention block (DFAB) and pyramid pooling module (PPM). Specifically, DFAB is parameter-free and is embedded in each layer of the network to better extract architectural footprints by refining the feature maps of different layers. It first uses a low-pass filter to filter out high-frequency noise in the feature map. Then, the feature map is reweighted in the transform domain to enhance the information more relevant to the building, and finally, a high-pass filter is used to reduce the loss of details. For the PPM, it is inserted in the middle of the encoder and decoder, which builds multi-scale feature maps by using different sizes of adaptive average pooling layers, and then stacks them together to obtain Better multi-scale object recognition. In this way, the proposed DFANet can effectively filter the background noise interference while enhancing the frequency details of buildings, highlighting the characteristics of the building itself and improving the extraction accuracy. We conduct extensive experiments on two commonly used real-world datasets, and the results demonstrate the validity and superiority of our proposal. The visualization and ablation analyses further demonstrate the critical role of our method. The main contributions of this paper can be summarized as follows:

(1) We propose a novel denoising frequency attention network (DFANet) for building footprint extraction in VHR images. It contributes to the enhancement of the frequency details of the building while filtering out the background noise interference, which in turn greatly improves the building extraction capability.
(2) We specifically design the denoising frequency attention block and pyramid pooling module to enable better extraction of building footprints by refining the feature mapping of different layers and constructing multi-scale fusion feature maps with adaptive average pooling layers of different sizes.
(3) Numerous experiments on public datasets demonstrate the advanced performance achieved by our method. In addition, both visualization analysis and ablation experiments confirm that our proposed DFAB and PPM have a positive effect on the improvement results.

The rest of this paper is organized as follows. Section 2 introduces some related work. Section 3 expounds the proposed approach in detail. In Sections 4 and 5, experimental results are reported and discussed. The conclusion and future work are in Section 6.

2. Related Works

Remote-sensing imagery can provide effective data support for humans to reform nature, and it has been widely used in Earth observation [20–22]. With the rapid development of aerial photography technology such as satellite and aviation, high-resolution remote-sensing images allow for observing detailed ground targets such as buildings, roads, and vehicles. In particular, building footprint extraction is of great significance for urban development planning and urban disaster prevention and mitigation, since buildings are one of the main man-made targets for humans to transform the Earth's surface [23–26]. Building footprint extraction has been a constant concern by scholars, and many building footprint extraction methods have been proposed in the past decade. These methods can be grouped into the following two categories: conventional building footprint extraction methods and deep-learning-based building footprint extraction methods. Here, we briefly review these methods as follows.

2.1. Conventional Building Footprint Extraction Methods

Building footprint extraction plays an important role in the interpretation and application of remote-sensing images [27]. In the early stage, scholars worked on extracting building footprints through different mathematical models or combining multiple types of data information. For instance, Reference [28] designed a fully automatic building footprint extraction approach from the differential morphological profile of high-resolution satellite imagery. In Reference [29], a Bayesian-based approach is proposed to extract building footprints through aerial LiDAR data. This method employs the shortest path algorithm and maximizes the posterior probability using linear optimization to automatically obtain building footprints. Sahar et al. utilized vector parcel geometries and their attributes to extract building footprints by using integrated aerial imagery and geographic information system (GIS) data [23]. These methods often require different types of data support to achieve building footprint extraction, and the results are not reliable enough [30,31]. In addition, scholars have devoted themselves to designing various hand-crafted features to automatically extract building footprints from high-resolution remote-sensing images. Zhang et al. devised a pixel shape index to extract buildings by classifying the shape and contour information of pixels [32]. Huang et al. proposed a morphological building index for automatic building extraction in [33]. Similarly, Huang et al. also developed a morphological shadow index for building extraction from high-resolution remote-sensing images [34]. Moreover, some methods use morphological attributes to achieve building footprint extraction [35,36]. In summary, these conventional approaches have been exploited to extract building footprints from high-resolution remote-sensing images.

2.2. Deep-Learning-Based Building Footprint Extraction Methods

Computational intelligence (CI) is a biology- and linguistics-driven computational paradigm [37,38]. In recent years, deep learning technology, as a main pillar, has been widely used in remote-sensing image interpretation with powerful layer-by-layer learning and nonlinear fitting capabilities, such as change detection [14], scene classification [39], semantic segmentation [40], object detection [41,42], etc. In this context, the building footprint extraction method based on deep learning has attracted the attention of many scholars. The building footprint extraction task can be treated as a single-objective semantic segmentation task [43]. Therefore, the direct idea is to use a deep learning-based semantic segmentation network for building footprint extraction, which can fully utilize mainstream deep neural networks (such as VGGNet [44], ResNet [45], etc.) to mine deep semantic features to recognize buildings. For example, compared with conventional methods, semantic segmentation networks such as fully convolutional network (FCN) [46] and U-Net [47] based on VGGNet can achieve a substantial improvement in the performance of building footprint extraction [17]. These methods promote the research of deep-learning-based building footprint extraction methods. According to this, recently, many deep-learning-based approaches have been proposed for building footprint extraction from high-resolution remote-sensing images in an end-to-end manner [43]. These recent methods can be broadly reviewed as follows.

As the spatial resolution of images continues to increase, the features of various building styles, such as material, color, texture, shape, scale, and distribution, have more obvious differences, which makes it difficult to accurately extract pixel-wise building footprints by using conventional semantic segmentation networks [48]. To overcome the above challenges, many novel networks based on multi-scale and attention structures have been proposed for building footprint extraction. For example, Ji et al. proposed a Siamese U-Net (SiU-Net) for multi-source building extraction [15]. SiU-Net [15] trains the network by inputting the down-sampled counterparts as the input of another Siamese branch to enhance the multi-scale perception ability of the network and improve the performance of building extraction. In [49], a novel network with an encoder–decoder structure, named building residual refine network (BRRNet), is devised for building extraction, which introduces a residual refinement module to enlarge the receptive field of the network, thus improving the performance of building extraction with various scales. Chen et al. proposed a context feature enhancement network (CFENet) to extract building footprints [50], which builds a spatial fusion module and focus enhancement module for enhancing multi-scale feature representation. Other similar networks can be found in [51,52]. In addition to these networks with multi-scale structures, attention-based networks have been able to enhance multi-scale feature representation, thus effectively improving building footprint extraction accuracy. For instance, Guo et al. developed a U-Net with an attention block for building extraction in [53]. In Reference [54], a scene-driven multitask parallel attention convolutional network is promoted for building extraction from high-resolution remote-sensing images. An attention-gate-based and pyramid network (AGPNet) with an encoder–decoder structure is designed for building extraction in [55], which is integrated with a grid-based attention gate and atrous spatial pyramid pooling module to enhance multi-scale features. Other attention-based building footprint extraction methods are available in [56–59].

Recently, some methods have introduced edge information and frequency information to enhance the recognition ability of buildings [48,60]. For instance, Zhu et al. proposed an edge-detail network for building extraction [61], which can consider the edge information of the images to enhance the identification ability to build footprints. In [62], a multi-task frequency–spatial learning network is promoted for building extraction. Zhao et al. adopted a multi-scale attention-guided UNet++ with edge constraint to achieve accurate building footprint segmentation in [63]. For other related papers, one can refer to the following studies [64–66]. In addition, advanced transformer-based networks have also received attention for building extraction, such as References [57,67,68]. These methods have largely contributed to the development of building footprint extraction.

3. Methodology

In this section, the proposed denoising frequency attention network (DFANet) is introduced in detail. Firstly, the overview of DFANet is demonstrated in Section 3.1. Then, the proposed denoising frequency attention block (DFAB) is illustrated in detail in Section 3.2. Finally, we introduce the pyramid pooling module (PPM) [69] in Section 3.3, which is a widely used module to better extract multi-scale objects.

3.1. Overview

To extract a fine building footprint in remote-sensing imagery, we employ the U-shape encoder–decoder architecture with skip connections as the backbone of DFANet, which is well proven in similar image segmentation tasks [47], as shown in Figure 1. It is well known that skip connections can help preserve detailed information in the deeper layers of the network, which can benefit the segmentation performance. Considering that there are plenty of small building objects that need to be well extracted, the backbone with such features can promote the detection of these objects.

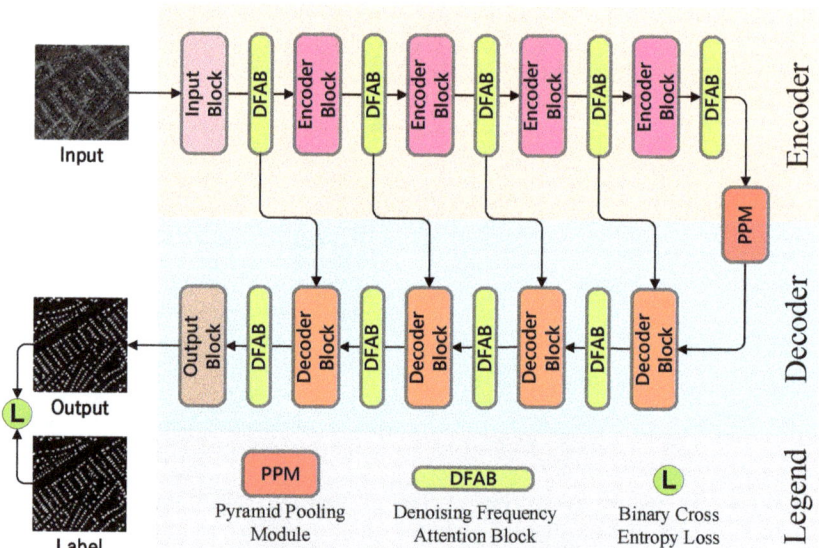

Figure 1. Overview of the proposed DFANet.

In terms of details, the backbone consists of four different blocks, i.e., the input block, the encoder block, the decoder block, and the output block. The input block contains two 3 × 3 convolutional layers with batch normalization (BN) and a rectified linear unit (ReLU) activation function, which fit the input remote-sensing image into the DFANet. The encoder block has two convolutional layers with the kernel size of 3 × 3, followed by BN and ReLU, too. The difference between them is that the latter has a 2 × 2 max pooling layer, which decreases the spatial size. The decoder block has the same convolutional layers as that of the encoder block, but with different convolutional configurations, i.e., input and output channel sizes. Different from the encoder block, the decoder block has a 2 × 2 bilinear interpolation layer instead of the max pooling layers. Moreover, the output block has only one 1 × 1 convolutional layer without BN and ReLU to generate the raw prediction of DFANet.

Apart from the backbone, the proposed DFAB is stacked in the network to acquire a better building footprint by refining the feature maps of different layers. To achieve this, the DFAB first utilizes a low-pass filter to filter out the noises in feature maps, since noises are usually in the high-frequency spectrum. Then, the feature maps are reweighted in the transformation domain to enhance the relevant information for building footprint extraction. Finally, since some detailed information is weakened by the low-pass filter, we employ a high-pass filter to avoid the loss of details. Moreover, the DFAB works without the parameters that need to be trained, and we can refine the feature maps of DFANet at a lower cost.

Moreover, to better deal with buildings of varied shapes and sizes, we employ the widely used PPM [69] to increase the receptive field of DFANet and acquire better cognition of multi-scale objects. The proposed DFAB and employed PPM will be demonstrated in detail below.

3.2. Denoising Frequency Attention Block

Attention-based techniques have been time-tested in the remote-sensing field and similar applications, such as building change detection [8] and building extraction [48]. These attention mechanisms usually obtain the attention scores or masks based on the data distribution of the feature maps in networks, and try to utilize acquired scores to reweight the feature maps for better performance. Notably, the features in networks contain the noises caused by input data and premature feature mapping at the early stage of training, based on which we can potentially poison the generated attention scores and downgrade the performance. Moreover, to acquire capable ability, most attention mechanisms need to be guided and adjusted through training over specific tasks, which limits their usability. Moreover, most building footprint extraction methods with attention techniques refine their features with spatial and channel attention mechanisms, which can be affected by the noises inside feature maps. And it is notable that frequency-based attention mechanisms have been invented and are well proven for change detection [60]. Based on these facts, the proposed DFAB makes efforts to utilize the transformation-based attention mechanism and kernel filters to refine the features of DFANet without training, which can potentially avoid the aforementioned limitations, as shown in Figure 2. In general, DFAB is parameter-free and is embedded in each layer of the network to better extract architectural footprints by refining the feature maps of different layers. It first uses a low-pass filter to filter out high-frequency noise in the feature map. Then, the feature map is reweighted in the transform domain to enhance the information more relevant to the building, and finally, a high-pass filter is used to reduce the loss of details.

The mathematical style of the DFAB can be shown as follows: firstly, let the input feature maps of DFAB be $f_i \in \mathbb{R}^{C \times H \times W}$, where C, H, and W represent the channel, height, and width sizes of f_i, respectively. To lower the high-frequency noise of input features, we utilize a low-pass filter, a Gaussian filter, to process the input feature maps. Different from other widely used low-pass filters, a Gaussian filter can preserve more detailed information due to its structure. And for fine-grained feature representation, we utilize a Gaussian filter with a size of 3×3 to suppress the noises, which can be denoted as:

$$f_L = Gaussian(f_i) \qquad (1)$$

where $Gaussian(\cdot)$ represents the 3×3 Gaussian kernel filter. Then, we use discrete cosine transform (DCT) and global average pooling (GAP) to screen the informative feature maps [70] and further lower the impact of the noises, which can be represented as follows:

$$A_s = Softmax(GAP(DCT(f_L))) \qquad (2)$$

where $DCT(\cdot)$ and $GAP(\cdot)$ denote the channel-wise DCT and GAP, respectively. Notably, the Softmax function is employed to further emphasize the relevant informative features and suppress the irrelevant features, which is represented as $Softmax(\cdot)$. With these procedures, the attention score $A_s \in \mathbb{R}^{C \times 1 \times 1}$ is obtained. Considering that the low-pass filter inevitably damages the high-frequency information of the input features, we employ a high-pass filter, the Laplacian filter, to extract and enhance the detailed information, which can be represented as:

$$f_H = Laplacian(f_L \otimes A_s) \tag{3}$$

where $Laplacian(\cdot)$ indicates a 3×3 Laplacian kernel filter, and $\otimes$ denotes the channel-wise multiplication. Finally, we utilize a residual path to make the output more stable and avoid gradient vanishing [45], which can be denoted as:

$$f_o = f_i \oplus f_H \tag{4}$$

where $\oplus$ denotes the pixel-wise addition.

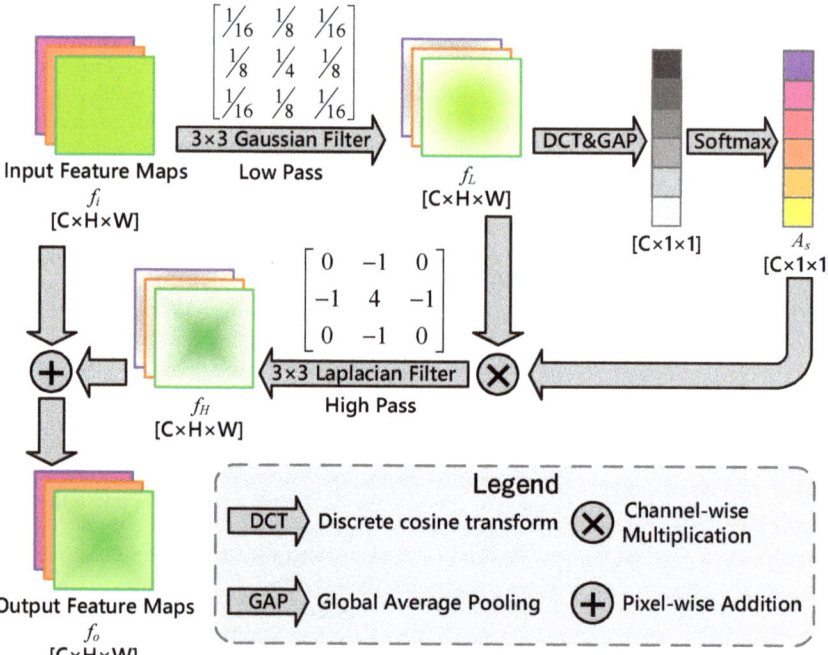

Figure 2. The illustration of the proposed DFAB.

To sum up, the DFAB proposed in this paper attempts to achieve a better fine-grained feature representation by utilizing an attention mechanism based on a parameter-free transformation and a kernel filter. Through DFAB, the refined feature maps with less noise and more informative details can potentially benefit the building extraction performance of the proposed DFANet.

3.3. Pyramid Pooling Module

Convolutional neural-network-based methods usually suffer from a limited receptive field, which downgrades the performance when detecting multi-scale objects. To alleviate this problem, the PPM was proposed in [69], which greatly improves the segmentation performance. Encouraged by its success in natural image segmentation tasks, we employ the PPM in the building footprint extraction tasks to tackle buildings with varied scales.

The PPM mainly utilizes the adaptive average pooling (AAP) layers of different sizes to construct multi-scale feature maps and then stacks them together to acquire better recognition of multi-scale objects. In the proposed DFANet, the PPM uses the same configuration as that of its original work. The detailed process of the PPM is shown in Figure 3, which also can be represented in mathematical style as follows:

Let the input feature maps of the PPM be $F_I \in \mathbb{R}^{C \times H \times W}$, where C, H, and W, denote the sizes of channel, height, and weight, respectively. The input features will be processed by AAP layers of four different sizes, i.e., 1×1, 2×2, 3×3, and 6×6, which can be represented as:

$$F_x = AAP_n(F_I) \tag{5}$$

where $F_x \in \mathbb{R}^{C \times n \times n}$ $\{x = 1, 2, 3, 4 | n = 1, 2, 3, 6\}$ is the processed features, and $AAP_n(\cdot)$ denotes AAP with an output size of n × n. Then, all of them will be compressed in channel dimension and up-sampled to H × W by convolutional layers and bilinear interpolation, respectively, which can be denoted as:

$$F_{xO} = Upsample(conv_x(F_x)) \tag{6}$$

where $conv_x(\cdot)$ and $Upsample(\cdot)$ indicate 1×1 convolutional layers and the bilinear interpolation, respectively. Finally, the feature maps with multi-scale information are stacked together with the input feature to better detect multi-scale objects, which can be demonstrated as:

$$F_O = F_I \odot F_{1O} \odot F_{2O} \odot F_{3O} \odot F_{4O} \tag{7}$$

where ⊙ denotes the channel-wise concatenation.

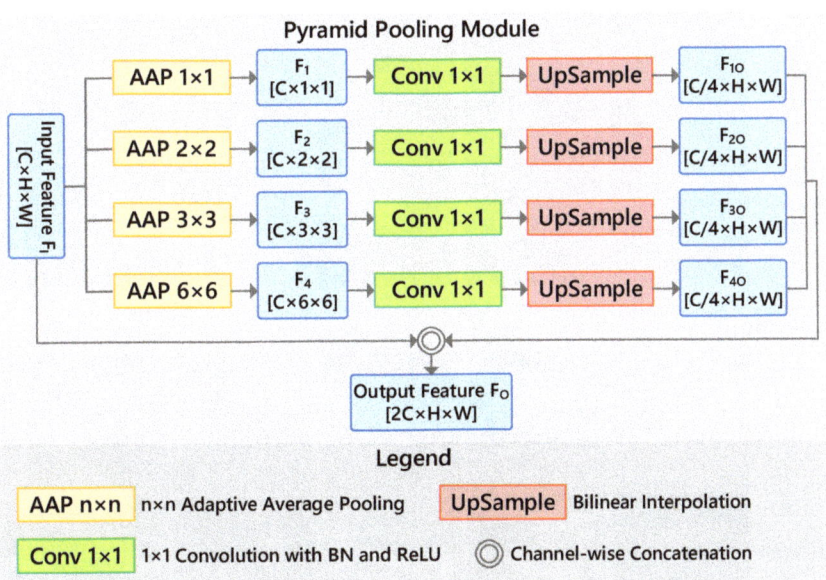

Figure 3. Architecture of the PPM.

To conclude, the PPM can increase the receptive field of convolutional neural networks by multi-scale pooling layers and better capture objects with varied sizes. As a result, we attempt to employ the PPM in the proposed DFANet to better deal with multi-scale building objects and further improve the building detection performance.

4. Experimental Results

In this section, we implement extensive experiments and ablation analysis to demonstrate the superior performance of the proposed method. First, the dataset, evaluation metrics, and implementation details are provided, and then six comparison algorithms are used to show that our method is able to achieve state-of-the-art performance, and finally, ablation analysis is implemented to demonstrate that each module contributes to the improvement of the results.

4.1. Datasets and Evaluation Metrics

In the experiments, two benchmark building detection datasets are employed to demonstrate the effectiveness of our proposed DFANet, namely the Massachusetts dataset [71] and the East Asia Dataset [15].

The Massachusetts dataset [71] was collected in the Boston area of the United States, which is approximately 340 square kilometers. This dataset contains a total of 151 aerial images of 1500×1500 pixels with a 1 m spatial resolution. In the original dataset version, 173, 4, and 10 of these images were used as training, validation, and test sets, respectively. In these experiments, consistent with [48], we sequentially crop each image into four non-overlapping 300 tiles of size 512×512. Therefore, the training set, validation set, and test set are composed of 548, 16, and 40 aerial image tiles, respectively. Some aerial image blocks are shown in Figure 4a. It can be seen that there are dense and sparse buildings in the Massachusetts dataset in the complex background at the same time, which puts forward strict requirements for the building extraction ability of the model in multiple scene categories.

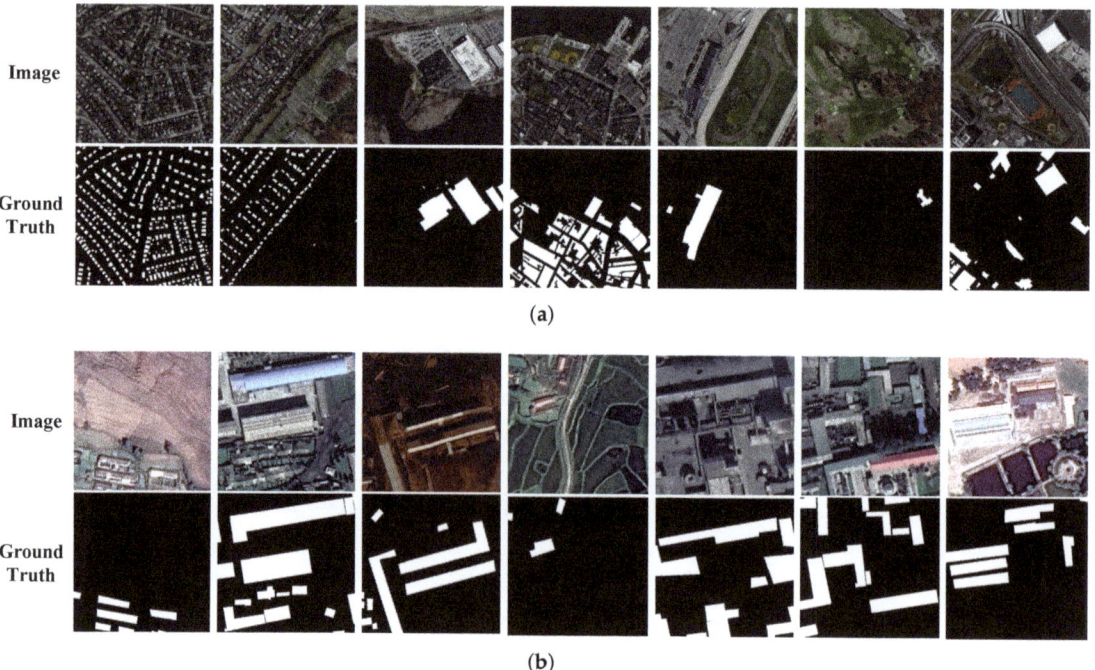

Figure 4. Some examples of two benchmark datasets: (**a**) Massachusetts dataset; (**b**) East Asia Dataset. The first row in each subplot is the aerial image tile, and the second row is the ground truth.

The East Asia Dataset [15] contains an area of 550 square kilometers in East Asia, collected from six adjacent satellite images with a spatial resolution of 2.7 m. The image size of this dataset is 512 × 512, and some aerial image tiles are shown in Figure 4b. In this experiments, consistent with [48], We selected the parts with buildings from the whole dataset, containing 3153 tiles and 903 tiles in the training and testing sets, respectively. Since these images are collected from different data sources but have similar architectural styles in the same geographical area, this dataset can be leveraged to accurately test and evaluate the generalization ability of deep models for building extraction.

In terms of evaluation metrics, four commonly used building detection indicators, namely Precision, Recall, F1-Score, and Intersection over Union (IOU), are employed to measure the performance of all the methods. Precision and Recall are the two most commonly used quantitative indicators. Precision refers to the percentage of buildings predicted to extract correctly, while Recall is the proportion of positive pixels in the building that extract ground truths that are predicted to be correct. Due to the imbalance between the number of building pixels and the number of non-building pixels in the dataset, the two comprehensive indicators of F1-Score and IOU are also considered, which more objectively reflects the ability of the model to handle the building detection task. Their detailed definitions are as follows:

$$Precision = \frac{TP}{TP + FP}, \qquad (8)$$

$$Recall = \frac{TP}{TP + FN}, \qquad (9)$$

$$F1\text{-}Score = \frac{2 \times Recall \times Precision}{Recall + Precision}, \qquad (10)$$

$$IOU = \frac{TP}{TP + FN + FP}. \qquad (11)$$

where TP and FP are the number of true-positive and false-positive pixels, respectively. Similarly, TN and FN represent the number of true-negative and false-negative pixels, respectively.

4.2. Implementation Details

In the experiments, we reproduced all the comparison methods and performed them under the same experimental conditions to ensure the fairness of the comparison with DFANet. We performed DFANet on the Pytorch platform of CUDA 11.6 by using a single NVIDIA RTX 3090 GPU with 24 GB video memory.

In the setting of hyperparameters, the batch size is set to 4, and the Adam optimizer is employed. In addition, the initial learning rate is set to 10^{-4}, with a weight decay rate of 10^{-5}. In addition, a multi-step learning rate delay is deployed to progressively update the learning rate during the training with gamma set to 0.9 and milestone set to [30, 35, 40, 45, 50, 55, 60, 65, 70]. It is worth mentioning that the experiments do not employ data augmentation strategies.

4.3. Comparison with Other Methods

4.3.1. Comparative Algorithms

To verify the effectiveness of our proposed DFANet, six excellent peers are selected as comparative algorithms, which are detailed as follows.

(1) **U-Net** [47] is built on the basis of FCN8s [46], which mainly includes a contraction path for extracting image features or context and an expansion path for precise segmentation.

(2) **PANet** [72] proposed a pyramid attention network to exploit the influence of global context information in semantic segmentation, and introduced feature pyramid attention and global attention upsampling to overcome the loss of localization information.
(3) **SiU-Net** [15] is designed based on a Siamese fully convolutional network, where the two branches of the network share weights, and the original image and its downsampled counterpart are used as input.
(4) **BRRNet** [49] consists of a prediction module and a residual refinement module. The prediction module obtains a larger receptive field by introducing dilated convolutions with different dilation rates, while the residual refinement module takes the output of the prediction module as input to improve the accuracy of building segmentation.
(5) **AGPNet** [55] is one of the state-of-the-art methods designed for architectural segmentation. It is an encoder–decoder structure that combines a grid-based attention gate and an atrous-space pyramid pooling module.
(6) **Res2-Unet** [73] is an end-to-end building detection network that employs granular-level multi-scale learning to expand the receptive field size of each bottleneck layer, focusing on pixels in complex background boundary regions.

4.3.2. Results on the Massachusetts Dataset

Table 1 shows the quantitative analysis results compared with various building extraction algorithms. It can be observed that in the two quantitative indicators of Precision and Recall, DFANet is behind the state-of-the-art (SOTA) algorithm (i.e., BRRNet), by 1.75% in Recall, but lags behind the SOTA, (i.e., U-Net) in the Precision indicator 5.24%. However, due to the data imbalance in quite a few images, these two indicators alone are not enough to reflect the performance of the algorithms. On two comprehensive indicators, DFANet can achieve the SOTA, outperforming BRRNet in F1-Score and IOU by 1.06% and 1.50%, respectively.

Table 1. Quantitative results of DFANet and comparative methods on the Massachusetts dataset. The best and second best results are marked in bold and underlined, respectively.

Methods	Precision (%)	Recall (%)	F1-Score (%)	IOU (%)
U-Net [47] (2015)	**88.66**	72.19	79.58	66.09
PANet [72] (2018)	<u>85.05</u>	42.02	56.25	39.13
SiU-Net [15] (2019)	84.82	75.80	80.06	66.74
BRRNet [49] (2020)	79.48	**81.46**	<u>80.46</u>	<u>67.31</u>
AGPNet [55] (2021)	84.72	74.86	79.48	65.95
Res2-Unet [73] (2022)	81.04	65.65	72.64	56.91
DFANet (Ours)	83.42	<u>79.71</u>	**81.52**	**68.81**

In addition to quantitative analysis, we also provide visual results for some cases in the Massachusetts dataset, as shown in Figure 5. It can be observed from the visualized results that DFANet has a more robust monitoring ability for the buildings, whether it is dense building changes or sparse building scenes. Take the first case in Figure 5 to illustrate that for the building scene similar to the background, other comparison algorithms inevitably have a large number of missing or false detection pixels, while our proposed DFANet can accurately detect most of the buildings. In addition, we can also conclude from the visualization results that the correct detection in building edges of DFANet is significantly better than other comparison algorithms.

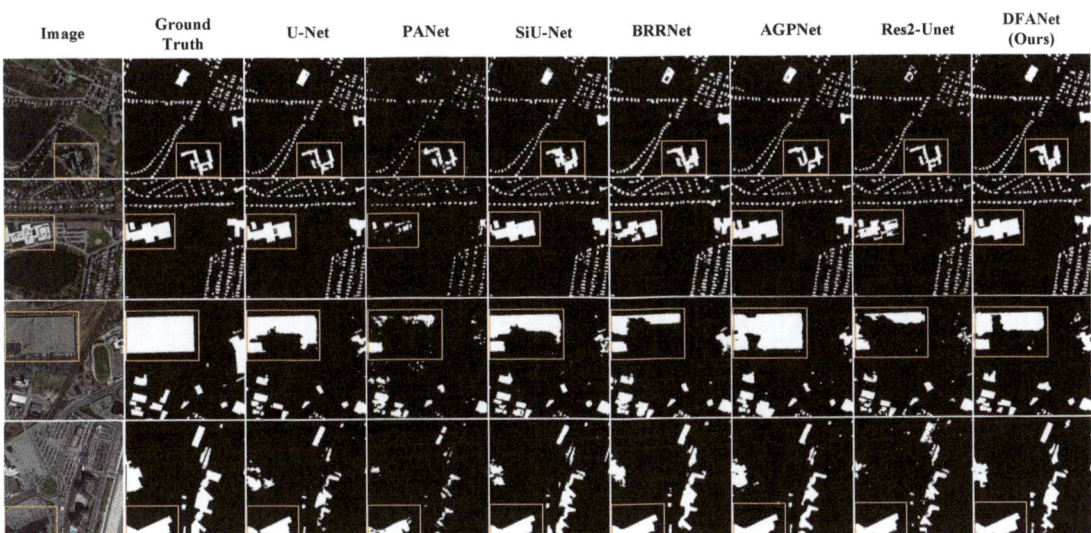

Figure 5. Some case visualization results of the Massachusetts dataset. Each column from left to right is the image, T2 image, ground truth, U-Net, PANet, SiU-Net, BRRNet, AGPNet, Res2-Unet and our proposed DFANet.

4.3.3. Results of the East Asia Dataset

Table 2 shows the quantitative results of DFANet and comparative methods of the East Asia dataset. Although DFANet does not perform well in the indicator of Precision on the East Asia dataset, it leads the previous SOTA by 2.80% in the Recall indicator. However, these two indicators cannot be directly related to the effectiveness of the algorithms due to the problem of data imbalance. On the other hand, in terms of comprehensive indicators, DFANet can still reach the SOTA and exceeds AGPNet 0.18% in F1-Score and 0.25% in IOU.

Table 2. Quantitative results of DFANet and comparative methods of the East Asia dataset. The best and second-best results are marked in bold and underlined, respectively.

Methods	Precision (%)	Recall (%)	F1-Score (%)	IOU (%)
U-Net [47] (2015)	**88.41**	71.22	78.89	65.14
PANet [72] (2018)	86.29	66.60	75.18	60.23
SiU-Net [15] (2019	<u>88.29</u>	70.85	78.62	64.77
BRRNet [49] (2020)	84.06	<u>78.02</u>	80.93	67.97
AGPNet [55] (2021)	86.37	76.59	<u>81.19</u>	<u>68.34</u>
Res2-Unet [73] (2022)	84.07	69.14	75.88	61.14
DFANet (Ours)	81.93	**80.82**	**81.37**	**68.59**

Some cases of visualization results of the East Asia dataset are shown in Figure 6. As shown in the fourth case in Figure 6, the buildings are actually quite similar to the background scene, and it is even difficult to distinguish them with human eyes. Algorithms such as PANet, SiU-Net, BRRNet, and Res2-Unet missed detection, while only U-Net, AGPNet, and DFANet can accurately identify the buildings to a large extent. But compared with U-Net and AGPNet, DFANet is more excellent in building edge detection. For densely building scenes, DFANet also outperforms other comparative algorithms.

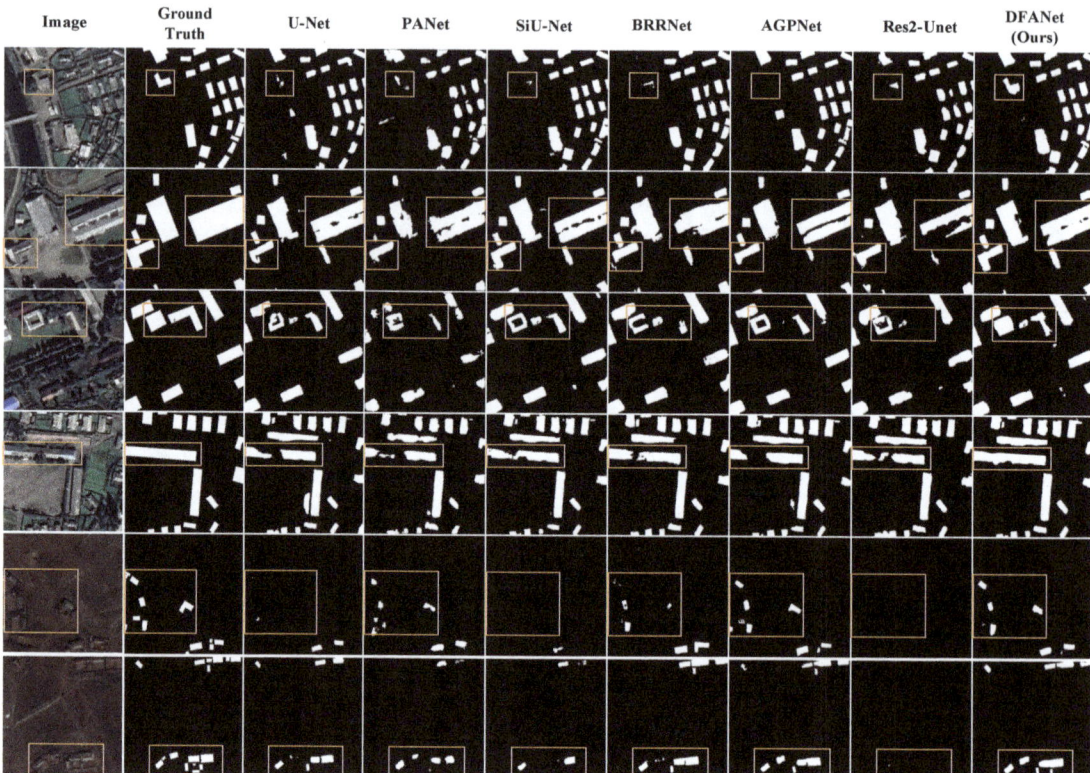

Figure 6. Some case visualization results of the East Asia dataset. Each column from left to right is the image, T2 image, ground truth, U-Net, PANet, SiU-Net, BRRNet, AGPNet, Res2-Unet, and our proposed DFANet.

5. Discussion

During the implementation of DFANet, it is still challenging to visualize the critical role that our proposed modules play in detection performance. In other words, we would like to actively explore the relationship between the proposed modules and the improvement of building footprint extraction accuracy. We evaluate and analyze the proposed DFAB and PPM modules on two benchmark datasets with four quantitative metrics (i.e., Precision, Recall, F1-Score, and IOU). The quantitative results of the ablation experiments in the Massachusetts dataset and the East Asia dataset are shown in Tables 3 and 4, respectively. It can be clearly concluded that compared with the backbone, the design of the DFAB and PPM both can improve the overall performance of the network, and the combination of these two contributions further improves the ability of the model to detect the buildings, rather than influencing each other. Specifically, in terms of two key comprehensive indicators, the DFAB, PPM, and their combination are, respectively, 1.26%, 0.68%, and 2.36% in F1-Score and 1.75%, 0.93%, and 3.30% in IOU higher than the backbone in the Massachusetts dataset. Meanwhile, in the East Asia dataset, the DFAB, PPM, and their combination are, respectively, 0.34%, 0.79%, and 0.86% in F1-Score and 0.49%, 1.13%, and 1.22% in IOU, better than the backbone.

Table 3. Ablation study of the proposed DFANet on Massachusetts dataset. Notation: the best results are marked in bold.

Methods	Precision (%)	Recall (%)	F1-Score (%)	IOU (%)
Backbone	80.63	77.74	79.16	65.51
Backbone + DFAB	81.48	79.39	80.42	67.26
Backbone + PPM	84.20	75.90	79.84	66.44
Backbone + DFAB + PPM (DFANet)	**83.42**	**79.71**	**81.52**	**68.81**

Table 4. Ablation study of the proposed DFANet on East Asia dataset. Notation: the best results are marked in bold.

Methods	Precision (%)	Recall (%)	F1-Score (%)	IOU (%)
Backbone	86.68	75.02	80.51	67.37
Backbone + DFAB	84.73	77.31	80.85	67.86
Backbone + PPM	83.83	78.93	81.30	68.50
Backbone + DFAB + PPM (DFANet)	**81.93**	**80.82**	**81.37**	**68.59**

In addition to the analysis of quantitative results, some case visualization results of feature map and heat map of the East Asia dataset are shown in Figure 7. It can be observed that the PPM can better capture building features of different shapes and sizes in the backbone network, while the DFAB can enhance the relevant information of the building to refine the feature map of each floor at a lower cost.

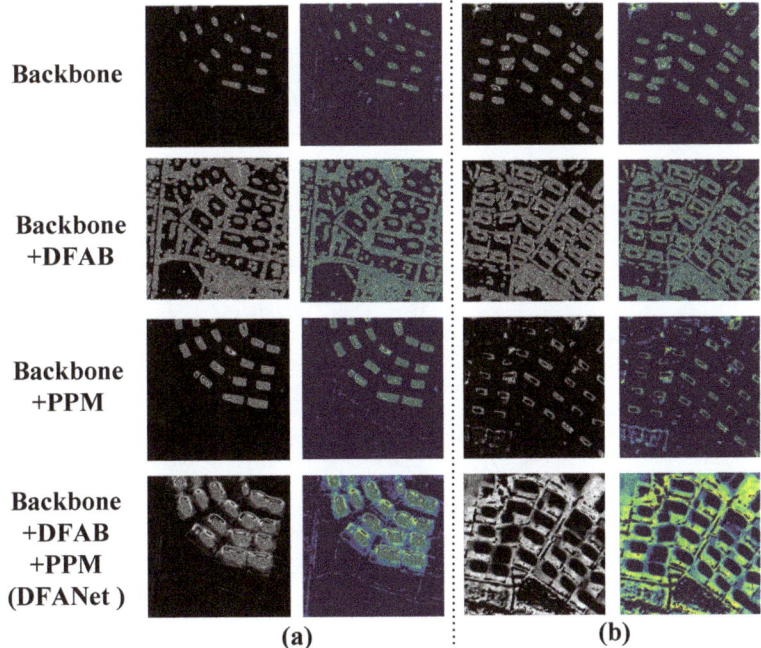

Figure 7. Visualization results of feature map and heat map of two cases (**a,b**) in the East Asia dataset. Notation: in each subgraph, the left one is the feature map, and the right one is the heat map.

6. Conclusions

In this article, a novel denoising frequency attention network (DFANet) is proposed for building footprint extraction in VHR remote-sensing images. The proposed DFANet contains three parts: a U-shape backbone network, a denoising frequency attention block (DFAB), and a pyramid pooling module (PPM). In the proposed DFANet, we devised a parameter-free DFAB, which can enhance the relevant information about buildings, thereby refining the feature maps of each layer at a lower cost. In addition, in order to better capture building features of varied shapes and sizes, we also introduced a widely used PPM to enlarge the receptive field of our proposed DFANet. Experiments on two publicly available large building footprint extraction datasets demonstrate that our proposed DFANet is able to achieve competitive performance compared to other state-of-the-art methods. Moreover, sufficient ablation experiments show that introducing our designed parameter-free DFAB can effectively improve the building detection performance. In future work, we will further study this method from the following two aspects. On the one hand, we will use more building extraction datasets to further verify the robustness of the method. On the other hand, we will test the feasibility of the DFAB in other tasks.

Author Contributions: Conceptualization, L.L. and T.L.; methodology, L.L., T.L. and F.J.; validation, L.L. and B.H.; investigation, L.L. and P.Z.; writing—original draft preparation, L.L., T.L. and F.J.; writing—review and editing, L.L., T.L. and G.W. All authors have read and agreed to the published version of the manuscript.

Funding: This work is partially supported by the National Science Foundation of China Funding Project for Department of Education of Shaanxi Province of China (Grant No. 22JC063), Natural Science and Technology Project Plan in Yulin of China (Grant No. CXY-2022-94, CXY-2022-92, CXY-2022-93, CXY-2021-102-04, CXY-2021-102-02, CXY-2021-102-01, CXY-2021-102-03, CXY-2021-102-05, CXY-2021-94-02), Natural Science Basic Research Plan in Shaanxi Province of China (2021NY-208), Scientific Research Program Funded by Yulin National High Tech Industrial Development Zone (Program No. CXY-2021-55, CXY-2021-57, CXY-2021-32, CXY-2021-40, 2022HX234), and Thanks for the help.

Data Availability Statement: Data is contained within the article.

Conflicts of Interest: The authors declare no conflict of interest.

References

1. Lv, Z.; Liu, T.; Benediktsson, J.A.; Falco, N. Land cover change detection techniques: Very-high-resolution optical images: A review. *IEEE Geosci. Remote. Sens. Mag.* **2021**, *10*, 44–63. [CrossRef]
2. Gong, M.; Li, J.; Zhang, Y.; Wu, Y.; Zhang, M. Two-path aggregation attention network with quad-patch data augmentation for few-shot scene classification. *IEEE Trans. Geosci. Remote. Sens.* **2022**, *60*, 1. [CrossRef]
3. Gong, Y.; Xiao, Z.; Tan, X.; Sui, H.; Xu, C.; Duan, H.; Li, D. Context-aware convolutional neural network for object detection in VHR remote sensing imagery. *IEEE Trans. Geosci. Remote. Sens.* **2019**, *58*, 34–44. [CrossRef]
4. Jiang, F.; Gong, M.; Zheng, H.; Liu, T.; Zhang, M.; Liu, J. Self-Supervised Global-Local Contrastive Learning for Fine-Grained Change Detection in VHR Images. *IEEE Trans. Geosci. Remote. Sens.* **2023**, *61*, 1–13. . [CrossRef]
5. Liu, P.; Liu, X.; Liu, M.; Shi, Q.; Yang, J.; Xu, X.; Zhang, Y. Building footprint extraction from high-resolution images via spatial residual inception convolutional neural network. *Remote. Sens.* **2019**, *11*, 830. [CrossRef]
6. Zhang, Y.; Gong, M.; Li, J.; Zhang, M.; Jiang, F.; Zhao, H. Self-supervised monocular depth estimation with multiscale perception. *IEEE Trans. Image Process.* **2022**, *31*, 3251–3266. [CrossRef]
7. Zhu, Q.; Liao, C.; Hu, H.; Mei, X.; Li, H. MAP-Net: Multiple attending path neural network for building footprint extraction from remote sensed imagery. *IEEE Trans. Geosci. Remote. Sens.* **2020**, *59*, 6169–6181. [CrossRef]
8. Liu, T.; Gong, M.; Lu, D.; Zhang, Q.; Zheng, H.; Jiang, F.; Zhang, M. Building change detection for VHR remote sensing images via local–global pyramid network and cross-task transfer learning strategy. *IEEE Trans. Geosci. Remote. Sens.* **2021**, *60*, 1. [CrossRef]
9. Sun, Y.; Hua, Y.; Mou, L.; Zhu, X.X. CG-Net: Conditional GIS-aware network for individual building segmentation in VHR SAR images. *IEEE Trans. Geosci. Remote. Sens.* **2021**, *60*, 1. [CrossRef]
10. Kadhim, N.; Mourshed, M. A shadow-overlapping algorithm for estimating building heights from VHR satellite images. *IEEE Geosci. Remote. Sens. Lett.* **2017**, *15*, 8–12. [CrossRef]
11. Wu, Y.; Liu, J.; Gong, M.; Gong, P.; Fan, X.; Qin, A.; Miao, Q.; Ma, W. Self-Supervised Intra-Modal and Cross-Modal Contrastive Learning for Point Cloud Understanding. *IEEE Trans. Multimed.* **2023**, 1–13. . [CrossRef]

12. Gong, M.; Zhao, Y.; Li, H.; Qin, A.; Xing, L.; Li, J.; Liu, Y.; Liu, Y. Deep Fuzzy Variable C-Means Clustering Incorporated with Curriculum Learning. *IEEE Trans. Fuzzy Syst.* **2023**, 1–15. . [CrossRef]
13. Zhang, Y.; Gong, M.; Zhang, M.; Li, J. Self-Supervised Monocular Depth Estimation With Self-Perceptual Anomaly Handling. *IEEE Trans. Neural Netw. Learn. Syst.* **2023**, ahead of print. [CrossRef] [PubMed]
14. Wu, Y.; Li, J.; Yuan, Y.; Qin, A.; Miao, Q.G.; Gong, M.G. Commonality autoencoder: Learning common features for change detection from heterogeneous images. *IEEE Trans. Neural Netw. Learn. Syst.* **2021**, *33*, 4257–4270. [CrossRef] [PubMed]
15. Ji, S.; Wei, S.; Lu, M. Fully convolutional networks for multisource building extraction from an open aerial and satellite imagery data set. *IEEE Trans. Geosci. Remote. Sens.* **2018**, *57*, 574–586. [CrossRef]
16. Zhang, Y.; Gong, M.; Li, J.; Feng, K.; Zhang, M. Autonomous perception and adaptive standardization for few-shot learning. *Knowl.-Based Syst.* **2023**, *277*, 110746. [CrossRef]
17. Yuan, J. Learning building extraction in aerial scenes with convolutional networks. *IEEE Trans. Pattern Anal. Mach. Intell.* **2017**, *40*, 2793–2798. [CrossRef]
18. Liu, T.; Gong, M.; Jiang, F.; Zhang, Y.; Li, H. Landslide inventory mapping method based on adaptive histogram-mean distance with bitemporal VHR aerial images. *IEEE Geosci. Remote. Sens. Lett.* **2021**, *19*, 1–5. [CrossRef]
19. Wu, Y.; Liu, J.; Yuan, Y.; Hu, X.; Fan, X.; Tu, K.; Gong, M.; Miao, Q.; Ma, W. Correspondence-Free Point Cloud Registration Via Feature Interaction and Dual Branch [Application Notes]. *IEEE Comput. Intell. Mag.* **2023**, *18*, 66–79. [CrossRef]
20. Lv, Z.; Zhong, P.; Wang, W.; You, Z.; Shi, C. Novel Piecewise Distance based on Adaptive Region Key-points Extraction for LCCD with VHR Remote Sensing Images. *IEEE Trans. Geosci. Remote. Sens.* **2023**, *61*. [CrossRef]
21. Li, J.; Li, H.; Liu, Y.; Gong, M. Multi-fidelity evolutionary multitasking optimization for hyperspectral endmember extraction. *Appl. Soft Comput.* **2021**, *111*, 107713. [CrossRef]
22. Lv, Z.; Zhang, P.; Sun, W.; Benediktsson, J.A.; Li, J.; Wang, W. Novel Adaptive Region Spectral-Spatial Features for Land Cover Classification with High Spatial Resolution Remotely Sensed Imagery. *IEEE Trans. Geosci. Remote. Sens.* **2023**, *61*, 5609412. [CrossRef]
23. Sahar, L.; Muthukumar, S.; French, S.P. Using aerial imagery and GIS in automated building footprint extraction and shape recognition for earthquake risk assessment of urban inventories. *IEEE Trans. Geosci. Remote. Sens.* **2010**, *48*, 3511–3520. [CrossRef]
24. Van Etten, A.; Hogan, D.; Manso, J.M.; Shermeyer, J.; Weir, N.; Lewis, R. The multi-temporal urban development spacenet dataset. In Proceedings of the IEEE/CVF Conference on Computer Vision and Pattern Recognition, Nashville, TN, USA, 20–25 June 2021; pp. 6398–6407.
25. Ma, H.; Liu, Y.; Ren, Y.; Yu, J. Detection of collapsed buildings in post-earthquake remote sensing images based on the improved YOLOv3. *Remote. Sens.* **2019**, *12*, 44. [CrossRef]
26. Li, H.; Li, J.; Zhao, Y.; Gong, M.; Zhang, Y.; Liu, T. Cost-sensitive self-paced learning with adaptive regularization for classification of image time series. *IEEE J. Sel. Top. Appl. Earth Obs. Remote. Sens.* **2021**, *14*, 11713–11727. [CrossRef]
27. Song, W.; Haithcoat, T.L. Development of comprehensive accuracy assessment indexes for building footprint extraction. *IEEE Trans. Geosci. Remote. Sens.* **2005**, *43*, 402–404. [CrossRef]
28. Shackelford, A.K.; Davis, C.H.; Wang, X. Automated 2-D building footprint extraction from high-resolution satellite multispectral imagery. In Proceedings of the IGARSS 2004 IEEE International Geoscience and Remote Sensing Symposium, Anchorage, AK, USA, 20–24 September 2004; IEEE: Piscataway, NJ, USA, 2004; Volume 3, pp. 1996–1999.
29. Wang, O.; Lodha, S.K.; Helmbold, D.P. A bayesian approach to building footprint extraction from aerial lidar data. In Proceedings of the 3rd International Symposium on 3D Data Processing, Visualization, and Transmission (3DPVT'06), Washington, DC, USA, 14–16 June 2006; IEEE: Piscataway, NJ, USA, 2006; pp. 192–199.
30. Zabuawala, S.; Nguyen, H.; Wei, H.; Yadegar, J. Fusion of LiDAR and aerial imagery for accurate building footprint extraction. In *Image Processing: Machine Vision Applications II*; SPIE: Bellingham, WA, USA, 2009; Volume 7251, pp. 337–347.
31. Wang, J.; Zeng, C.; Lehrbass, B. Building extraction from LiDAR and aerial images and its accuracy evaluation. In Proceedings of the 2012 IEEE International Geoscience and Remote Sensing Symposium, Munich, Germany, 22–27 July 2012; IEEE: Piscataway, NJ, USA, 2012; pp. 64–67.
32. Zhang, L.; Huang, X.; Huang, B.; Li, P. A pixel shape index coupled with spectral information for classification of high spatial resolution remotely sensed imagery. *IEEE Trans. Geosci. Remote. Sens.* **2006**, *44*, 2950–2961. [CrossRef]
33. Huang, X.; Zhang, L. A Multidirectional and Multiscale Morphological Index for Automatic Building Extraction from Multispectral GeoEye-1 Imagery. *Photogramm. Eng. Remote. Sens.* **2011**, *77*, 721–732. [CrossRef]
34. Huang, X.; Zhang, L. Morphological building/shadow index for building extraction from high-resolution imagery over urban areas. *IEEE J. Sel. Top. Appl. Earth Obs. Remote. Sens.* **2011**, *5*, 161–172. [CrossRef]
35. Ma, W.; Wan, Y.; Li, J.; Zhu, S.; Wang, M. An automatic morphological attribute building extraction approach for satellite high spatial resolution imagery. *Remote. Sens.* **2019**, *11*, 337. [CrossRef]
36. Li, J.; Cao, J.; Feyissa, M.E.; Yang, X. Automatic building detection from very high-resolution images using multiscale morphological attribute profiles. *Remote. Sens. Lett.* **2020**, *11*, 640–649. [CrossRef]
37. Wu, Y.; Ding, H.; Gong, M.; Qin, A.; Ma, W.; Miao, Q.; Tan, K.C. Evolutionary multiform optimization with two-stage bidirectional knowledge transfer strategy for point cloud registration. *IEEE Trans. Evol. Comput.* **2022**, 1. [CrossRef]
38. Wu, Y.; Zhang, Y.; Ma, W.; Gong, M.; Fan, X.; Zhang, M.; Qin, A.; Miao, Q. Rornet: Partial-to-partial registration network with reliable overlapping representations. *IEEE Trans. Neural Netw. Learn. Syst.* **2023**, 1–14. . [CrossRef] [PubMed]

39. Li, J.; Gong, M.; Liu, H.; Zhang, Y.; Zhang, M.; Wu, Y. Multiform Ensemble Self-Supervised Learning for Few-Shot Remote Sensing Scene Classification. *IEEE Trans. Geosci. Remote. Sens.* **2023**, *61*, 4500416. [CrossRef]
40. Yuan, X.; Shi, J.; Gu, L. A review of deep learning methods for semantic segmentation of remote sensing imagery. *Expert Syst. Appl.* **2021**, *169*, 114417. [CrossRef]
41. Hoeser, T.; Kuenzer, C. Object detection and image segmentation with deep learning on earth observation data: A review-part I: Evolution and recent trends. *Remote. Sens.* **2020**, *12*, 1667. [CrossRef]
42. Hoeser, T.; Bachofer, F.; Kuenzer, C. Object detection and image segmentation with deep learning on Earth observation data: A review—Part II: Applications. *Remote. Sens.* **2020**, *12*, 3053. [CrossRef]
43. Luo, L.; Li, P.; Yan, X. Deep learning-based building extraction from remote sensing images: A comprehensive review. *Energies* **2021**, *14*, 7982. [CrossRef]
44. Simonyan, K.; Zisserman, A. Very deep convolutional networks for large-scale image recognition. *arXiv* **2014**, arXiv:1409.1556.
45. He, K.; Zhang, X.; Ren, S.; Sun, J. Deep residual learning for image recognition. In Proceedings of the IEEE Conference on Computer Vision and Pattern Recognition, Las Vegas, NV, USA, 26 June–1 July 2016; pp. 770–778.
46. Long, J.; Shelhamer, E.; Darrell, T. Fully convolutional networks for semantic segmentation. In Proceedings of the IEEE Conference on Computer Vision and Pattern Recognition, Boston, MA, USA, 7–12 June 2015; pp. 3431–3440.
47. Ronneberger, O.; Fischer, P.; Brox, T. U-net: Convolutional networks for biomedical image segmentation. In Proceedings of the Medical Image Computing and Computer-Assisted Intervention–MICCAI 2015: 18th International Conference, Munich, Germany, 5–9 October 2015; Proceedings, Part III 18; Springer: Berlin/Heidelberg, Germany, 2015; pp. 234–241.
48. Gong, M.; Liu, T.; Zhang, M.; Zhang, Q.; Lu, D.; Zheng, H.; Jiang, F. Context-content collaborative network for building extraction from high-resolution imagery. *Knowl.-Based Syst.* **2023**, *263*, 110283. [CrossRef]
49. Shao, Z.; Tang, P.; Wang, Z.; Saleem, N.; Yam, S.; Sommai, C. BRRNet: A fully convolutional neural network for automatic building extraction from high-resolution remote sensing images. *Remote. Sens.* **2020**, *12*, 1050. [CrossRef]
50. Chen, J.; Zhang, D.; Wu, Y.; Chen, Y.; Yan, X. A context feature enhancement network for building extraction from high-resolution remote sensing imagery. *Remote. Sens.* **2022**, *14*, 2276. [CrossRef]
51. Ma, J.; Wu, L.; Tang, X.; Liu, F.; Zhang, X.; Jiao, L. Building extraction of aerial images by a global and multi-scale encoder-decoder network. *Remote. Sens.* **2020**, *12*, 2350. [CrossRef]
52. Ji, S.; Wei, S.; Lu, M. A scale robust convolutional neural network for automatic building extraction from aerial and satellite imagery. *Int. J. Remote. Sens.* **2019**, *40*, 3308–3322. [CrossRef]
53. Guo, M.; Liu, H.; Xu, Y.; Huang, Y. Building extraction based on U-Net with an attention block and multiple losses. *Remote. Sens.* **2020**, *12*, 1400. [CrossRef]
54. Guo, H.; Shi, Q.; Du, B.; Zhang, L.; Wang, D.; Ding, H. Scene-driven multitask parallel attention network for building extraction in high-resolution remote sensing images. *IEEE Trans. Geosci. Remote. Sens.* **2020**, *59*, 4287–4306. [CrossRef]
55. Deng, W.; Shi, Q.; Li, J. Attention-gate-based encoder–decoder network for automatical building extraction. *IEEE J. Sel. Top. Appl. Earth Obs. Remote. Sens.* **2021**, *14*, 2611–2620. [CrossRef]
56. Yang, H.; Wu, P.; Yao, X.; Wu, Y.; Wang, B.; Xu, Y. Building extraction in very high resolution imagery by dense-attention networks. *Remote. Sens.* **2018**, *10*, 1768. [CrossRef]
57. Yuan, W.; Xu, W. MSST-Net: A multi-scale adaptive network for building extraction from remote sensing images based on swin transformer. *Remote. Sens.* **2021**, *13*, 4743. [CrossRef]
58. Tian, Q.; Zhao, Y.; Li, Y.; Chen, J.; Chen, X.; Qin, K. Multiscale building extraction with refined attention pyramid networks. *IEEE Geosci. Remote. Sens. Lett.* **2021**, *19*, 1–5. [CrossRef]
59. Zhou, D.; Wang, G.; He, G.; Long, T.; Yin, R.; Zhang, Z.; Chen, S.; Luo, B. Robust building extraction for high spatial resolution remote sensing images with self-attention network. *Sensors* **2020**, *20*, 7241. [CrossRef] [PubMed]
60. Zheng, H.; Gong, M.; Liu, T.; Jiang, F.; Zhan, T.; Lu, D.; Zhang, M. HFA-Net: High frequency attention siamese network for building change detection in VHR remote sensing images. *Pattern Recognit.* **2022**, *129*, 108717. [CrossRef]
61. Zhu, Y.; Liang, Z.; Yan, J.; Chen, G.; Wang, X. ED-Net: Automatic building extraction from high-resolution aerial images with boundary information. *IEEE J. Sel. Top. Appl. Earth Obs. Remote. Sens.* **2021**, *14*, 4595–4606. [CrossRef]
62. Yu, B.; Chen, F.; Wang, N.; Yang, L.; Yang, H.; Wang, L. MSFTrans: A multi-task frequency-spatial learning transformer for building extraction from high spatial resolution remote sensing images. *GISci. Remote Sens.* **2022**, *59*, 1978–1996. [CrossRef]
63. Zhao, H.; Zhang, H.; Zheng, X. A multiscale attention-guided UNet++ with edge constraint for building extraction from high spatial resolution imagery. *Appl. Sci.* **2022**, *12*, 5960. [CrossRef]
64. Jung, H.; Choi, H.S.; Kang, M. Boundary enhancement semantic segmentation for building extraction from remote sensed image. *IEEE Trans. Geosci. Remote. Sens.* **2021**, *60*, 1–12. [CrossRef]
65. Xu, Z.; Xu, C.; Cui, Z.; Zheng, X.; Yang, J. CVNet: Contour Vibration Network for Building Extraction. In Proceedings of the IEEE/CVF Conference on Computer Vision and Pattern Recognition, New Orleans, LA, USA, 18–24 June 2022; pp. 1383–1391.
66. Chen, S.; Shi, W.; Zhou, M.; Zhang, M.; Xuan, Z. CGSANet: A Contour-Guided and Local Structure-Aware Encoder–Decoder Network for Accurate Building Extraction From Very High-Resolution Remote Sensing Imagery. *IEEE J. Sel. Top. Appl. Earth Obs. Remote. Sens.* **2021**, *15*, 1526–1542. [CrossRef]
67. Wang, L.; Fang, S.; Meng, X.; Li, R. Building extraction with vision transformer. *IEEE Trans. Geosci. Remote. Sens.* **2022**, *60*, 1–11. [CrossRef]

68. Hu, Y.; Wang, Z.; Huang, Z.; Liu, Y. PolyBuilding: Polygon transformer for building extraction. *ISPRS J. Photogramm. Remote. Sens.* **2023**, *199*, 15–27. [CrossRef]
69. Zhao, H.; Shi, J.; Qi, X.; Wang, X.; Jia, J. Pyramid scene parsing network. In Proceedings of the IEEE Conference on Computer Vision and Pattern Recognition, Honolulu, HI, USA, 21–26 July 2017; pp. 2881–2890.
70. Feng, D.; Chu, H.; Zheng, L. Frequency Spectrum Intensity Attention Network for Building Detection from High-Resolution Imagery. *Remote. Sens.* **2022**, *14*, 5457. [CrossRef]
71. Mnih, V. *Machine Learning for Aerial Image Labeling*; University of Toronto: Toronto, ON, Canada, 2013.
72. Li, H.; Xiong, P.; An, J.; Wang, L. Pyramid attention network for semantic segmentation. *arXiv* **2018**, arXiv:1805.10180.
73. Chen, F.; Wang, N.; Yu, B.; Wang, L. Res2-Unet, a New Deep Architecture for Building Detection from High Spatial Resolution Images. *IEEE J. Sel. Top. Appl. Earth Obs. Remote. Sens.* **2022**, *15*, 1494–1501. [CrossRef]

Disclaimer/Publisher's Note: The statements, opinions and data contained in all publications are solely those of the individual author(s) and contributor(s) and not of MDPI and/or the editor(s). MDPI and/or the editor(s) disclaim responsibility for any injury to people or property resulting from any ideas, methods, instructions or products referred to in the content.

Article

Micro-Expression Spotting Based on VoVNet, Driven by Multi-Scale Features

Jun Yang, Zilu Wu and Renbiao Wu *

Tianjin Key Laboratory for Advanced Signal Processing, Civil Aviation University of China, Tianjin 300300, China; junyang@cauc.edu.cn (J.Y.); 2021021098@cauc.edu.cn (Z.W.)
* Correspondence: rbwu@cauc.edu.cn; Tel.: +86-22-24092003

Abstract: Micro-expressions are a type of real emotional expression, which are unconscious and difficult to hide. Identifying these expressions has great potential applications in areas such as civil aviation security, criminal interrogation, and clinical medicine. However, because of their characteristics such as short duration, low intensity, and sparse action units, this makes micro-expression spotting difficult. To address this problem and inspired by object detection methods, we propose a VoVNet-based micro-expression spotting model, driven by multi-scale features. Firstly, VoVNet is used to achieve the extraction and reuse of different scale perceptual field features to improve the feature extraction capability. Secondly, multi-scale features are extracted and fused using the Feature Pyramid Network module, incorporating optical flow features, and by realizing the interactive fusion of fine-grained feature information and semantic feature information. Finally, the model is trained and optimized on CAS(ME)^2 and SAMM Long Video. The experimental results show that the F1 score of the proposed model is improved by 0.1963 and 0.2441 on the two datasets compared with the baseline method, which outperforms the most popular spotting methods.

Keywords: micro-expression spotting; multi-scale; optical flow

1. Introduction

Facial expressions are mainly divided into micro-expressions and macro-expressions [1]. Micro-expressions are facial expressions that are unconsciously revealed by humans. When micro-expressions occur, the changes to the facial features are insignificant, mainly characterized by short duration, low intensity, and sparse facial action units. However, compared with macro-expressions, they can realistically reveal people's emotions. Therefore, micro-expression research has a large application value in the fields of civil aviation security screening [2], criminal interrogation [3], and clinical medicine [4].

Research related to micro-expressions is divided into two categories: micro-expression spotting and micro-expression recognition. Micro-expression spotting refers to locating the clips of micro-expressions in a video. Micro-expression recognition refers to the classification of a detected micro-expression slice, and then the classification results are applied to different clips. Micro-expression recognition research is more mature, while micro-expression spotting is still in the preliminary research stage. In this paper, inspired by object detection methods, a multi-scale feature fusion method is applied to micro-expression spotting to improve the accuracy of the micro-expression spotting model.

The object detection method consists of three parts: backbone, neck, and head [5]. The backbone part serves to perform feature extraction, where high quality features retain more information in the image and make subsequent detection more accurate. The neck part serves to perform feature fusion, which aims to fuse different features and enrich the feature connotation. The head part is used to predict the results, such as the location and the classification of the result. Similar to object detection, in micro-expression spotting, facial features are extracted in the backbone part, the extracted features are fused in the neck part, and finally the location and category of the micro-expressions are output in the head part.

In feature extraction, a simple backbone network will ignore the detailed information of micro-expressions, while a complex backbone network will slow down the model's speed. Therefore, we use VoVNet [6] for feature extraction and to concatenate the feature maps of each layer in the end, which not only achieves feature reuse and improves feature extraction capability, but also reduces the model parameters and improves the model's training speed. Different levels of feature maps have different focuses. The shallow feature maps mainly reflect the content, such as the light and dark of an image; the deep feature maps express the overall structural information. Therefore, in the neck part, the Feature Pyramid Network (FPN) [7] is applied to fuse the deep-level features with the shallow-level features, making the whole feature richer.

The optical flow method is widely used in the computer field, which can provide key information for many vision tasks and help to improve performance. As an important method in computer vision and image processing, optical flow can provide dynamic features about facial motion, combining temporal and spatial information to improve the accuracy of micro-expression spotting. At the same time, the optical flow method is robust to common factors such as facial occlusion, illumination change, and noise. It enables the network to be more able to deal with various interference factors in the actual scene. Optical flow is incorporated into the features, and the motion information is extracted by analyzing the pixel changes between consecutive frames, which can better capture the change in micro-expressions.

The organizational structure of this paper is as follows: the first section introduces the background and significance of this paper; the second section introduces the current status of micro-expression spotting; the third section, the micro-expression spotting based on VoVNet, driven by multi-scale features is introduced in detail; the fourth section shows the analysis of the experimental results; and the fifth section summarizes the work of this paper.

2. Related Work

In the early stage of micro-expression spotting, the algorithms were mainly focused on traditional methods. Shreve [8] calculated the optical flow from the onset frame to each frame of the video sequence and determined the micro-expression interval according to the magnitude of the optical flow change. Moilanen [9] used a local binary pattern (LBP) to analyze the feature difference between consecutive frames for micro-expression spotting. Patel [10] computed optical flow over local spatial regions and used a heuristic algorithm to filter out non-micro-expressions. This could detect the onset frame, the vertex frame, and the offset frame. Li [11] proposed using a local temporal pattern (LTP) and a local binary pattern (LBP) for micro-expression spotting and used them as the benchmark for the Micro-Expression Spotting Challenge, 2019. Later, He Y [12] proposed the MDMD method using the maximum difference of optical flow features to detect micro-expressions.

In recent years, deep learning methods have been widely used in various fields, and more and more experts and scholars are exploring the use of deep learning methods for micro-expression spotting and recognition. Xia [13] applied machine learning to micro-expression spotting and considered the relationship between frames and used adaboost to predict the probability of a certain frame as a micro-expression. Hong [14] used a sliding window to detect micro-expressions in samples with a fixed number of frames and treated micro-expression spotting as a binary classification task. Nag [15] proposed a joint architecture of temporal and spatial information to detect the onset frame and offset frame of micro-expressions. Verburg M [16] applied the computed HOOF features into a recurrent neural network (RNN) for micro-expression localization, which combined deep learning and traditional methods and applied them to micro-expression spotting. Pan et al. [17] proposed putting each frame of a video into the local bilinear convolutional neural network (LBCNN) to judge whether each frame belonged to a micro-expression, a macro-expression, or a natural expression. Yap et al. [18] proposed a 3D-CNN model that compared each frame with a reference frame, which is a pure deep learning scheme. Liong et al. [19] proposed a shallow optical flow three-stream CNN (SOFTNet), which used different optical flow components in three channels to capture different motion information. Fang Y [20] used the phase calculated by the Riesz Pyramid to represent motion and used CNN to calculate the probability that each frame is a micro-expression. Many of these micro-expression spotting methods draw on the idea of micro-expression recognition to judge whether a clip or a certain frame in a video is a micro-expression. This is essentially a classification problem and does not locate the clips in the video where the micro-expression occurs. Li J et al. [21] first introduced the self-supervised learning method into the construction of the micro-expression spotting model. By using auxiliary tasks in a large number of unsupervised videos, a model with temporal and spatial features of micro-expressions was constructed. Cao [22] designed a micro-expression spotting framework based on outlier spotting. Song [23] proposed a BERT network-based micro-expression spotting algorithm composed of candidate fragment generation, a spatio-temporal feature extraction module, and a grouping module.

Object detection methods based on deep learning are widely used in areas such as facial detection [24], pedestrian detection [25], and license plate detection [26]. Inspired by object detection, some scholars began to apply the methods of object detection in the spatial dimension to micro-expression spotting in the temporal dimension. For example, Yu et al. proposed using the detection method for micro-expression spotting and achieved good results in the Facial Micro-Expression (FME) Challenge. In this paper, we draw on the methods and ideas of object detection to carry out micro-expression spotting research and propose a VoVNet-based micro-expression spotting method driven by multi-scale features.

3. Proposed Method

3.1. Micro-Expression Spotting Method Based on VoVNet

Although micro-expressions are short in duration, there is still a process of facial change. Here, we define the starting point where the micro-expression occurs as the onset frame, the frame where the micro-expression changes most significantly as the apex frame, and the offset frame of the micro-expression as the offset frame. The main task of micro-expression spotting is to locate the apex frame and offset frame of the micro-expression. Figure 1 shows the structure of the micro-expression spotting model. Firstly, the micro-expression samples and the corresponding optical flow are concatenated and input into the VoVNet for feature extraction. Secondly, the fusion of the extracted features is performed by the FPN module. Finally, the micro-expression spotting results are output. In the whole process, feature extraction and fusion play a key role in ensuring the accuracy of the micro-expression spotting. Figure 1 shows the network structure of the micro-expression spotting.

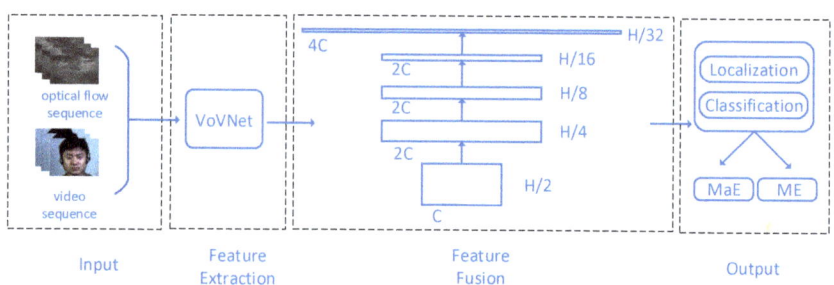

Figure 1. Structure of the micro-expression spotting model.

3.2. Optical Flow

Optical flow is the displacement of pixels due to the motion of objects in a continuous sequence of image frames. Calculating the optical flow between different frames can obtain the motion trajectory of the object in the image sequence because the micro-expressions occur as tiny details and are not easy to find; however, optical flow has good performance for the estimation of motion in a small range. Tiny movements in specific areas of the face can be detected by calculating optical flow. Micro-expressions are continuous actions, and optical flow can extract rich features from continuous image frames and capture the temporal correlation of local areas in the image. Compared with static images, optical flow can provide dynamic change information and capture the motion information of an image sequence. By combining optical flow features with raw video, micro-expressions can be spotted more accurately.

The optical flow method is based on three assumptions: (1) that the illumination remains constant between two frames; (2) that the motion of the same pixel between two frames is small; and (3) that the motion of adjacent pixels is similar. Let I(x,y,t) be the brightness value at the position (x,y) at time t, and the distance the pixel moves in dt time be (dx,dy). Because the brightness value between two frames is unchanged, we can achieve Equation (1).

$$I(x,y,t) = I(x+dx, y+dy, t+dt), \tag{1}$$

Equation (1) is expanded by the Taylor series, and Equation (2) is obtained by removing the general terms and dividing by dt.

$$\frac{\partial I}{\partial x}\frac{dx}{dt} + \frac{\partial I}{\partial y}\frac{dy}{dt} + \frac{\partial I}{\partial t} = 0, \tag{2}$$

If p,q are the horizontal and vertical directions of the pixel to obtain the velocity component then:

$$p = \frac{dx}{dt}, \, q = \frac{dy}{dt} \tag{3}$$

By bringing p and q into Equation (2), the optical flow change of each pixel of the picture can be obtained.

According to Liong S T et al. [27], the TVL1 optical flow method is more robust and accurate than other methods in the study of micro-expression. Therefore, this article also uses the TVL1 method.

3.3. VoVNet Module

Related studies have proven that features with multiple receptive fields can capture richer visual information [28–30]. Since the features are inconspicuous when micro-expressions occur, they are mainly manifested in the weak intensity of facial muscle changes and sparse facial action units. Therefore, to improve the extraction capability of micro-expression features, VOVNet is used. By fusing the features of different receptive fields, VoVNet can extract the relevant features of the long-range facial action unit and improve the performance of micro-expression spotting. VoVNet is mainly composed of One-Shot Aggregation (OSA) modules, as shown in Figure 2. The OSA module consists of multiple convolution layers, each of which is bi-directionally connected. One is used to connect to the next convolution layer to generate features with a larger receptive field, and the other is used to connect to the last layer to achieve feature splicing and reuse. This structure is designed to enhance the feature extraction capability of the network by fusing features with different receptive fields. It does not cause redundancy of features and improves the efficiency of the model.

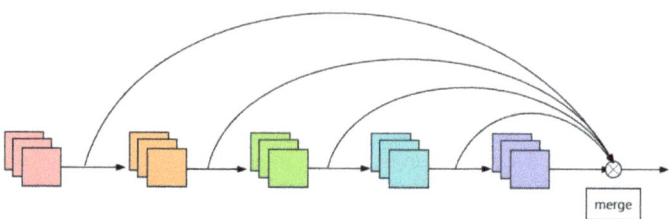

Figure 2. OSA module structure. The convolved feature graphs are changed and finally fused.

Memory Access Cost (MAC) is an important measure of model processing speed. VoVNet is not only strong in feature extraction, but also fast in computation, mainly because of the small MAC. The MAC is calculated as shown in Equation (4). Let the number of input and output channels of one convolution layer of the OSA module be c_1 and c_2, respectively, and the size of the feature map is h × w; then, the FLOPs of 1 × 1 convolution is $B = h \times w \times c_1 \times c_2$. Equation (5) is derived from the mean inequality and the MAC is minimized when $c_1 = c_2$. Therefore, when the number of input and output channels in the middle layer of the OSA module is the same, the model MAC is minimized and the model processing speed is fastest.

$$\text{MAC} = h \times w \times (c_1 + c_2) + c_1 \times c_2, \tag{4}$$

$$\text{MAC} \geq 2\sqrt{h \times w \times B} + \frac{B}{h \times w}, \tag{5}$$

VoVNet consists of three convolution layers and four OSA modules. Each OSA module consists of five convolution layers with the same input and output channels to minimize the value of the MAC. The number of feature channels is gradually increased by superimposing multiple OSA modules, and the superposition of feature maps of different sizes makes the features more abundant. Feature fusion is performed after feature extraction. The specific network structure is shown in Table 1.

Table 1. VoVNet network architecture.

Type	VoVNet
Inception	3 × 3conv, 64, stride = 2 3 × 3conv, 128, stride = 2
OSA 1	3 × 3conv, 64, ×5 concat: 1 × 1conv, 128
OSA 2	3 × 3conv, 80, ×5 concat: 1 × 1conv, 256
OSA 3	3×3conv, 96, ×5 concat: 1 × 1conv, 384
OSA 4	3 × 3conv, 112, ×5 concat: 1 × 1conv, 1

3.4. FPN Module

In object detection, feature fusion can effectively improve model performance and generalization ability. FPN, as a common feature fusion module in object detection, improves detection accuracy by constructing a feature pyramid structure, extracting and fusing multi-scale features from different levels.

The feature pyramid consists of multiple levels, each with a different resolution and receptive field. This design enables the model to analyze and process micro-expression sequences at different scales. The bottom pyramid layers contain features at lower levels, while the features at higher levels are more abstract and semantic. Combining these features can obtain more comprehensive and accurate features, which can help to improve the accuracy of micro-expression detection. Each level will extract the features of the micro-expression sequence, which can improve the ability to understand and analyze the micro-expression sequence by transferring information. Low-level features can provide background and global information for higher-level features so that the model can better detect micro-expressions. Because features at different levels obtain information at different scales, they are robust in detection.

The pyramid model can obtain feature maps of different scales through one-dimensional convolution, and rich multi-scale and multi-level feature representations can be obtained through multi-level feature extraction and combination. Thus, the accuracy of micro-expression spotting is improved. The specific network structure is shown in Table 2.

Table 2. FPN network architecture.

Type	FPN
layer 1	3 × 1conv, 512 × 64, stride = 2
layer 2	3 × 1conv, 1024 × 32, stride = 2
layer3	3 × 1conv, 1024 × 16, stride = 2
layer4	3 × 1conv, 1024 × 8, stride = 2
layer5	3 × 1conv, 2048 × 4, stride = 2

3.5. Loss Function

The loss function can calculate the difference between the predicted result and the true label. The lower the loss value, the stronger the ability of micro-expression training. Classification loss, boundary frame loss, and IOU loss are calculated, respectively, in micro-expression spotting.

The first is classification loss, which is a measure of the ability to classify the target species. Because there are more macro-expressions than micro-expressions in the video sample, focal loss [31] is used to solve the category imbalance problem. Focal loss introduced w and pt to adjust the weights of samples to be unequal, reduce the emphasis on easily identifiable samples, and increase the emphasis on samples that are difficult to classify. The alph is a balancing parameter standing at 0.25 and w changes the weight of the sample. The proportion of different samples in the equation is different, which makes the model pay more attention to the small number of samples. Pt reduces the weight of samples that are easy to classify and increases the weight of samples that are difficult to classify by calculating probabilities. This makes the model pay more attention to those samples that are difficult to classify, improving the model's learning ability for difficult samples. Equation (6) is the calculation equation for focal loss.

$$\text{Focal\_loss} = -w(1-pt)^2 \times log(pt), \tag{6}$$

$$\text{pt} = \begin{cases} p & positive\ sample \\ 1-p & negative\ sample \end{cases}, \tag{7}$$

$$\text{w} = \begin{cases} alph & positive\ sample \\ 1-alph & negative\ sample \end{cases}, \tag{8}$$

In addition to classification losses, positioning losses are used to measure the difference between the predicted bounding box and the true bounding box. This difference is optimized to better regulate the location of the predicted bounding box. When the absolute difference between the predicted value and the target value is large, the smooth L1 loss function adopts the square function, and the loss growth rate slows down. It is more robust in the face of outliers and large error boundary boxes. The equation for the smooth L1 loss function is as follows:

$$\text{L1\_loss} = \begin{cases} 1/2x^2 & t < 1 \\ |x| - 0.5 & t \geq 1 \end{cases}, \qquad (9)$$

Finally, IOU loss is a simple and intuitive method to calculate the overlap between the predicted bounding box and the real bounding box. It is not affected by the shape and size of the target and only considers the overlap degree of the two bounding boxes, which is suitable for different targets. By minimizing the IOU loss, the model parameters can be optimized to make the predicted bounding box closer to the real bounding box. Let the left abscissa of the predicted and true bounding boxes be x_{p1} and x_{t1}, and the right abscissa of the bounding boxes be x_{p2} and x_{t2}. Equation (10) is the equation of IOU loss function.

$$\begin{aligned} \text{IOU\_loss} &= \text{inter}/\text{union}, \\ \text{Inter} &= \min(x_{t2}, x_{p2}) - \max(x_{p1}, x_{t1}, \\ \text{Union} &= (x_{p2} - x_{p1}) + (x_{t2} - x_{t1}) - \text{inter}, \end{aligned} \qquad (10)$$

$$\text{Loss} = \text{Focal\_loss} + \text{L1\_loss} + \text{IOU\_loss}, \qquad (11)$$

The combination of classification loss, positioning loss, and IOU loss can comprehensively evaluate the performance of object detection. Classification loss is used to evaluate the accuracy of the model for target classification. Positioning loss is used to assess the accuracy of the model for the target position. IOU loss assesses the accuracy of the boundary box matching. Equation (11) is the calculation equation of the final loss function. Target spotting usually requires the accurate classification of targets and the accurate location of targets. Combining these loss functions can simplify the model training process. It can improve the stability and convergence of training, and reduce the difficulty of hyper-parameter adjustment so that the model has the ability to perform classification and positioning at the same time.

4. Experiment
4.1. Dataset

Currently, the available micro-expression datasets are very limited and differ in resolution, frame rate, and generation methods. Authoritative datasets that have been released mainly include CASME [32], SMIC [33], CASME II [34], SAMM [35], CAS(ME)^2 [36], SAMM Long Videos [37], MMEW [38], and CASME III [39]. The CASME, CASME II, SMIC, and SAMM only contain micro-expression samples, while the CAS(ME)^2, CASME III, SAMM Long Videos, and MMEW contain not only micro-expression video samples but also macro-expression video samples. CAS(ME)^2 was released by the Chinese Academy of Sciences in 2018. The subjects of CAS(ME)^2 are 22 Asians, and the data are divided into two parts: part A and part B. Part A includes 87 long videos of micro-expressions and macro-expressions. Part B includes 300 cropped macro-expression samples and 57 cropped micro-expression samples. The average duration of each video is 148 s. CASME III manually labeled 1030 micro-expressions and 2264 macro-expressions. The SAMM Long Videos are extended from the SAMM and include a total of 147 long videos. Compared with CAS(ME)^2, SAMM Long Videos have a longer video duration with higher resolution and frame rates. The MMEW was released in 2021 and contains 300 micro-expression video samples and 900 macro-expression video samples. Table 3 shows the details of the commonly used datasets of macro-expressions and micro-expressions.

CAS(ME)^2 and SAMM Long Videos were used in the Facial Micro-Expression (FME) Challenge [40] to validate the micro-expression spotting model. Therefore, in order to ensure the comparability of the results, CAS(ME)^2 and SAMM Long Videos were also selected as the micro-expression spotting dataset in this paper.

Table 3. Micro-expression dataset details.

Dataset		Time	Resolution	Frame Rate	Number of Participants	Number of Samples	Number of Emotions
CAS(ME)^2		2018	640 × 480	30	22	300 (macro) 57 (micro)	4
SAMM Long Videos		2019	2040 × 1088	200	29	343 (macro) 159 (micro)	/
MMEW		2021	1920 × 1080	90	36	900 (macro) 300 (micro)	7
CASME III	A B C	2022	1280 × 720	30	100 116 31	3364 (macro) 1030 (micro)	7

The dataset is divided into two categories: micro-expression and macro-expression. Micro-expressions are extremely brief and tiny changes in human facial expressions, typically lasting between 1/25 and 1/5 of a second. These small facial changes are often very rapid and imperceptible and often occur when people are trying to mask or hide their true feelings. Macro-expression is relative to micro-expression, which refers to the expression changes that are more significant and last longer. Whether micro-expression or macro-expression, both are expressions of the human face in different emotional or psychological states, and all involve the movement and change of the facial muscles. Figure 3 shows micro-expression and macro-expression samples in the SAMM Long Videos dataset. The human eye is difficult to distinguish, and a computer is needed for recognition.

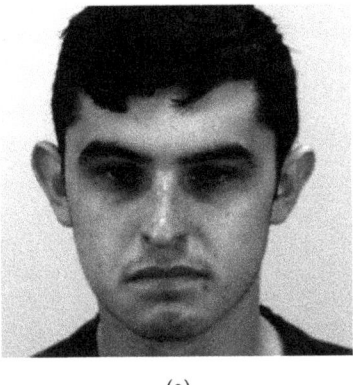 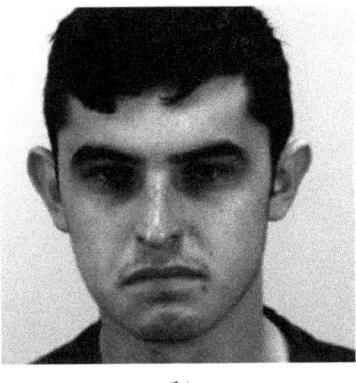

(a) (b)

Figure 3. (a) MMEW dataset macro-expression sample; (b) MMEW dataset micro-expression sample.

4.2. Experimental Environment and Hyper-Parameters

The configurations of the computer used for training and validation of the micro-expression spotting model are as follows:
(1) Operating system: 64-bit Ubuntu16.04.1.;
(2) Development environment: PyTorch1.2.0.;
(3) CPU: Intel® Xeon(R) Gold 5218R CPU @ 2.10 GHz × 46;
(4) GPU: Quadro RTX5000;
(5) Memory: 128 GB.
The hyper-parameters of the micro-expression spotting model are as follows:
(1) Optimizer: Adam;
(2) Learning rate: 0.005;

(3) Batch size: the batch size of CAS(ME)^2 is 32, and the batch size of SAMM Long Videos is 2.

4.3. Evaluation Metrics

Intersection over Union (IOU) [41] is used in object detection. IOU is the intersection of the predicted box and the real box divided by their union. When the value of IOU is greater than a certain threshold, it proves that the target is correctly boxed. Equation 12 shows the equation for micro-expression spotting IOU. Where, $W_{spotted}$ is the micro-expression clips obtained by the micro-expression spotting model, $W_{groundTrut}$ is the clips of the real micro-expression, k is the threshold of IOU, which is generally set to a constant. When the intersection of $W_{spotted}$ and $W_{groundTrut}$ divided by their union is greater than k, it proves that the micro-expression clips are detected correctly.

$$\frac{W_{spotted} \cap W_{groundTrut}}{W_{spotted} \cup W_{groundTrut}} \geq k, \qquad (12)$$

As shown in Figure 4, AC are the clips where a micro-expression occurs and BD are the clips detected by the micro-expression model. BC is the intersection of $W_{spotted}$ and $W_{groundTrut}$, AD is the union of $W_{spotted}$ and $W_{groundTrut}$.

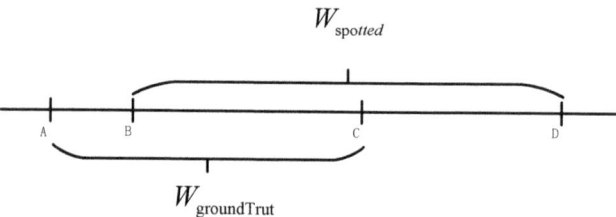

Figure 4. Micro-expression spotting IoU.

The micro-expression spotting performance is evaluated with an F1 score. The equation of the F1 score is shown in Figure 4. TP is the number of positive samples correctly identified. FP is the number of negative samples predicted as positive samples, i.e., the number of false detections. TN is the number of negative samples correctly identified. FN is the number of positive samples detected as negative samples, i.e., the number of missed detections. There are two main reasons for using the F1 score as the evaluation metric of the micro-expression spotting model:

(1) If there is no micro-expression in a single video or no micro-expression is detected in the video, the denominator of recall or precision will be 0. Using the F1 score as the evaluation metric will avoid this situation;

(2) Since the databases are apparently unbalanced, the sample size of micro-expressions is smaller than that of the macro-expressions. An F1 score will give us a fair evaluation of how well the model performs on all the classes rather than biasing only a few certain classes [36].

$$\text{F1-score} = 2 \times \frac{recall \times precision}{recall\, precision} = \frac{2TP}{2TPFPFN}, \qquad (13)$$

$$\text{Recall} = \frac{TP}{TPFN}, \qquad (14)$$

$$\text{Precision} = \frac{TP}{TPFP} \qquad (15)$$

4.4. Results and Discussion

Following [1], we use Leave-One-Subject-Out (LOSO) cross-validation to report the performance on micro-expression spotting. One micro-expression video sample is taken as the test set and the remaining samples are used as the training set.

The loss value of a model training can intuitively measure the quality of model training. Figure 5 shows the change of loss value when the model is trained on two datasets, respectively. From Figure 5, it can be seen that the loss value of the model decreases and converges as the number of iterations increases, and finally converges to a smooth state. This indicates that the model can reach a smooth convergence state.

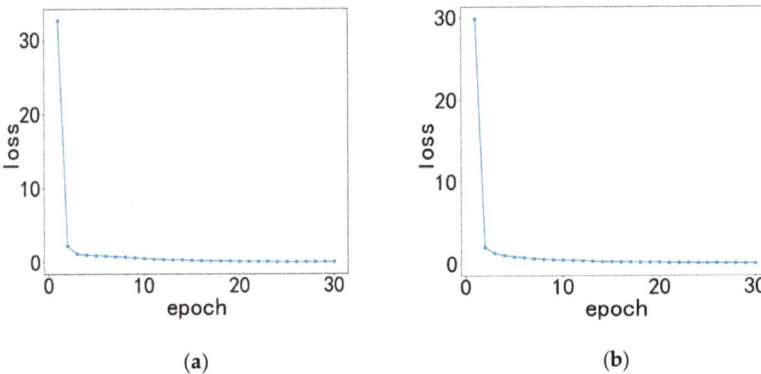

Figure 5. (a) Describes the changes in loss for the SAMM Long Video dataset; (b) describes the changes in loss for the CAS(ME)^2 dataset.

To evaluate the model performance, the proposed method is compared with the baseline method of the Facial Micro-Expression (FME) Challenge, traditional methods, and deep learning methods. Table 4 provides a detailed comparison of the models. With the SAMM Long Video, compared with the baseline method, the performance of the proposed method is significantly improved for both macro- and micro-expression spotting, with an improvement of 0.1986 and 0.1217 in the F1 score, respectively. With the CAS(ME)^2, compared with the baseline method, the proposed method improves the F1 score of macro- and micro-expression spotting by 0.2597 and 0.0571. In the overall performance of both macro- and micro-expression spotting, the method proposed in this paper outperforms the most popular spotting methods, such as MDMD, STCAN, and SOFTNet.

Table 4. Experimental results.

Model	SAMM Long Video			CAS(ME)^2		
	MaE	ME	Overall	MaE	ME	Overall
Baseline [11]	0.1863	0.0409	0.1193	0.0401	0.0118	0.0304
MDMD [12]	0.0629	0.0364	0.445	0.1196	0.0082	0.0376
STCAN [42]	0.1469	0.0125	0.1257	0.1250	0.0250	0.1168
SOFTNet [19]	0.2169	0.1520	0.1881	0.2410	0.1173	0.2022
Article	0.3849	0.1626	0.3156	0.2998	0.0689	0.2745

4.5. Ablation Experiment

The ablation experiment in this experiment verifies the influence of different modules on the model and reflects the superiority of the network. We perform replacement experiments on the optical flow module and feature extraction separately.

Optical flow features provide temporal dimension information for micro-expression detection. We compare the results of only the video features with the results of adding optical flow features. In the SAMM Long Video dataset, the F1 score of the method with an optical flow module increased by 0.1986 for macro-expression spotting and 0.2597 for micro-expression spotting. In the CAS(ME)^2 dataset, the F1 score of the method with the optical flow module increased by 0.0115 for macro-expression spotting and 0.0345 for micro-expression spotting. The results show that optical flow improves the micro-expression detection ability. Table 5 shows the effect of the optical flow module.

Table 5. Optical flow module ablation experiment.

Type	SAMM Long Video			CAS(ME)^2		
	MaE	ME	Overall	MaE	ME	Overall
No optical flow	0.2500	0.0696	0.2162	0.2883	0.0344	0.2620
Optical flow	0.3849	0.1626	0.3156	0.2998	0.0689	0.2745

The second stage is feature extraction, which is compared with the feature extraction network with better performance in target detection. ResNet shows good performance in target detection [43]. Residual links help train deeper networks in object detection. They also help solve degradation problems and are more stable in model performance. Dense connectivity in DenseNet enables features from each layer to interact directly with subsequent layers, enabling feature reuse. It can improve the detection performance. ResNet and DenseNet can extract richer and more meaningful features, and their structure is similar to VoVNet. Therefore, VoVNet is compared with ResNet and DenseNet.

A SAMM Long Video sample occupies a large storage space, and DenseNet training requires a large number of parameters. Due to the limitation of server GPU memory, we only used the CAS(ME)^2 dataset for progressive ablation experiments. Table 6 shows the results of VoVNet compared with other models in detail. The results show that VoVNet has the best feature extraction ability in micro-expression detection.

Table 6. Feature extraction module ablation experiment.

Model	CAS(ME)^2		
	MaE	ME	Overall
ResNet	0.2495	0.0421	0.2253
DenseNet	0.3026	0.0459	0.2596
VoVNet	0.2998	0.0689	0.2745

5. Discussion

To address the problem that micro-expressions are difficult to detect, a VoVNet-based micro-expression spotting model driven by multi-scale features is proposed in this paper. VoVNet is used for feature extraction; it integrates the features of different receptive fields to improve the model's performance. The FPN model is used in feature fusion to fuse features of different sizes and achieve deep fusion of fine-grained and semantic features, which reduces the loss of feature information and improves model robustness. Finally, the LOSO cross-validation is used to evaluate the performance of the model. The experimental results show that compared with other popular methods, the micro-expression spotting method proposed in this paper can improve the performance of micro-expression spotting to a certain extent. In addition to micro-expression spotting, the method proposed in this paper can also be applied to video behavior recognition tasks, such as abnormal behavior detection, action recognition, and gesture recognition in surveillance videos. It can also be applied to medical image processing, such as lesion detection, disease classification, and diagnosis. By extracting and analyzing the features in medical images, it can assist doctors in the diagnosis and treatment of diseases.

Since micro-expression and macro-expression samples are not balanced, we used attention mechanisms and other methods to compensate for this deficiency. Due to the large dataset and many model parameters, our next step will explore the use of a lighter model for feature extraction. What is more, the importance of the three loss functions will be considered. These losses can be weighted, and the weights can be optimized to take advantage of the results.

Author Contributions: Methodology, J.Y.; validation, Z.W.; investigation, J.Y.; writing—original draft preparation, Z.W.; writing—review and editing, Z.W and R.W.; capital, R.W. All authors have read and agreed to the published version of the manuscript.

Funding: This research was funded by "the Open Fund of Tianjin Key Lab for Advanced Signal Processing, Civil Aviation University of China", grant number 2022ASP-TJ03, and supported by "the Fundamental Research Funds for the Central Universities of China", grant number 3122023011.

Data Availability Statement: Not applicable.

Conflicts of Interest: The authors declare no conflict of interest.

References

1. Yu, W.W.; Yang, K.F.; Yan, H.M.; Li, Y.J. Weakly-supervised Micro-and Macro-expression Spotting Based on Multi-level Consistency. *arXiv* **2023**, arXiv:2305.02734.
2. Weinberger, S. Airport security: Intent to deceive? *Nature* **2010**, *465*, 412–416. [CrossRef] [PubMed]
3. Owayjan, M.; Kashour, A.; Al Haddad, N.; Fadel, M.; Al Souki, G. The design and development of a lie detection system using facial micro-expressions. In Proceedings of the 2012 2nd International Conference on Advances in Computational Tools for Engineering Applications (ACTEA), Beirut, Lebanon, 12–15 December 2012; pp. 33–38.
4. Russell, T.A.; Green, M.J.; Simpson, I.; Coltheart, M. Remediation of facial emotion perception in schizophrenia: Concomitant changes in visual attention. *Schizophr. Res.* **2008**, *103*, 248–256. [CrossRef] [PubMed]
5. Yu, W.W.; Jiang, J.; Li, Y.J. LSSNet: A two-stream convolutional neural network for spotting macro-and micro-expression in long videos. In Proceedings of the 29th ACM International Conference on Multimedia, Virtual, China, 20–24 October 2021; pp. 4745–4749.
6. Lee, Y.; Hwang, J.; Lee, S.; Bae, Y.; Park, J. An energy and GPU-computation efficient backbone network for real-time object detection. In Proceedings of the IEEE/CVF Conference on Computer Vision and Pattern Recognition Workshops, Long Beach, CA, USA, 16–17 June 2019.
7. Lin, T.Y.; Dollár, P.; Girshick, R.; He, K.; Hariharan, B.; Belongie, S. Feature pyramid networks for object detection. In Proceedings of the IEEE Conference on Computer Vision and Pattern Recognition, Honolulu, HI, USA, 21–26 July 2017; pp. 2117–2125.
8. Shreve, M.; Godavarthy, S.; Manohar, V.; Goldgof, D.; Sarkar, S. Towards macro-and micro-expression spotting in video using strain patterns. In Proceedings of the 2009 Workshop on Applications of Computer Vision (WACV), Snowbird, UT, USA, 7–8 December 2009; pp. 1–6.
9. Moilanen, A.; Zhao, G.; Pietikäinen, M. Spotting rapid facial movements from videos using appearance-based feature difference analysis. In Proceedings of the 2014 22nd International Conference on Pattern Recognition, Stockholm, Sweden, 24–28 August 2014; pp. 1722–1727.
10. Patel, D.; Zhao, G.; Pietikäinen, M. Spatiotemporal integration of optical flow vectors for micro-expression detection. In Proceedings of the Advanced Concepts for Intelligent Vision Systems: 16th International Conference, ACIVS 2015, Catania, Italy, 26–29 October 2015; Springer International Publishing: Cham, Switzerland, 2015; pp. 369–380.
11. Li, J.; Soladié, C.; Séguier, R.; Wang, S.-J.; Yap, M.H. Spotting micro-expressions on long videos sequences. In Proceedings of the 2019 14th IEEE International Conference on Automatic Face & Gesture Recognition, Lille, France, 14–18 May 2019; pp. 1–5.
12. He, Y.; Wang, S.J.; Li, J.; Yap, M.H. Spotting macro-and micro-expression intervals in long video sequences. In Proceedings of the 2020 15th IEEE International Conference on Automatic Face and Gesture Recognition, Buenos Aires, Argentina, 16–20 November 2020; pp. 742–748.
13. Xia, Z.; Feng, X.; Peng, J.; Peng, X.; Zhao, G. Spontaneous micro-expression spotting via geometric deformation modeling. *Comput. Vis. Image Underst.* **2016**, *147*, 87–94. [CrossRef]
14. Hong, X.; Tran, T.K.; Zhao, G. Micro-expression spotting: A benchmark. *arXiv* **2017**, arXiv:1710.02820.
15. Nag, S.; Bhunia, A.K.; Konwer, A.; Roy, P.P. Facial micro-expression spotting and recognition using time contrasted feature with visual memory. In Proceedings of the ICASSP 2019—2019 IEEE International Conference on Acoustics, Speech and Signal Processing (ICASSP), Brighton, UK, 12–17 May 2019; pp. 2022–2026.

16. Verburg, M.; Menkovski, V. Micro-expression detection in long videos using optical flow and recurrent neural networks. In Proceedings of the 2019 14th IEEE International Conference on Automatic Face & Gesture Recognition, Lille, France, 14–18 May 2019; pp. 1–6.
17. Pan, H.; Xie, L.; Wang, Z. Local bilinear convolutional neural network for spotting macro-and micro-expression intervals in long video sequences. In Proceedings of the 2020 15th IEEE International Conference on Automatic Face and Gesture Recognition, Buenos Aires, Argentina, 16–20 November 2020; pp. 749–753.
18. Yap, C.H.; Yap, M.H.; Davison, A.; Kendrick, C.; Li, J.; Wang, S.-J.; Cunningham, R. 3d-cnn for facial micro-and macro-expression spotting on long video sequences using temporal oriented reference frame. In Proceedings of the 30th ACM International Conference on Multimedia, Lisboa, Portugal, 10–14 October 2022; pp. 7016–7020.
19. Liong, G.B.; See, J.; Wong, L.K. Shallow optical flow three-stream CNN for macro-and micro-expression spotting from long videos. In Proceedings of the 2021 IEEE International Conference on Image Processing (ICIP), Anchorage, AK, USA, 19–22 September 2021; pp. 2643–2647.
20. Fang, Y.; Deng, D.; Wu, L.; Jumelle, F.; Shi, B. RMES: Real-Time Micro-Expression Spotting Using Phase from Riesz Pyramid. *arXiv* **2023**, arXiv:2305.05523.
21. Li, J.; Dong, Z.; Liu, Y.; Wang, S.-J.; Zhuang, D. A micro-expression spotting method based on human attention mechanism. *Adv. Psychol. Sci.* **2019**, *30*, 2143–2153. [CrossRef]
22. Cao, R. *Micro-Expression Detection for Long Videos Based on Outlier Detection*; South Western University of Finance and Economics: Chengdu, China, 2022.
23. Li Song, Y. *Research on Micro-Expression Spotting and Recognition Based on Convolutional Neural Networks*; Shandong University: Jinan, China, 2021.
24. Liu, L. Inverted Non-maximum Suppression for more Accurate and Neater Face Detection. *arXiv* **2023**, arXiv:2305.10593.
25. Ci, Y.; Wang, Y.; Chen, M.; Tang, S.; Bai, L.; Zhu, F.; Zhao, R.; Yu, F.; Qi, D.; Ouyang, W. UniHCP: A Unified Model for Human-Centric Perceptions. In Proceedings of the IEEE/CVF Conference on Computer Vision and Pattern Recognition, Vancouver, BC, Canada, 17–24 June 2023; pp. 17840–17852.
26. Oublal, K.; Dai, X. An advanced combination of semi-supervised Normalizing Flow & Yolo (YoloNF) to detect and recognize vehicle license plates. *arXiv* **2022**, arXiv:2207.10777.
27. Liong, S.T.; Gan, Y.S.; Zheng, D.; Li, S.-M.; Xu, H.-X.; Zhang, H.-Z.; Lyu, R.-K.; Liu, K.-H. Evaluation of the spatio-temporal features and gan for micro-expression recognition system. *J. Signal Process. Syst.* **2020**, *92*, 705–725. [CrossRef]
28. Szegedy, C.; Liu, W.; Jia, Y.; Sermanet, P.; Reed, S.; Anguelov, D.; Erhan, D.; Vanhoucke, V.; Rabinovich, A. Going deeper with convolutions. In Proceedings of the IEEE Conference on Computer Vision and Pattern Recognition, Boston, MA, USA, 7–12 June 2015; pp. 1–9.
29. Liu, S.; Huang, D. Receptive field block net for accurate and fast object detection. In Proceedings of the European Conference on Computer Vision (ECCV), Munich, Germany, 8–14 September 2018; pp. 385–400.
30. Lee, J.; Kim, H.; Park, E.; Cui, X.; Kim, H. Wide-residual-inception networks for real-time object detection. In Proceedings of the 2017 IEEE Intelligent Vehicles Symposium (IV), Los Angeles, CA, USA, 11–14 June 2017; pp. 758–764.
31. Lin, T.-Y.; Goyal, P.; Girshick, R.; He, K.; Dollár, P. Focal loss for dense object detection. In Proceedings of the IEEE International Conference on Computer Vision, Venice, Italy, 22 October 2017; pp. 2980–2988.
32. Yan, W.J.; Wu, Q.; Liu, Y.J.; Wang, S.-J.; Fu, X. CASME database: A dataset of spontaneous micro-expressions collected from neutralized faces. In Proceedings of the 2013 10th IEEE International Conference and Workshops on Automatic Face and Gesture Recognition (FG), Shanghai, China, 22–26 April 2013; pp. 1–7.
33. Li, X.; Pfister, T.; Huang, X.; Zhao, G.; Pietikäinen, M. A spontaneous micro-expression database: Inducement, collection and baseline. In Proceedings of the 2013 10th IEEE International Conference and Workshops on Automatic Face and Gesture Recognition, Shanghai, China, 22–26 April 2013; pp. 1–6.
34. Yan, W.J.; Li, X.; Wang, S.J.; Zhao, G.; Liu, Y.J.; Chen, Y.H.; Fu, X. CASME II: An improved spontaneous micro-expression database and the baseline evaluation. *PLoS ONE* **2014**, *9*, e86041. [CrossRef]
35. Davison, A.K.; Lansley, C.; Costen, N.; Tan, K.; Yap, M.H. Samm: A spontaneous micro-facial movement dataset. *IEEE Trans. Affect. Comput.* **2016**, *9*, 116–129. [CrossRef]
36. Qu, F.; Wang, S.J.; Yan, W.J.; Li, H.; Wu, S.; Fu, X. CAS(ME)^2: A Database for Spontaneous Macro-Expression and Micro-Expression Spotting and Recognition. *IEEE Trans. Affect. Comput.* **2017**, *9*, 424–436. [CrossRef]
37. Yap, C.H.; Kendrick, C.; Yap, M.H. Samm long videos: A spontaneous facial micro-and macro-expressions dataset. In Proceedings of the 2020 15th IEEE International Conference on Automatic Face and Gesture Recognition, Buenos Aires, Argentina, 16–20 November 2020; pp. 771–776.
38. Ben, X.; Ren, Y.; Zhang, J.; Wang, S.J.; Kpalma, K.; Meng, W.; Liu, Y.J. Video-based facial micro-expression analysis: A survey of datasets, features and algorithms. *IEEE Trans. Pattern Anal. Mach. Intell.* **2021**, *44*, 5826–5846. [CrossRef] [PubMed]
39. Li, J.; Dong, Z.; Lu, S.; Wang, S.J.; Yan, W.J.; Ma, Y.; Liu, Y.; Huang, C.; Fu, X. CAS (ME)3: A third generation facial spontaneous micro-expression database with depth information and high ecological validity. *IEEE Trans. Pattern Anal. Mach. Intell.* **2022**, *45*, 2782–2800. [CrossRef] [PubMed]
40. Li, J.; Soladie, C.; Seguier, R. Local temporal pattern and data augmentation for micro-expression spotting. *IEEE Trans. Affect. Comput.* **2020**, *14*, 811–822. [CrossRef]

41. Yu, J.; Jiang, Y.; Wang, Z.; Cao, Z.; Huang, T. Unitbox: An advanced object detection network. In Proceedings of the 24th ACM international conference on Multimedia, Amsterdam, The Netherlands, 15–19 October 2016; pp. 516–520.
42. Pan, H.; Xie, L.; Wang, Z. Spatio-temporal convolutional attention network for spotting macro-and micro-expression intervals. In Proceedings of the 1st Workshop on Facial Micro-Expression: Advanced Techniques for Facial Expressions Generation and Spotting, Virtual, China, 24 October 2021; pp. 25–30.
43. He, K.; Gkioxari, G.; Dollár, P.; Girshick, R. Mask r-cnn. In Proceedings of the IEEE International Conference on Computer Vision, Venice, Italy, 22–29 October 2017; pp. 2961–2969.

Disclaimer/Publisher's Note: The statements, opinions and data contained in all publications are solely those of the individual author(s) and contributor(s) and not of MDPI and/or the editor(s). MDPI and/or the editor(s) disclaim responsibility for any injury to people or property resulting from any ideas, methods, instructions or products referred to in the content.

Article

PSRGAN: Perception-Design-Oriented Image Super Resolution Generative Adversarial Network

Tao Wu [1,†], Shuo Xiong [2,*,†], Hui Liu [1], Yangyang Zhao [3,*], Haoran Tuo [1], Yi Li [1], Jiaxin Zhang [1] and Huaizheng Liu [1]

[1] National Model Software Institute, Huazhong University of Science and Technology, Wuhan 430074, China; wutao1972@hust.edu.cn (T.W.); liuh_@hust.edu.cn (H.L.); thr@hust.edu.cn (H.T.); liyi99@hust.edu.cn (Y.L.); jiaxinzhang@hust.edu.cn (J.Z.); liuhuaizheng@hust.edu.cn (H.L.)
[2] PSS Lab of Big Data and National Communication Strategy, MOE, Huazhong University of Science and Technology, Wuhan 430074, China
[3] Hytera Communication Co., Ltd., Shenzhen 518057, China
* Correspondence: xiongshuo@hust.edu.cn (S.X.); yangyangzhao0803@gmail.com (Y.Z.)
† These authors contributed equally to this work.

Abstract: Among recent state-of-the-art realistic image super-resolution (SR) intelligent algorithms, generative adversarial networks (GANs) have achieved impressive visual performance. However, there has been the problem of unsatisfactory perception of super-scored pictures with unpleasant artifacts. To address this issue and further improve visual quality, we proposed a perception-design-oriented PSRGAN with double perception turbos for real-world SR. The first-perception turbo in the generator network has a three-level perception structure with different convolution kernel sizes, which can extract multi-scale features from four $\frac{1}{4}$ size sub-images sliced by original LR image. The slice operation expands adversarial samples to four and could alleviate artifacts during GAN training. The extracted features will be eventually concatenated in later 3×2 upsampling processes through pixel shuffle to restore SR image with diversified delicate textures. The second-perception turbo in discriminators has cascaded perception turbo blocks (PTBs), which could further perceive multi-scale features at various spatial relationships and promote the generator to restore subtle textures driven by GAN. Compared with recent SR methods (BSRGAN, real-ESRGAN, PDM_SR, SwinIR, LDL, etc.), we conducted an extensive test with a ×4 upscaling factor on various datasets (OST300, 2020track1, RealSR-Canon, RealSR-Nikon, etc.). We conducted a series of experiments that show that our proposed PSRGAN based on generative adversarial networks outperforms current state-of-the-art intelligent algorithms on several evaluation metrics, including NIQE, NRQM and PI. In terms of visualization, PSRGAN generates finer and more natural textures while suppressing unpleasant artifacts and achieves significant improvements in perceptual quality.

Keywords: perception design; image super resolution; generative adversarial network; artifact suppression; intelligent computing

1. Introduction

Single-image super-resolution (SISR) aims to reconstruct a high-resolution (HR) image from a low-resolution (LR) one. The traditional methods for solving the SR problems are mainly interpolation-based methods [1–4] and reconstruction-based methods [5–7]. Intelligent computing has also been applied in the field of image super-resolution. Super-resolution methods based on genetic algorithms, guided by imaging models, utilize optimization techniques to seek the optimal estimation of the original image. At its core, this approach transforms the problem of reconstructing multiple super-resolved images into a linear system of equations. The convolutional neural network (CNN) has greatly promoted the vigorous development of SR field and demonstrates vast superiority over traditional methods. The main reason it achieves good results is due to its strong capability of learning rich features from big data in an end-to-end manner [8]. CNN-based SR methods often use

PSNR as the evaluation metric; although some SR methods achieve good results for PSNR, it is still not completely satisfactory in terms of perception.

The generative adversarial network (GAN) [9] has achieved impressive visual performance in the field of super-resolution (SR) since the pioneering work of SRGAN [10]. GANs have proven their capability to generate more realistic images with high perceptual quality. In pursuit of further enhancing visual quality, Wang et al. proposed ESRGAN [11]. Given the challenges of collecting well-paired datasets in real-world scenarios, unsupervised GANs have been introduced [12,13]. BSRGAN [14] and real-ESRGAN [15] are dedicated to simulating the practical degradation process to obtain better visual results on real datasets.

However, perceptual dissatisfaction accompanied by unpleasant artifacts still exists in GAN-based SR models because of insufficient design in either generators or discriminators. In GAN-based SR methods, it is obvious that the decisive capability to recover naturally finer textures in generators is dependent largely on the guidance of discriminators through GAN training, but discriminators are usually cloned from well-known networks (U-net [16], VGG [17], etc.) suitable for image segmentation or classification, which might not fully lead generators to restore subtle textures in SR. Moreover, the design of generators should be perceptive enough to extract multi-scale image features from low-resolution (LR) images and mitigate artifacts.

Research hypotheses and questions: Perceived quality improvement: How can we design a network structure of PSRGAN to suppress artifact generation in images, and how can we achieve the effect of suppressing artifacts? Generative adversarial network image quality assessment: Which evaluation metrics are used to assess the generated images to ensure their perceived quality is enhanced? Adversarial training stability: How can we ensure the stability and convergence of our PSRGAN training? To address these issues and further improve the visual quality of the restored SR images, we redesigned both generators and discriminators; the contributions of this paper are mainly in four aspects:

- We present a novel perception-design-oriented PSRGAN with double perception turbos, which can generate real-world SR images with naturally finer textures while suppressing unpleasant artifacts by ×4 upscaling factors (see Figure 1).
- We design the first-perception turbo in the generator network, characterized by slice operation and a three-level perception structure, which can extract multi-scale features from sliced sub-images and mitigate artifacts.
- We propose the second-perception turbo in the discriminator network with cascaded perception turbo blocks, which can further promote the generator to restore subtle textures.
- We demonstrate that the proposed PSRGAN has achieved state-of-the-art perceptual capabilities calculated by NIQE, NRQM, and PI.

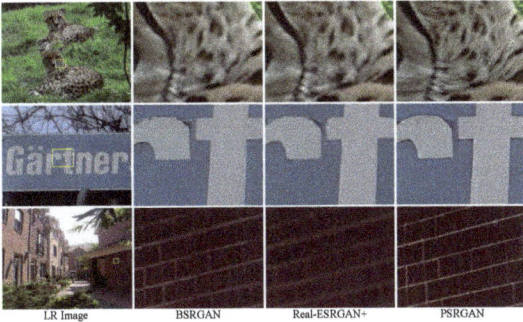

Figure 1. Comparisons of visual quality among BSRGAN [14], real-ESRGAN+ [1], and PSRGAN on real-life images by ×4 upscaling. The PSRGAN can generate naturally finer textures and remove or alleviate annoying artifacts for real-world images. Zoom in for best view.

2. Related Work

Single-image super-resolution: SRCNN [18] is the first method to apply deep learning to SR reconstruction, and a series of learning-based works are subsequently proposed [19–23]. ESPCN [24] introduces an efficient sub-pixel convolution layer to perform the feature extraction stages in the LR space instead of HR space. VDSR [19] uses a very deep convolutional network. EDSR [25] removes the batch normalization layers from the network. SRGAN [10] first uses the GAN network for the SR problem and proposes perceptual loss, including adversarial loss and content loss. Based on human perceptual characteristics, the residual in the residual dense block strategy (RRDB) is exploited to implement various depths in network architectures [11,26]. ESRGAN [11] introduces the residual-in-residual dense block (RRDB) into the generator. RealSR [27] estimates various blur kernels and real noise distributions to synthesize different LR images. CDC [28] proposes a divide-and-conquer SR network. Luo et al., in [29], propose a probabilistic degradation model (PDM). Shao et al., in [30], propose a sub-pixel convolutional neural network (SPCNN) for image SR reconstruction.

Perceptual-driven approaches: The PSNR-oriented approaches lead to overly smooth results and a lack of high-frequency details, and the results sometimes do not agree with the subjective human perception. In order to improve the perceptual quality of SR results, the perceptual-driven approach is proposed. Based on the idea of perceptual similarity [31], Li Feifei et al. propose perceptual loss in [32]. Then, textures matching loss [33] and contextual loss [34] are introduced. ESRGAN [11] improves the perceptual loss by using the features before activation and wins the PIRM perceptual super-resolution challenge [35]. Christian Szegedy et al. propose inception [36], which can extract more features with the same amount of computation, thus improving the training results. For the purpose of extracting multi-scale information and enhance the feature discriminability, RFB-ESRGAN [8] applies the receptive field block (RFB) [37] to super resolution and wins the NTIRE 2020 perceptual extreme super-resolution challenge. There is still plenty of room for perceptual quality improvement [38].

The design of discriminator networks: The discriminator in SRGAN is VGG-style, which is trained to distinguish between SR images and GT images [10]. ESRGAN borrows ideas from relativistic GAN to improve the discriminator in SRGAN [11]. Real-ESRGAN improves the VGG-style discriminator in ESRGAN to an U-Net design [15]. In [39], Alejandro et al. propose a novel convolutional network architecture named "stacked hourglass", which captures and consolidates information across all scales of the image. Inspired by [39], we propose a new discriminator structure, which can guide the generator to recover finer textures. All the related work as Table 1 shows.

Table 1. Related work on design of discriminator networks.

Different Methods	Design of Discriminator Networks
SRGAN	VGG-style, which is trained to distinguish between SR images
ESRGAN	borrows ideas from relativistic GAN to improve the discriminator in SRGAN
Real-ESRGAN	proposed an U-Net design
RFB-ESRGAN	proposed stacked hourglass network which captures and consolidates information across all scales of the image

Artifact suppression: The instability of the training of GANs often leads to the introduction of many perceptually unpleasant artifacts while generating details in the GAN-based SR networks [40]. There have been several SR models focusing on solving the problem. Zhang et al. propose a supervised pixel-wise generative adversarial network (SPGAN) to obtain higher-quality face images [41]. Gong et al., in [42], overcome the effect of artifacts in the super-resolution of remote sensing images using self-supervised hierarchical perceptual loss. Real-ESRGAN uses spectral normalization (SN) regularization to stabilize the training dynamics [15]. We propose a algorithm named "image slice and multi-scale feature extraction", which can generate more delicate textures and suppress artifacts.

The evaluation metrics: The DCNN-based SR approaches have two main optimization objectives: the distortion metric (e.g., PSNR, SSIM, IFC, and VIF [43–45]) and perceptual quality (e.g., the human opinion score; no-reference quality measures such as Ma's score [46], NIQE [47], BRISQUE [48], and PI [49]) [50]. Yochai et al. in [49] have revealed that distortion and perceptual quality are contradictory and there is always a trade-off between the two. Algorithms that are superior in terms of perceptual quality tend to be poorer in terms of, e.g., PSNR and SSIM. However, sometimes there is also inconsistency between the results observed by human eyes and these perceptual quality metrics. Because the no-reference metrics do not always match perceptual visual quality [51], some SR models such as SRGAN perform mean-opinion-score (MOS) tests to quantify the perceptual ability of different methods [10]. We use NIQE, NRQM, and PI as our image quality metrics, which do not depend on the GT image to measure the perceptual quality of the reconstructed image [52]. The related work on evaluation metrics as Table 2 shows.

Table 2. Related work on evaluation metrics.

Evaluation Metrics	Advantage	Disadvantage
Distortion metrics	Simple calculation	Greater inconsistency with perceived quality
Human opinion score	Consistent with visual perception	High labor costs
No-reference quality measures	Balancing consistency with perceived quality and computational cost	There is some inconsistency with visual perception

The transformer: Vaswani et al. in [36] propose a new simple network architecture, transformer, based solely on attention mechanisms, dispensing with recurrence and convolutions entirely. Transformer continues to show amazing capabilities in the NLP domain. Many researches have started to try to apply the powerful modeling ability of transformer to the field of computer vision [53]. In [54], Yang et al. propose TTSR, in which LR and HR images are formulated as queries and keys in transformer, respectively, to encourage joint feature learning across LR and HR images. Swin transformer [55] combines the advantages of convolution and transformer. Liang et al. in [56] propose SwinIR based on Swin transformer. Vision transformer is computationally expensive and consumes high GPU memory, so Lu et al. in [57] propose ESRT, which uses efficient transformers (ET), a lightweight version of the transformer structure.

3. Proposed Methods

To further improve perceptual quality as well as mitigate artifacts in SISR, we proposed a novel perception-design-oriented super resolution generative adversarial network (PSRGAN) with double perception turbos. In this section, we first introduce the generator network-containing first-perception turbo (GPT) and then describe the construction of the discriminator network with the second-perception turbo (DPT). At last, we discuss the perceptual loss function used.

3.1. Generator Network

The generator network consists of two components: first-perception turbo, and the feature blending and upsampling component (FBUC) as shown in Figure 2.

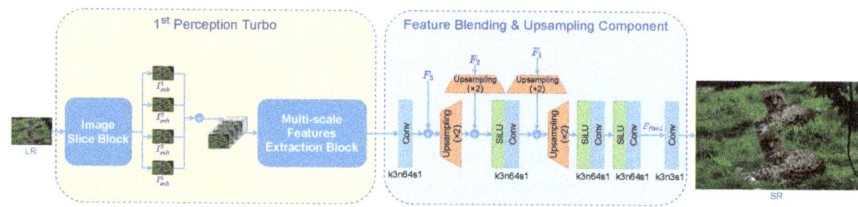

Figure 2. Architecture of generator network with corresponding kernel size (k), number of feature maps (n), and stride (s) indicated for each convolutional layer, where F_1, F_2, and F_3 are multi-scale features extracted by MFEB described in Figure 3.

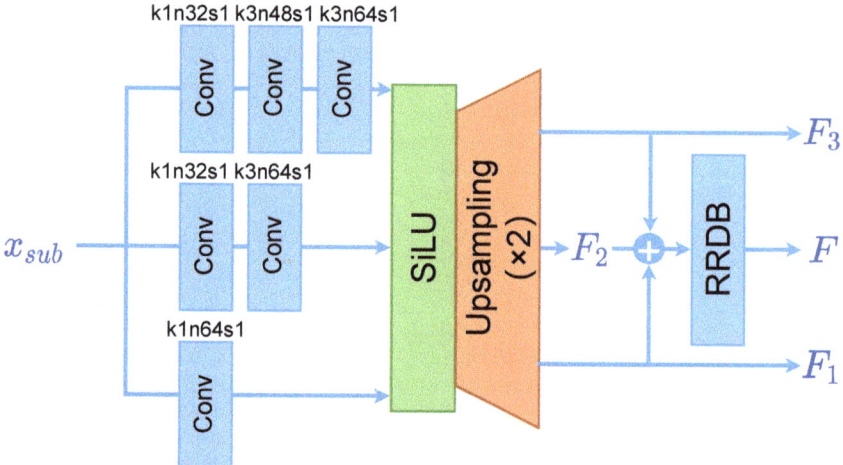

Figure 3. Design of MFEB in first-perception turbo.

The first perception turbo has two major blocks: the image slice block (ISB) and the multi-scale feature-extraction block (MFEB). The image slice block (ISB) produces four $\frac{1}{4}$ size sub-images (I_{sub}^1, I_{sub}^2, I_{sub}^3, and I_{sub}^4) from the low-resolution image I^{LR} via pixel reassembly. Specifically, suppose I^{LR} has the resolution of $2m \cdot 2n$ pixels or padding to $2m \cdot 2n$ pixels; the sliced sub-images are $m \cdot n$ pixels. If the upper left pixel is denoted as $(0, 0)$, and the lower right pixel is denoted as $(2m - 1, 2n - 1)$, the relationship of the pixels between I^{LR} and the sub-images can be formulated as below.

$$\begin{cases} I^{LR} = \{(k, t) \mid 0 \leq k < 2m,\ 0 \leq t < 2n,\ k, t \in N \cup 0\} \\ I_{sub}^1 = \{(2p, 2q) \mid 0 \leq p < m,\ 0 \leq q < n,\ p, q \in N \cup 0\} \\ I_{sub}^2 = \{(2p+1, 2q) \mid 0 \leq p < m,\ 0 \leq q < n\} \\ I_{sub}^3 = \{(2p, 2q+1) \mid 0 \leq p < m,\ 0 \leq q < n\} \\ I_{sub}^4 = \{(2p+1, 2q+1) \mid 0 \leq p < m,\ 0 \leq q < n\} \end{cases} \quad (1)$$

The slice method above has the following characteristics:

- The slice splits the LR image to multiple detail adversarial sub-images while preserving the pixel integrity of the LR image.
- The subsequent MFEB could extract multi-scale features from smaller adversarial samples; thus, the generator is capable of generating diverse and delicate textures.
- The slice weakens the correlations among noisy pixels in I^{LR}, which can effectively reduce noises and further alleviate artifacts in the restored SR image. Although the correlations among adjacent pixels might be also impaired, the meaningful semantic features will be eventually recovered in the SR image through GAN training.

The multi-scale feature extraction block (MFEB, Figure 3): It has been proven that each learned filter has its specific functionality and that a reasonably larger filter size could grasp richer structural information, which in turn could lead to better results [18]. The MFEB is perceptually designed to extract diverse image features from the LR image by three groups of convolutional layers inspired by inception networks [36], as depicted in Figure 3. Please refer to Appendix B for more detail.

The first convolution group has a tiny receptive field, used to retain micro subtle features, denoted as k1-n64-s1.

The second convolution group has a medium receptive field, used to capture moderate features, denoted as k1-n32-s1, k3-n64-s1.

The third convolution group has a large receptive field, used to seize macro features, denoted as k1-n32-s1, k3-n48-s1, k3-n64-s1.

The outputs of the three convolution groups are activated using the Sigmoid weighted liner unit (SiLU) and then ×2 upsampled via pixel-shuffle to obtain multi-scale features F_1, F_2, F_3. The process can be formulated as:

$$F_i = [SiLU(Convs_i(x_{sub}))] \uparrow_s, i \in \{1,2,3\}. \quad (2)$$

where $Convs_i(x_{sub}), i \in \{1,2,3\}$ denote the three convolution groups, SiLU is the activation function, $\uparrow$ denotes upsampling, s denotes the scale factor and $s = 2$ in this block, and $F_i, i \in \{1,2,3\}$ indicate the 3-scale feature maps extracted. Subsequently, the obtained feature maps F_1, F_2, F_3 are added in the channel dimension as input, residual in residual dense block (RRDB) [11] is adopted to further capture semantic information and improve the recovered textures, and the output is denoted as F. The formal processing in the first-perception turbo is described in Algorithm 1.

Algorithm 1 Image slice and multi-scale feature extraction

Input: LR images set $\mathcal{X}$.
Output: Multi-scale features F_1, F_2, F_3, deeper features F.
1: **for all** I_{LR} such that $I_{LR} \in \mathcal{X}$ **do**
2:   generate $I_{sub}^1, I_{sub}^2, I_{sub}^3, I_{sub}^4$ through slice operation from I_{LR}.
3:   Get x_{sub} by merging the four sub-images $I_{sub}^1, I_{sub}^2, I_{sub}^3, I_{sub}^4$ in color channel dimension.
4:   **for all** i such that $1 \leq i \leq 3$ **do**
5:     input x_{sub} to $Convs_i, SiLU, 2UP$ obtain F_i,
6:   **end for**
7:   generate $F = RRDB(F_1 + F_2 + F_3)$,
8: **end for return** F_1, F_2, F_3, F.

Feature blending and upsampling component (FBUC, Figure 2): The FBUC reassembles the obtained multi-scale features to generate the corresponding I^{SR} counterpart of I^{LR}. In the upsampling phase, the FBUC upsamples I^{LR} with diversfied features F as the input via pixel shuffle and gradually blends the features extracted by the MFEB. The upsampling process can be formulated as follows:

$$F_{final} = f_{Conv-SiLU}(f_{Conv-SiLU}(f_{Conv-SiLU}((F+F_3)\uparrow_s + (F_2)\uparrow_s) + (F_1)\uparrow_s)\uparrow_s) \quad (3)$$

where '+' denotes concatenation operation, $\uparrow$ denotes upsampling, s denotes the scale factor, and $s = 2$. $f_{Conv-SiLU}$ denotes one convolutional kernel, SiLU is the activation function, and F_{final} denotes the final features obtained from the FBUC. F_{final} is passed through a triple convolutional layer with the kernel size of 3×3 and finally outputs I^{SR}, which is ×4 upscaling according to the original I^{LR}.

3.2. Discriminator Network

We proposed a novel discriminator containing the pre-processing block, cascaded perception turbo blocks (PTBs), and the post-processing block. The structure of the discriminator is depicted in Figure 4.

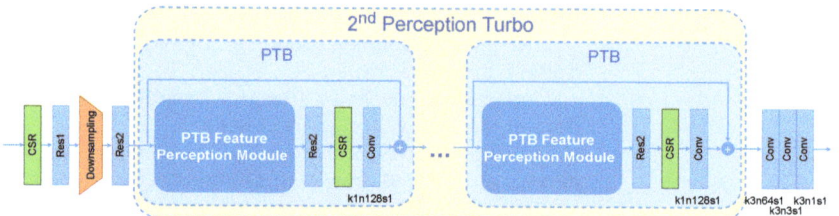

Figure 4. Discriminator network structure with second-perception turbo. The structure of CSR, Res1, and Res2 are shown in Figure 5.

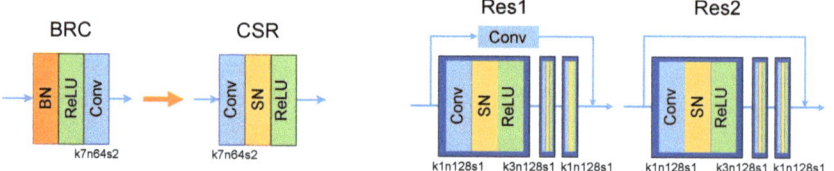

Figure 5. (**Left**): Differences between BRC and CSR; (**right**): structure of Res1 and Res2 in PTBs.

The pre-processing block is utilized for the initial feature perception of I^{SR} and I^{HR}. As shown in Figure 4, it includes a CSR block, two residual blocks, and a downsampling layer. The CSR block consists of a convolution layer, an SN layer, and a ReLU activation function. The specific structure of the two residual blocks Res1 and Res2 is shown in the Figure 5.

The second-perception turbo is the core structure of this discriminator, which consists of cascaded PTBs. In order to further promote the generator to restore subtle textures, we proposed the PTB structure and made the following four improvements on the basis of hour-glass module [39]:

- As shown in the Figure 5, we adopt the CSR structure instead of BRC, which consists of the BN layer, the ReLU activation function, and the convolutional layer. It has been proven that removing the BN layers can prevent BN artifacts of SR images, improve the performance, and reduce the computational complexity in the SR task [25]. In addition, we improve the perceptual loss by using the features before activation, which could provide stronger supervision for brightness consistency and texture recovery [11].
- In the upsampling procedure, we use pixel-shuffle instead of nearest neighbor interpolation, which may lose pixel information.
- In the downsampling layer, we use convolution instead of Maxpool2d operation, which may lose the integrity of feature map.
- We enlarge the input channels of PTB to 128, which improves the perceptive capabilities of the discriminator.

The post-processing block consists of three convolutional layers to further learn features and output a feature map that benefits the computation of adversarial loss.

Based on the above improvements, the discriminator could further perceive multi-scale features at various spatial relationships and promote the generator to restore subtle textures driven by GAN.

3.3. Perception Loss

We introduced the loss function similar to ESRGAN, which is a hybrid weighted loss function that takes into account pixel-level recovery and visual perception effects and is able to achieve better super-resolution quality. Therefore, the total loss function of the generator L_G is a weighted combination of several losses: the adversarial loss L_{GAN}, pixel loss L_{Pixel}, and perceptual loss L_{Percep}. The loss function of the discriminator L_D is the adversarial loss L_{GAN}. The L_G is described as follows:

$$L_G = \alpha L_{GAN} + \beta L_{Pixel} + \gamma L_{Percep} \qquad (4)$$

where $L_{Pixel} = \mathbb{E}_{x_i} \| G(x_i) - y \|_1$ is the one-norm distance between the recovered image $G(x_i)$ and HR image y; it thus evaluates the average degree of approximation of I^{SR} and I^{HR} over pixels. α, β, γ are coefficients to balance different loss terms. Moreover, L_{Percep} is gained by introducing a fine-tuned VGG19 network to calculate the one-norm distance between the recovered image $G(x_i)$ and high-level features of y. It is used to evaluate the approximation of I^{SR} and I^{HR} in human perception. The perceptual loss is calculated as follows:

$$L_{Percep} = \mathbb{E}_{x_i} \| VGG(G(x_i)) - VGG(y) \|_1 \qquad (5)$$

L_{GAN} aims to distinguish the SR image from the HR image by the superior perceptive capability of the discriminator, which could help to learn sharper edges and more detailed textures; it can be formulated as follows:

$$L_{GAN} = -\mathbb{E}_{x_{hr}}[log(1 - D(x_{hr}, x_{sr}))] - \mathbb{E}_{x_{sr}}[log(D(x_{sr}, x_{hr}))] \qquad (6)$$

4. Experiments

In this section, we will discuss our PSRGAN model trained in RGB three channels.

4.1. Training Details

The experiments are performed with a scaling factor of ×4 between LR and HR images; we obtain corresponding four-times smaller LR images by degrading the HR pictures, which are cropped to size 400 × 400 using the high-order [15] algorithm. Meanwhile, the patch size of cropped HR is 256 × 256, and the patch size of LR is 64 × 64. When training, the batch size is set to 12 × 2, which means that we use two GPUs and the batch size per GPU is 12.

The training process is divided into two stages. One is the pre-training generator, and the other is conducting GAN training combined with the generator and discriminator. First, in the pre-training process, we purely train the generator with the L1 loss. The learning rate is 2×10^{-4}, and the sum of the iteration is 0.4 million. Then, we employ the pre-training generator model as an initialization for the generator. The GAN is trained with a combination of L1 loss, perception loss, and GAN loss, with weights of 1, 1, and 0.1, respectively. The learning rate is set to 1×10^{-4} for both the generator and discriminator, and the sum of iteration is 0.28 million. Pre-training with L1 loss is beneficial to obtain more visually pleasing results by avoiding undesired local optima for the generator. Moreover, it can help the discriminator to distinguish more on the textures part so that the discriminator can receive relatively better super-resolved images during GAN training.

For optimization, we use Adam [58] with $\beta 1 = 0.9$, $\beta 2 = 0.99$. We alternately update the generator and discriminator network until the model converges. We implement our models with the PyTorch framework and train them using NVIDIA GeForce RTX 3090 GPUs.

4.2. Data

For training, we use the DIV2K dataset [59], the Flickr2K dataset [21], and the OutdoorSceneTraining(OST) dataset [60] as training datasets. We employ these large datasets with rich textures, which help to generate SR pictures with more natural and subtle textures [11].

We evaluate our models on widely used benchmark datasets, including OST300 [60], PIRM_Self_val [35], 2020track1 [51], RealSR-Canon [61], DRealSR_Test_x4 [28], and RealSR-

Nikon [61]. In particular, the images from RealSR-Canon and RealSR-Nikon are the center subimages of original images, and those larger than $1K \times 1K$ are cropped to $1K \times 1K$.

4.3. Qualitative Results

Due to the accessibility of SR methods, we compare our PSRGAN with several state-of-the-art methods, including BSRGAN, PDM_SR, SwinIR [56], LDL [40], ESRGAN, and real-ESRGAN+. We have shown some representative qualitative results with NIQE in Figure 6 and Table 3. More detailed results calculated by NRQM and PI are presented in Tables 4–6. It can be observed from the figure that the results of our proposed PSRGAN outperforms previous approaches in both details and clearness, with fewer artifacts. For instance, PSRGAN can produce clearer, more natural lion fur (see 0901) and more detailed wall structures (see OST_278) than BSRGAN and LDL, whose textures are unnatural, skewed, and contain unpleasing noise. Compared with PSRGAN, ESRGAN and real-ESRGAN+ fail to produce enough details. Moreover, PSRGAN is capable of boosting visual sharpness (see DSC_1454_x1), while other methods either produce blurry structures (ESRGAN, PDM_SR, and SwinIR) or do not generate enough details (BSRGAN). In addition, previous GAN-based methods sometimes introduced unpleasant artifacts such as BSRGAN and real-ESRGAN+. Our PSRGAN eliminates these artifacts and obtains cleaner results (see Canon_40_x1).

Table 3. NIQE scores on diverse testing datasets—the lower, the better. Colors R, G, and B indicate the best first, second, and third NIQE results among models on each dataset row. The calculation method of NIQE is derived from the basic SR package of PyTorch 1.11.0 + cu113.

	Bicubic	BSRGAN	PDM_SR	SwinIR	LDL	ESRGAN	real-ESRGAN+	PSRGAN
OST300	7.600	3.309	4.319	2.921	2.817	3.501	2.806	2.735
DRealSR_Test_x4	9.772	4.803	7.667	4.698	5.250	8.644	4.846	4.533
RealSR-Canon	13.480	5.998	10.015	4.956	5.637	13.096	5.352	4.499
RealSR-Nikon	13.017	6.377	9.544	4.819	5.712	12.443	5.180	5.164
PIRM_Self_val	7.747	3.808	5.132	3.683	3.539	3.516	3.350	3.330
2020track1	7.596	3.783	4.101	3.618	3.958	7.440	3.820	3.411

Table 4. NIQE scores on diverse testing datasets—the lower, the better. Colors R, G, and B indicate the best first, second, and third NIQE results among models on each dataset row. The calculation method of NIQE is in PIRM2018 derived from https://github.com/roimehrez/PIRM2018 (accessed on 1 June 2023).

	Bicubic	BSRGAN	PDM_SR	SwinIR	LDL	ESRGAN	real-ESRGAN+	PSRGAN
OST300	7.612	3.414	4.308	3.034	4.56	3.551	2.929	2.826
DRealSR_Test_x4	9.766	4.818	7.635	9.765	8.372	8.632	4.848	4.543
RealSR-Canon	13.442	6.046	10.008	4.985	13.187	13.101	5.346	4.512
RealSR-Nikon	13.006	6.435	9.537	4.834	12.39	12.446	5.176	5.169
PIRM_Self_val	7.746	3.838	5.195	3.716	2.986	3.511	3.363	3.311
2020track1	7.606	3.813	4.096	7.606	3.249	7.217	3.835	3.423

Table 5. NRQM scores on diverse testing datasets—the higher, the better. Colors R, G, and B indicate the best first, second, and third NRQM results among models on each dataset row. The calculation method of NRQM is in PIRM2018 derived from https://github.com/roimehrez/PIRM2018 (accessed on 1 June 2023).

	Bicubic	BSRGAN	PDM_SR	SwinIR	LDL	ESRGAN	real-ESRGAN+	PSRGAN
OST300	3.266	6.319	5.737	6.58	5.683	6.236	6.576	6.714
DRealSR_Test_x4	2.576	5.264	3.536	2.576	3.317	3.244	5.295	5.551
RealSR-Canon	2.337	4.571	2.484	4.861	2.548	2.476	5.743	6.131
RealSR-Nikon	2.366	4.635	2.597	5.249	2.866	2.681	5.69	5.839
PIRM_Self_val	3.76	8.091	6.096	8.191	8.393	8.401	8.347	8.524
2020track1	3.307	6.219	5.99	3.307	6.493	6.591	6.133	6.504

Table 6. PI scores on diverse testing datasets—the lower, the better. Colors R, G, and B indicate the best first, second, and third PI results among models on each dataset row. The calculation method of PI is in PIRM2018 derived from https://github.com/roimehrez/PIRM2018 (accessed on 1 June 2023).

	Bicubic	BSRGAN	PDM_SR	SwinIR	LDL	ESRGAN	real-ESRGAN+	PSRGAN
OST300	7.173	3.548	4.286	3.227	4.438	3.658	3.176	3.056
DRealSR_Test_x4	8.595	4.777	7.05	8.595	7.527	7.694	4.777	4.495
RealSR-Canon	10.552	5.738	8.762	5.062	10.319	10.313	4.802	4.191
RealSR-Nikon	10.32	5.9	8.47	4.793	9.762	9.883	4.743	4.665
PIRM_Self_val	6.994	2.874	4.549	2.763	2.297	2.555	2.509	2.394
2020track1	7.15	3.797	4.053	7.15	3.378	5.313	3.851	3.459

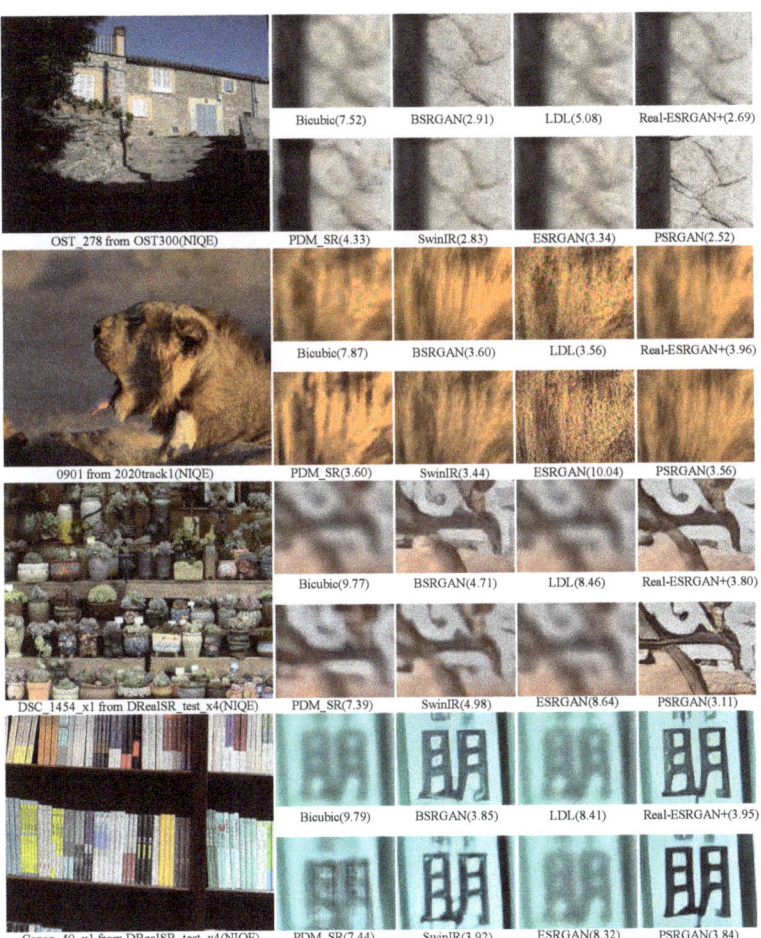

Figure 6. Qualitative results of PSRGAN. PSRGAN produces more subtle textures and clearer structures, e.g., animal texture and building structure, as well as fewer unpleasant artifacts, e.g., artifacts in fonts. Zoom in for best view.

Although the NIQE score of PSRGAN is not always best, we still believe that exploring the effect of focusing on the human visual perception of real pictures is crucial for SR; after all, the existing perception indexes do not reflect all the problems. Please refer to Appendix C for more qualitative results.

4.4. Ablation Study

In order to study the effects of each component in the proposed PSRGAN, we gradually modify the discriminators of PSRGAN and compare their differences. The overall visual comparison is illustrated in Figure 7. Each column represents a model with its configurations shown at the top. The red sign indicates the best performance. A detailed discussion is provided as Table 7 follows.

Table 7. Model with different configurations.

	Second	Third	Fourth	Fifth
PTBs	3	5	5	7
Channels	128	128	256	128

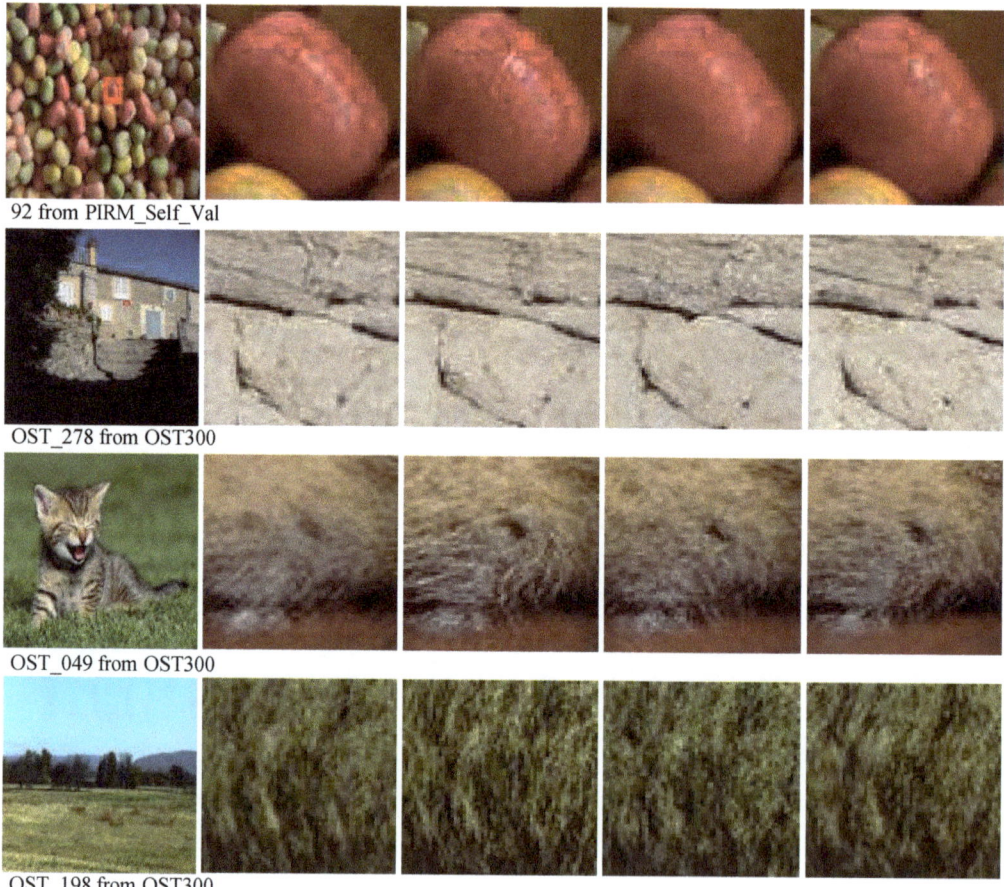

Figure 7. Visual comparisons of different configurations in PSRGAN. The red sign indicates the best performance.

Number of PTBs: The discriminator with the optimal number of cascaded PTBs has a strong representation capacity to capture semantic information, which can further improve the recovered textures, especially for regular structures like the wall of image OST_278 in Figure 6. We set the order of the number to 2, 3, 4, 5, 6, and 7 for experimentation, respectively. For simplicity, we only demonstrate the results of 3, 5, and 7 numbers; the experimental results are depicted in Figure 7. As shown, when the number is 5, the results are relatively sharper with richer textures than others. For some cases, a prominent difference can be observed from the second, third and fifth column in Figure 7.

Channel size of PTB: The different channel sizes of PTB influence the perceptive capabilities of the discriminator. We have tested on 3, 128, and 256 channels. For simplicity, we only demonstrate the results of 128 and 256 channels, as shown in Figure 7. When the channel size is 128, the results are clearer and have fewer artifacts.

Cross verification between PTBs and U-net: Please refer to Appendix A for details.

4.5. Running Times

Our method achieves moderate GPU run times for both training and testing, thanks to its design characteristics. Our model achieves outstanding super-resolution performance, reaching a superior level of quality after a rigorous training regimen of 490 k iterations. Our model exhibits test times on multiple datasets that are comparable to existing state-of-the-art models. Notably, when compared to SwinIR and LDL, our model demonstrates a significant advantage in test time efficiency. The algorithms were trained and tested on a server with NVIDIA GeForce RTX 3090 GPUs. Tables 8 and 9 compare the running times of different state-of-the-art models.

Table 8. The GPU run times for training of different networks. The unit is the number of iterators, and k represents thousands. Since Bicubic is not an adversarial neural network, there is no number of iterators.

	Bicubic	BSRGAN	PDM_SR	SwinIR	LDL	ESRGAN	real-ESRGAN+	PSRGAN
GAN Training Times (iters)	None	1000 k	200 k	500 k	400 k	400 k	400 k	490 k

Table 9. The GPU run times of different networks on diverse datasets. The unit is time, where m stands for minutes and s stands for seconds.

	Bicubic	BSRGAN	PDM_SR	SwinIR	LDL	ESRGAN	real-ESRGAN+	PSRGAN
OST300	54 s	5 m 4 s	5 m 13 s	23 m 54 s	7 m 15 s	5 m 36 s	5 m 16 s	5 m 29 s
DRealSR_Test_x4	1 m 2 s	5 m 47 s	5 m 46 s	21 m 56 s	8 m 34 s	6 m 21 s	5 m 58 s	6 m 20 s
RealSR-Canon	17 s	2 m	2 m 1 s	9 m 6 s	2 m 20 s	2 m	2 m 3 s	2 m 9 s
RealSR-Nikon	22 s	2 m 31 s	2 m 30 s	9 m 26 s	3 m 12 s	2 m 31 s	2 m 34 s	2 m 42 s
PIRM_Self_val	1 s	6 s	6 s	17 s	19 s	5 s	7 s	7 s
2020track1	10 s	53 s	54 s	2 m 56 s	1 m 18 s	55 s	56 s	58 s

5. Discussion

In this study, we present the perception-design-oriented image super resolution generative adversarial network (PSRGAN), an innovative approach that fuses generative adversarial networks (GANs) and human perceptual insights. Through extensive experiments and analysis of the model, we have achieved the following major achievement.

Perceptually guided super-resolution enhancement: We successfully combined human perceptual insights and used them to guide super-resolution processes. This resulted in sharper, more realistic, and more human-perceivable high-resolution image generation, as illustrated by Figure 6, where our PSRGAN generates more detailed textures of animal hairs, fewer artifacts, and a sharper edge in text-related images.

The experimental results: Our extensive experiments show that PSRGAN achieves significant performance gains on multiple datasets and tasks. Quantitative evaluations show that PSRGAN outperforms traditional super-resolution methods (real-ESRGAN+, ESRGAN, and BSRGAN) on multiple standard image quality metrics such as NIQE, NRQM, and PI. More encouragingly, the images generated by PSRGAN are closer to the high-resolution original images in terms of human perception.

Limitations: Despite our satisfactory achievements, we have to recognize some limitations of PSRGAN. Computational requirements: the training and inference of PSRGAN requires a large number of computational resources, which may be a challenge for some applications. Data diversity: while our model performs well on multiple datasets, performance may be degraded in specific domains or with uneven data distribution.

In my opinion, the SR network will definitely develop in the direction of breaking through its current limitations in the future, and the trend of super-resolution application is to reduce the computational burden and to apply it to diversified datasets.

6. Conclusions

We have presented a PSRGAN model that achieves superior perceptual quality both in terms of evaluation metrics and visual effects. According to the experimental results, our proposed PSRGAN based on generative adversarial networks outperforms current state-of-the-art intelligent algorithms (BSRGAN, real-ESRGAN, PDM_SR, SwinIR, LDL, etc.) on several evaluation metrics (NIQE, NRQM and PI), with a $\times 4$ upscaling factor on various datasets (OST300, DRealSR_Test_x4, RealSR-Canon, etc.). The PSRGAN model mainly consists of two kinds of perception turbo (PT), GPT in the generator network, and DPT in the discriminator network. In terms of visual effects, the proposed image slice block mitigates the artifacts and noise in the reconstructed image, the three-level perception structure in GPT which could extract diversified textures. The cascaded PTBs in DPT could further promote the generator to restore subtle textures.

Author Contributions: All authors contributed to the study conception and design. T.W. and Y.Z. participated in the design of the network structure, S.X. is responsible for the budget and paper quality and revision, and the network implementation was carried out by Y.L. and H.T. Material preparation, data collection, and analysis were performed by H.T., H.L. (Huaizheng Liu) and J.Z. The model training and experimental results collection was carried out by Y.L., H.T. and H.L. (Huaizheng Liu). Y.Z. participated in the system integration and testing. The first draft of the manuscript was written by H.L. (Hui Liu) and J.Z. All of the authors commented on previous versions of the manuscript. All authors have read and agreed to the published version of the manuscript

Funding: This work was supported by Tencent Technology (Shenzhen) Co., Ltd.

Data Availability Statement: The calculation method of NIQE is derived from the following resources available in the public domain: https://github.com/roimehrez/PIRM2018 (accessed on 1 June 2023). The verification program is available at https://drive.google.com/file/d/1AZmkgvgfcBicTP9tM5X-gahnirskm6-1/view?usp=share_link (accessed on 1 June 2023). The datasets analyzed during the current study are derived from the following resources available in the public domain: https://github.com/XPixelGroup/BasicSR/blob/master/docs/DatasetPreparation.md (accessed on 1 June 2023).

Acknowledgments: The authors would like to thank Tencent Company for helpful budget and resource on topics related to this work, special the Qilong Kou, the department of Tencent Institute of Games.

Conflicts of Interest: The authors have no competing interests to declare that are relevant to the content of this article. This work did not involve human participants or animal research.

Appendix A. Cross Verification between PTBs and U-Net

In PSRGAN, we now call its generator network PSRNet and its discriminator network PTBs. In this section, we further compare the differences between two kinds of GANs, PSRNet+PTBs, and PSRNet+U-net on diverse testing datasets. From the results in Table A1, we can conclude that using PTBs can promote the generator to restore more perceptive SR images driven by GAN; more qualitative comparisons are shown in Figure A1.

OST_99 from OST300(NIQE) Bicubic(7.52) PSRNet+U-net(2.69) PSRGAN(2.48)

OST_164 from OST300(NIQE) Bicubic(7.87) PSRNet+U-net(3.35) PSRGAN(3.01)

Figure A1. Qualitative comparisons on representative real-world samples with ×4 upscaling factors. PSRNet+PTBs outperforms PSRNet+U-net in terms of both restoring texture details (See OST_99) and producing clearer results (See OST_164).

Table A1. NIQE scores on several diverse testing datasets. The lower, the better.

	PIRM_self_val	OST300	RealSR-Nikon	RealSR-Canon
PSRNet+U-net	3.527	2.830	5.673	5.896
PSRGAN (PSRNet+PTBs)	3.330	2.735	5.164	4.499

Appendix B. Structure of Multi-Scale Feature Extraction Block

We conducted experiments on the number of convolutional groups for multi-scale feature-extraction block (MFEB) in the generator network. As the experimental results in Table A2 show, the SR results show better performance when the number of convolutional groups is three.

Table A2. NIQE scores of feature extraction block at different scales on diverse testing datasets; the lower, the better. The calculation method of NIQE is derived from the basic SR package of PyTorch 1.11.0+cu113.

Groups	1	2	3	4	5
OST300	6.650362	6.635382	**6.520303**	6.626211	6.61622
DRealSR_Test_x4	7.892549	7.932709	**7.818715**	7.993731	7.821493
RealSR-Canon	**10.179904**	10.313314	10.208351	10.32831	10.3463
RealSR-Nikon	10.445691	10.491598	10.409443	10.582925	**10.378877**
PIRM_Self_val	6.717716	6.717983	**6.653905**	6.699813	6.694974
2020track1	6.596391	6.583975	**6.46227**	6.60103	6.526587

Appendix C. More Qualitative Results

Figure A2. More qualitative results of PSRGAN and NIQE are provided for reference. [×4 upscaling].

References

1. Duchon, C.E. Lanczos filtering in one and two dimensions. *J. Appl. Meteorol. Climatol.* **1979**, *18*, 1016–1022. [CrossRef]
2. Zhang, L.; Wu, X. An edge-guided image interpolation algorithm via directional filtering and data fusion. *IEEE Trans. Image Process.* **2006**, *15*, 2226–2238. [CrossRef] [PubMed]
3. Wu, Y.; Ding, H.; Gong, M.; Qin, A.; Ma, W.; Miao, Q.; Tan, K.C. Evolutionary multiform optimization with two-stage bidirectional knowledge transfer strategy for point cloud registration. *IEEE Trans. Evol. Comput.* **2022**. [CrossRef]
4. Wu, Y.; Zhang, Y.; Ma, W.; Gong, M.; Fan, X.; Zhang, M.; Qin, A.; Miao, Q. Rornet: Partial-to-partial registration network with reliable overlapping representations. *IEEE Trans. Neural Netw. Learn. Syst.* **2023**. [CrossRef] [PubMed]
5. Dai, S.; Han, M.; Xu, W.; Wu, Y.; Gong, Y.; Katsaggelos, A.K. Softcuts: A soft edge smoothness prior for color image super-resolution. *IEEE Trans. Image Process.* **2009**, *18*, 969–981. [PubMed]
6. Sun, J.; Xu, Z.; Shum, H.Y. Image super-resolution using gradient profile prior. In Proceedings of the 2008 IEEE Conference on Computer Vision and Pattern Recognition, Anchorage, Alaskapp, 23–28 June 2008; pp. 1–8.
7. Yan, Q.; Xu, Y.; Yang, X.; Nguyen, T.Q. Single image superresolution based on gradient profile sharpness. *IEEE Trans. Image Process.* **2015**, *24*, 3187–3202. [PubMed]
8. Shang, T.; Dai, Q.; Zhu, S.; Yang, T.; Guo, Y. Perceptual extreme super-resolution network with receptive field block. In Proceedings of the IEEE/CVF Conference on Computer Vision and Pattern Recognition Workshops, Seattle, WA, USA, 13–19 June 2020; pp. 440–441.
9. Goodfellow, I.; Pouget-Abadie, J.; Mirza, M.; Xu, B.; Warde-Farley, D.; Ozair, S.; Courville, A.; Bengio, Y. Generative adversarial networks. *Adv. Neural Inf. Process. Syst.* **2020**, *63*, 139–144. [CrossRef]
10. Ledig, C.; Theis, L.; Huszár, F.; Caballero, J.; Cunningham, A.; Acosta, A.; Aitken, A.; Tejani, A.; Totz, J.; Wang, Z.; et al. Photo-realistic single-image super-resolution using a generative adversarial network. In Proceedings of the IEEE Conference on Computer Vision and Pattern Recognition, Honolulu, HI, USA, 21–26 July 2017; pp. 4681–4690.

11. Wang, X.; Yu, K.; Wu, S.; Gu, J.; Liu, Y.; Dong, C.; Qiao, Y.; Change Loy, C. Esrgan: Enhanced super-resolution generative adversarial networks. In Proceedings of the European Conference on Computer Vision (ECCV) Workshops, Munich, Germany, 8–14 September 2018.
12. Yuan, Y.; Liu, S.; Zhang, J.; Zhang, Y.; Dong, C.; Lin, L. Unsupervised image super-resolution using cycle-in-cycle generative adversarial networks. In Proceedings of the IEEE Conference on Computer Vision and Pattern Recognition Workshops, Salt Lake City, UT, USA, 18–23 June 2018; pp. 701–710.
13. Zhang, Y.; Liu, S.; Dong, C.; Zhang, X.; Yuan, Y. Multiple cycle-in-cycle generative adversarial networks for unsupervised image super-resolution. *IEEE Trans. Image Process.* **2019**, *29*, 1101–1112. [CrossRef]
14. Zhang, K.; Liang, J.; Van Gool, L.; Timofte, R. Designing a practical degradation model for deep blind image super-resolution. In Proceedings of the IEEE/CVF International Conference on Computer Vision, Montreal, BC, Canada, 11–17 October 2021; pp. 4791–4800.
15. Wang, X.; Xie, L.; Dong, C.; Shan, Y. real-ESRGAN: Training real-world blind super-resolution with pure synthetic data. In Proceedings of the IEEE/CVF International Conference on Computer Vision, Montreal, BC, Canada, 11–17 October 2021; pp. 1905–1914.
16. Ronneberger, O.; Fischer, P.; Brox, T. U-net: Convolutional networks for biomedical image segmentation. In Proceedings of the Medical Image Computing and Computer-Assisted Intervention–MICCAI 2015: 18th International Conference, Munich, Germany, 5–9 October 2015; Proceedings, Part III 18; Springer: Berlin/Heidelberg, Germany, 2015; pp. 234–241.
17. Simonyan, K.; Zisserman, A. Very deep convolutional networks for large-scale image recognition. *arXiv* **2014**, arXiv:1409.1556.
18. Dong, C.; Loy, C.C.; He, K.; Tang, X. Learning a deep convolutional network for image super-resolution. In Proceedings of the Computer Vision–ECCV 2014: 13th European Conference, Zurich, Switzerland, 6–12 September 2014; Proceedings, Part IV 13; Springer: Berlin/Heidelberg, Germany, 2014; pp. 184–199.
19. Kim, J.; Lee, J.K.; Lee, K.M. Accurate image super-resolution using very deep convolutional networks. In Proceedings of the IEEE Conference on Computer Vision and Pattern Recognition, Las Vegas, NV, USA, 27–30 June 2016; pp. 1646–1654.
20. Lai, W.S.; Huang, J.B.; Ahuja, N.; Yang, M.H. Deep laplacian pyramid networks for fast and accurate super-resolution. In Proceedings of the IEEE Conference on Computer Vision and Pattern Recognition, Honolulu, HI, USA, 21–26 July 2017; pp. 624–632.
21. Timofte, R.; Agustsson, E.; Van Gool, L.; Yang, M.H.; Zhang, L. Ntire 2017 challenge on single-image super-resolution: Methods and results. In Proceedings of the IEEE Conference on Computer Vision and Pattern Recognition Workshops, Honolulu, HI, USA, 21–26 July 2017; pp. 114–125.
22. Haris, M.; Shakhnarovich, G.; Ukita, N. Deep back-projection networks for super-resolution. In Proceedings of the IEEE Conference on Computer Vision and Pattern Recognition, Salt Lake City, UT, USA, 18–23 June 2018; pp. 1664–1673.
23. Dong, C.; Loy, C.C.; Tang, X. Accelerating the super-resolution convolutional neural network. In Proceedings of the Computer Vision–ECCV 2016: 14th European Conference, Amsterdam, The Netherlands, 11–14 October 2016; Proceedings, Part II 14; Springer: Berlin/Heidelberg, Germany, 2016; pp. 391–407.
24. Shi, W.; Caballero, J.; Huszár, F.; Totz, J.; Aitken, A.P.; Bishop, R.; Rueckert, D.; Wang, Z. Real-time single image and video super-resolution using an efficient sub-pixel convolutional neural network. In Proceedings of the IEEE Conference on Computer Vision and Pattern Recognition, Las Vegas, NV, USA, 26 June–1 July 2016; pp. 1874–1883.
25. Lim, B.; Son, S.; Kim, H.; Nah, S.; Mu Lee, K. Enhanced deep residual networks for single-image super-resolution. In Proceedings of the IEEE Conference on Computer Vision and Pattern Recognition Workshops, Honolulu, HI, USA, 21–26 July 2017; pp. 136–144.
26. Musunuri, Y.R.; Kwon, O.S. Deep residual dense network for single-image super-resolution. *Electronics* **2021**, *10*, 555. [CrossRef]
27. Ji, X.; Cao, Y.; Tai, Y.; Wang, C.; Li, J.; Huang, F. Real-world super-resolution via kernel estimation and noise injection. In Proceedings of the IEEE/CVF Conference on Computer Vision and Pattern Recognition Workshops, Seattle, WA, USA, 13–19 June 2020; pp. 466–467.
28. Wei, P.; Xie, Z.; Lu, H.; Zhan, Z.; Ye, Q.; Zuo, W.; Lin, L. Component divide-and-conquer for real-world image super-resolution. In Proceedings of the Computer Vision–ECCV 2020: 16th European Conference, Glasgow, UK, 23–28 August 2020; Proceedings, Part VIII 16; Springer: Berlin/Heidelberg, Germany, 2020; pp. 101–117.
29. Luo, Z.; Huang, Y.; Li, S.; Wang, L.; Tan, T. Learning the degradation distribution for blind image super-resolution. In Proceedings of the IEEE/CVF Conference on Computer Vision and Pattern Recognition, New Orleans, LA, USA, 18–24 June 2022; pp. 6063–6072.
30. Wang, X.; Yu, K.; Dong, C.; Loy, C.C. Recovering realistic texture in image super-resolution by deep spatial feature transform. In Proceedings of the IEEE Conference on Computer Vision and Pattern Recognition, Salt Lake City, UT, USA, 18–23 June 2018; pp. 606–615.
31. Shao, G.; Sun, Q.; Gao, Y.; Zhu, Q.; Gao, F.; Zhang, J. Sub-Pixel Convolutional Neural Network for Image super-resolution Reconstruction. *Electronics* **2023**, *12*, 3572. [CrossRef]
32. Bruna, J.; Sprechmann, P.; LeCun, Y. super-resolution with deep convolutional sufficient statistics. *arXiv* **2015**, arXiv:1511.05666.
33. Johnson, J.; Alahi, A.; Fei-Fei, L. Perceptual losses for real-time style transfer and super-resolution. In Proceedings of the Computer Vision–ECCV 2016: 14th European Conference, Amsterdam, The Netherlands, 11–14 October 2016; Proceedings, Part II 14; Springer: Berlin/Heidelberg, Germany, 2016; pp. 694–711.
34. Sajjadi, M.S.; Scholkopf, B.; Hirsch, M. Enhancenet: Single-image super-resolution through automated texture synthesis. In Proceedings of the IEEE International Conference on Computer Vision, Venice, Italy, 22–29 October 2017; pp. 4491–4500.

35. Mechrez, R.; Talmi, I.; Zelnik-Manor, L. The contextual loss for image transformation with non-aligned data. In Proceedings of the European Conference on Computer Vision (ECCV), Munich, Germany, 8–14 September 2018; pp. 768–783.
36. Blau, Y.; Mechrez, R.; Timofte, R.; Michaeli, T.; Zelnik-Manor, L. The 2018 PIRM challenge on perceptual image super-resolution. In Proceedings of the European Conference on Computer Vision (ECCV) Workshops, Munich, Germany, 8–14 September 2018.
37. Szegedy, C.; Liu, W.; Jia, Y.; Sermanet, P.; Reed, S.; Anguelov, D.; Erhan, D.; Vanhoucke, V.; Rabinovich, A. Going deeper with convolutions. In Proceedings of the IEEE Conference on Computer Vision and Pattern Recognition, Boston, MA, USA, 7–12 June 2015; pp. 1–9.
38. Liu, S.; Huang, D. Receptive field block net for accurate and fast object detection. In Proceedings of the European Conference on Computer Vision (ECCV), Munich, Germany, 8–14 September 2018; pp. 385–400.
39. Zhang, K.; Gu, S.; Timofte, R. Ntire 2020 challenge on perceptual extreme super-resolution: Methods and results. In Proceedings of the IEEE/CVF Conference on Computer Vision and Pattern Recognition Workshops, Seattle, WA, USA, 13–19 June 2020; pp. 492–493.
40. Newell, A.; Yang, K.; Deng, J. Stacked hourglass networks for human pose estimation. In Proceedings of the Computer Vision–ECCV 2016: 14th European Conference, Amsterdam, The Netherlands, 11–14 October 2016; Proceedings, Part VIII 14; Springer: Berlin/Heidelberg, Germany, 2016; pp. 483–499.
41. Liang, J.; Zeng, H.; Zhang, L. Details or artifacts: A locally discriminative learning approach to realistic image super-resolution. In Proceedings of the IEEE/CVF Conference on Computer Vision and Pattern Recognition, New Orleans, LA, USA, 18–24 June 2022; pp. 5657–5666.
42. Zhang, M.; Ling, Q. Supervised pixel-wise GAN for face super-resolution. *IEEE Trans. Multimed.* **2020**, *23*, 1938–1950. [CrossRef]
43. Gong, Y.; Liao, P.; Zhang, X.; Zhang, L.; Chen, G.; Zhu, K.; Tan, X.; Lv, Z. Enlighten-GAN for super resolution reconstruction in mid-resolution remote sensing images. *Remote Sens.* **2021**, *13*, 1104. [CrossRef]
44. Sheikh, H.R.; Bovik, A.C.; De Veciana, G. An information fidelity criterion for image quality assessment using natural scene statistics. *IEEE Trans. Image Process.* **2005**, *14*, 2117–2128. [CrossRef]
45. Sheikh, H.R.; Bovik, A.C. Image information and visual quality. *IEEE Trans. Image Process.* **2006**, *15*, 430–444. [CrossRef]
46. Wang, Z.; Bovik, A.C.; Sheikh, H.R.; Simoncelli, E.P. Image quality assessment: From error visibility to structural similarity. *IEEE Trans. Image Process.* **2004**, *13*, 600–612. [CrossRef]
47. Ma, C.; Yang, C.Y.; Yang, X.; Yang, M.H. Learning a no-reference quality metric for single-image super-resolution. *Comput. Vis. Image Underst.* **2017**, *158*, 1–16. [CrossRef]
48. Mittal, A.; Soundararajan, R.; Bovik, A.C. Making a "completely blind" image quality analyzer. *IEEE Signal Process. Lett.* **2012**, *20*, 209–212. [CrossRef]
49. Mittal, A.; Moorthy, A.K.; Bovik, A.C. No-reference image quality assessment in the spatial domain. *IEEE Trans. Image Process.* **2012**, *21*, 4695–4708. [CrossRef]
50. Blau, Y.; Michaeli, T. The perception-distortion tradeoff. In Proceedings of the IEEE Conference on Computer Vision and Pattern Recognition, Salt Lake City, UT, USA, 18–23 June 2018; pp. 6228–6237.
51. Vasu, S.; Thekke Madam, N.; Rajagopalan, A. Analyzing perception-distortion tradeoff using enhanced perceptual super-resolution network. In Proceedings of the European Conference on Computer Vision (ECCV) Workshops, Munich, Germany, 8–14 September 2018.
52. Lugmayr, A.; Danelljan, M.; Timofte, R. Ntire 2020 challenge on real-world image super-resolution: Methods and results. In Proceedings of the IEEE/CVF Conference on Computer Vision and Pattern Recognition Workshops, Seattle, WA, USA, 13–19 June 2020; pp. 494–495.
53. Cai, J.; Zeng, H.; Yong, H.; Cao, Z.; Zhang, L. Toward real-world single-image super-resolution: A new benchmark and a new model. In Proceedings of the IEEE/CVF International Conference on Computer Vision, Seoul, Republic of Korea, 27 October–2 November 2019; pp. 3086–3095.
54. Vaswani, A.; Shazeer, N.; Parmar, N.; Uszkoreit, J.; Jones, L.; Gomez, A.N.; Kaiser, Ł.; Polosukhin, I. Attention is all you need. *Adv. Neural Inf. Process. Syst.* **2017**, *30*.
55. He, E.; Chen, Q.; Zhong, Q. SL-Swin: A transformer-Based Deep Learning Approach for Macro-and Micro-Expression Spotting on Small-Size Expression Datasets. *Electronics* **2023**, *12*, 2656. [CrossRef]
56. Yang, F.; Yang, H.; Fu, J.; Lu, H.; Guo, B. Learning texture transformer network for image super-resolution. In Proceedings of the IEEE/CVF Conference on Computer Vision and Pattern Recognition, Seattle, WA, USA, 13–19 June 2020; pp. 5791–5800.
57. Liu, Z.; Lin, Y.; Cao, Y.; Hu, H.; Wei, Y.; Zhang, Z.; Lin, S.; Guo, B. Swin transformer: Hierarchical vision transformer using shifted windows. In Proceedings of the IEEE/CVF International Conference on Computer Vision, Montreal, BC, Canada, 11–17 October 2021; pp. 10012–10022.
58. Liang, J.; Cao, J.; Sun, G.; Zhang, K.; Van Gool, L.; Timofte, R. Swinir: Image restoration using swin transformer. In Proceedings of the IEEE/CVF International Conference on Computer Vision, Montreal, BC, Canada, 11–17 October 2021; pp. 1833–1844.
59. Lu, Z.; Li, J.; Liu, H.; Huang, C.; Zhang, L.; Zeng, T. transformer for single-image super-resolution. In Proceedings of the IEEE/CVF Conference on Computer Vision and Pattern Recognition, New Orleans, LA, USA, 18–24 June 2022; pp. 457–466.

60. Kingma, D.P.; Ba, J. Adam: A method for stochastic optimization. *arXiv* **2014**, arXiv:1412.6980.
61. Agustsson, E.; Timofte, R. Ntire 2017 challenge on single-image super-resolution: Dataset and study. In Proceedings of the IEEE Conference on Computer Vision and Pattern Recognition Workshops, Honolulu, HI, USA, 21–26 July 2017; pp. 126–135.

Disclaimer/Publisher's Note: The statements, opinions and data contained in all publications are solely those of the individual author(s) and contributor(s) and not of MDPI and/or the editor(s). MDPI and/or the editor(s) disclaim responsibility for any injury to people or property resulting from any ideas, methods, instructions or products referred to in the content.

Article

Optimal Scheduling of Emergency Materials Based on Gray Prediction Model under Uncertain Demand

Bing Li * and Qi Liu

School of Economics, Wuhan University of Technology, Wuhan 430070, China
* Correspondence: 11539@whut.edu.cn

Abstract: In the context of long-term infectious disease epidemics, guaranteeing the dispatch of materials is important to emergency management. The epidemic situation is constantly changing; it is necessary to build a reasonable mechanism to dispatch emergency resources and materials to meet demand. First, to evaluate the unpredictability of demand during an epidemic, gray prediction is inserted into the proposed model, named the Multi-catalog Schedule Considering Costs and Requirements Under Uncertainty, to meet the material scheduling target. The model uses the gray prediction method based on pre-epidemic data to forecast the possible material demand when the disease appears. With the help of the forecast results, the model is able to achieve cross-regional material scheduling. The key objective of material scheduling is, of course, to reach a balance between the cost and the material support rate. In order to fulfil this important requirement, a multi-objective function, which aims to minimize costs and maximize the material support rate, is constructed. Then, an ant colony algorithm, suitable for time and region problems, is employed to provide a solution to the constructed function. Finally, the validity of the model is verified via a case study. The results show that the model can coordinate and deploy a variety of materials from multiple sources according to changes in an epidemic situation and provide reliable support in decisions regarding the dynamic dispatch of emergency materials during an epidemic period.

Keywords: emergency material scheduling; gray prediction; ant colony algorithm; demand forecasting; multi-objective optimization

Citation: Li, B.; Liu, Q. Optimal Scheduling of Emergency Materials Based on Gray Prediction Model under Uncertain Demand. *Electronics* 2023, 12, 4337. https://doi.org/10.3390/electronics12204337

Academic Editor: Javid Taheri

Received: 8 September 2023
Revised: 17 October 2023
Accepted: 17 October 2023
Published: 19 October 2023

Copyright: © 2023 by the authors. Licensee MDPI, Basel, Switzerland. This article is an open access article distributed under the terms and conditions of the Creative Commons Attribution (CC BY) license (https://creativecommons.org/licenses/by/4.0/).

1. Introduction

COVID-19 is a severe global public health emergency that has had a profound impact on medical systems and social economies [1]. During the outbreak of large-scale infectious diseases, the scheduling of emergency supplies is necessary to ensure medical treatment and the continuation of normal life. Thus, it is important to establish an emergency resources supply system fully tailored to the epidemic process. Among the issues linked with emergencies, methods of efficiently dispatching resources require attention. There are many factors affecting dispatching, including external factors, such as region and time, and internal factors, such as material supply and demand. A state of uncertainty and emergency increases the difficulty of dispatching materials. Therefore, the first factor that must be considered is the prediction of the possible demand through scientific methods. A two-stage location-routing model has been proposed for guiding resource allocation when the requirements and infrastructure are unknown [2]. The model has a lower computational cost because of its simple calculation process. Then, case-based reasoning (CBR) and the Dempster–Shafer theory have been employed to improve the accuracy in forecasting emergency material demand [3]. A good method is necessary not only for estimating demand but also for the organization of the supply chain and the coordination of the relationship between the parties in order to enhance the effectiveness of the material distribution. A two-stage MADA-B mechanism was designed to research the supply and demand of multi-attribute emergency materials, which combines a multi-attribute double auction (MADA) with bargaining and can perfectly match buyers with sellers through the game playing of the transaction price and quantity [4]. After demand matching is completed, the subsequent production plan becomes the new focus. Then, a fuzzy linear programming model was provided to solve the aggregate production planning problem. Its advantage is the incorporation of uncertainty of the customer demands, and unit holding and backordering costs of the production plan [5]. In one work, a method based on the timed-colored Petri net (TCPN) model was proposed to model the cooperation of actions with time analysis [6]. After the production of materials, timeliness needs to be considered in the selection of transportation methods. After an in-depth discussion of the cold chain model selection problem, taking into account economic and environmental objectives from both business and financial aspects, a value-based management method is provided as a new shipping approach [7]. The method effectively solves material planning by cutting out unnecessary actions. Other methods focus on the quick construction of the supply chain according to the criterion of reaction speed. Based on this idea, a hybrid algorithm combining artificial immunity with ant colony optimization has been developed, the transportation scheme of which has a shorter response time and covers more demand points [8]. With the hierarchical timed color Petri net (HTCPN) model and the skyline operator, a multi-objective optimization (MOO) model for a fire emergency response was established, which not only shortened the response time but also reduced resource consumption [9]. It must be noted that the above methods assume that materials are directly transported from the supply side to the demand side. They do not take into account cross-regional transportation, which is more likely in epidemic situations. To overcome this disadvantage, an inter-regional emergency cooperation network that includes system construction, organization and coordination, and mechanism design is proposed to offer an optimal countermeasure for city cooperation [10]. Transit points need to be considered when cross-regional issues are involved. The location of transit points will affect transportation efficiency. Considering this, a multi-objective optimization model for the selection of rescue stations has been established to improve efficiency [11]. In the research into transit points for cross-regional issues, the requirement for warehouses becomes obvious because it is nearly impossible to match the rate of supply with the rate of consumption. A mixed-integer programming model for uncertain requirements controlled by time and cost provides a helpful solution for emergency warehouse location and distribution [12]. Additionally, when stocks are available, a simulation–optimization approach based on the stochastic counterpart or sample path has been shown to optimize the pharmaceutical supply chain by managing the records of the stocks [13]. Due to the uncertainty of epidemics and the timeliness of drugs, medical demand is difficult to predict and handle. For that, a deterministic MILP model and a robust optimization model are used to deal with the demand uncertainty while integrating warehouse selection, inventory strategy and delivery route optimization of the VMI [14].

The above examples from the literature show different solutions for emergency events. However, all of them ignore the fact that the degrees of urgency of different requirements play a role in the response, especially when the emergency supplies are not enough to meet all of the requirements. In this situation, the distribution of materials has to consider the degree of urgency. An optimization model combines the location hazard index (LHI) with the response time; the LHI measures the potential hazard of a location, while the response time provides resource allocation in response to an emergency situation [15]. From the observation of multiple independent emergency events, a deep ensemble multitask model integrating four subnetworks has been proposed. It can improve the medical dispatch process by classifying the degree of emergency based on clinical data, environmental data and other factors [16]. In the case of an epidemic outbreak, a hybrid multi-verse optimizer algorithm based on the multi-verse optimization algorithm and the differential evolution algorithm can effectively reduce the distribution cost by considering the urgency of the demand for emergency supplies [17]. Numerous studies have comprehensively discussed good solutions for dispatching materials by recreating the scene of the emergency.

The pre-emergency warning process has become another research hotspot. A study has formulated a multi-objective mixed-integer non-linear programming model to determine the location and number of relief centers, with their prepositioned inventory level, in the pre-emergency stage. The decision provided by the model can minimize costs and transportation distances [18].

The above literature examples discuss the various factors that support a reasonable resource-scheduling solution to advance the development of emergency management. However, most of the studies concentrate on static analysis to optimize resource scheduling, which means that the variations in the requirements and degrees of emergency are totally ignored in the process. In addition, the works mainly focus on the post-stage response, and the pre-stage early warning mechanism is rarely involved. In order to offer a solution incorporating all factors, a coordinated allocation model of multiple materials based on the gray prediction model is proposed in this work and is named the Multi-catalog Schedule Considering Costs and Requirements Under Uncertainty. If the number of infectious members of the population can be forecast, then the materials that will subsequently be required can be prepared. Thus, by collecting information on historical infectious diseases, the model uses a gray prediction algorithm to predict the number of infectious diseases in the future. According to the prediction results, the demand relative to infectious disease is determined, and this includes both medical materials and general goods. At the same time, the cost is also considered. With the goal of reducing the cost and meeting demand, a multi-object function is defined and takes into consideration the type of relief material, the time difference, and trans-regional coordination. This model contains numerous variables from different angles, meaning it is difficult to set the initial solutions. The ant colony model does not require much for the initial solutions and has few parameters, meaning that it is suitable for combinational optimization problems such as material dispatch. Therefore, an ant colony model is designed to solve our problem. The contributions of this work are as follows:

(1) The gray prediction algorithm is used to predict the number of confirmed cases at various times. Then, the degree of emergency can be estimated, and the predicted data can be used to guide material scheduling. The application of this prediction module means that our model can play a certain role in early warning systems.

(2) Both external and internal factors are considered in order to expand the scope of the model's application and improve the satisfaction of the solution provided by the proposed model. External factors include distances and the time of transportation. The internal factor comprises the maximum level of production. Then, an objective function for cross-regional scheduling is defined, in which the uncertainty of requirements and different types of goods in a period of time are taken into account.

(3) In order to obtain the final schedule, the model uses the ant colony algorithm to solve the objective function. There are numerous integer variables in the function, and the initial solution is a three-dimensional matrix. Thus, the model records the directions of each ant's action in each dimension in the matrix and defines a utility function, which is used to calculate the effect of the ant's every choice. Unlike the pheromone, the calculated results will help shorten the time required to obtain the result of the model by adjusting the probability of picking the direction in the course of each ant's actions.

This paper consists of five sections. Section 1 mainly describes the latest achievements regarding the research issues in this paper and discusses their advantages and disadvantages. Then, the model and the research value proposed in this paper are briefly introduced. Section 2 provides a detailed introduction to the theories used in the model. Section 3 consists of the building and solving processes of the model. The results of the model are verified and presented using examples in Section 4. Finally, the conclusions are discussed in Section 5.

2. Preliminaries

2.1. Gray Prediction

The gray prediction method GM(1,1) is a prediction system that can contain both known and unknown information. Based on the rule of data change, it generates a sequence with strong regularity and then the corresponding differential equation is built to predict the developed values of the data. Compared with other prediction methods, the gray prediction model only needs a few samples to drive, which is suitable to deal with the emergency because emergency always happens in a short time, and it is hard to gather enough observations during it. Therefore, in this paper, the gray prediction model is used to complete the prediction job [19]. The model is defined as follows [20].

We assume that the reference data column is $x^0 = \left(x^0(1), x^0(2), \ldots, x^0(n)\right)$, whose 1-AGO is as follows:

$$x^{(1)} = \left(x^{(1)}(1), x^{(1)}(2), \ldots, x^{(1)}(n)\right) \tag{1}$$

$$x^{(1)} = \left(x^{(0)}(1), \sum_{i=1}^{2} x^{(0)}(i) \ldots, \sum_{i=1}^{n} x^{(0)}(i)\right) \tag{2}$$

Formula (1) is the accumulating generation operator (1-AGO) of the reference data column, and it is obtained via Formula (2). In Formula (2), $x^{(1)}(k) = \sum_{i=1}^{k} x^{(0)}(i), k = 1, 2, \ldots, n$. n is the number of observations. The mean generated sequence of $x^{(1)}$ is $z^{(1)}$, where $k = 2, 3, \ldots, n$:

$$z^{(1)} = \left(z^{(1)}(2), z^{(1)}(3), \ldots, z^{(1)}(n)\right) \tag{3}$$

$$z^{(1)}(k) = 0.5x^{(1)}(k) + 0.5x^{(1)}(k-1) \tag{4}$$

The gray differential equation is established:

$$x^{(0)}(k) + az^{(1)}(k) = b, k = 2, 3, \ldots n \tag{5}$$

In Formula (5), a, b are the parameters of the equation. The values of a, b are calculated by the immediate mean of the original data series. It is worth noting that when performing the immediate mean calculation, since the first data point does not have the previous data point, it needs to be averaged with the second data point. The whitening differential equation corresponding to Formula (5) is as follows:

$$\frac{dx^{(1)}}{dt} + ax^{(1)}(t) = b \tag{6}$$

$$u = [a, b]^T \tag{7}$$

$$Y = \left[x^{(0)}(2), x^{(0)}(3), \ldots, x^{(0)}(n)\right]^T \tag{8}$$

$$B = \begin{bmatrix} -z^{(1)}(2) & 1 \\ -z^{(1)}(3) & 1 \\ \vdots & \vdots \\ -z^{(1)}(n) & 1 \end{bmatrix} \tag{9}$$

According to least squares, the estimated value of u for minimizing $J(u) = (Y - Bu)^T (Y - Bu)$ is obtained as $\hat{u} = [\hat{a}, \hat{b}]^T = (B^T B)^{-1} B^T Y$. To solve the whitening differential equation, the formula is as follows:

$$\hat{x}^{(1)}(k+1) = \left(x^{(0)}(1) - \frac{\hat{b}}{\hat{a}}\right) e^{-\hat{a}k} + \frac{\hat{b}}{\hat{a}} \tag{10}$$

$$k = 0, 1, \ldots, n-1$$

The model accuracy is mainly verified using three items: a residual test, a correlation test, and a posterior error test. The residual test refers to the point-by-point comparison of the residual difference between the calculated value and the actual value. First, we calculate $\hat{x}^{(1)}(k+1)$ according to the method. Then, the predicted value of the original sequence is calculated according to Formula (11).

$$\hat{x}^{(0)}(k) = \hat{x}^{(1)}(k) - \hat{x}^{(1)}(k-1) \tag{11}$$

$$\Delta^{(0)}(k) = \left| x^{(0)}(k) - \hat{x}^{(0)}(k) \right| \tag{12}$$

$$\varphi_k = \frac{\Delta^{(0)}(k)}{x^{(0)}(k)} \tag{13}$$

$$\overline{\Phi} = n^{-1} \sum_{k=1}^{n} \varphi_k \tag{14}$$

$$k = 1, 2, \ldots, n$$

The absolute residual sequence $\Delta^{(0)}$ is formed from the results of Formulas (11) and (12). The relative residual sequence Φ is formed from the results of Formula (13). Then, the average relative residual is shown in Formula (14). For the given α, the model can be regarded as qualified when $\overline{\Phi} < \alpha$ and $\varphi_n < \alpha$ are both true.

The correlation degree test refers to the comparison of the similarities between the computed sequence curves and real sequence curves. The correlation coefficient is defined as Formula (17):

$$\hat{X} = \{\hat{x}(1), \hat{x}(2), \ldots, \hat{x}(n)\} \tag{15}$$

$$X_i = \{x_i(1), x_i(2), \ldots, x_i(n)\} \tag{16}$$

$$\eta_i(k) = \frac{\text{minmin}|\hat{x}(k) - x_i(k)| + \rho \text{maxmax}|\hat{x}(k) - x_i(k)|}{|\hat{x}(k) - x_i(k)| + \rho \text{maxmax}|\hat{x}(k) - x_i(k)|} \tag{17}$$

$$i = 1, 2, \ldots, m; k = 1, 2, \ldots, n$$

$|\hat{x}(k) - x_i(k)|$ is the absolute error of sequence $\hat{X}$ and X_i at k point. $\min|\hat{x}(k) - x_i(k)|$ represents the minimum distance between the corresponding points in sequence $\hat{X}$ and X when i remains the same. $\text{minmin}|\hat{x}(k) - x_i(k)|$ aims to traverse i to find the minimum value in the result of $\min|\hat{x}(k) - x_i(k)|$. The calculation process of $\text{maxmax}|\hat{x}(k) - x_i(k)|$ is the same as $\text{minmin}|\hat{x}(k) - x_i(k)|$, except that $\text{maxmax}|\hat{x}(k) - x_i(k)|$ is looking for the maximum. $\rho(0 < \rho < 1)$ is the resolution. Usually, when $\rho = 0.5$ and $\eta_i(k) > 0.6$ where $i = 1, 2, \ldots, m$, the model is considered as qualified.

The posteriori error test refers to testing the statistical characteristics of the residual distribution. A series of statistical indicators needs to be calculated. The following Formula (18) is the average of the original sequence. Formula (19) is the standard deviation of the original sequence. Formula (20) is the mean of the residual. Formula (21) is the standard deviation of the residual:

$$\overline{x^{(0)}} = n^{-1} \sum_{i=1}^{n} x^{(0)}(i) \tag{18}$$

$$S_1 = \sqrt{\left[\frac{\sum_{i=1}^{n}\left[x^{(0)}(i) - \overline{x^{(0)}}\right]^2}{n-1}\right]} \tag{19}$$

$$\overline{\Delta^{(0)}} = n^{-1} \sum_{i=1}^{n} \Delta^{(0)}(i) \tag{20}$$

$$S_2 = \sqrt{\left[\frac{\sum_{i=1}^{n}\left[\Delta^{(0)}(i) - \overline{\Delta^{(0)}}\right]^2}{n-1}\right]} \tag{21}$$

Calculate the variance ratio: $C = S_2 \times S_1^{-1}$. S_1 is the variance calculated from the original sequence x^0. S_2 is the variance calculated from the residual sequence $\Delta^{(0)}$. Calculate the small residual probability: $p = P\left\{\left|\Delta^{(0)}(i) - \overline{\Delta^{(0)}}\right| < 0.6745 S_1\right\}$. Generally, when $C < 0.65$ and $p > 0.7$, the model is acceptable.

2.2. Ant Colony Algorithm

The ant colony algorithm is an intelligent optimization algorithm. The basic ACO model is described by the following three formulas [21]:

$$P_{ij}(t) = \begin{cases} \frac{[\tau_{ij}(t)]^\alpha \eta_{ij}^\beta}{\sum_{l \in A_k}[\tau_{il}(t)]^\alpha \eta_{il}^\beta}, & if\ s_j \in A_k \\ 0, & otherwise \end{cases} \tag{22}$$

$$\tau_{ij}(t+1) = \rho \tau_{ij}(t) + \sum_{k=1}^{m} \Delta \tau_{ij}^k(t) \tag{23}$$

$$\Delta \tau_{ij}^k(t) = \begin{cases} \frac{1}{L_k}, & if\ ant\ k\ moves\ from\ s_i\ to\ s_j\ at\ step\ t \\ 0, & otherwise \end{cases} \tag{24}$$

In the ant colony algorithm, an ant chooses the next destination at each iteration until it has completed its journey. For example, at iteration t, the ant k moves from s_i to s_j. s_j belongs to the set A_k for the feasible location. $P_{ij}(t)$ is the probability that the ant will go from s_i to s_j at time t. The heuristic values $\eta_{ij} = 1/d_{ij}$, where d_{ij} is the distance between s_i and s_j. The amount of pheromone trail $\tau_{ij}(t)$ maintained at the connection between s_i and s_j represents the learned desirability of choosing s_j when at s_i point. $\tau_{ij}(t+1)$ is the pheromone concentration on the s_i to s_j route in the next time period. It is calculated via the addition of the heuristic values and the experience acquired by the ants. The possibility of this step follows Formula (22), where α and β are positive constants. The pheromone trail on the path from s_i to s_j is updated as Formula (23) where ρ is the pheromone evaporation coefficient expressed by a constant within interval (0, 1) and m is the total number of ants. $\Delta \tau_{ij}^k(t)$ is the pheromone trail deposited by ant k as in Formula (24). L_k is the length of the tour taken by ant k at step t. If ant k does not go from s_i to s_j at time t, then the pheromone left by ant k along this path is 0.

3. Problem Description and Optimal Model

3.1. Problem Description

Due to the large number of viruses and the constant emergence of new variants, epidemic outbreaks have the characteristic of being sudden and uncertain. According to the scale of the epidemic, it can be divided into two stages: a stable period and an outbreak period [22]. As shown in Figure 1, the number of cases increased significantly in April 2022; the data for this period are about nine times higher than those for March 2022 and about fourteen times higher than those for April 2021. Then, the number of cases fall back to the normal range in May 2022. Therefore, April 2022 can be classified as the outbreak period. The remaining months are classified as stable.

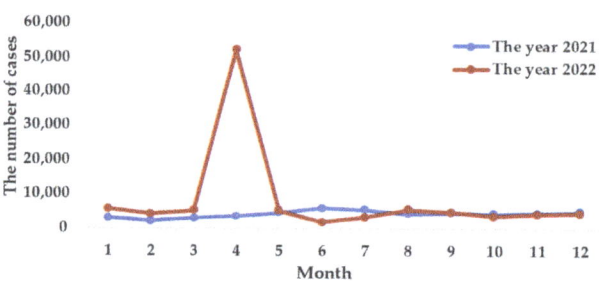

Figure 1. The report of legal infectious diseases in Shanghai.

The difference in the data in April between the two years is very large in Figure 1, which verifies the uncertainty feature of the outbreak. Because of the uncertainty of the outbreak, the additional demand for resources with an outbreak is difficult to estimate. For example, in order to solve the problem of material distribution during the peak in April 2022, an e-commerce platform first added 3246 couriers to Shanghai. However, it was found that the increase in staff was not enough. Then, another 1754 staff members were reassigned to Shanghai. It can be seen that the uncertain requirements and the dynamic situation of the epidemic are the main difficulties in resource allocation.

This paper focuses on solving the problem by coordinating the dispatch of various anti-epidemic materials in multiple regions and multiple periods, considering the changes in the emergency situation and the premise of uncertain demand.

3.2. Model Building

The following assumptions are made for the model: (1) There are three parties involved in the emergency supply system, including responsible organizations in the epidemic areas, suppliers of class A resources and suppliers of class B resources. (2) Three types of supplies—daily necessities, medical supplies and testing materials—are needed. Class A suppliers can provide daily necessities and testing materials; class B suppliers can provide medical supplies and daily necessities. (3) The threshold of requirements is set as *per*%, which means that at least *per*% of materials on the demand list must be met. (4) The production cycle of the suppliers is a unit time t, and the entire epidemic period is T. The process from producing goods to delivering them is shown in Figure 2, and the time difference between the production of a resource and its delivery is shown in Figure 3. The model parameters are shown in Table 1.

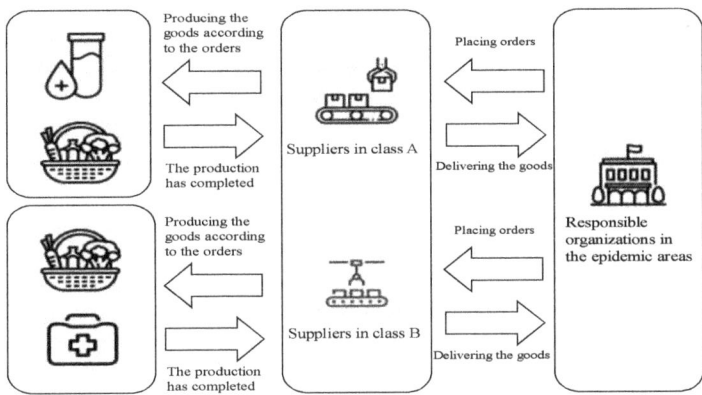

Figure 2. The process between the production of goods and their delivery.

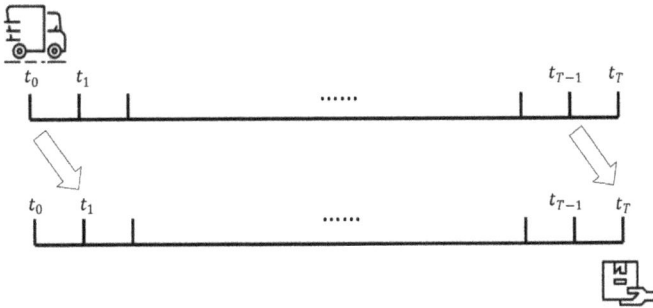

Figure 3. The time between the production of a resource and its delivery.

Table 1. Model parameters' definition.

Variables	Introduction	Variable Types
n	$n \in N$, N is the set of the epidemic areas	
m	$m \in M$, M is the set of suppliers in class A	Index variables
k	$k \in K$, K is the set of suppliers in class B	
t	Time t, $t = 0, 1, 2, \ldots, T$	
$p_n(t)$	The number of confirmed cases in area n at time t	
$lq_{mn}(t)$	The transportation volume of testing materials provided by the suppliers in class A	
$cq_{mn}(t)$	The transportation volume of daily necessities provided by the suppliers in class A	
$mq_{kn}(t)$	The transportation volume of medical supplies provided by the suppliers in class B	
$tq_{kn}(t)$	The transportation volume of daily necessities provided by the suppliers in class B	
al_m	The unit price of testing materials for class A	
ac_m	The unit price of daily necessities for class A	
bc_k	The unit price of daily necessities for class B	
bm_k	The unit price of medical supplies for class B	Parameter variables
ap_m	The shipment price of one item provided by class A for one kilometer	
bp_k	The shipment price of one item provided by class B for one kilometer	
s_{in}	Distance, $i = m, k$	
$ld_n(t)$	The requirement for testing materials in epidemic areas	
$md_n(t)$	The requirement for medical supplies in affected areas	
$cd_n(t)$	The requirement for daily necessities in affected areas	
max_{jm}	The maximum production capacity provided by suppliers in class A.	
max_{jk}	The maximum production capacity provided by suppliers in class B.	
ε_j	The penalty factor dependent on the difference between the requirement and real provision of goods.	
α_m	When Class A suppliers produce test materials, $\alpha_m = 1$; otherwise, $\alpha_m = 0$.	Decision variables
β_k	When Class B suppliers produce medical supplies, $\beta_k = 1$; otherwise, $\beta_k = 0$.	
j	$j = 1, 2, 3$ where j represents three kinds of materials. This is set as: 1 indicating testing materials, 2 indicating medical supplies, and 3 indicating daily necessities.	

The responsible organizations in the epidemic areas issue detailed information to the suppliers cataloged into A and B in stages according to the material demand according to type and quantity. The suppliers produce and transport the materials based on the orders, and the organizations pay the bill when the materials are delivered. The costs are computed as follows:

$$C_{A1} = \sum_{m \in M} lq_{mn}(t) \alpha_m (al_m + s_{mn} ap_m) \tag{25}$$

$$C_{A3} = \sum_{m \in M} cq_{mn}(t)(1 - \alpha_m)(ac_m + s_{mn} ap_m) \tag{26}$$

$$C_{B2} = \sum_{k \in K} mq_{kn}(t) \beta_k (bm_k + s_{kn} bp_k) \tag{27}$$

$$C_{B3} = \sum_{k \in K} tq_{kn}(t)(1 - \beta_k)(bc_k + s_{kn} bp_k) \tag{28}$$

There are two situations that can arise in the process of material supply, namely material shortage and material oversupply. The shortage of materials is not conducive to the implementation of emergency measures, while the oversupply of materials will generate carrying costs. The penalty cost is employed to describe the impact of these two scenarios and is calculated as follows:

$$CF_1 = \left| ld_n(t) - \sum_{m \in M} lq_{mn}(t) \right| \varepsilon_1 \tag{29}$$

$$CF_2 = \left| md_n(t) - \sum_{k \in K} mq_{kn}(t) \right| \varepsilon_2 \tag{30}$$

$$CF_3 = \left| cd_n(t) - \sum_{m \in M} cq_{mn}(t) - \sum_{k \in K} tq_{kn}(t) \right| \varepsilon_3 \tag{31}$$

A good solution should be generated via the selection of suitable suppliers to meet requirements at a low cost. Based on this idea, the objective functions are defined as follows:

$$\min f_{cost} = \sum_t^T C_{A1} + C_{A2} + C_{B2} + C_{B3} \tag{32}$$

$$\min f_{punish} = \sum_t^T \sum_{n \in N} CF_1 + CF_2 + CF_3 \tag{33}$$

s.t.

$$lq_{mn}(t) \leq max_{1m} \tag{34}$$

$$mq_{kn}(t) \leq max_{2k} \tag{35}$$

$$cq_{mn}(t) \leq max_{3m} \tag{36}$$

$$tq_{kn}(t) \leq max_{3k} \tag{37}$$

$$per\% \times ld_n(t+1) \leq lq_{mn}(t) \tag{38}$$

$$per\% \times md_n(t+1) \leq mq_{kn}(t) \tag{39}$$

$$per\% \times cd_n(t+1) \leq cq_{mn}(t) + tq_{kn}(t) \tag{40}$$

$$\alpha_m, \beta_k \in \{0, 1\} \tag{41}$$

$$t = 0, 1, 2, \ldots, T-1, \forall m \in M, n \in N, k \in K$$

Formulas (34)–(37) indicate the amount of materials transported by category A and B suppliers. They suggest that the amount of all the materials should not exceed their own production capacity. Formulas (38)–(40) indicate that all the materials transported by the suppliers in category A and B should meet at least $per\%$ of the needs of the epidemic area. Formula (41) indicates the decision variables by which materials are produced by class A and B suppliers.

3.3. Model Analysis

First, the model is built to achieve the goal of reducing costs while meeting material requirements. The cost is represented by money, an entity whose value as a commodity is equal to its value as money. Thus, the numerical value of currency can represent the value of goods [23]. However, this is a very complex problem that needs to consider both economic factors and living security. With a limited budget, it is helpful to consider economic factors, and living security is crucial. Therefore, two objective functions $\min f_{cost}$ and $\min f_{punish}$ are respectively defined to minimize the cost and the difference between of supply quantity and the required quantity. To sum up, the problem studied in this paper is still an optimization problem in essence. In order to solve it, there are two main ways to build the framework of the model: one is called predict-then-optimize, and the other is called Smart "Predict, then Optimize" (SPO) [24]. These two modes have different focuses on prediction. Predict-then-Optimize attaches great importance to the accuracy of prediction, while SPO pays more attention to the bias cost of decisions in similar situations. Considering that the prediction part of the paper aims at material demand, the accurate matching of material demand and supply is one of the most important requirements in the rescue process, so this paper chose the predict-then-optimize framework to establish the model.

Second, the number of confirmed cases, denoted as $p_n(t)$, is a dynamic variable affected by time; as a sequenced result, the amount of various emergency materials expressed as $ld_n(t), md_n(t), cd_n(t)$ are also changed. This improves the uncertainty and increases the difficulty of this problem. In this work, the number of confirmed cases at time t is set as the first parameter affecting others because the requirement for supplies at a given time in the epidemic area is mainly affected by the number of infected people [25]. Formula (42) is the prediction formula where $p_n(t)$ is the result of the gray prediction model. To obtain the value of $p_n(t)$, the number of confirmed patients in θ periods before time t is taken as the input for the gray prediction method, which is used to predict the possible number of confirmed patients at the following times. Adjusting θ can change the input number of variables in the gray prediction model so as to adjust the prediction results. The specific adjustment analysis is discussed in the subsequent experiment. Then, the material requirement is obtained by converting the predicted results through Formulas (43)–(45). $ld_n(t)$, $md_n(t)$ and $cd_n(t)$ are determined by $p_n(t)$. xd, yd, and zd are respectively the demand coefficients of the three types of materials.

$$p_n(t) = f_{GM(1,1)}(p_n(t - \theta)) \tag{42}$$

$$ld_n(t) = xd \cdot p_n(t) \tag{43}$$

$$md_n(t) = yd \cdot p_n(t) \tag{44}$$

$$cd_n(t) = zd \cdot p_n(t) \tag{45}$$

The model randomly generates several groups of feasible solutions and uses the ant colony algorithm to optimize each group of feasible solutions. Finally, we compare the optimization results to obtain the resource procurement allocation scheme. The original ant colony algorithm mentioned above relies on the experience of all ants to drive. This method is limited to high-dimensional problems because the large solution space weakens the effect of the rule of thumb of ants. Therefore, for high-dimensional problems, randomness is added to help expand the search scope of the solution while considering the experience accumulation of ants [26]. Inspired by this, this paper proposes an alternative treatment to help ants explore the solution space. The process of optimizing feasible solutions is as follows. In the optimization process, the model aims to achieve lower costs by changing the transportation schedule at time t. So, at time t, the model sets $LQ(t) = \left\{ lq_{ij}(t) \middle| i \in M, K; j \in N \right\}$ as the transport matrix, and $lq_{ij}(t)$ represents the amount of materials transported by supplier i to responsible organization j, which is also the number of orders issued by responsible organization j to supplier i. The difference between the transportation volume before adjustment and the volume after is $\Delta lq_{ij}(t)$. The adjustment directions are divided into three categories: increase, decrease and unchanged. $lq_{ij}'(t)$ is set as the transportation volume at time t after adjustment, and its relationship with $lq_{ij}(t)$ is shown in Formula (46).

$$lq_{ij}'(t) = lq_{ij}(t) + d_{ij} \times \Delta lq_{ij}(t) \tag{46}$$

$$D^t = \{d_{ij} | i \in M, K; j \in N\} \tag{47}$$

d_{ij} denotes the direction of adjustment, which belongs to $\{1, 0, -1\}$. D^t is the set of d_{ij} at time t. If we assume $TD = \{td\}$ is the set of all the directions that the ant can choose, then D^t belongs to TD. The initial solution should be able to explain the origin and the end of the transportation and the transportation volumes at any moment, meaning that it should be a three-dimensional matrix. In the original ant colony algorithm, each iteration indicates that each ant has finished its journey. For this model, it signifies that every $lq_{ij}(t)$ in the solution has changed, where $t \in T$, $i \in M, K$, $j \in N$. However, there are so many variables that it is hard for the model to obtain the final scheme, even with the help of the remaining pheromone trail. Therefore, this paper sets another utility function to lead an ant to reach its destination faster. Formulas (48)–(55) explain the mechanism of the utility function.

$$f_{ant}\left(lq_{ij}(t)\right) = \gamma f_{cost}(t) + \omega f_{punish}(t) \tag{48}$$

$$\Delta f_{ant} = f_{ant}\left(lq_{ij}'(t)\right) - f_{ant}\left(lq_{ij}(t)\right) \tag{49}$$

$$g_{ant} = \begin{cases} 1, & \Delta f_{ant} > 0 \\ 0, & \Delta f_{ant} \leq 0 \end{cases} \tag{50}$$

$$P\left(D^{t+1} = td\right) = P_{td}(c) + g_{ant} \times \Delta f_{ant} \times f_{ant}\left(lq_{ij}(t)\right)^{-1} \tag{51}$$

$$P_{td' \neq td}\left(D^{t+1} = td'\right) = P_{td}(c) - g_{ant} \times \Delta f_{ant} \times \left(f_{ant}\left(lq_{ij}(t)\right) \times (|TD| - 1)\right)^{-1} \tag{52}$$

$$\Delta \tau_{td}^{ant}(c) = \begin{cases} \sum_{t, D^t = td} \Delta f_{ant}, & \text{if ant choose } td \text{ at time } t \text{ during step } c \\ 0, & \text{otherwise} \end{cases} \tag{53}$$

$$\tau_{td}(c+1) = \rho \tau_{td}(c) + \frac{\sum_{ant} \Delta \tau_{td}^{ant}(c)}{\sum_{td \in TD} \sum_{ant} \Delta \tau_{td}^{ant}(c)} \tag{54}$$

$$P_{td}(c) = \frac{\tau_{td}(c)^\alpha \eta_{td}^\beta}{\sum_{td \in TD} \tau_{td}(c)^\alpha \eta_{td}^\beta} \tag{55}$$

If the *ant* chooses the direction *td* at time *t*, then $D^t = td$. $f_{ant}\left(lq_{ij}(t)\right)$ is the utility function that consists of $f_{cost}(t)$ and $f_{punish}(t)$. γ, ω are used to adjust the weight. Δf_{ant} is the difference in the transportation volume before and after the change at time *t*. g_{ant} represents the effect of *ant* making this change. $P(D^{t+1} = td)$ is the probability of choosing direction *td* at time $t + 1$. At the same time, the probability of picking the other directions decrease equally as Formula (52). *c* represents the number of iterations of the optimization process. Then, as in Formulas (53)–(55), after all ants have finished their journey, they exchange experiences and then move on to the next iteration. The solution process for the algorithm is shown in Figure 4.

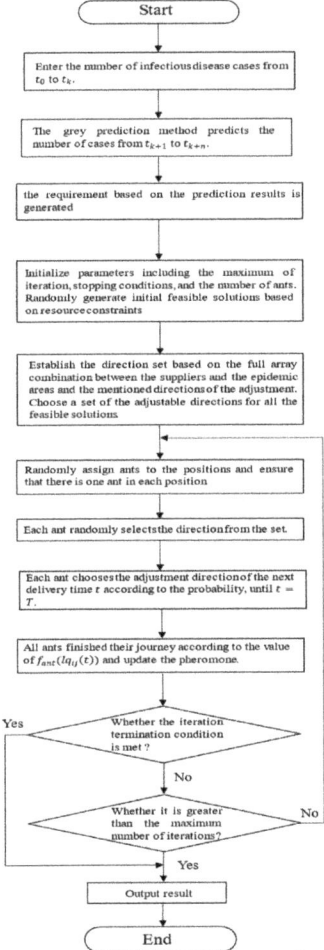

Figure 4. Flow chart of the MS-CR-U.

Now, the complete model named the Multi-catalog Schedule Considering Costs and Requirements Under Uncertainty (MS-CR-U) has been introduced. First, the uncertainty caused by the dynamic characteristics of epidemics is measured through the gray prediction method. A multi-catalog model means that the types of materials and catalogs of suppliers are both partitioned because most of the suppliers focus on fixed goods. The production ability, cost and requirements are taken into the objective functions defined by the model to improve the application. Finally, the ant colony algorithm is employed to provide the solution for the model. The details of the model designed based on the ant colony algorithm are as follows:

Step 1: Enter the number of infectious disease cases from t_0 to t_k.
Step 2: After the gray prediction method predicts the number of cases from t_{k+1} to t_{k+n}, the requirement based on the prediction results is generated according to Formulas (42)–(45).
Step 3: Initialize parameters, including the maximum iterations, stopping conditions and the number of ants. Randomly generate initial feasible solutions based on resource constraints according to Formulas (34)–(41).
Step 4: Establish the direction set based on the full array combination between the suppliers and the epidemic areas and the mentioned directions of the adjustment. Choose a set of adjustable directions for all feasible solutions.
Step 5: Randomly assign ants to the positions and ensure that there is one ant in each position.
Step 6: Each ant randomly selects the direction from the set.
Step 7: Each ant chooses the adjustment direction of the next delivery time according to the Formulas (50)–(52), until $t = T$.
Step 8: All ants finish their journey and update the pheromone according to the Formulas (53)–(55).
Step 9: Check the stopping criterion. If yes, go to Step 11; otherwise, go to Step 10.
Step 10: Check whether the upper limit is reached. If yes, continue; otherwise, go to Step 5.
Step 11: Output the result.

4. Data Analysis and Prediction Results

The problem solved using the MS-CR-U is to build a complete method for coordinating and dispatching multiple anti-epidemic materials under the condition of varied requirements during the epidemic period. In order to foresee possible situations, the number of historical infectious disease cases is used to sum up past experience. Additionally, it should be noted that climate is an important factor affecting the occurrence and spread of infectious diseases [27]. Thus, the mean temperature and precipitation data from 2020 to 2022 for 34 cities are shown in Figure 5. After observing the data, three types of characteristic climate items can be described, which are called the south type, north type and north–south junction. As the spread of infectious diseases is also related to the population size, in order to control the variables, this paper selects three cities with similar population sizes from the three climate types to collect statistics for infectious diseases. The data came from the websites of the health commissions of the three cities. As the date of the earliest data in the three cities is not consistent, the data from January 2018 to August 2022 are uniformly utilized for collation.

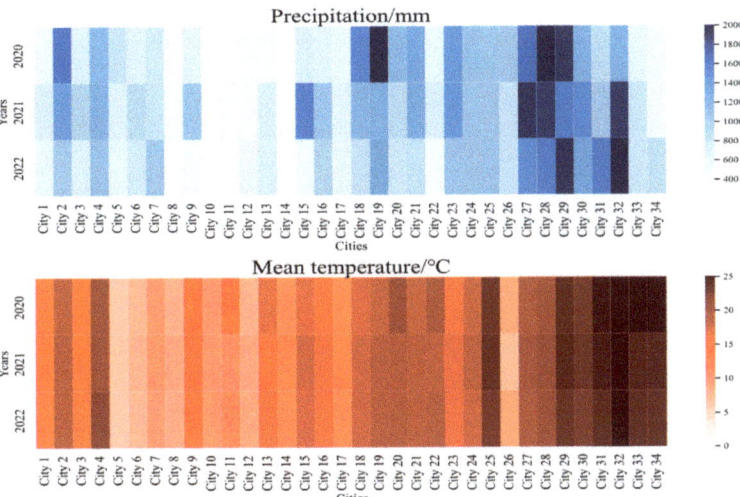

Figure 5. Heat map of precipitation and average temperature.

4.1. Data Analysis

As shown in Figure 6a, in January 2019, there was a peak in the outbreak of infectious diseases in City 3. Within one month, the growth rate of infectious disease was as high as 425.5%. According to a public report, from December 2018 to January 2019, the temperatures of City 3 dropped significantly. In early December 2018, the temperature in City 3 remained around 10 to 20 degrees, but in early January 2019, the temperature dropped to −1 to 5 degrees. Within a month, the average temperature dropped by 52.25% and the Air Quality Index (AQI) increased by 19.15%. Based on the situation that climate change is predicted to increase the frequency and intensity of extreme weather events, amplifying air pollution levels and exacerbating respiratory diseases [28], and many people were infected with influence because they could not adapt to the temperature change. That is why the number of cases in City 3 soared within a month. Between the end of 2019 and the beginning of 2020, there was a small peak in Cities 2 and 3. Due to a series of epidemic prevention measures taken after the outbreak, the total number of infectious diseases in the three cities decreased by 57.7% in 2020. People adopted the habit of wearing masks, which effectively limited the spread of infectious diseases. During 2022, the number of cases in Cities 2 and 3 increased slightly at different time points. On account of the continuous mutations in the novel coronavirus in the process of transmission, the spread of new strains led to repeated outbreaks.

As shown in Figure 6b, various indicators in the data for the three cities are discussed. From 2018 to 2021, the mean, median and standard deviation for City 1 were significantly lower than those for Cities 2 and 3, indicating that the epidemic scale in City 1 was smaller than in the others, on the whole. Vertically, the three indexes for City 1 are close, meaning that the distribution of the number of cases in each month is relatively average and the outbreak scale is relatively stable. The annual mean and median for Cities 2 and 3 are similar, and the difference between them and the standard deviation is large. This means that the number of cases in each month fluctuates within a similar amplitude and the scale of outbreaks is highly variable.

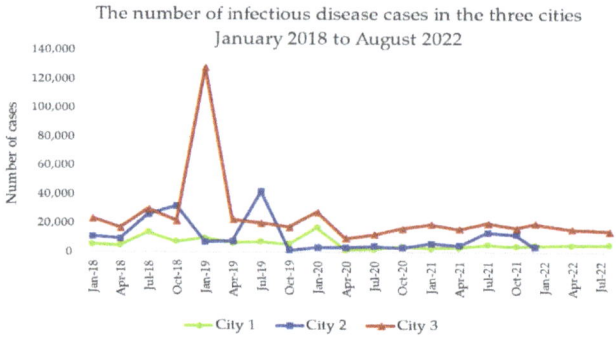

(**a**) The number of infectious disease cases.

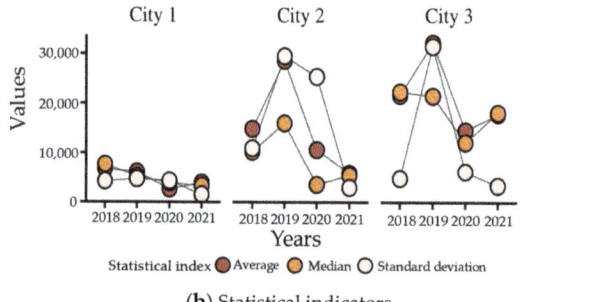

(**b**) Statistical indicators.

Figure 6. (**a**) The number of infectious disease cases in three cities from January 2018 to August 2022; (**b**) statistical indicators of the three cities from 2018 to 2021.

4.2. Demand Forecasting

After the analysis of infectious disease data in these three cities, the gray prediction method is used to predict the number of cases in the three cities from August 2021 to August 2022. The model and prediction results are evaluated. The results are reached in two ways. (1) In order to compare the results, gray prediction, SVM [29], the random forest model [30] and LSTM [31] are used to predict the data. The three criteria of the mean absolute error (MAE), mean absolute percentage error (MAPE), and root-mean-square percentage error (RMSPE) is set to measure the performance. (2) The gray prediction model is also evaluated via its own three test methods. The test results are shown in Table 2.

Table 2. Comparison of the test indexes among the prediction methods.

Methods	City 1			City 2			City 3		
	MAE	MAPE	RMSPE	MAE	MAPE	RMSPE	MAE	MAPE	RMSPE
SVM	5520	1.66	0.95	15,261	1.60	0.87	11,642	0.41	0.17
RF	2660	0.86	0.49	5069	0.67	0.39	11,992	0.52	0.29
LSTM	1152	0.43	0.27	6705	0.95	0.46	8235	0.29	0.13
GM(1,1)	618	0.18	0.08	4040	0.40	0.18	5936	0.24	0.16

For City 1 and City 2, the three indicators of the gray prediction are superior to the other three methods. For City 3, the root-mean-square of the gray prediction is slightly inferior to that of LSTM, but other indicators are also superior to those of other models. Because the gray prediction model relies on the analysis of the change rule in the short term to realize the prediction of the next stage, further analysis is conducted on the data for the three cities. It is found that the growth rate of the number of cases in City 3 from October 2018 to January 2019 is not only higher than the average growth rate of City 1 and City 2 but is also higher than the average growth rate of City 3 from January to September 2018. The change rule of data is broken in a short period of time, which means that the root-mean-square percentage of the gray prediction was slightly higher than that of the LSTM model. However, LSTM requires a large number of samples in the training process to improve its accuracy, while the gray prediction method only needs a small number of samples to complete the prediction. In addition, the gray prediction model outperforms LSTM in two of the three indexes. Given that the sample size is small, gray prediction has more advantages in dealing with this paper.

In addition to the above three indicators, gray prediction has three special testing methods. The results of the three testing methods are shown in Table 3. For the posterior difference test, when $C < 0.65, p > 0.7$, the method is qualified; for the residual test, when $\alpha = 0.05$ and the residual test value is less than α, the method is tested. For the correlation degree test, when $\rho = 0.5$ and $\eta(k)$ is greater than 0.6, it is qualified. With the results in Table 3, the values of the three indicators all meet the standards, proving that the model is suitable for this topic. The predicted results given by the gray prediction model of the number of cases in the three cities from August 2021 to August 2022 are shown in Figure 7.

Table 3. The results of the three test criteria for gray prediction.

	City 1	City 2	City 3
posterior-variance-test	$\overline{C} = 0.46, \overline{p} = 0.81$	$\overline{C} = 0.40, \overline{p} = 0.73$	$\overline{C} = 0.42, \overline{p} = 0.76$
residual test ($\alpha = 0.05$)	$\overline{\Phi} = 0.034$	$\overline{\Phi} = 0.045$	$\overline{\Phi} = 0.049$
correlation test ($\rho = 0.5$)	$\eta(k) = 0.71$	$\eta(k) = 0.88$	$\eta(k) = 0.81$

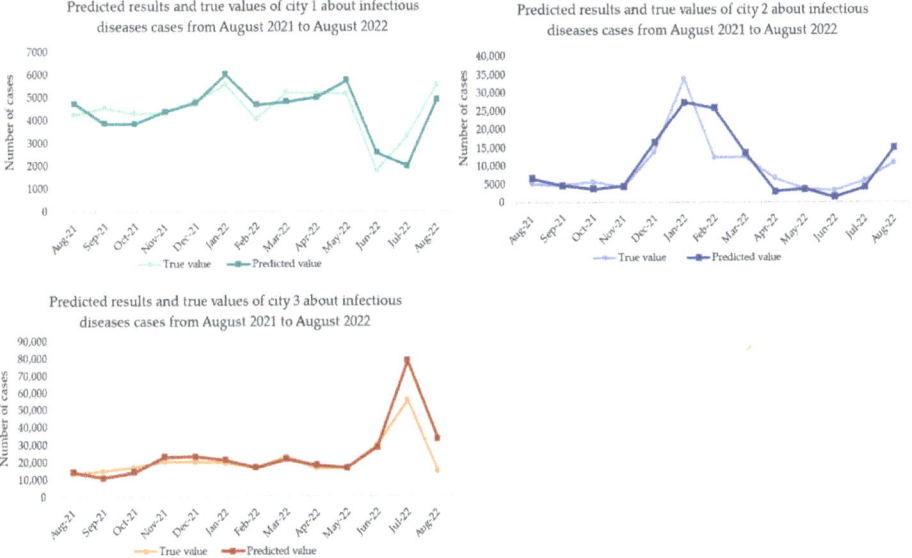

Figure 7. The predicted results given by the gray prediction model and true values for the three cities for infectious disease cases from August 2021 to August 2022.

Compared with the above indicators, this paper uses the gray prediction model to complete the prediction job in the model. Considering that there are two parameters in the gray prediction model, the paper studied their influence on the gray prediction model by adjusting them, and the results are shown in Figure 8.

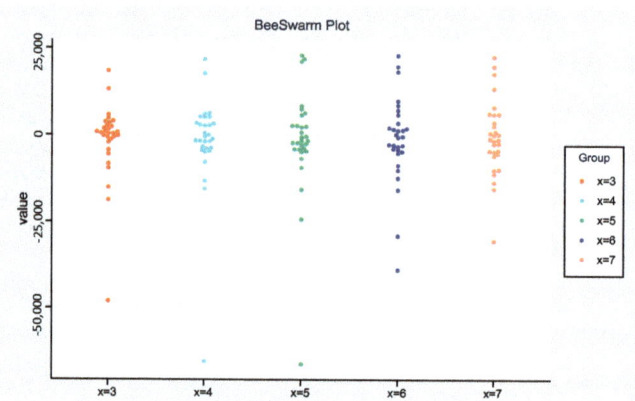

Figure 8. The difference between the true and predicted values when $y = 1$.

The two parameters of the gray prediction model are the number of input variables x and the number of outputs y. As shown in Figure 8, we changed the value of x and fix y. The results generally indicate that when y is fixed, the larger x is, the larger the gap is between the true and predicted values. It is concluded that for every unit increase in x, MAE will increase by 25.52% on average. Since the degree of dispersion is more obvious when $x = 6$ and 7, the remaining three cases are chosen for further analysis. Figure 9 shows that a change in y also causes a change in prediction accuracy. Increasing y will decrease the accuracy of gray prediction model. For every additional unit of y, MAPE increases by 0.55 on average. By comparing the MAE and MAPE of each group x and y, $x = 4$ and $y = 1$ are finally selected.

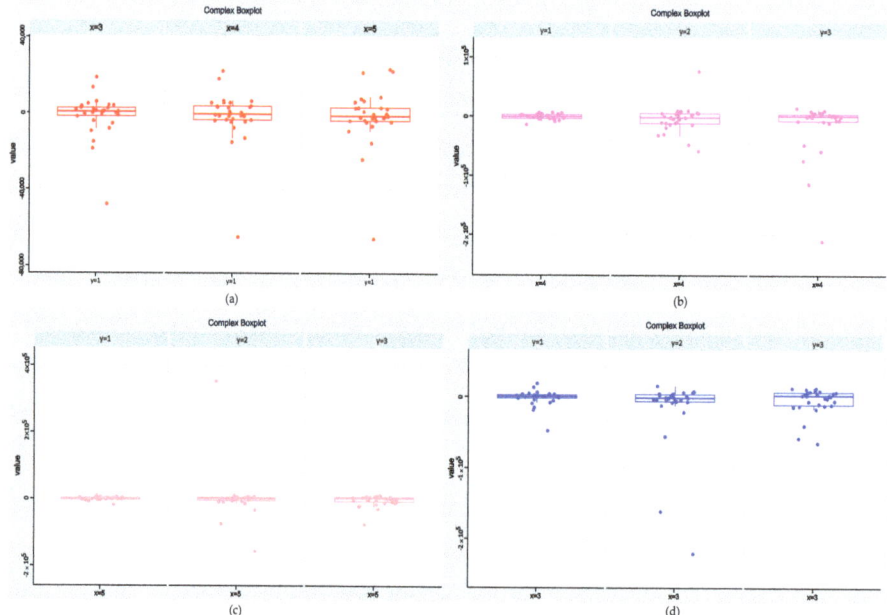

Figure 9. (**a**) It shows the effect of changing x on the error when $y = 1$; (**b**–**d**) show the effect of changing y on prediction accuracy when x is fixed.

4.3. Experimental Design

As shown in Figure 7, the number of cases in City 2 increased significantly from November 2021 to December 2021 and reached 232.76% within a month. After four months, the number of infectious diseases fell back into the original range, which implies the epidemic broke out suddenly, in a short period of time. This situation is consistent with the problems discussed in this paper. Therefore, we chose City 2 as the discussed site. The period T of the epidemic is set from September 2021 to April 2022, for which the unit of time t denotes one month. The period from September 2021 to November 2021 is treated as the pre-stage, and the period from December 2021 to April 2022 is treated as the post-stage. Nine cities are randomly selected as the locations of suppliers, among which five are the locations of suppliers in class A and four are the locations of class B suppliers. Table 4 shows the monthly demand for materials in the epidemic area. Tables 5 and 6 show class A and class B suppliers' production capacity, material pricing and the distance between epidemic area and them. The gray prediction model is used to predict the number of cases from October 2021 to April 2022. According to the predicted results, the monthly demand for daily essential materials, testing materials and medical materials in epidemic areas is obtained.

Table 4. The demand for materials per unit of time in the epidemic areas.

T	Type of Materials		
	Daily Necessities	Test Materials	Medical Supplies
t_1	11,221	748	3740
t_2	13,264	884	4421
t_3	48,769	3251	16,256
t_4	81,906	5460	27,302
t_5	77,244	5149	25,748
t_6	40,638	2709	13,546
t_7	9033	602	3011

Table 5. Class A suppliers' production capacity, material pricing and transportation distance.

	Daily Necessities		Test Materials		Transportation Cost	
	Productive Capacity	Material Pricing	Productive Capacity	Material Pricing	Transport Distance	Shipping Unit Price
A_1	25,000	34	2400	6.5	1171	18
A_2	25,000	40	2500	8	1293	12
A_3	26,000	45	2800	7	1021	17
A_4	22,000	35	2500	5.5	1090	16
A_5	28,000	43	2600	6	1397	19

Table 6. Class B suppliers' production capacity, material pricing and transportation distance.

	Daily Necessities		Medical Materials		Transportation Cost	
	Productive Capacity	Material Pricing	Productive Capacity	Material Pricing	Transport Distance	Shipping Unit Price
B_1	24,000	33	12,000	148	695	13
B_2	27,000	37	18,000	128	692	12
B_3	26,000	37	16,000	185	821	14
B_4	25,000	30	14,000	160	721	15

The penalty function in the objective function contains the weight coefficients. Sensitivity analysis of parameters was performed before weights were determined and the result is presented as Figure 10. ST values of $\varepsilon_1, \varepsilon_2, \varepsilon_3$ are 0.36, 0.33 and 0.31, and the S1 values are the same as ST. It is concluded that $\varepsilon_1, \varepsilon_2, \varepsilon_3$ generally has the same influence on the penalty value. In order to ensure that each material is of similar importance, we set $per = 80$ and $\varepsilon_1 = \varepsilon_2 = \varepsilon_3 = \gamma = \omega = 1$. Then, the solution for the model is compared with the solution for the random configuration model.

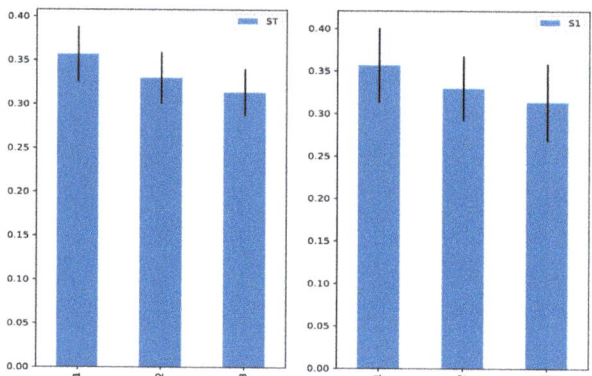

Figure 10. Sensitivity analysis of weight parameters of penalty function.

Heuristic algorithms should find a balance between intensification and diversification [32]. Therefore, extensive parameter tuning and sensitivity analysis are needed for algorithmic design. In ACO, the number of ants affect the performance of the algorithm to some extent. This paper adjusts the number of ants to compare the optimization performance and optimization time of the algorithm. Figure 11 shows the results of the comparison. Generally, as the ant population increases, the cost of the emergency plan decreases but the algorithm takes longer. The optimization results and optimization time increase by an average of 6.8% and 21.19% for each increase of 10 ants. Finally, this paper determine that the number of ants is 50. In total, 50 groups of solutions satisfying the constraint conditions are randomly generated, and these 50 groups of feasible solutions are taken as the solutions for the stochastic resource allocation model. The costs of these 50 schemes are calculated. The resource procurement allocation scheme provided by the MS-CR-U is compared with the original random scheme. At the same time, we calculate the demand satisfaction rate of the MS-CR-U to further verify the feasibility of the solution. The results are shown in Table 7. The optimization process is shown in Figure 12. Compared with the random resource allocation model, the cost of the procurement allocation scheme provided by the MS-CR-U decrease by 55.59% on average.

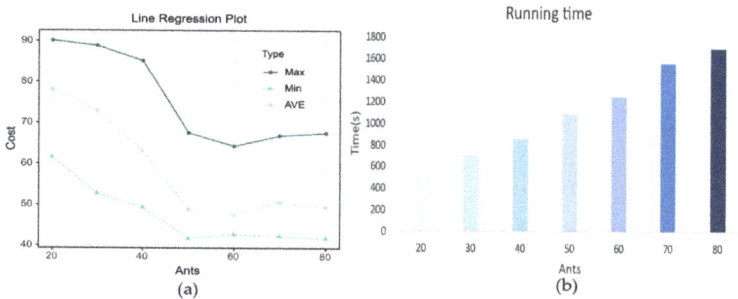

Figure 11. The optimization performance and optimization time of the algorithm. (**a**) The cost of different solutions obtained by adjusting the ant population. (**b**) The time taken to solve the model under different ant population.

Table 7. Comparison of the cost results of the different models.

Unit: $\times 10^8$ CNY	Random Resource Allocation Model	MS-CR-U
Maximum cost	139.75	67.46
Minimum cost	72.85	41.75
Average cost	108.60	48.23

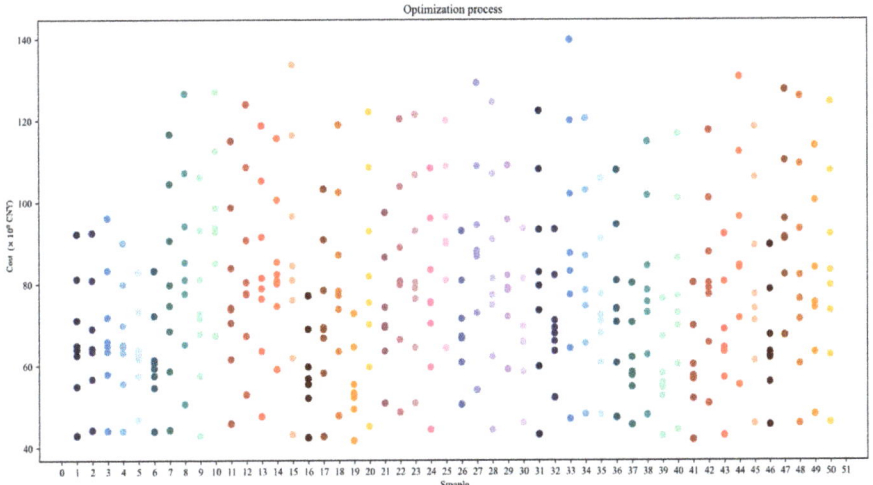

Figure 12. The model optimization process. Different colors indicate different solutions.

$\alpha_M = \{\alpha_m | m = 1, 2, 3, 4, 5\}$ is the set of decision variables for class A suppliers. When class A suppliers produce test materials, $\alpha_m = 1$; otherwise, $\alpha_m = 0$. $\beta_K = \{\beta_k | k = 1, 2, 3, 4\}$. When class B suppliers produce medical supplies, $\beta_k = 1$; otherwise, $\beta_k = 0$. Formula (56) shows the production arrangements reached by the suppliers in class A and B and the responsible organizations. Formula (57) is the cost of the solution given by the model. Formula (58) is the penalty cost calculated using the model. The final solution given by the MS-CR-U is shown in Table 8. At this time, the required cost of the solution is CNY 4.175 billion. The penalty cost means that the solution is short of 4124 items, including 41 testing material items, 1321 medical material items, and 2762 daily essential items.

$$\alpha_M = [1, 1, 1, 0, 1], \beta_M = [1, 0, 0, 1] \tag{56}$$

$$\min f_{cost} = 41.75 \times 10^8 \tag{57}$$

$$\min f_{punish} = 4124 \tag{58}$$

Table 8. A and B supplier emergency materials transportation plans during the epidemic period.

Time	A_1	A_2	A_3	A_4	A_5	B_1	B_2	B_3	B_4
t_0	0	742	0	0	0	3738	11,218	0	0
t_1	0	856	0	0	0	4415	13,256	0	0
t_2	0	2472	776	0	0	11,984	26,982	21,781	4272
t_3	158	2489	2782	22,000	35	12,000	27,000	26,000	14,000
t_4	63	2479	2600	22,000	10	11,976	27,000	26,000	13,772
t_5	0	2482	223	0	0	12,000	27,000	13,644	1554
t_6	0	561	34	0	0	2992	9017	0	0

To summarize, the MS-CR-U in this paper can be used to predict the number of cases in the future based on historical epidemic information and can convert the prediction results in order to obtain the demand for different materials. The requirements for various materials are taken as the input for the proposed model to generate a reasonable schedule. Thus, it is helpful in the procurement and allocation plan of emergency supplies before and after the outbreak of an epidemic. The results show that the MS-CR-U is superior to the random resource allocation model in terms of cost. Furthermore, the demand satisfaction rate of three types of emergency materials is calculated, with the guaranteed rate of living essentials being about 99.26%, the guaranteed rate of testing materials being approximately 99.27%, and the guaranteed rate of medical materials being about 99.27%. The total results prove that the scheme given by the MS-CR-U is feasible.

5. Conclusions

This paper mainly studies the method of coordinating suppliers to complete the scheduling of multiple materials in a period of time under the circumstances of uncertain demand and a dynamic epidemic situation. This paper considers the two stages, the stable period and the outbreak period, aiming to minimize the cost and meet material demand, and proposes a coordinated allocation model of multiple materials based on the gray prediction model. In view of uncertain demand, the gray prediction method is used to predict the number of confirmed cases in the following time period, and this number is utilized to estimate the possible emergency demand. Then, the Multi-catalog Schedule Considering Costs and Requirements Under Uncertainty is completed to find the final solution, which is based on the ant colony algorithm. In the proposed model, the optimization direction is represented by the adjacency matrix. The effect of selection by a single ant each time is calculated via the establishment of a utility function to adjust the probability of each direction and screen out the optimal direction. Finally, examples and related indicators demonstrate the qualifications of the model. We found that the cost of the material scheduling model is superior to other models when material demand is guaranteed. Thus, the model can provide support in decisions regarding material scheduling during an epidemic. The main consideration of this paper is the problem of demand uncertainty in emergencies. Considering the impact of emergency events on the market, the future work plan will be further discussed and studied on the influence of material price changes on decision-making based on the paper.

Author Contributions: Methodology, B.L.; software, Q.L. All authors have read and agreed to the published version of the manuscript.

Funding: This research was funded by the National Natural Science Foundation of China (72004174).

Data Availability Statement: The meteorological data come from http://www.meteomanz.com/index?l=1 (accessed on 15 September 2022). The infectious disease statistics come from https://wsjkw.sh.gov.cn/; http://wjw.beijing.gov.cn/English/; https://wsjkw.cq.gov.cn/ (accessed on 15 September 2022). No new data were created.

Conflicts of Interest: The authors declare no conflict of interest.

References

1. Li, M.; Zhang, C.; Ding, M.; Lv, R. A Two-Stage Stochastic Variational Inequality Model for Storage and Dynamic Distribution of Medical Supplies in Epidemic Management. *Appl. Math. Model.* **2022**, *102*, 35–61. [CrossRef] [PubMed]
2. Caunhye, A.M.; Zhang, Y.; Li, M.; Nie, X. A Location-Routing Model for Prepositioning and Distributing Emergency Supplies. *Transp. Res. Part E Logist. Transp. Rev.* **2016**, *90*, 161–176. [CrossRef]
3. Fei, L.; Wang, Y. Demand Prediction of Emergency Materials Using Case-Based Reasoning Extended by the Dempster-Shafer Theory. *Socio-Econ. Plan. Sci.* **2022**, *84*, 101386. [CrossRef]
4. Zhang, M.; Kong, Z. A Multi-Attribute Double Auction and Bargaining Model for Emergency Material Procurement. *Int. J. Prod. Econ.* **2022**, *254*, 108635. [CrossRef]
5. Iris, C.; Cevikcan, E. A Fuzzy Linear Programming Approach for Aggregate Production Planning. In *Supply Chain Management under Fuzziness*; Springer: Berlin/Heidelberg, Germany, 2014; pp. 355–374.

6. Zhou, J.; Reniers, G. Petri-net Based Cooperation Modeling and Time Analysis of Emergency Response in the Context of Domino Effect Prevention in Process Industries. *Reliab. Eng. Syst. Saf.* **2022**, *223*, 108505. [CrossRef]
7. Zhang, X.; Lam, J.S.L.; Iris, Ç. Cold Chain Shipping Mode Choice with Environmental and Financial Perspectives. *Transp. Res. Part D Transp. Environ.* **2020**, *87*, 102537. [CrossRef]
8. Zhang, Q.; Xiong, S. Routing Optimization of Emergency Grain Distribution Vehicles Using the Immune Ant Colony Optimization Algorithm. *Appl. Soft Comput.* **2018**, *71*, 917–925. [CrossRef]
9. Liu, Q.; He, R.; Zhang, L. Simulation-Based Multi-Objective Optimization for Enhanced Safety of Fire Emergency Response in Metro Stations. *Reliab. Eng. Syst. Saf.* **2022**, *228*, 108810. [CrossRef]
10. Liu, J.; Dong, C.; An, S. Integration and Modularization: Research on Urban Cross-Regional Emergency Cooperation Based on the Network Approach. *Int. J. Disaster Risk Reduct.* **2022**, *82*, 103375. [CrossRef]
11. Feng, J.R.; Gai, W.M.; Li, J.Y. Multi-Objective Optimization of Rescue Station Selection for Emergency Logistics Management. *Saf. Sci.* **2019**, *120*, 276–282. [CrossRef]
12. Wang, B.C.; Qian, Q.Y.; Gao, J.J.; Tan, Z.Y.; Zhou, Y. The Optimization of Warehouse Location and Resources Distribution for Emergency Rescue under Uncertainty. *Adv. Eng. Inform.* **2021**, *48*, 101278. [CrossRef]
13. Franco, C.; Alfonso-Lizarazo, E. Optimization under Uncertainty of the Pharmaceutical Supply Chain in Hospitals. *Comput. Chem. Eng.* **2020**, *135*, 106689. [CrossRef]
14. Shang, X.; Zhang, G.; Jia, B.; Almanaseer, M. The Healthcare Supply Location-Inventory-Routing Problem: A Robust Approach. *Transp. Res. Part E Logist. Transp. Rev.* **2022**, *158*, 102588. [CrossRef]
15. Rebeeh, Y.; Pokharel, S.; Abdella, G.M.; Hammuda, A. A Framework Based on Location Hazard Index for Optimizing Operational Performance of Emergency Response Strategies: The Case of Petrochemical Industrial Cities. *Saf. Sci.* **2019**, *117*, 33–42. [CrossRef]
16. Ferri, P.; Sáez, C.; Félix-De Castro, A.; Juan-Albarracín, J.; Blanes-Selva, V.; Sánchez-Cuesta, P.; García-Gómez, J.M. Deep Ensemble Multitask Classification of Emergency Medical Call Incidents Combining Multimodal Data Improves Emergency Medical Dispatch. *Artif. Intell. Med.* **2021**, *117*, 102088. [CrossRef] [PubMed]
17. Liu, H.; Sun, Y.; Pan, N.; Li, Y.; An, Y.; Pan, D. Study on the Optimization of Urban Emergency Supplies Distribution Paths for Epidemic Outbreaks. *Comput. Oper. Res.* **2022**, *146*, 105912. [CrossRef]
18. Abazari, S.R.; Aghsami, A.; Rabbani, M. Prepositioning and Distributing Relief Items in Humanitarian Logistics with Uncertain Parameters. *Socio-Econ. Plan. Sci.* **2021**, *74*, 100933. [CrossRef]
19. Ceylan, Z. Short-Term Prediction of COVID-19 Spread Using Grey Rolling Model Optimized by Particle Swarm Optimization. *Appl. Soft Comput.* **2021**, *109*, 107592. [CrossRef]
20. Tseng, F.M.; Yu, H.C.; Tzeng, G.H. Applied Hybrid Grey Model to Forecast Seasonal Time Series. *Technol. Forecast. Soc. Change* **2001**, *67*, 291–302. [CrossRef]
21. Dorigo, M.; Di Caro, G. Ant colony optimization: A new meta-heuristic. In Proceedings of the 1999 Congress on Evolutionary Computation-CEC99 (Cat. No. 99TH8406), Washington, DC, USA, 6–9 July 1999; Volume 1472, pp. 1470–1477.
22. Anzai, A.; Nishiura, H. Doubling Time of Infectious Diseases. *J. Theor. Biol.* **2022**, *554*, 111278. [CrossRef]
23. Lapavitsas, C. Money and the Analysis of Capitalism: The Significance of Commodity Money. *Rev. Radic. Political Econ.* **2000**, *32*, 631–656. [CrossRef]
24. Elmachtoub, A.N.; Grigas, P. Smart "Predict, Then Optimize". *Manag. Sci.* **2022**, *68*, 9–26. [CrossRef]
25. Shokouhifar, M.; Ranjbarimesan, M. Multivariate Time-Series Blood Donation/Demand Forecasting for Resilient Supply Chain Management during COVID-19 Pandemic. *Clean. Logist. Supply Chain* **2022**, *5*, 100078. [CrossRef]
26. Zhu, Q.; Yang, Z.; Ma, W. A Quickly Convergent Continuous Ant Colony Optimization Algorithm with Scout Ants. *Appl. Math. Comput.* **2011**, *218*, 1805–1819. [CrossRef]
27. Chew, A.W.Z.; Wang, Y.; Zhang, L. Correlating Dynamic Climate Conditions and Socioeconomic-Governmental Factors to Spatiotemporal Spread of COVID-19 via Semantic Segmentation Deep Learning Analysis. *Sustain. Cities Soc.* **2021**, *75*, 103231. [CrossRef]
28. Tran, H.M.; Tsai, F.-J.; Lee, Y.-L. The Impact of Air Pollution on Respiratory Diseases in an Era of Climate Change: A Review of the Current Evidence. *Sci. Total Environ.* **2023**, *898*, 166340. [CrossRef]
29. van den Burg, G.J.J.; Groenen, P.J.F. GenSVM: A generalized multiclass support vector machine. *J. Mach. Learn. Res.* **2016**, *17*, 1–42.
30. Athey, S.; Tibshirani, J.; Wager, S. Generalized Random Forests. *Ann. Stat.* **2019**, *47*, 1148–1178. [CrossRef]
31. Shi, X.; Chen, Z.; Wang, H. Convolutional LSTM network: A machine learning approach for precipitation nowcasting. In Proceedings of the 29th Advances in Neural Information Processing Systems, Montreal, QC, Canada, 7–12 December 2015; Volume 1, pp. 802–810.
32. Iris, Ç.; Pacino, D.; Ropke, S. Improved Formulations and an Adaptive Large Neighborhood Search Heuristic for the Integrated Berth Allocation and Quay Crane Assignment Problem. *Transp. Res. Part E Logist. Transp. Rev.* **2017**, *105*, 123–147. [CrossRef]

Disclaimer/Publisher's Note: The statements, opinions and data contained in all publications are solely those of the individual author(s) and contributor(s) and not of MDPI and/or the editor(s). MDPI and/or the editor(s) disclaim responsibility for any injury to people or property resulting from any ideas, methods, instructions or products referred to in the content.

Article

AHP-Based Network Security Situation Assessment for Industrial Internet of Things

Junkai Yi [1] and Lin Guo [2,*]

[1] School of Automation, Key Laboratory of Modern Measurement and Control Technology Ministry of Education, Beijing Information Science & Technology University, Beijing 100192, China; yijk@bistu.edu.cn
[2] School of Automation, Beijing Information Science & Technology University, Beijing 100192, China
* Correspondence: 2021020382@bistu.edu.cn

Abstract: The Industrial Internet of Things (IIoT) is used in various industries to achieve industrial automation and intelligence. Therefore, it is important to assess the network security situation of the IIoT. The existing network situation assessment methods do not take into account the particularity of the IIoT's network security requirements and cannot achieve accurate assessment. In addition, IIoT transmits a lot of heterogeneous data, which is subject to cyber attacks, and existing classification methods cannot effectively deal with unbalanced data. To solve the above problems, this paper first considers the special network security requirements of the IIoT, and proposes a quantitative evaluation method of network security based on the Analytic Hierarchy Process (AHP). Then, the average under-/oversampling (AUOS) method is proposed to solve the problem of unbalance of network attack data. Finally, an IIoT network security situation assessment classifier based on the eXtreme Gradient Boosting (XGBoost) is constructed. Experiments show that the situation assessment method proposed in this paper can more accurately characterize the network security state of the IIoT. The AUOS method can achieve data balance without generating too much data, and does not burden the training of the model. The classifier constructed in this paper is superior to the traditional classification algorithm.

Keywords: Industrial Internet of Things; network security situation assessment; Analytic Hierarchy Process; data sampling

Citation: Yi, J.; Guo, L. AHP-Based Network Security Situation Assessment for Industrial Internet of Things. *Electronics* **2023**, *12*, 3458. https://doi.org/10.3390/electronics12163458

Academic Editors: Yue Wu, Kai Qin, Qiguang Miao and Maoguo Gong

Received: 6 July 2023
Revised: 12 August 2023
Accepted: 13 August 2023
Published: 15 August 2023

Copyright: © 2023 by the authors. Licensee MDPI, Basel, Switzerland. This article is an open access article distributed under the terms and conditions of the Creative Commons Attribution (CC BY) license (https://creativecommons.org/licenses/by/4.0/).

1. Introduction

The Internet of Things (IoT) is one of the fastest-growing technologies. With the development of IoT technology, information from various fields can be integrated into comprehensive applications [1]. The IIoT combines the emerging technologies of the IoT with industrial control systems (ICS) to enable an intelligent industrial ecosystem by providing potential solutions for automating manufacturing processes and effectively controlling production chains, significantly increasing manufacturing efficiency, improving product quality, and reducing costs and resource consumption. However, web-dependent IIoT faces huge challenges in terms of cybersecurity [2]. By the end of 2022, the China National Vulnerability Database (CNVD) had recorded 3141 industrial system vulnerabilities and 1443 IoT end device vulnerabilities. According to the "2019 China Internet Network Security Situation Overview" released by the National Computer Network Emergency Response Technical Team/Coordination Center of China (CNCERT/TT), about 41% of the existing IIoT devices in China have high-risk vulnerabilities in their systems. The most serious problems are exposed in electric power systems and urban rail transportation industries.

In 1988, Endsley [3] proposed situation awareness as acquiring and understanding environmental factors and predicting future states under certain spatial and temporal conditions. Cyberspace situational awareness (CSA) was first proposed by Tim Bass [4] in

1999. Network situation awareness is to determine the current network security states and predict its future state trends by analyzing the environmental factors of the system [5]. The process can be divided into four steps: data collection, situation understanding, situation assessment, and situation prediction. Network security situation assessment (NSSA) is the core of network situation awareness, which can analyze the current network security states in real time [6]. NSSA enables early detection of security risks and threats in the network so that measures can be taken to stop these threats before they occur [7]. The research of NSSA for the IIoT is very important to ensure the stable operation, data confidentiality, and environmental security of the IIoT.

There have been relatively few NSSA studies on IIoT. IIoT systems have different requirements for information confidentiality, system availability, and data security than information systems. The NSSA of traditional information systems does not take into account its particularities, and is therefore not well suited to assessing the network condition of the IIoT. IIoT integrates various networks and devices, and the network environment is complex, so the amount of data collected by IIoT is large and the data distribution is uneven. Large-scale network data cannot be directly used as NSSA, which will affect the efficiency of evaluation [8]. Both undersampling and oversampling can only deal with the data imbalance problem of binary classification, and cannot realize the balanced sampling of multi-class data [9]. Aiming at the above problems, this paper first studies NSSA for the IIoT based on the AHP. Then, the average under-/oversampling method is proposed to deal with the imbalance of different attack data volumes. Finally, the IIoT network security situation assessment classifier is constructed based on the XGBoost to improve the effectiveness of the model. A ToN-IoT dataset was used in the experiment. The dataset is derived from a test bench created for the Industry 4.0 network.

The major contributions of this paper are as follows:

(1) An NSSA method for the IIoT is proposed, which uses binary classification and multi-classification results of attack traffic to quantify the network situation and uses the AHP to obtain influence weights of each attack type for the IIoT.

(2) Using the XGBoost algorithm to build a classification model to judge whether the IIoT has been attacked, and what the type of attack is. An average under-/oversampling method is proposed to solve the problem of attack data imbalance, and the sampling method used for a certain type of attack data is determined by the ratio of its data volume to the average value of the total data volume.

(3) Experiments show that the NSSA method proposed in this paper is more suitable for industrial control systems, and the attack classification model constructed in this paper has high accuracy under the condition of a large amount of data and imbalance of various types of data, laying a foundation for effective network security situation assessment.

The rest of this article is organized as follows. Section 2 gives an overview of some related work. Section 3 describes the theory related to the construction of an IIoT network situational assessor. Section 4 details the quantification and evaluation methods of NSSA for the IIoT. The experimental results are presented in Section 5. Finally, Section 6 summarizes this paper and discusses future work.

2. Related Works

Today, a number of prominent studies on network security situational assessment techniques for traditional security areas have been performed, and the assessment methods are relatively mature, but the research on situational assessment for the IIoT is still in the development stage.

Liu et al. [10] studied the characteristics of wireless networks and proposed an NSSA method based on BIPMU to improve the performance and accuracy of NSSA. Zhao et al. [11] analyzed NSSA in the big data environment, selected multi-source data in the big data environment, proposed a parallel reduction algorithm based on an attribute importance matrix to reduce the number of attributes of data sources, and used the particle swarm optimization algorithm to calculate the situation value of a wavelet neural network. Nikoloudakis et al. [12] proposed a situation awareness framework based on machine learning to handle heterogeneous attack data. This framework used the real-time awareness function provided by the SDN paradigm to detect network entities and evaluate known vulnerabilities. Experiments showed that this framework improved the accuracy of threat detection. Zhang et al. [13] used a combination of long- and short-term memory networks and decision tree algorithms to assess the time series problem of security posture. The method improved the accuracy of the algorithm, but without taking into account the existence of data category imbalance, meaning that the experimental results were not well optimized. Chen et al. [14] used SVM and gravitational search algorithms to design an NSSA method with better global optimization function. Han et al. [15] designed a quantitative NSSA method for wirelessly connected intelligent robot clusters using convolutional neural networks.

Khaleghi et al. [16] built a three-layer SMM by embedding context-dynamic quantitative security measures (QSM) into the security measurement model (SMM). The model considered the network's deterrence against threats, resilience against attacks, and ability to withstand shocks, and accurately measured the security effectiveness of the entire network and its context components. Cai et al. [17] established a three-layer distribution Internet of Things (PDIoT) security evaluation index system and used the entropy weight method and cloud model theory to evaluate the security risks of PDIoT. Venkataramanan et al. [18] proposed a model for detecting the resistance of microgrids to attacks. The model considered all cyber-physical layers of the microgrid and quantified the state of cyber-physical security using theories such as graph theory analysis, availability probability models, and attack graph metrics. The model was used experimentally to assess the resilience of the microgrid after an attack. Basumallik et al. [19] studied the state of large-scale power system outages caused by coordinated attacks and evaluated the state of the power grid after attacks by using the semi-Markov method and defined three indicators. Sarkar et al. [20] proposed a power system framework consisting of a computing system, a SCADA system, and other software systems and created a concrete example based on this framework, for use in evaluating the cyber-physical impact of the power system under different cyber attacks. Zhang et al. [21] used a fuzzy reasoning algorithm to mine and identify network attack correlation, and realized the perception and control of network security situation. Li et al. [22] combined the entropy weight method and grey correlation analysis method to put forward the ADN situation assessment index systems and assessment method considering network attack. This method avoided the dependence of traditional assessment on expert experience and took into account the differences in assessment in different scenarios. Umunnakwe et al. [23] proposed a model for ranking the importance of multiple components, which integrated industry vulnerabilities into the network risk assessment of power systems. Experiments showed that the model provided operators with different system protection strategies. Fan et al. [24] used the multi-observation Hidden Markov Model (HMM) based on the attack characteristics to quantify the network state and obtain the security status evaluation value of the software-defined network. Liu et al. [25] used the D-S evidence theory to fuse the measured indicators and obtain the device threat value. Then, AHP was used to calculate the weights of different devices, and finally, the network threat situation value was obtained using a weighted method. Based on fuzzy AHP, Zheng et al. [26] conducted hierarchical modeling of industrial control system equipment and attack behavior, carried out security risk assessment and analysis, calculated system risk value, and deployed more effective defense measures. Shang et al. [27] adopted a method based on the attack tree model to model the industrial control system, calculated the node interval probability by fuzzy reasoning, and obtained the probability of each attack path in the system. Spyridon et al. [28] adopted the method of fuzzy probabilistic Bayesian networks to conduct the dynamic security risk assessment of industrial control systems from the perspective of dynamic characteristics, which is more in line with the application of actual systems. Dong et al. [29] used object-oriented Bayesian networks

(OOBN) for structural modeling and designed a prototype of the power information test systems. Experiments showed that this method could be effectively applied to the security risk assessment of the power systems network.

Bhandari et al. [30] proposed feature selection during the data preprocessing stage, combining sequencer search and Chi-square attribute evaluation, and then using Bayesian networks to identify attack types. Yang et al. [31] proposed an NSSA method for network attack behavior classification, aiming at the problems whereby it is difficult to extract features using traditional network security situation assessment methods, and with poor timeliness. Sen et al. [32] proposed a multi-stage network attack detection framework. Introducing the DOMCA correlation method constructs a multi-source intelligence knowledge base for use in reconstructing complex attack activities, improving detection accuracy. Experiments demonstrated that DOMCA could reliably detect multi-stage network attacks. Al Ghazo et al. [33] studied the interdependencies between vulnerabilities, proposed an automatic attack graph generator, and conducted experiments in a SCADA network. The experiments showed that the attack graph generator was able to take into account the vulnerability exploitation conditions and other security properties in detail. Based on the idea of artificial immunity, Wang et al. [34] proposed a dynamic network intrusion detection and prediction model based on a fuzzy fractional ordinary differential equation. Tian et al. [35] proposed a network attack detection method based on URL analysis to address the problem whereby there are increased numbers of attacks on network servers in the case of cloud Internet of Things systems. This method normalizes the URLs of edge devices, integrates multiple concurrent depth models to analyze URLs, and performs web attack detection. Experiments showed that this method was able to effectively improve the accuracy of network attack detection. Tang et al. [36] proposed an optimized cloud model based on the impact function to evaluate DDoS attacks. In this method, a V support vector machine (V-SVM) was established to identify DDoS attacks. Xi et al. [37] proposed a framework for NSSA by analyzing three dimensions: threat, vulnerability, and stability, in which the decision layer incorporated the results of the sub-assessments and quantified impact factors such as threats based on CVSS. The experiments demonstrated the effectiveness of the framework using alert information.

In summary, although existing IIoT network security situation assessment methods have achieved certain results, the following problems are still present:

- NSSA methods based on machine learning usually feature high precision, but existing situation assessment models based on machine learning do not fully consider the industrial characteristics of the IIoT systems, and their assessment results are not applicable to IIoT systems.
- The IIoT network connects a variety of heterogeneous networks with complex structures and a huge amount of data. The modeling of industrial control systems, and then the analysis of the model from different angles to evaluate the network security of the system, required a lot of logical and mathematical operations, resulting in the efficiency of NSSA realization being low, and possessing certain limitations. In addition, system modeling relies on expert experience, and there is a lack of reasonable quantitative standards, meaning that there is a certain subjectivity to the process of evaluation.
- In some studies analyzing network security from threat detection, the researchers did not process the unbalanced sample data in the industrial control dataset, resulting in a small number of samples with low extraction accuracy, thus affecting the overall effect.

Based on the existing research on industrial control system network risk assessment methods, this paper considers the impact of the confrontation between attackers and defenders on industrial control system network security, and further studies risk assessment methods. Considering the unbalanced characteristics of industrial control data samples, this paper proposes a multi-class sampling method.

3. Theoretical Research on NSSA for the IIoT
3.1. Design of the AHP for the IIoT

The IIoT has many features that are different from those of information systems. In information systems, the key assets to be protected include information, such as bank account data, credit card records, customer records, and so on. The security of information systems mainly refers to the confidentiality of data, and sometimes it may be necessary to shut down the network for hours, no matter the cost, in order to protect data security. In contrast, the key asset of the IIoT is the availability of the plant or infrastructure. For example, the plant must run continuously without shutting down the network.

Confidentiality (C), Integrity (I), and Availability (A) are three basic attributes of network security. Availability has the highest priority in the IIoT [38,39]. Considering the differences in cybersecurity characteristics between the IIoT and information systems, Table 1 shows the different rankings of CIA between the IIoT and information systems.

Table 1. CIA Ranking.

Feature	Information Systems	IIoT
Confidentiality	Low	High
Integrity	Medium	Medium
Availability	High	Low

AHP is a subjective evaluation method suitable for analyzing multi-factor and multi-level problems [40]. This paper uses AHP and IIoT security features to determine the CIA weight coefficients of various attack impact values. The operation steps of this method can be divided into four aspects, as follows:

1. Establishment of hierarchical structure model: The purpose of decision making, and decisive factors are analyzed, and a hierarchical structure diagram is constructed according to the relationship between them.
2. Construction of a judgment matrix: The decision factors are compared in pairs to determine the value of the relatively important factors among them, which is generally determined using the nine-point method.
3. Hierarchical sorting: The weight of each decision factor is solved by the sum-product method using the judgment matrix.
    - Each column of the judgment matrix B is normalized;
    - The values of each column of the normalized judgment matrix are added to obtain a one-dimensional vector;
    - The one-dimensional vector is normalized to obtain the approximate solution W of the desired feature vector. The maximum characteristic root λ_{max} of the judgment matrix is calculated according to (1), where n is the dimension of the judgment matrix, and w_i is the weight of the ith decision factor.

$$\lambda_{max} = \frac{1}{n}\sum_{i=1}^{n}\frac{BW}{w_i} \qquad (1)$$

4. Consistency check: The CR value is calculated to determine whether the values of paired decision factors in the judgment matrix have been correctly defined.
    - The calculation of CI is shown in (2);
    - The random consistency RI values are listed in Table 2;
    - CR is calculated as shown in (3). Smaller values of CR indicate better consistency of the judgment matrix. Generally, if the CR value is less than 0.1, the judgment matrix meets the consistency test.

Table 2. Random consistency, RI.

n	3	4	5	6	7	8	9
RI	0.52	0.89	1.12	1.26	1.36	1.41	1.46

$$CI = \frac{\lambda_{\max} - n}{n - 1} \quad (2)$$

$$CR = \frac{CI}{RI} \quad (3)$$

3.2. Average Under-/Oversampling (AUOS)

IIoT systems in different industries are subject to different types of attacks. When studying attack traffic, it is common to encounter unbalanced data distributions. When training models using multiple types of data, if the amount of data in a particular category is too small, the model cannot fully learn the characteristics of that type of data, which leads to a decrease in model accuracy. If the amount of data of a certain type is too large, the model may be over-fitted, and the learning ability of the model will be weakened.

The traditional multiclass data undersampling method reduces the number of other classes based on the class with the smallest amount of data. If the amount of data in a category is extremely small, the total data volume will drop dramatically, which is not conducive to model learning. The traditional multiclass data oversampling method increases the number of other categories according to the category with the largest data volume, resulting in a sharp increase in the total data volume, causing difficulties in model learning, and a decrease in the operation rate. To solve this problem, an average under-/oversampling method is proposed in this paper to balance the data. The steps of the method are as follows:

1. Calculate the threshold value.
   - Suppose that the size of the dataset S is m, there are j types, and the data size of each class is x_j;
   - Calculate the average data volume *average* of the dataset according to (4).

$$average = \frac{m}{j} \quad (4)$$

2. Perform data sampling.
   - The data of type $i\{i \in (1, 2, \ldots, j)\}$ are extracted from S and denoted as S_i, and the remaining dataset is S_{1-i};
   - The train–test–split method is used in Python to divide the dataset S_{1-i} and extract the *average* size of the dataset, denoted as S_{1-i}^{train};
   - All types of data in S_{1-i}^{train} are converted into the same label, and the label is not i;
   - S_{1-i}^{train} and S_i are combined into S_i^{train}. The sampling method of the dataset S_i^{train} is judged according to step 3, and the data of type i in the sampled S_i^{train} are extracted and recorded as S_{deal}.

3. Judge the sampling methods with the threshold: If $w_i > 2$, undersampling is used for this type. if $w_i < 0.5$, oversampling is used for this type. If w_i = *average*, no processing is performed for this type of data;
   - The coefficient factor w_i of each class is calculated according to (5);

$$w_i = \frac{x_i}{average} \quad (5)$$

   - The random undersampling method is used for undersampling;

- The SMOTE (Synthetic Minority Oversampling Technique) method is used for oversampling

4. Merge the datasets: The unprocessed categories of data in S keep their original labels and quantities, and the label of S_{deal} is restored to i. The unprocessed data in S and S_{deal} are combined as the training set S_{train}.

The AUOS algorithm is shown in Algorithm 1.

Algorithm 1: AUOS algorithm pseudo code

Input: original train dataset S
Output: resampled dataset S_{train}
1 $m, j, x_j \leftarrow S$;
2 $average = m/j$;
3 **for** ($i = 1; i \leq j; i++$) **do**
4    $w_i = x_i / average$
5   **if** $w_i \neq 1$ **then**
6      $S_i, S_{1-i} \leftarrow S$; //The data of type i is extracted from S.
7      $S_{1-i}^{train} \leftarrow S_{1-i}$; //$S_{1-i}$ size is $average$ extracted from S_{1-i} using the
8   //train-test-split method.
9      $S_{1-i}^{train} \leftarrow S_{1-i}^{train}$;
10     $S_i^{train} \leftarrow S_{1-i}^{train} + S_i$;
11   **if** $w_i > 2$ **then**
12       $S_{deal} \leftarrow S_i^{train}$;
13   **end if**
14   **if** $w_i < 0.5$ **then**
15       $S_{deal} \leftarrow S_i^{train}$;
16   **end if**
17   **end if**
18   **if** $w_i = 1$ **then**
19     $S_i \leftarrow S_i$;
20   **end if**
21   $S_{train} \leftarrow S_i, S_{deal}$;
22 **end for**
23 **return** S_{train}

3.3. Construction of NSSA Classifier for the IIoT

The IIoT combines the emerging technologies related to the IoT with ICS, and while it greatly improves the efficiency and automation of production, it also increases its potential to be attacked. Given the characteristics of high-dimensional attack data and large sample size, in this paper, the XGBoost strong classifier is designed to improve the accuracy of NSSA.

XGBoost is characterized by high accuracy, strong flexibility, and prevention of overfitting. It is often used in data mining [41]. XGBoost belongs to the ensemble learning boosting algorithms, and is composed of multiple Gradient Boosting Decision trees (GBDT).

The algorithm structure of XGBoost is shown in Figure 1. XGBoost is a boosted tree model. The idea of the XGBoost algorithm is to keep adding trees and to keep splitting features to grow a tree. Each time a tree is added, a new function is learned to fit the residuals of the last prediction. The parameters of the nodes of the already-trained tree remain unchanged, and a new tree is added. The features of a sample fall to a corresponding leaf node in each tree, each leaf node corresponds to a score, and finally, the scores corresponding to each tree are added to the predicted value of the sample.

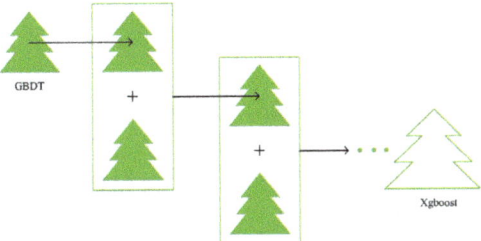

Figure 1. Algorithm structure of XGBoost.

Assume that the collected data sample is $S = \{(x_1, y_1), (x_2, y_2) \ldots, (x_n, y_n)\}$. There are n samples, each of which has m-dimension characteristics, and the predicted value of a single sample is:

$$\tilde{y}_i = \sum_{k=1}^{t} f_k(x_i) = \tilde{y}_i^{t-1} + f_t(x_i) \tag{6}$$

$$f(x_i) = w_{q(x_i)} \tag{7}$$

where $w_{q(x_i)}$ is the fraction of sample x_i in a leaf node $q(x_i)$, $q(x_i)$ represents the leaf node of sample x_i after judgment, and $f_k(x_i)$ represents the leaf node values of kth regression tree in a single sample x_i.

XGBoost adopts a greedy algorithm to perform optimization tree by tree. Supposing the current regression tree has T base learners in total, then the objective function of the XGBoost will be:

$$obj = \sum_{i=1}^{n} l(y_i, \tilde{y}_i) + \sum_{t=1}^{T} \Omega(f_t) \tag{8}$$

$$\Omega(f_t) = \gamma T + \frac{1}{2} \lambda \sum_{t=1}^{T} w_t^2 \tag{9}$$

The first half of (8) represents the error between the predicted values and the true values, and the second half is the increased regularization term, as specified in (9).

γ is the penalty parameter for controlling the depth of the tree, and λ controls the leaf node score w_t to prevent overfitting. The optimization objective of a single tree is as follows:

$$\operatorname{argmin}[\sum_{i=1}^{n} l(y_i, \tilde{y}_i) + \sum_{t=1}^{T} \Omega(f_t)] \tag{10}$$

Bring Formulas (6) and (7) into Formula (8) to expand:

$$obj = \gamma T + \sum_{t=1}^{T} [\sum_{i \in n} l(y_i, \tilde{y}_i^{t-1} + w_t)] + \frac{1}{2} \lambda w_t^2 \tag{11}$$

The loss function is obtained by Taylor second-order expansion:

$$obj \approx \gamma T + \sum_{t=1}^{T} [w_t G_i + \frac{1}{2} w_t^2 (\lambda + H_i)] \tag{12}$$

$$G_i = \sum_{i \in n} g_i \tag{13}$$

$$H_i = \sum_{i \in n} h_i \tag{14}$$

where g_i is the first step gradient and h_i is the second step gradient, both of which are constants. The optimization objective at this time is:

$$\operatorname*{argmin}[\sum_{t=1}^{T}(w_t G_i + \frac{1}{2}w_t^2(\lambda + H_i))] \tag{15}$$

Calculating the quadratic Equation (15) yields:

$$w_i = -\frac{G_i}{H_i + \lambda} \tag{16}$$

The objective function of XGBoost can be divided into two parts. The first half is the error between the predicted and true values, and the second half is the regularization term, which controls the complexity of the model. By transforming the objective function, a quadratic function about the fraction of a leaf node can be obtained, and the optimal w and the objective function value can be solved.

When XGBoost is used to implement classification, the selection of the decision tree number, maximum tree depth, and learning rate has an important influence on the classification effect.

- The number of decision trees refers to the maximum number of iterations. The larger the value, the stronger the learning ability of the model and the easier it is to overfit;
- The maximum tree depth is used to control model overfitting;
- The learning rate determines the step size when iterating the decision tree and controls the iteration rate. The slower the rate, the more likely the model is to find the best value more accurately.

4. Proposed NSSA Model for the IIoT

4.1. NSSA Framework

The NSSA model designed for the IIoT in this paper is shown in Figure 2. The model can be divided into three parts.

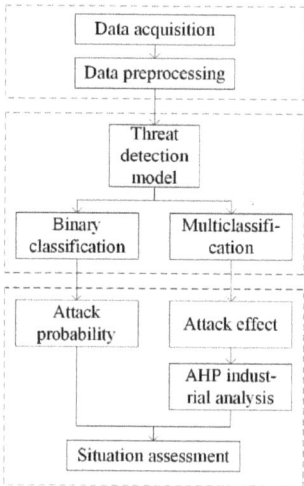

Figure 2. NSSA model for the IIoT.

1. Situation acquisition.

Traffic acquisition modules are deployed in the control layer, information management layer, and Internet edge of the IIoT, respectively, to collect normal and attack events. The collected traffic is processed by removing redundancy, simplifying features, filling defaults, converting data formats, and so on.

2. Situation understanding.

The threat detection model is used to train the dataset. Binary classification is used to determine whether each piece of data constitutes external attack traffic in order to determine attack probability, and multiple classification is used to determine the attack type in order to determine attack influence. The combination of the two is used to calculate the network security situation value.

3. Situation quantitative assessment.

The AHP is used, in combination with the characteristics of the IIoT, to determine the influence weight coefficients of various attacks. The classification results of the detection model are combined in order to quantify the cybersecurity situation of the IIoT. Network security situation assessment is performed by dividing the network risk level.

4.2. Network Situation Quantification

In this paper, the network security situation of the IIoT is studied, and the threat severity and influence of network attacks arising from attack traffic are determined.

1. Severity of threat:

The threat severity is determined by the attack probability within a time, as shown in (17). If the data in clause i is normal traffic, I_i is marked with 0; otherwise, it is marked with 1; M represents the total network traffic within a time.

$$p = \frac{\sum_{i=1}^{M} I_i}{M} \quad (17)$$

2. Threat influence.

Due to the differences in structural characteristics and security requirements between IIoT and information systems, quantitative assessments of threat influence used in information systems networks cannot be fully applied to IIoT networks. Therefore, the formula for calculating the IIoT network threat influence in this paper is as follows:

$$v_i = \varepsilon(xC_i + yI_i + zA_i) \quad (18)$$

where C, I and A represent the CIA scores of specific attack types, and x, y and z are determined by the AHP analysis of the IIoT characteristics. Since the scores of C, I, and A are all reduced after multiplying by their weights, in order to control the security situation value to within the interval [0, 1], v_i is expanded ε times. ε is the reciprocal value of the maximum value of cumulative CIA score.

This paper focuses on the security of the IIoT network environment represented by ToN-IoT dataset. Different types of attack have different impacts on the system. The ToN-IoT dataset contains nine types of attack traffic. Table 3, below, presents an overview of the nine types of attack and determines the CIA rating of each attack based on its characteristics. The specific levels and scoring settings are shown in Table 3 [42], where h represents high impact, l represents low impact, and n represents no impact.

3. Network security situation value.

The IIoT network security situation value calculation is shown in (19) [43].

$$V = \frac{p \times \sum_{i=1}^{n} v_i \times t_i}{M - m} \quad (19)$$

where m indicates the normal traffic within this period, n indicates the attack type within this period, v_i indicates the influence score of a specific attack type, and t_i indicates the duration of a specific attack.

Table 3. Attack characteristics.

Attack Type	Attack Impact	Confidentiality	Integrity	Availability
backdoor	Attackers use backdoors to secretly access other systems, and backdoors are also used by intruders as vulnerabilities to attack other systems.	h	h	l
ddos	This type of attack causes servers or multiple hosts to fail to communicate with each other.	n	n	h
dos	The victim host cannot receive and process external requests or respond to external requests promptly.	n	n	h
injection	The attack causes database information leakage, remote control of the server, the installation of a backdoor, and other hazards.	h	h	l
mitm	Intruders place themselves between clients and servers to intercept confidential data or manipulate incorrect information within it.	h	n	l
password	The attack may result in the disclosure of user information or the inability to send emails.	l	l	n
ransomware	Dissemination of sensitive information to extort money from victims, resulting in leakage of user information.	h	n	n
scanning	The attacker obtains port information by scanning for the next attack.	l	n	n
xss	The attack can launch damaging behaviors such as leaking user data, tampering with website pages, and ddos attacks.	h	h	l

h represents high impact, l represents low impact, and n represents no impact.

4.3. Network Situation Severity Levels

The security risks faced by IIoT networks are divided into five levels, as shown in Table 4. When the quantitative security situation value is 0, the network has no attack traffic and is in a secure condition. The higher the situation value, the worse the network security condition.

Table 4. Network security situation evaluation level.

Low	Lower	Medium	Higher	High
[0, 0.2]	[0.2, 0.4]	[0.4, 0.6]	[0.6, 0.8]	[0.8, 1]

5. Experiment and Result Analysis

5.1. Simulation Environment

Most of the research on NSSA has focused on datasets such as NSL-KDD, CICIDS2017, KDDCup-99, and UNSW_NB15. These datasets are huge and redundant and do not come from industrial control system networks.

The ToN_IoT dataset was collected from a large-scale network of Industry 4.0 testbeds designed by Cyber Range and IoT LABS in collaboration with others. The Industry 4.0 testbed is deployed using multiple virtual machines and hosts with the Windows, Linux, and Kali operating systems to simulate the interconnect between the Internet of Things, the cloud, and Edge/Fog three-tier systems. The data in ToN_IoT are collected from network traffic, the Windows audit trail, the Linux audit trail, and telemetry data from IoT services, and can be used to test AI for a variety of cybersecurity applications, such as in intrusion detection systems, threat intelligence, and threat search. In this experiment, ToN_IoT's Train_Test_Network traffic packet is used, which has a file size of 66.6 MB and contains 400,000 pieces of data, including nine types of common industrial network attack traffic and normal traffic.

PyCharm Community Edition 2021 is used to simulate the experiment. The hardware environment consisted of a 3 GHz CPU and 16 GB memory, and the operating system was Windows 10.

5.2. Data Preprocessing

1. Feature numeralization and default processing.

In the Train_Test_Network packet, some of the classification features are in the form of characters, and there are a large number of default values in the data. In the experiment, the LabelEncoder package of scikit-learn is used to quickly convert each feature into 0, 1, 2, ..., and the default value is set to 0.

2. Data sampling and partitioning.

The Train_Test_Network packet contains more than 400,000 pieces of traffic, which is a huge amount of data. To speed up model training, in this experiment, the data are simplified to 165,976 pieces through stratified sampling according to attack categories. The raw data distribution is shown in Figure 3.

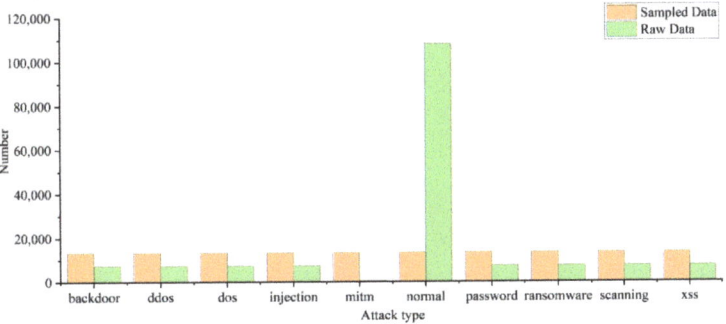

Figure 3. Distribution of the dataset.

In a binary classification, the ratio of normal traffic to attack traffic is about 2:1. The difference between the two does not cause huge errors in model classification. In multiple classification, by observing the original data distribution in Figure 3, it can be found that the amount of mitm attack traffic data is too small and the amount of normal traffic data is too large. Therefore, the average undersampling method proposed in this paper is adopted to balance the various kinds of data, and the data distribution after processing is shown in Figure 3.

In this experiment, the Python package train_test_split is used to divide the dataset into the training set and the test set according to a ratio of 0.2. The training set contains 132,780 pieces of data, and the test set contains 33,196 pieces of data.

3. Feature normalization.

To avoid there being a large gap between the maximum value and the minimum value of some classification features, which would affect the classification effect of the model, Equation (20) is used in the experiment to normalize each feature data and summarize it within the interval [0, 1].

$$x = \frac{x - x_{min}}{x_{max} - x_{min}} \tag{20}$$

where x_{max}, x_{min} are the maximum and minimum values of this feature, respectively.

5.3. Binary Classification

Binary classification can be used to determine whether the traffic is attack traffic. In this experiment, four indexes, including recall rate, precision rate, F1, and training duration T, are used to judge the efficiency of a binary classification model. The higher the value of recall rate, precision rate, and F1, the better the training effect of the model; and the shorter the training duration, the higher the efficiency of the model.

The recall rate refers to the probability of all samples being correctly predicted from among the actual positive samples, calculated as shown in (21).

$$recall = \frac{TP}{TP+FN} \quad (21)$$

The precision rate refers to the probability of all samples predicted to be positive being positive, calculated as shown in (22).

$$precision = \frac{TP}{TP+FP} \quad (22)$$

The recall rate and precision rate are inversely proportional to each other. To synthesize the performance of the two, a balance point should be found between them. F1 can be used to evaluate the performance of them both together. It can be calculated as shown in (23).

$$F1 = \frac{2 \times precision \times recall}{precision + recall} \quad (23)$$

TP (True Positive): indicates the amount of normal traffic that was judged to be normal traffic.

FN (False Negative): indicates the amount of normal traffic that was judged to be attack traffic.

TN (True Negative): indicates the amount of actual attack traffic that was judged to be attack traffic.

FP (False Positive): indicates the amount of attack traffic that was judged to be normal traffic.

In this paper, the effectiveness of four classification algorithms—Support Vector Machine (SVM), K-Nearest Neighbour (KNN), Random Forest (RF) and XGBoost—is compared using the ToN_IoT dataset. For each model, we empirically selected the parameters that had the greatest impact on its classification effectiveness for tuning, using a mesh search combined with cross-validation to determine the optimal parameters for each model. The optimal parameter settings for each model are shown in Table 5. The binary classification results for the four models are shown in Table 6.

Table 5. Optimal parameters for each model.

Model	Parameter Setting
SVM	C: 10; kernel: rbf; gamma: 0.1
KNN	n_neighbors: 35; p: 1; weights: distance
RF	n_estimators: 40; min_samples_leaf: 1; max_depth: 10
XGBoost	n_estimators: 40; learning_rate: 0.5; max_depth: 10

Table 6. Results of model binary classification.

Model	Recall	Precision	F1	T
SVM	0.944	0.864	0.912	1246 s 871 ms
KNN	0.986	0.966	0.976	30 ms
RF	0.995	0.983	0.989	3 s 672 ms
XGBoost	0.998	0.998	0.998	2 s 611 ms

From Table 6, it can be seen that SVM has the worst binary classification effect. SVM involves the calculation of a matrix of the order M (where m is the number of samples) when solving for the support vector. As this experiment adopts big data training, SVM classification consumes a large amount of memory space, the training time is too long, and the training accuracy is poor. The shortest time required for big data classification can be seen for KNN, while XGBoost achieves the best classification effect. Compared with RF, which is also composed of decision trees, the time required is also relatively short.

5.4. Multiple Classification

The model can use multiple classification to determine the specific attack type of attack traffic. In this experiment, the recall rate, precision rate, and F1 of each attack type are used to judge the multi-classification efficiency of each model. The multi-classification effects of the four models are shown in Figures 4–6. The confusion matrix generated by using XGBoost combined with the average under-/oversampling method designed in this paper for processing multiple classifications is shown in Figure 7.

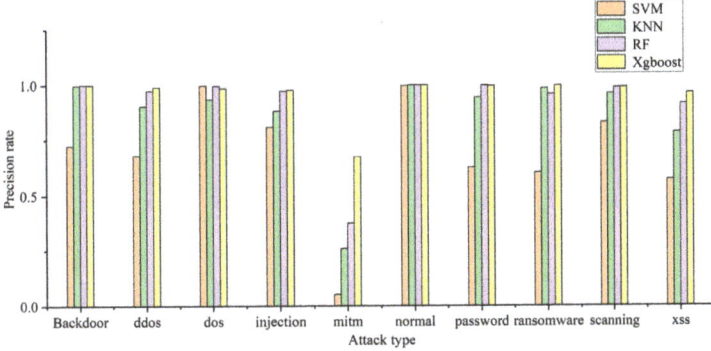

Figure 4. Model precision rate of multiple classification.

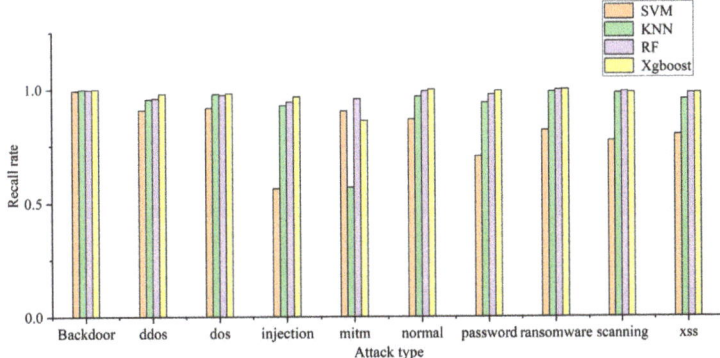

Figure 5. Model recall rate of multiple categories.

Figures 4–6 describe the precision rates, recall rates, and F1 scores for each of the four models. As can be seen from the figures, the SVM model has a low detection precision for small data, where the precision for mitm-type attacks is only 5.2%, and the F1 score is 9.7%. Due to the lack of available training data, SVM models are not sensitive to such attacks. Compared with the other three classification models, the XGBoost model built in this paper demonstrates improved detection precision for mitm-type attacks, reaching 67%. In addition, when detecting normal traffic, it achieves high scores of 99% for precision, recall and F1. Compared with the SVM, KNN and RF models, the proposed model improves the F-score by 26%, 8% and 3%, respectively.

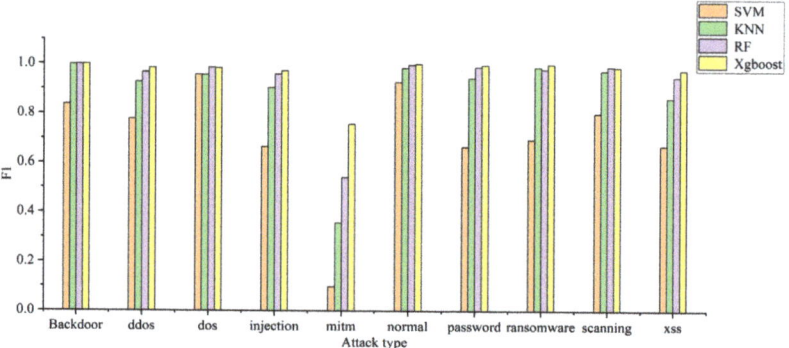

Figure 6. Model F1 of multiple classification.

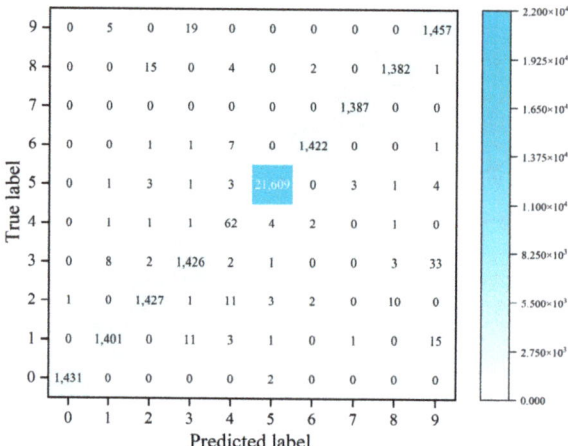

Figure 7. Confusion matrix of the XGBoost + AUOS.

The experimental results show that the proposed model is superior to the other models in terms of precision rate, recall rate and F1 score, and the detection precision of small-data attack categories is improved without decreasing the detection performance for most attack categories.

After performing sampling using the AUOS method proposed in this paper, the data volume for nine types of attack attains a balance. This is because a large number of samples in the dataset used in this paper have a portion of their features missing, and the sparse perception algorithm adopted by XGBoost is able to automatically learn the splitting direction of the sample. XGBoost adds a regular term to the objective function and performs second-order Taylor expansion to improve the classification effect of the model.

5.5. NSSA Results

1. Quantification of NSSA for the IIoT

The judgment matrix is determined by combining Table 1 and the nine-point scale method of the AHP. The weight value of CIA is generated using the sum-product method. The results are shown in Table 7.

Table 7. CIA weighting factors.

Feature	Weight	λ_{max}	CI	RI	CR
Confidentiality	10.616%				
Integrity	26.050%	3.039	0.019	0.520	0.037
Availability	63.335%				

In this experiment, the data in the training and testing package are reduced to 300,000 pieces and divided into 60 groups, on average. The data distribution of some of the groups is shown in Figure 8. In combination with the CIA weighting generated in Table 7, Formulas (17)–(19) are used to calculate the situation value of each group. The security situation curves are shown for each stage of the IIoT, as well as for information systems, in Figure 9.

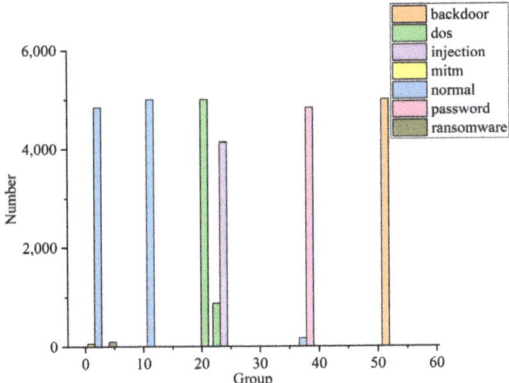

Figure 8. Partial data distribution.

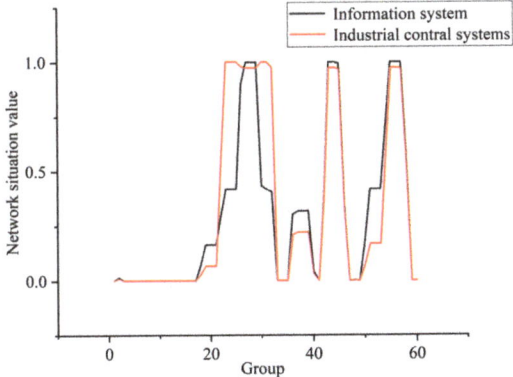

Figure 9. Network security situation curve.

From the analysis presented in Figures 8 and 9, it can be seen that most of the data in the first group represent normal traffic, with only a small number of mitm and ransomware attacks, and the security risk of this group is very low. All of the data of the 10th group represent normal traffic, and so its security status is good. The traffic in group 23 all represents dos attacks, so the security risk faced by IIoT is much higher than in the case of information systems. In group 25, most of the traffic represents injection attacks, while a small amount represents dos attacks. In this case, information systems face a higher level of risk. The traffic in group 36 mainly comprises password attacks, but a small portion is normal traffic. Password attacks do not affect the availability of the attacked host, but the information integrity and confidentiality of the host are affected. Therefore, the security risk of the system is lower at this time, and the level of risk faced by the IIoT is lower than in the case of information systems. The traffic in group 55 consists entirely of backdoor attacks. The successful use of backdoor attacks can seriously affect the integrity and confidentiality of the host's information, and can also impact the availability of the host. At this point, the system faces a high level of risk, and the level of risk faced by information systems is higher than that faced by the IIoT.

From the above analysis, it can be seen that the method of NSSA for the IIoT based on AHP proposed in this study has good application value. Compared with the quantitative evaluation method for the traditional network situation, this method considers the network characteristics of the IIoT and can more fully describe the network security situation of the IIoT.

2. Quantification of NSSA for each classification model

In this experiment, the test set data are divided into 43 groups. The IIoT network situation curve drawn using the classification results of different models is shown in Figure 10. Each dataset in the test set uniformly contains a very small number of different attacks. In this case, the network security status value is very low, and the risk to the network is very low. Compared with each curve, the NSSA results obtained using the XGBoost model designed in this paper are closest to the real values, while the evaluation effect of SVM is the worst.

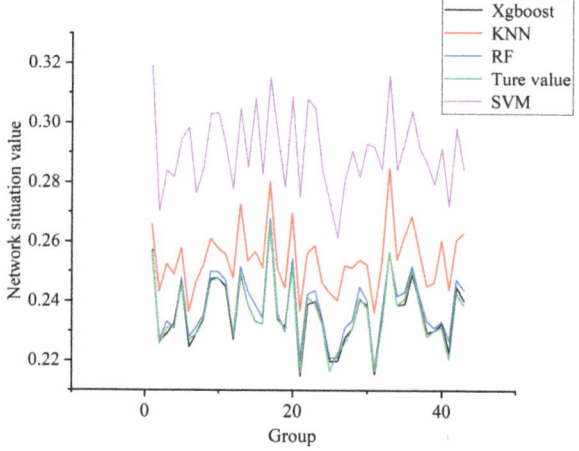

Figure 10. Network security situation curve of each model for the IIoT.

6. Conclusions

To date, many studies have been performed on NSSA, including attack detection and situation assessment. However, there are relatively few studies on IIoT network posture. On the one hand, the complexity of the IIoT networks makes it difficult to obtain posture elements. On the other hand, IIoT has extensvie requirements in terms of achieving real-time performance. Because IIoT networks connect a variety of heterogeneous networks, there are a lot of logical and mathematical operations required in order to perform network security situation assessment based on knowledge-based reasoning, leading to low efficiency and certain limitations when implementing NSSA. In addition, in some industrial system situation acquisition studies, unbalanced data samples in industrial control datasets are not balanced, leading to there being a small number of samples with low extraction accuracy, thus affecting the overall effect. This paper undertakes further research on existing risk assessment methods for industrial control systems.

First of all, in this paper, the characteristics of the IIoT were analyzed, the AHP method was used to analyze the impact factors of the IIoT systems with respect to network security requirements, and the situation assessment results were quantified. Then, XGBoost was used to build a classification model to judge whether the IIoT has been subject to attack, and to determine the category of the attack. In order to solve the problem of unbalanced attack data, an average under-/oversampling method was proposed. The average data volume is taken as the threshold to determine the sampling method for different categories of data, so that the sample data volume will not have too much influence on the efficiency of the model. The experimental results showed that the NSSA method proposed in this paper is able to improve the accuracy of the IIoT network security situation assessment. Under conditions including unbalanced data categories and large sample sizes, the attack classification model constructed in this paper has high accuracy, thus laying a foundation for effective network security situation assessment.

At present, our analysis of the IIoT features only addresses the security of information assets. Using the NSSA model in this paper, it is possible to better understand the destructive power of cyber attacks on IIoT information assets that threaten their stable operation. In the future, we will study the characteristics of the IIoT more comprehensively, optimize its quantitative security metrics, and integrate various factors in order to determine the overall security of the IIoT networks. In addition, the complete dataset of ToN_IoT is used in this paper, and the data volume is large. Reducing the dimensionality of the data will be considered in the future, and the use of other advanced deep learning algorithms, such as CNN, will be continued for conducting experiments and optimizing the threat detection model.

Author Contributions: Conceptualization, J.Y.; Methodology, J.Y. and L.G.; Software, L.G.; Formal analysis, J.Y. and L.G.; Writing—original draft, L.G. All authors have read and agreed to the published version of the manuscript.

Funding: This research received no external funding.

Data Availability Statement: Files—CloudStor (aarnet.edu.au).

Conflicts of Interest: The authors declare no conflict of interest.

References

1. Qiu, J.; Tian, Z.; Du, C.; Zuo, Q.; Su, S.; Fang, B. A Survey on Access Control in the Age of Internet of Things. *IEEE Internet Things J.* **2020**, *7*, 4682–4696. [CrossRef]
2. Berger, S.; Buerger, O.; Roeglinger, M. Attacks on the Industrial Internet of Things—Development of a multi-layer Taxonomy. *Comput. Secur.* **2020**, *93*, 101790. [CrossRef]
3. Endsley, M.R. Design and Evaluation for Situation Awareness Enhancement. In Proceedings of the Human Factors and Ergonomics Society Annual Meeting, Chicago, IL, USA, 5–9 October 1988; Sage Publications: Los Angeles, CA, USA, 1988; Volume 32, pp. 101–197.
4. Bass, T.; Gruber, D. A glimpse into the future of ID. *Mag. Usenix Sage* **1999**, *24*, 40–49.
5. Tadda, G.P.; Salerno, J.S. Overview of Cyber Situation Awareness. In *Advances in Information Security*; Springer: Boston, MA, USA, 2009; pp. 15–35. [CrossRef]
6. Leau, Y.-B.; Manickam, S.; Chong, Y.-W. Network Security Situation Assessment: A Review and Discussion. In *Lecture Notes in Electrical Engineering*; Springer: Berlin/Heidelberg, Germany, 2015; pp. 407–414. [CrossRef]
7. Cheng, X.R.; Lang, S. Research on Network Security Situation Assessment and Prediction. In Proceedings of the 2012 Fourth International Conference on Computational and Information Sciences, Chongqing, China, 17–19 August 2012; pp. 864–867.
8. Zhang, J.; Feng, H.; Liu, B.; Zhao, D. Survey of Technology in Network Security Situation Awareness. *Sensors* **2023**, *23*, 2608. [CrossRef] [PubMed]
9. Wei, W.; Chen, Y.; Lin, Q.; Ji, J.; Wong, K.-C.; Li, J. Multi-objective evolving long–short term memory networks with attention for network intrusion detection. *Appl. Soft Comput.* **2023**, *139*, 110216. [CrossRef]
10. Liu, Z.; Yang, C.; Liu, Y.; Ding, Y. A BIPMU-based network security situation assessment method for wireless network. *Comput. Stand. Interfaces* **2023**, *83*, 103661. [CrossRef]

11. Zhao, D.; Liu, J. Study on network security situation awareness based on particle swarm optimization algorithm. *Comput. Ind. Eng.* **2018**, *125*, 764–775. [CrossRef]
12. Nikoloudakis, Y.; Kefaloukos, I.; Klados, S.; Panagiotakis, S.; Pallis, E.; Skianis, C.; Markakis, E.K. Towards a Machine Learning Based Situational Awareness Framework for Cybersecurity: An SDN Implementation. *Sensors* **2021**, *21*, 4939. [CrossRef]
13. Zhang, H.; Kang, C.; Xiao, Y. Research on Network Security Situation Awareness Based on the LSTM-DT Model. *Sensors* **2021**, *21*, 4788. [CrossRef]
14. Chen, Y.; Yin, X.; Sun, A.; Destech, P.I. Network Security Situation Assessment Model Based on GSA-SVM. In Proceedings of the 2018 International Conference on Computer, Communication and Network Technology (CCNT), Bengaluru, India, 10–12 July 2018; Book Network Security Situation Assessment Model Based on GSA-SVM, Series Network Security Situation Assessment Model Based on GSA-SVM 291; pp. 414–420.
15. Han, W.; Tian, Z.; Huang, Z.; Huang, D.; Jia, Y. Quantitative Assessment of Wireless Connected Intelligent Robot Swarms Network Security Situation. *IEEE Access* **2019**, *7*, 134293–134300. [CrossRef]
16. Khaleghi, M.; Aref, M.R.; Rasti, M. Context-Aware Ontology-based Security Measurement Model. *J. Inf. Secur. Appl.* **2022**, *67*, 103199. [CrossRef]
17. Cai, S.; Wei, W.; Chen, D.; Ju, J.; Zhang, Y.; Liu, W.; Zheng, Z. Security Risk Intelligent Assessment of Power Distribution Internet of Things via Entropy-Weight Method and Cloud Model. *Sensors* **2022**, *22*, 4663. [CrossRef] [PubMed]
18. Venkataramanan, V.; Hahn, A.; Srivastava, A. CP-SAM: Cyber-Physical Security Assessment Metric for Monitoring Microgrid Resiliency. *IEEE Trans. Smart Grid* **2020**, *11*, 1055–1065. [CrossRef]
19. Basumallik, S.; Eftekharnejad, S.; Johnson, B.K. The impact of false data injection attacks against remedial action schemes. *Int. J. Electr. Power Energy Syst.* **2020**, *123*, 106225. [CrossRef]
20. Sarkar, S.; Teo, Y.M.; Chang, E.-C. A cybersecurity assessment framework for virtual operational technology in power system automation. *Simul. Model. Pract. Theory* **2022**, *117*, 102453. [CrossRef]
21. Zhang, R.; Hu, Z. Access control method of network security authentication information based on fuzzy reasoning algorithm. *Measurement* **2021**, *185*, 110103. [CrossRef]
22. Li, J.; Liang, J.; Liu, Q.; Qi, D.; Zhang, J.; Chen, Y. Research on situation assessment of active distribution networks considering cyberattacks. *Front. Energy Res.* **2022**, *10*, 971725. [CrossRef]
23. Umunnakwe, A.; Sahu, K. Davis, and IEEE, Multi-Component Risk Assessment Using Cyber-Physical Betweenness Centrality. In Proceedings of the 2021 IEEE Madrid PowerTech, Madrid, Spain, 28 June–2 July 2021. Book Multi-Component Risk Assessment Using Cyber-Physical Betweenness Centrality, Series Multi-Component Risk Assessment Using Cyber-Physical Betweenness Centrality.
24. Fan, Z.; Xiao, Y.; Nayak, A.; Tan, C. An improved network security situation assessment approach in software defined networks. *Peer-to-Peer Netw. Appl.* **2019**, *12*, 295–309. [CrossRef]
25. Liu, Z.H.; Zhang, B.; Zhu, N.; Li, L.X. Hierarchical network threat situation assessment method for DDoS based on D-S evidence theory. In Proceedings of the 2017 IEEE International Conference on Intelligence and Security Informatics (ISI), Beijing, China, 22–24 July 2017; pp. 49–53.
26. Zheng, Y.; Zheng, S. Cyber Security Risk Assessment for Industrial Automation Platform, Book Cyber Security Risk Assessment for Industrial Automation Platform. In Proceedings of the 2015 International Conference on Intelligent Information Hiding and Multimedia Signal Processing (IIH-MSP), Adelaide, SA, Australia, 23–25 September 2015; Series Cyber Security Risk Assessment for Industrial Automation Platform. pp. 341–344.
27. Shang, W.; Gong, T.; Chen, C.; Hou, J.; Zeng, P. Information Security Risk Assessment Method for Ship Control System Based on Fuzzy Sets and Attack Trees. *Secur. Commun. Netw.* **2019**, *2019*, 3574675. [CrossRef]
28. Spyridon, V.G.; Stefanos, N.M. A Systematic Power-Quality Assessment and Harmonic Filter Design Methodology for Variable-Frequency Drive Application in Marine Vessels. *IEEE Trans. Ind. Appl.* **2015**, *51*, 1909–1919.
29. Dong, Y.; Sun, B.; Wang, G. Research on modeling method of power system network security risk assessment based on object-oriented Bayesian network. *Energy Rep.* **2021**, *7*, 289–295. [CrossRef]
30. Bhandari, P. Novel technique of extraction of principal situational factors for NSSA. *Int. J. Eng. Sci.* **2014**, *1*, 48–56.
31. Yang, H.; Zhang, Z.; Xie, L.; Zhang, L. Network security situation assessment with network attack behavior classification. *Int. J. Intell. Syst.* **2022**, *37*, 6909–6927. [CrossRef]
32. Sen, O.; van der Velde, D.; Wehrmeister, K.A.; Hacker, I.; Henze, M.; Andres, M. On using contextual correlation to detect multi-stage cyber attacks in smart grids. *Sustain. Energy Grids Netw.* **2022**, *32*, 100821. [CrossRef]
33. Al Ghazo, A.T.; Ibrahim, M.; Ren, H.; Kumar, R. A2G2V: Automatic Attack Graph Generation and Visualization and Its Applications to Computer and SCADA Networks. *IEEE Trans. Syst. Man Cybern. Syst.* **2020**, *50*, 3488–3498. [CrossRef]
34. Wang, Z.; Chen, L.; Song, S.; Cong, P.X.; Ruan, Q. Automatic cyber security risk assessment based on fuzzy fractional ordinary differential equations. *Alex. Eng. J.* **2020**, *59*, 2725–2731. [CrossRef]
35. Tian, Z.; Luo, C.; Qiu, J.; Du, X.; Guizani, M. A Distributed Deep Learning System for Web Attack Detection on Edge Devices. *IEEE Trans. Ind. Inform.* **2020**, *16*, 1963–1971. [CrossRef]
36. Tang, X.; Zheng, Q.; Cheng, J.; Sheng, V.S.; Cao, R.; Chen, M. A DDoS Attack Situation Assessment Method via Optimized Cloud Model Based on Influence Function. *Comput. Mater. Contin.* **2019**, *60*, 1263–1281. [CrossRef]
37. Xi, R.R.; Yun, X.C.; Hao, Z.Y. A Framework for Risk Assessment in Cyber Situational Awareness. *IET Inf. Secur.* **2019**, *13*, 149–156.

38. Dsouza, J.; Elezabeth, L.; Mishra, V.P.; Jain, R. Security in Cyber-Physical Systems. In Proceedings of the 2019 Amity International Conference on Artificial Intelligence (AICAI), Dubai, United Arab Emirates, 4–6 February 2019; pp. 840–844.
39. Swessi, D.; Idoudi, H. A Survey on Internet-of-Things Security: Threats and Emerging Countermeasures. *Wirel. Pers. Commun.* **2022**, *124*, 1557–1592. [CrossRef]
40. Wang, H.; Chen, Z.; Feng, X.; Di, X.; Liu, D.; Zhao, J.; Sui, X. Research on Network Security Situation Assessment and Quantification Method Based on Analytic Hierarchy Process. *Wirel. Pers. Commun.* **2018**, *102*, 1401–1420. [CrossRef]
41. Yang, C.-T.; Chan, Y.-W.; Liu, J.-C.; Kristiani, E.; Lai, C.-H. Cyberattacks detection and analysis in a network log system using XGBoost with ELK stack. *Soft Comput.* **2022**, *26*, 5143–5157. [CrossRef]
42. Peter, M.; Karen, K.; Sasha, R. Common Vulnerability Scoring System. *IEEE Secur. Priv.* **2006**, *4*, 85–89.
43. Yang, H.; Zeng, R.; Xu, G.; Zhang, L. A network security situation assessment method based on adversarial deep learning. *Appl. Soft Comput.* **2021**, *102*, 107096. [CrossRef]

Disclaimer/Publisher's Note: The statements, opinions and data contained in all publications are solely those of the individual author(s) and contributor(s) and not of MDPI and/or the editor(s). MDPI and/or the editor(s) disclaim responsibility for any injury to people or property resulting from any ideas, methods, instructions or products referred to in the content.

Article

Robust Zero Watermarking Algorithm for Medical Images Based on Improved NasNet-Mobile and DCT

Fangchun Dong [1], Jingbing Li [1,*], Uzair Aslam Bhatti [1], Jing Liu [2], Yen-Wei Chen [3] and Dekai Li [1]

1. School of Information and Communication Engineering, Hainan University, Haikou 570228, China; 21220854000140@hainanu.edu.cn (F.D.); uzairaslambhatti@hotmail.com (U.A.B.); 21220854000150@hainanu.edu.cn (D.L.)
2. Research Center for Healthcare Data Science, Zhejiang Laboratory, Hangzhou 311121, China; liujinglj@zhejianglab.com
3. Graduate School of Information Science and Engineering, Ritsumeikan University, Kusatsu 525-8577, Japan; chen@is.ritsumei.ac.jp
* Correspondence: jingbingli2008@hotmail.com; Tel.: +86-136-3765-8206

Abstract: In the continuous progress of mobile internet technology, medical image processing technology is also always being upgraded and improved. In this field, digital watermarking technology is significant and provides a strong guarantee for medical image information security. This paper offers a robustness zero watermarking strategy for medical pictures based on an Improved NasNet-Mobile convolutional neural network and the discrete cosine transform (DCT) to address the lack of robustness of existing medical image watermarking algorithms. First, the structure of the pre-training network NasNet-Mobile is adjusted by using a fully connected layer with 128 output and a regression layer instead of the original Softmax layer and classification layer, thus generating a regression network with 128 output, whereby the 128 features are extracted from the medical images using the NasNet-Mobile network with migration learning. Migration learning is then performed on the modified NasNet-Mobile network to obtain the trained network, which is then used to extract medical image features, and finally the extracted image features are subjected to DCT transform to extract low frequency data, and the perceptual hashing algorithm processes the extracted data to obtain a 32-bit binary feature vector. Before performing the watermark embedding, the watermark data is encrypted using the chaos mapping algorithm to increase data security. Next, the zero watermarking technique is used to allow the algorithm to embed and extract the watermark without changing the information contained in the medical image. The experimental findings demonstrate the algorithm's strong resistance to both conventional and geometric assaults. The algorithm offers some practical application value in the realm of medicine when compared to other approaches.

Keywords: NasNet-Mobile network; DCT; chaotic encryption; zero watermarking; migration learning

Citation: Dong, F.; Li, J.; Bhatti, U.A.; Liu, J.; Chen, Y.-W.; Li, D. Robust Zero Watermarking Algorithm for Medical Images Based on Improved NasNet-Mobile and DCT. *Electronics* 2023, 12, 3444. https://doi.org/10.3390/electronics12163444

Academic Editors: Yue Wu, Kai Qin, Qiguang Miao and Maoguo Gong

Received: 17 July 2023
Revised: 7 August 2023
Accepted: 13 August 2023
Published: 15 August 2023

Copyright: © 2023 by the authors. Licensee MDPI, Basel, Switzerland. This article is an open access article distributed under the terms and conditions of the Creative Commons Attribution (CC BY) license (https://creativecommons.org/licenses/by/4.0/).

1. Introduction

The network is disseminating more data as communication technology advances, whereby digital watermarking technology is being updated and iterated regularly to stop the leaking of user information, and it is gradually becoming a trend to protect the privacy of user information with the help of digital watermarking technology to provide security for personal information [1]. Medical images in medical diagnoses play a crucial role in medical diagnosis, treatment, and scientific research, providing a wealth of clinical data that helps doctors make more accurate diagnoses and more effective treatment plans [2]. The development of technology has promoted the integration of modern information technology with medical care, and more and more physicians and patients are using telemedicine to diagnose [3]. However, with the widespread dissemination of medical image information on the internet, the security and integrity of patient information faces serious challenges [4]. In this context, medical image watermarking technology has emerged to provide technical support for protecting the privacy of patient information. By embedding invisible or imperceptible watermark data in medical images, medical image watermarking technology achieves copyright protection, integrity verification, and content authentication of medical images [5]. This technique requires embedding watermarks without affecting image quality and diagnostic accuracy and good robustness and invisibility to resist common image attack processing [6].

Spatial domain watermarking technique and frequency domain watermarking technique are two common traditional watermarking techniques [7]. Spatial domain watermarking uses techniques like least significant bit (LSB) replacement and pixel value mapping to insert watermarking information directly in the original data [8]. Such methods are relatively simple, but vulnerable to image attacks. Wang, Huanying et al. proposed a color image watermarking method to obtain the elements of QR decomposition in the spatial domain and perform watermark embedding and extraction in the spatial domain [9]. Basha, Shaik Hedayath et al. used ESP algorithm to compute Euclidean spatial points for watermark embedding process and used Diffie-Hellman key exchange protocol to recover the watermark, wherein the algorithm has some resistance to JPEG compression, cropping, rotation, and other attacks [10]. Cao, H. et al. used quantization technique for watermark embedding extraction by studying the relationship between the DFT DC component and the domain pixel values [11]. The frequency domain watermarking technique converts the original data to the frequency domain and then embeds the watermark information in the converted data [12]. The frequency domain watermarking approach is considerably more secure and attack-resistant than the spatial domain watermarking method [13]. Tang, Ming et al. proposed a robust watermarking algorithm based on DWT and SVD by first applying FRFT transform to the original image and the watermarked image to obtain the magnitude of the image, next applying DWT transform to it, and finally applying SVD to the low frequency sub-band of the second level DWT of the original image and the magnitude of the watermarked image to construct a new matrix to embed the watermark using singular values, and using FRFT transform for watermark encryption to improve the algorithm security, which has good robustness in attacks such as rotation, clipping, Gaussian filtering, and median filtering [14]. Jing, Liu. et al. combine the use of DTCWT-DCT transform and perceptual hashing technique to achieve watermark embedding and extraction using zero watermarking technique. The suggested method performs well against geometric and conventional assaults, and particularly good at resisting geometric attacks [15].

With the development of image local feature extraction algorithms, more and more researchers are applying feature extraction algorithms in the field of watermarking technology [16]. The traditional local feature extraction algorithms mainly include SIFT, SURF, KAZE, etc. [17–19]. They have excellent rotation invariance and scale invariance in image feature extraction and matching. Binary feature extraction algorithms have faster run speeds, and the mainstream ones include BRIEF, ORB, BRISK, etc. [20–22]. Watermarking researchers often combine feature extraction algorithms with frequency domain watermarking techniques. Hamidi, Mohamed. et al. exploit SIFT's geometric invariance to improve watermarking's robustness against geometric attacks and the proposed algorithm combining DWT-DCT and SIFT has good robustness [23]. Soualmi et al. proposed an imperceptible watermarking method for medical image tampering detection by combining SURF descriptors with Weber descriptors (WD) and Arnold algorithm, applying SURF technique to the region of interest (ROI) of medical images and then selecting the region around the SURF points to insert the watermark, thus embedding and extracting the watermark using Weber descriptors [24]. Cheng, Zeng et al. used the KAZE feature extraction algorithm to extract original image features. The extracted features were then DCT transformed to obtain the feature sequence of medical images using perceptual hashing, while embedding and extracting watermarks using the zero-watermarking technique. The proposed KAZE-DCT algorithm has better resistance to geometric attacks, but less resistant to conventional attacks [25].

In recent years, deep learning-based watermarking algorithms have gradually become popular among watermarking technology researchers [26]. Deep learning models for image processing are used in image watermarking systems [27]. Compared with traditional watermarking methods, deep learning-based algorithms can better adapt to different image contents and provide higher robustness and security [28]. Yu, Fan et al. used Inception V3 convolutional neural network to extract image features and then encrypted the embedded watermark using the chaotic mapping system. The algorithm is resistant to a wide range of geometric attacks but is less resistant to conventional attacks [29]. Wenxing, Zhang et al. proposed a method to train the GoogLeNet network using migration learning, and the trained network is used to extract the image features and encrypts the watermark using two-dimensional Henon chaos cryptography, and the proposed GoogLeNet-DCT algorithm has strong resistance to geometric attacks [30].

Based on the studies above, at the current stage, most medical image algorithms still do not fully mitigate the problem of ownership protection, and most of these algorithms can only defend against a small number of attacks. Therefore, watermarking researchers should investigate new robust watermarking algorithms that can cope with more types of attacks. The algorithm proposed in this paper is highly resistant to many conventional and geometric attacks.

The main contributions of this study are as follows:

(1) Proposed a zero-watermarking algorithm for medical images based on improved NasNet-Mobile and DCT.
(2) Double encryption of the watermark using Chen chaos mapping and Arnold transform dislocation.
(3) Changing the NasNet-Mobile network structure to train the medical image dataset and extract robust features.
(4) The proposed algorithm can withstand most of the conventional and geometric attacks and the algorithm is robust.

2. Fundamental Principles

2.1. NasNet-Mobile Convolutional Neural Network

NasNet-Mobile is a lightweight neural network architecture [31] to achieve high-performance, low-latency image recognition tasks. Developed by the Google Brain team and based on Neural Architecture Search (NAS) technology, NasNet-Mobile's network architecture aims to maintain accuracy while significantly reducing computational resource requirements and power consumption. Compared with the original version of NasNet, NasNet-Mobile is optimized in terms of network hierarchy and parameters to provide better performance while reducing computational complexity. The NasNet-Mobile network structure consists of basic modules (Cells), NASNet search space, reinforcement learning, and transfer (Skip) connections. In this paper, the NasNet-Mobile network is applied to digital watermarking.

In NasNet-Mobile, the basic components are Cell structures, and there exist two types of Cell structures called Normal Cells and Reduction Cells, which are a sub-network of multiple convolutional layers with reusable and combinable characteristics. NasNet-Mobile forms the entire network by stacking these basic modules (Normal Cells and Reduction Cells) together. This modular design allows NasNet-Mobile to be highly flexible and can be adapted to different task requirements and resource constraints. The network model architecture is depicted in Figure 1 and the best-performing Normal Cell and Reduction Cell structures are depicted in Figure 2.

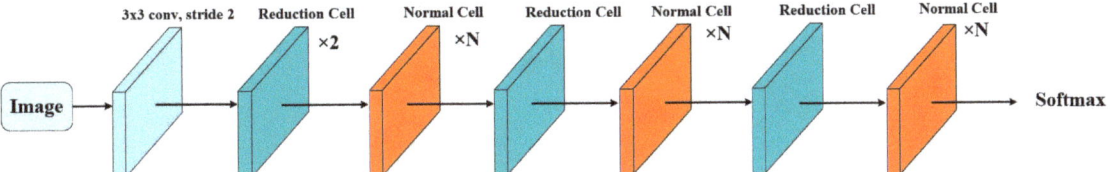

Figure 1. Network model architecture.

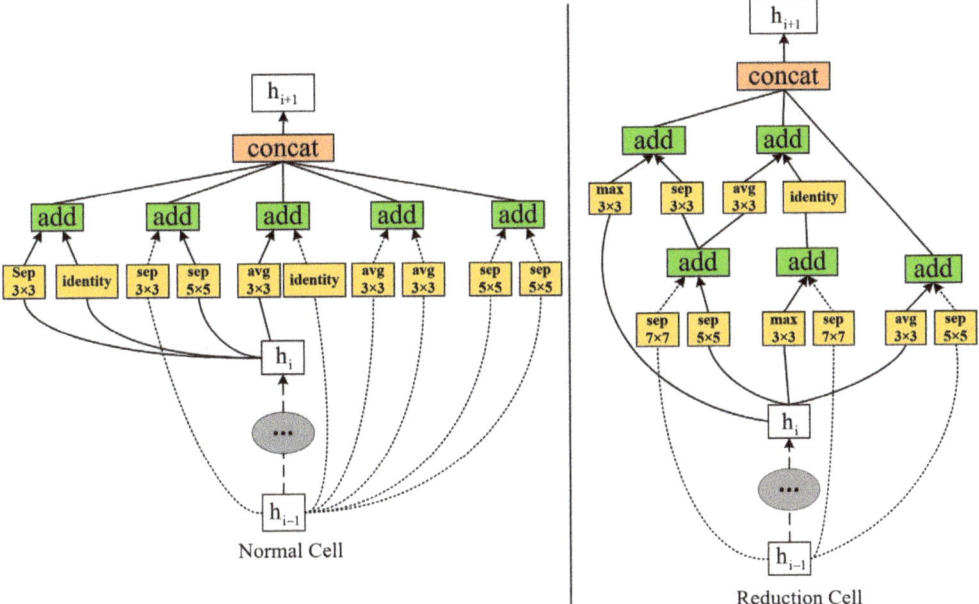

Figure 2. The architecture of the best convolutional cells.

2.2. Discrete Cosine Transform (DCT)

The DCT transform is commonly used for lossy data compression of images with separability and energy concentration. The principle of 1D-DCT is shown in Equation (1). In this case, 2D-DCT applies the one-dimensional discrete cosine transform to two-dimensional data, dividing the two-dimensional image into several small blocks, and then applying the discrete cosine transform to each block to convert the high-frequency signals in the small blocks into low-frequency signals. The 2D-DCT is shown in Equation (3):

$$F(u) = C(u) \sum_{i=0}^{N-1} f(i) \cos\left[\frac{(i+0.5)u\pi}{N}\right] \quad (1)$$

$$C(u) = \begin{cases} \sqrt{\frac{1}{N}}, & u = 0 \\ \sqrt{\frac{2}{N}}, & u = 1, 2, \ldots, M-1 \end{cases} \quad (2)$$

$$F(u,v) = C(u)C(v) \sum_{x=0}^{M-1} \sum_{y=0}^{N-1} f(x,y) \cos\left[\frac{(x+0.5)u\pi}{M}\right] \cos\left[\frac{(y+0.5)v\pi}{N}\right] \quad (3)$$
$$u = 0, 1, \ldots, M-1; v = 0, 1, \ldots, N-1$$

$$C(u) = \begin{cases} \sqrt{\frac{1}{M}}, & u = 0 \\ \sqrt{\frac{2}{M}}, & u = 1, 2, \ldots, M-1 \end{cases} \quad (4)$$

$$C(v) = \begin{cases} \sqrt{\frac{1}{N}}, & v = 0 \\ \sqrt{\frac{2}{N}}, & v = 1, 2, \ldots, N-1 \end{cases} \quad (5)$$

2.3. Chen Chaotic System

The Chen chaotic system is a particular type of three-dimensional nonlinear dynamical system. Equation (6) is used to define the Chen chaotic system. Encrypting images with the Chen chaotic system is common, mainly by generating a sequence of random numbers to obfuscate and permute the image pixels for data protection.

$$\begin{array}{c} \frac{dx}{dt} = a(y-x) \\ \frac{dy}{dt} = (c-a)x - xz + cy \\ \frac{dz}{dt} = xy - bz \end{array} \quad (6)$$

where a, b, and c are the parameters of the Chen chaotic system, and x, y, and z denote the three state variables of the system, respectively.

2.4. Arnold Mapping

Arnold mapping is a discrete-time mapping widely used in studying dynamical systems and chaos theory. Arnold mapping is a linear mapping defined in a two-dimensional toroidal space as shown in Equation (7). Arnold mapping mainly achieves the encryption of the original image by dislocating the pixels of the image and using a key to control the number of iterations, thus making the original image unrecognizable.

$$\begin{pmatrix} x_{n+1} \\ y_{n+1} \end{pmatrix} = \begin{pmatrix} 1 & b \\ a & ab+1 \end{pmatrix} \begin{pmatrix} x_n \\ y_n \end{pmatrix} \mathrm{mod} N \quad (7)$$

where (x_n, y_n) is the coordinate of the original point, (x_{n+1}, y_{n+1}) is the coordinate of the mapped point, a, b, N should be positive integers, and N is the image pixel size.

3. Zero Watermark Algorithm

This paper proposes a robust zero watermarking algorithm for medical images based on an improved NasNet-Mobile convolutional neural network and discrete cosine transform (DCT), combining NasNet-Mobile network, DCT transform, and perceptual hash function, watermarked image encryption using Chen chaotic system and Arnold transform dislocation dual encryption algorithm, using zero watermarking technique to embed and extract watermark, which has good effect in geometric attacks and some conventional attacks, and can blindly extract watermark.

3.1. NasNet-Mobile Pre-Trained Network Migration Learning

3.1.1. NasNet-Mobile Network Restructuring

The NasNet-Mobile network structure uses the idea of repetitive stacking, and the network itself has a strong feature extraction capability. To further improve the accuracy of image feature extraction, we adapt the structure of the pre-trained network NasNet-Mobile by using a fully connected layer with 128 output and a regression layer instead of the original Softmax layer and classification layer, thus generating a regression network with 128 output, and selecting the fully connected layer with output value of 128 for extracting feature values of medical images, as shown in Figure 3. After experiments, the improved network has better feature extraction capability.

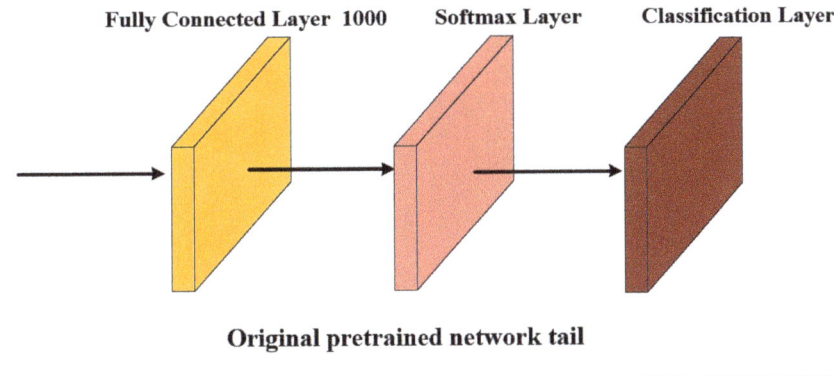

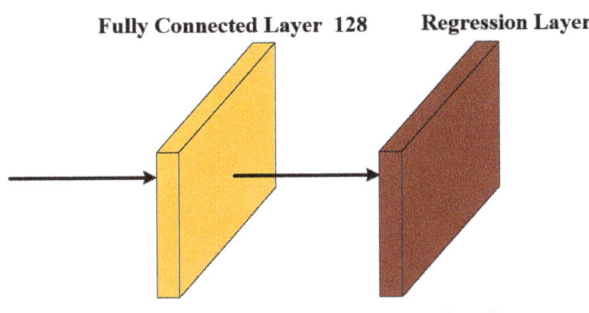

Figure 3. NasNet-Mobile network model adjustment.

3.1.2. Dataset Creation

The datasets in this paper are sourced from Medical Imaging Park and the American Institutes for Research, employing the datasets from the categories of the brain, abdomen, chest, bones, and muscles. We selected 350 original medical images as the training set, 150 original medical images as the validation set, and 100 original medical images as the test set, and some of the medical images are shown in Figure 4. To improve the algorithmis capacity to extract visual features, we perform data enhancement on the selected dataset as shown in Table 1. Because the NasNet-Mobile pre-training network requires the input image pixels to be 224 × 244, the image size needs to be set to 224 × 224, so that we get 37,450 training sets with 224 × 224 pixels and 16,050 validation sets. We perform 2D-DCT transform on the training and test set images and select 128 low-frequency components of 16 × 8 as the data set labels.

3.1.3. Training Network

The programming Matlab 2022b was used for this experiment and the NasNet-Mobile pre-trained network from the Neural Network Toolbox was selected. The computer configuration used for the experiments was a processor (AMD Ryzen7 5800H with Radeon Graphics), a graphics card (NVIDIA GeForce RTX 3060 Laptop GPU 6 G), and memory (Samsung DDR4 3200 MHz 16 G). We trained the NasNet-Mobile pre-trained network. During training, the initial learning rate is set at 0.001. At each iteration, the model will use thirty samples for weight update and is trained for four rounds. At the beginning of each round, the training data will be reordered randomly, and after every 1000 iterations, the model will be evaluated using validation data. After the training, we save the well-trained grid and use the fully connected layer with an output value of 128 at the tail end of the network as the feature values for image feature extraction.

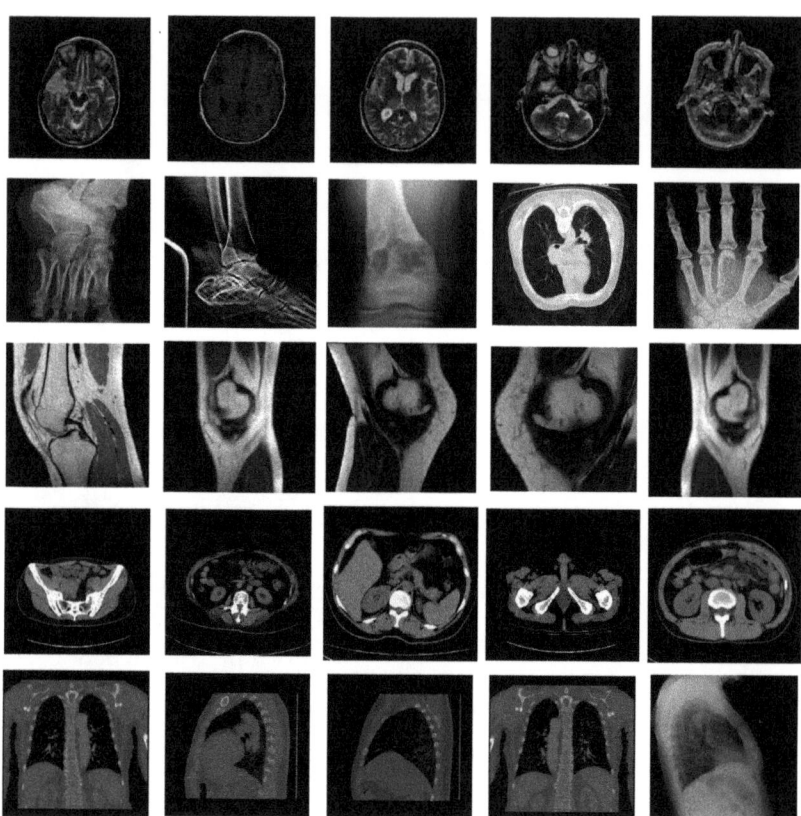

Figure 4. Some medical images in the dataset.

Table 1. Data Set Enhancement Methods.

Enhanced Type	Intensity	Number of New Images
JPEG compression (%)	5, 10, 15, 20	4
Gaussian noise (%)	2, 4, 6, 8, 10, 12, 14, 16	8
Median filter [3 × 3] (times)	5, 10, 15, 20	4
Median filter [5 × 5] (times)	5, 10, 15, 20	4
Median filter [7 × 7] (times)	5, 10, 15, 20	4
Clockwise rotation (°)	5, 10, 15, 20, 25, 30, 35, 40, 45, 50, 55, 60	12
Anticlockwise rotation (°)	5, 10, 15, 20, 25, 30, 35, 40, 45, 50, 55, 60	12
Y-axis shear (%)	5, 10, 15, 20, 25, 30, 35, 40	8
Scaling	0.2, 0.4, 0.6, 0.8, 1.0, 1.2, 1.4, 1.6, 1.8, 2.0	10
Right-shift (%)	5, 10, 15, 20, 25, 30, 35, 40	8
Left-shift (%)	5, 10, 15, 20, 25, 30, 35, 40	8
Down-shift (%)	5, 10, 15, 20, 25, 30, 35, 40	8
X-axis shear (%)	5, 10, 15, 20, 25, 30, 35, 40	8
Up-shift (%)	5, 10, 15, 20, 25, 30, 35, 40	8

3.2. NasNet-Mobile Feature Extraction

In this paper, we use a trained NasNet-Mobile network to extract medical image features and get 128 feature values $N(i,j)$, after DCT transformation of the extracted eigenvalues, 128 DCT transformed feature values $D(i,j)$ are obtained, then select the 32 low frequency coefficients $V(i,j)$ of feature values $D(i,j)$, perform sign transformation on the low frequency coefficients $V(i,j)$, set the elements greater than 0 in the matrix to 1 and the other elements to 0 to get the 32 bit hash value $H(i,j)$, and $H(i,j)$ for the binary feature sequence. The specific steps are shown in Figure 5.

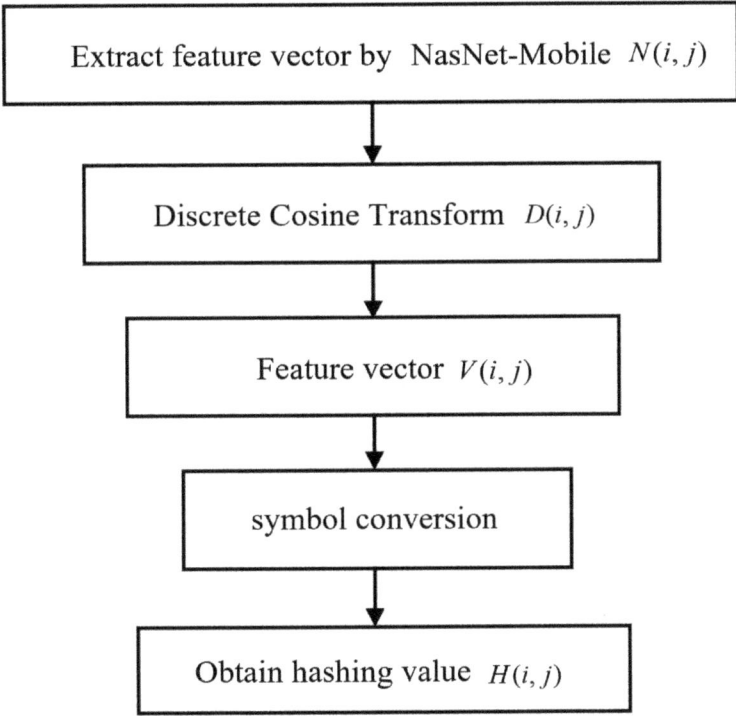

Figure 5. Image feature extraction flow chart.

3.3. Watermark Encryption

Chen chaos system and Arnold chaos mapping are used to encrypt the picture twice in order to improve the anti-interference and security of the embedded watermark. Firstly, the initial values of the Chen chaos system are set as follows: $x = 2, y = 1, z = 3, a = 35, b = 3, c = 28$. Subsequently, the system enters the chaotic state to obtain the chaotic sequence, and then the chaos matrix is obtained by binarization. XOR operation is performed on the chaotic matrix and the original watermark to obtain the watermark encrypted by the Chen chaos system $C(i,j)$, and finally, the watermark $C(i,j)$ is dislocated by Arnold chaos mapping to obtain the encrypted watermark $L(i,j)$. The parameters of Arnold chaos mapping in this paper are set as $a = 3, b = 5$, and the number of iterations is 10. The watermark encryption process is shown in Figure 6.

3.4. Embedding Watermarks

We embed the encrypted watermark into the medical image, whereby first the trained NasNet-Mobile network performs feature extraction on the original image to obtain the hash value $H(i,j)$, and then the binary feature sequence is XOR operation with the encrypted watermark to obtain the logical key used to extract the watermark $K(i,j)$. This embedding watermark method uses the zero-watermark embedding technique, which does not alter the original image. The specific embedding watermark steps are shown in Figure 7.

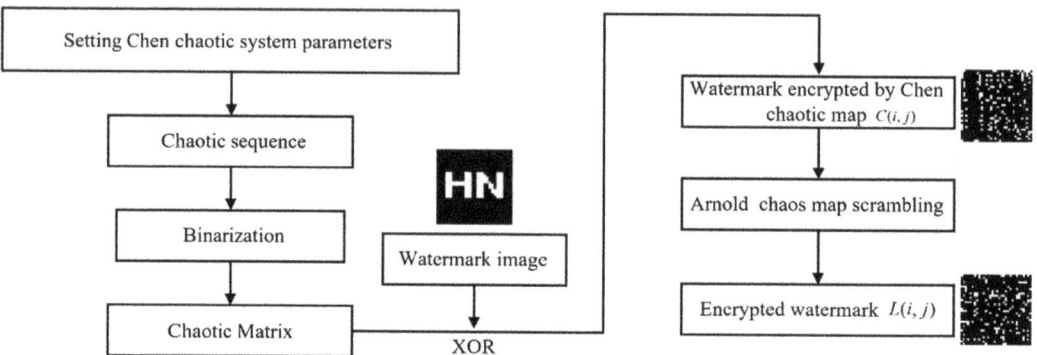

Figure 6. Watermark encryption flow chart.

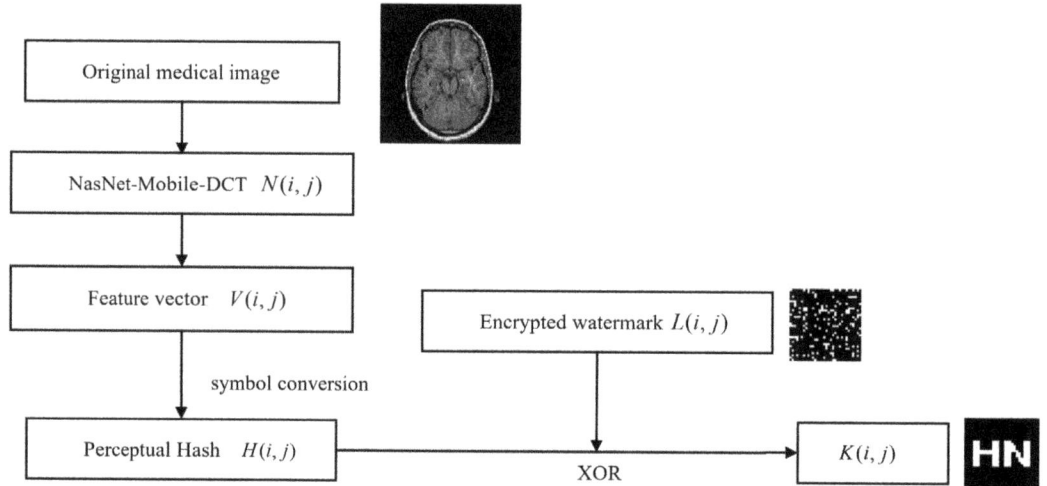

Figure 7. Embed watermark flow chart.

3.5. Watermark Extraction and Decryption

Finally, watermark extraction and decryption are performed. Firstly, the trained NasNet-Mobile network is used to extract features from the image after the attack and obtain the hash value $H'(i,j)$, the extracted encrypted watermark $L'(i,j)$ is obtained by performing the XOR operation between $H'(i,j)$ and the logical key $K(i,j)$, the encrypted watermark $L'(i,j)$ is obtained by the Arnold inverse transformation to the watermark encrypted by Chen chaos system $C'(i,j)$. Finally, the watermark is restored by the initial value of Chen chaos system. The specific watermark extraction step is shown in Figure 8.

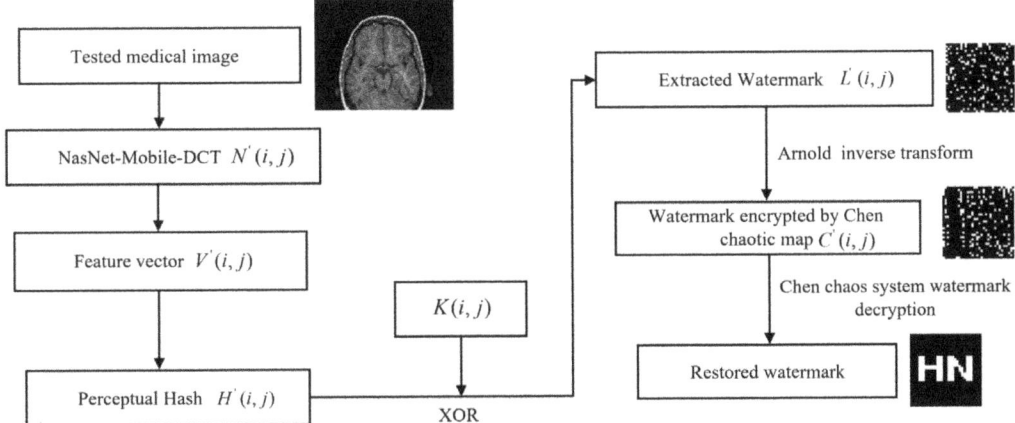

Figure 8. Watermark extraction and decryption flow chart.

4. Experiments and Results

This paper uses MATLAB 2022b software to simulate and experiment on medical images. Since the network input image pixel is 224 × 224, the medical image pixel used for testing is 224 × 224. In this paper, three medical images from the test set are chosen at random for testing, and the watermark image pixel size is chosen as 32 × 32, as seen in Figure 9. The normalized correlation coefficient (NC), as shown in Equation (8), is employed to determine how well the method can withstand assault by comparing how similar the original watermark is to the watermark that was retrieved from the picture after attack. The peak signal-to-noise ratio (PSNR), as shown in Equation (9), is used to represent the quality of the image. In the case of medical images without any attacks, the NC values are all 1.

$$NC = \frac{\sum_i \sum_j W_{(i,j)} W'_{(i,j)}}{\sum_i \sum_j W^2_{(i,j)}} \quad (8)$$

$$PSNR = 10\lg \left[\frac{MN \max_{i,j}(I(i,j))^2}{\sum_i \sum_j (I(i,j) - I'(i,j))^2} \right] \quad (9)$$

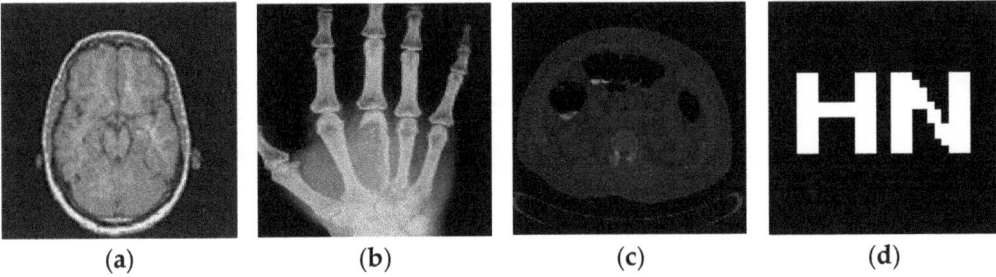

Figure 9. Tested images and watermarks. Brain image (**a**), palm image (**b**), abdominal image (**c**), watermark image (**d**).

4.1. Testing Different Images

Before testing the anti-attack performance of medical images, we first need to test ten different medical images with the algorithm, as shown in Figure 10. At the same time, their correlation coefficients are calculated to verify whether the algorithm can distinguish different medical images. The outcomes of the experiment are displayed in Table 2. The outcomes demonstrate that the NasNet-Mobile-DCT algorithm's NC values for different medical pictures are less than 0.5, which proves that the algorithm can distinguish different medical images.

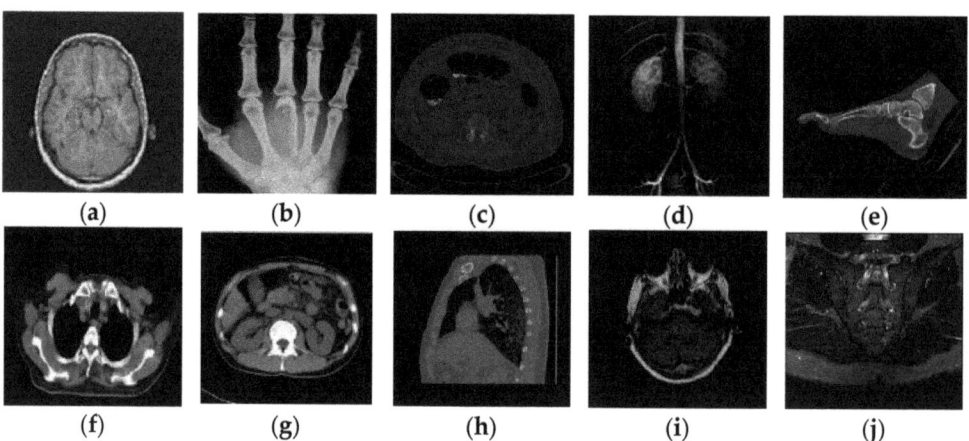

Figure 10. Different medical images within the test (a–j).

Table 2. Correlation coefficient values between different images (32 bits).

Image	(a)	(b)	(c)	(d)	(e)	(f)	(g)	(h)	(i)	(j)
(a)	1.00									
(b)	0.14	1.00								
(c)	0.42	0.25	1.00							
(d)	0.39	0.22	0.37	1.00						
(e)	0.18	0.30	0.33	0.34	1.00					
(f)	0.41	0	0.41	0.41	0.27	1.00				
(g)	0.43	0.07	0.05	0.24	0.07	0.10	1.00			
(h)	0.23	0.29	0.27	0.21	0.43	0.38	0.32	1.00		
(i)	0.39	0.03	0.17	0.35	0.06	0.18	0.33	0.39	1.00	
(j)	0.30	0.03	0.14	0.10	0.03	0.23	0.31	0.23	0.32	1.00

4.2. Conventional Attacks

The NasNet-Mobil-DCT algorithm is used to perform different levels of conventional attacks on medical images that already contain encrypted watermarks, and then the watermarks are extracted, and Figure 11 displays the conventionally attacked images along with the extracted watermarks. Then the algorithm's robustness for conventional attacks is observed, and Table 3 displays the trial outcomes. The findings demonstrate that the Gaussian attack strength is 0.02 and 0.04, the NC value is greater than 0.85, even if the Gaussian attack strength is 0.10, the NC value is greater than 0.55, which indicates that the proposed algorithm has certain ability to resist Gaussian attack. The NC value is greater than 0.85 even when the JPEG compression quality is 5%, and when the quality of the JPEG compression is greater than 20%, the NC value is 1, which indicates that the proposed algorithm has good robustness to JPEG compression attack. When the attack strength is 20 times [5 × 5] median filtering, the measured NC values are higher than 0.74, even if the attack intensity is 10 times [7 × 7] median filter, the NC value is greater than 0.70, and this shows that the algorithm is effectively resistant to median filtering. Experimental results show that the algorithm proposed in this paper has good resistance to conventional attacks.

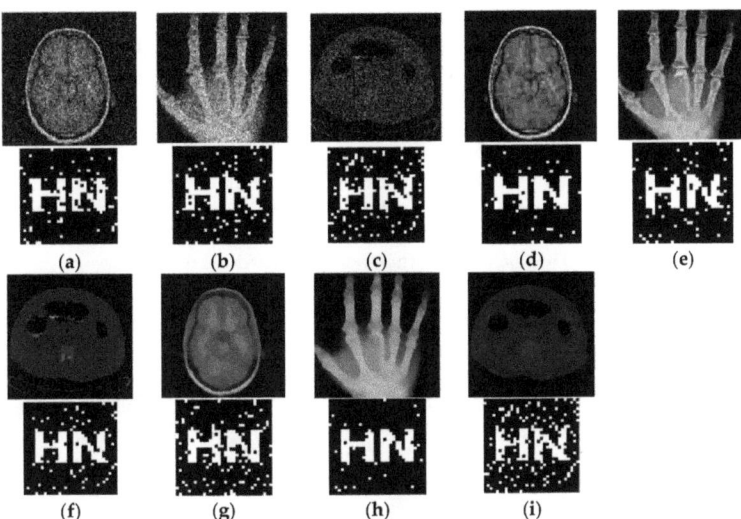

Figure 11. Medical images and watermarks for conventional attacks. (**a**–**c**) denote medical images and extracted watermarks after a Gaussian attack intensity of 0.06; (**d**–**f**) denote medical images and extracted watermarks at a compression quality of 5%; (**g**–**i**) denote medical images and extracted watermarks after 20 Me-dian filtering [5 × 5] attacks.

Table 3. Experimental data of watermarking based on conventional attacks.

Conventional Attacks		PSNR (dB)			NC		
	Intensity	Img1	Img2	Img3	Img1	Img2	Img3
Gaussian noise	0.02	17.81	16.76	17.29	1.00	0.93	0.94
	0.04	15.12	14.06	14.55	0.86	0.93	0.89
	0.06	13.65	12.55	13.04	0.85	0.88	0.82
	0.08	12.66	11.42	12.04	0.67	0.87	0.76
	0.10	11.86	10.67	11.21	0.56	0.85	0.63
JPEG compression	25%	33.39	32.03	34.27	1.00	1.00	1.00
	20%	32.51	31.17	33.39	1.00	1.00	1.00
	15%	31.25	30.03	32.37	0.90	0.94	1.00
	10%	29.26	28.39	30.65	0.95	1.00	0.88
	5%	26.46	25.16	27.68	0.95	0.86	0.88
Median filtering [5 × 5]	5 (times)	25.13	27.00	28.35	1.00	0.86	0.83
	10 (times)	24.29	25.99	27.60	0.92	0.92	0.83
	15 (times)	23.86	25.48	27.24	0.89	0.92	0.83
	20 (times)	23.56	25.09	27.07	0.84	0.92	0.75
Median filtering [7 × 7]	5 (times)	22.49	24.75	26.61	1.00	0.86	0.83
	10 (times)	21.77	23.14	25.70	0.72	0.86	0.83

4.3. Geometric Attacks

The NasNet-Mobil-DCT algorithm is robust under conventional attacks and the following tests are performed on geometric attacks. The medical images that already contain the encrypted watermark are subjected to different degrees of rotation attack, scaling attack, translation attack, X-axis shearing attack, and Y-axis shearing after extracting the watermark, and Figure 12 displays the extracted watermark and medical images following the geometric attack. Following that, the algorithm's resistance to geometrical assaults is seen, and the experimental findings are displayed in Table 4. The experimental findings demonstrate that the NC values were higher than 0.85 when the images were rotated by 5, 15, and 30 degrees, even after rotating the observed picture by 60 degrees, the NC value remains higher than 0.80, it shows that the algorithm can effectively fend against rotational attacks. When the scaling ratio is equal to 0.3 and 2.0, the NC value exceeds 0.86, and this suggests that the algorithm is rather resistant to scaling attacks. When the measured cryptomedical images were shifted upwards by 5%, the NC values were all greater than 0.92, the NC value exceeds to 0.75 when it is shifted to the up by 35%, the NC value is higher than or equal to 0.75 when the measured encrypted medical image is shifted to the right by 25%, demonstrating the algorithm's strong robustness to translation attacks. When the encrypted medical images are cut by 20% on the Y-axis, the NC value is greater than 0.85, even when the encrypted medical image is cropped 40% on the Y-axis, the NC value is greater than 0.82, when they are cut by 40% on the X-axis, the NC values are greater than 0.80, indicating that the algorithm has strong resistance to shear attacks. In conclusion, the algorithm proposed in this paper performs well against multiple geometric attacks.

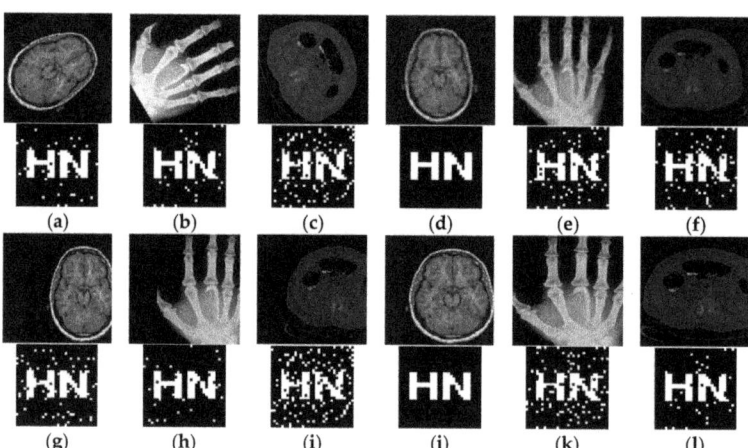

Figure 12. Medical images and watermarks for geometric attacks. (**a–c**) represent the medical image and extracted watermark after a 60-degree clockwise rotation attack; (**d–f**) represent the medical image and extracted watermark at a scaling of 0.3; (**g–i**) represent the medical image and extracted watermark after a 25% right shift; (**j–l**) denote the medical image and extracted watermark after a 20% X-axis clipping of the medical image and the extracted watermark.

Table 4. Experimental data of watermarking based on geometric attacks.

Geometric Attacks		PSNR (dB)			NC		
	Intensity	Img1	Img2	Img3	Img1	Img2	Img3
Rotation (clockwise)	5°	18.36	14.63	22.50	0.95	0.94	0.94
	15°	15.05	10.06	19.58	0.95	0.87	0.94
	30°	14.56	9.14	18.11	1.00	0.86	1.00
	45°	13.99	8.24	17.72	1.00	0.80	0.93
	60°	13.68	7.44	17.03	0.95	0.94	0.83
Scaling	0.3	20.97	21.32	25.67	1.00	0.88	0.88
	0.6	27.13	27.25	29.70	1.00	1.00	0.94
	1.5	46.44	43.72	45.19	1.00	1.00	0.93
	2.0	46.40	43.61	44.94	1.00	1.00	0.93

Table 4. *Cont.*

Geometric Attacks	Intensity	PSNR (dB)			NC		
		Img1	Img2	Img3	Img1	Img2	Img3
Right translation	5%	14.60	10.37	19.13	1.00	1.00	0.93
	15%	12.98	8.12	16.04	0.95	0.92	0.89
	25%	11.34	6.62	15.25	0.90	0.92	0.75
	40%	10.11	5.75	14.50	0.90	0.80	0.82
Up translation	5%	14.67	13.42	17.99	0.95	0.92	1.00
	15%	13.17	8.81	15.08	1.00	0.92	0.82
	25%	11.97	7.08	14.32	1.00	0.73	0.82
	35%	11.08	6.06	13.34	1.00	0.92	0.76
Y-axis cropping	10%	15.66	15.14	18.75	1.00	0.86	1.00
	20%	15.26	12.27	16.21	1.00	0.86	0.89
	30%	14.95	11.29	15.02	1.00	0.86	0.83
	40%	14.69	10.57	14.48	0.95	0.94	0.83
X-axis cropping	10%	14.70	10.00	19.52	1.00	0.94	1.00
	20%	13.14	8.80	18.07	1.00	0.81	0.94
	30%	12.55	7.48	17.04	1.00	0.75	0.86
	40%	12.14	7.70	16.67	1.00	0.81	0.88

4.4. Algorithm Comparison

To demonstrate the robustness of the NasNet-Mobil-DCT algorithm and use this algorithm to compare with other algorithms, this comparison experiment uses a brain image as the experimental object, as shown in Figure 9a, because this image is often used by a wide range of medical image watermarking researchers in comparative experiments and is representative. The comparison data are shown in Figure 13, in which black represents the DCT algorithm [32], green represents the DWT-DCT algorithm [33], blue represents the SIFT-DCT algorithm [34], purple represents the KAZE-DCT algorithm [25], orange represents the Inception V3-DCT algorithm [34], and red represents the NasNet-Mobil-DCT algorithm proposed in this paper. The NasNet-Mobil-DCT algorithm offers strong resilience to conventional and geometric attacks, as observed from the experimental data.

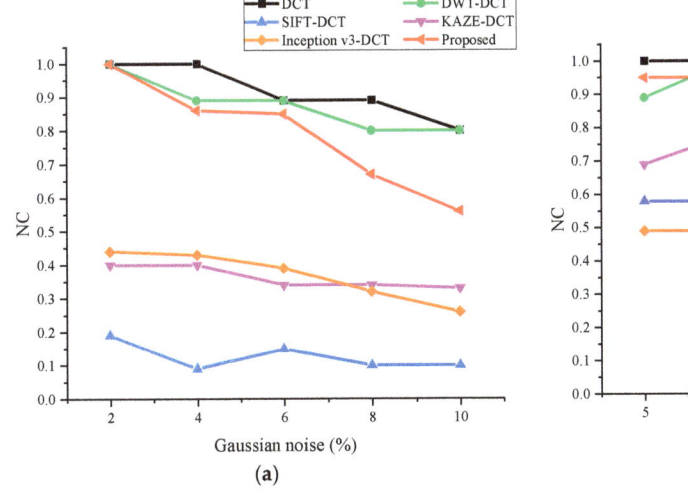

Figure 13. *Cont.*

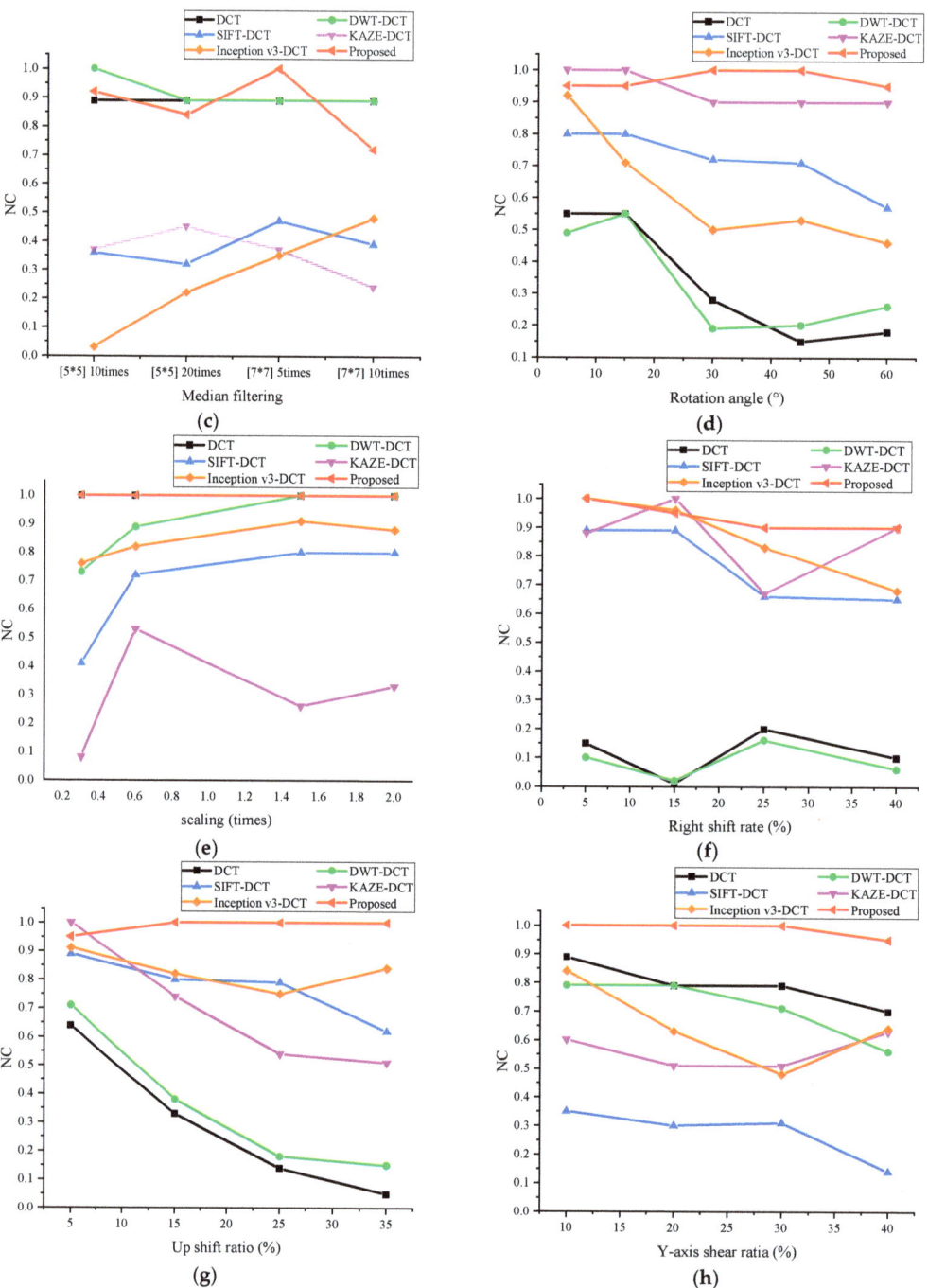

Figure 13. Algorithm comparison results. Comparison of NC values between different algorithms, where (**a**–**h**) indicate the results after Gaussian noise, JPEG compression, median filter, clockwise rotation, scaling, right-shift, up-shift, and Y-axis shear attacks, respectively.

5. Conclusions

In this paper, we propose a robust zero watermarking algorithm for medical images based on improved NasNet-Mobile convolutional neural network and discrete cosine transform (DCT), which uses deep learning algorithm, chaotic encryption technique, perceptual hashing algorithm, and zero watermarking technique to provide security for medical image watermarking information. Before watermark embedding, Chen chaotic system and Arnold mapping algorithm are used to double encrypt the watermarked data, which improves the security of the data, and then migration learning is carried out on the improved NasNet-Mobile network to get the trained medical image feature extraction network, and finally, the extracted image features are subjected to DCT transformation to extract the low-frequency data and the extracted data are processed by the perceptual hash algorithm to get the 32-bit binary feature vectors, and finally, the zero-watermarking technology is utilized for encrypting the medical images. The experimental results show that the algorithm proposed in this paper can resist a variety of conventional attacks, and at the same time, it is excellent in resisting geometric attacks such as rotation, translation, scaling, shearing, etc., and shows strong robustness. Therefore, the algorithm can be used for medical images. In the next research, we will improve the algorithm and look for algorithms that can extract image features more effectively to cope with the watermarking techniques' weak resistance against various attacks.

Author Contributions: Formal analysis, validation, data curation, and writing—original draft preparation, F.D.; funding acquisition, J.L. (Jingbing Li); supervision, J.L. (Jing Liu); software, Y.-W.C.; investigation, D.L. Data curation, Supervision, Resources, Writing—original draft, U.A.B. All authors have read and agreed to the published version of the manuscript.

Funding: This work was supported in part by the Natural Science Foundation of China under Grants 62063004, the Key Research Project of Hainan Province under Grant ZDYF2021SHFZ093, the Hainan Provincial Natural Science Foundation of China under Grants 2019RC018 and 619QN246, and the post doctor research from Zhejiang Province under Grant ZJ2021028.

Data Availability Statement: Data is contained within this article.

Conflicts of Interest: The authors declare no conflict of interest.

References

1. Evsutin, O.; Melman, A.; Meshcheryakov, R. Digital Steganography and Watermarking for Digital Images: A Review of Current Research Directions. *IEEE Access* **2020**, *8*, 166589–166611. [CrossRef]
2. Tian, Y.; Fu, S. A Descriptive Framework for the Field of Deep Learning Applications in Medical Images. *Knowl.-Based Syst.* **2020**, *210*, 106445. [CrossRef]
3. Amine, K.; Fares, K.; Redouane, K.M.; Salah, E. Medical Image Watermarking for Telemedicine Application Security. *J. Circuits Syst. Comput.* **2022**, *31*, 2250097. [CrossRef]
4. Venkateswarlu, I.B. Fast Medical Image Security Using Color Channel Encryption. *Braz. Arch. Biol. Technol.* **2020**, *63*, e20180473. [CrossRef]
5. Thabit, R. Review of Medical Image Authentication Techniques and Their Recent Trends. *Multimed. Tools Appl.* **2021**, *80*, 13439–13473. [CrossRef]
6. Raj, N.R.N.; Shreelekshmi, R. A Survey on Fragile Watermarking Based Image Authentication Schemes. *Multimed. Tools Appl.* **2021**, *80*, 19307–19333. [CrossRef]
7. Verma, V.S.; Jha, R.K. An Overview of Robust Digital Image Watermarking. *IETE Tech. Rev. (Inst. Electron. Telecommun. Eng. India)* **2015**, *32*, 479–496. [CrossRef]
8. Kumar, S.; Singh, B.K. Entropy Based Spatial Domain Image Watermarking and Its Performance Analysis. *Multimed. Tools Appl.* **2021**, *80*, 9315–9331. [CrossRef]
9. Wang, H.; Su, Q. A Color Image Watermarking Method Combined QR Decomposition and Spatial Domain. *Multimed. Tools Appl.* **2022**, *81*, 37895–37916. [CrossRef]
10. Basha, S.H.; Jaison, B. A Novel Secured Euclidean Space Points Algorithm for Blind Spatial Image Watermarking. *EURASIP J. Image Video Process.* **2022**, *2022*, 21. [CrossRef]
11. Cao, H.; Hu, F.; Sun, Y.; Chen, S.; Su, Q. Robust and Reversible Color Image Watermarking Based on DFT in the Spatial Domain. *Optik* **2022**, *262*, 169319. [CrossRef]

12. Chopra, A.; Gupta, S.; Dhall, S. Analysis of Frequency Domain Watermarking Techniques in Presence of Geometric and Simple Attacks. *Multimed. Tools Appl.* **2020**, *79*, 501–554. [CrossRef]
13. Tian, C.; Wen, R.-H.; Zou, W.-P.; Gong, L.-H. Robust and Blind Watermarking Algorithm Based on DCT and SVD in the Contourlet Domain. *Multimed. Tools Appl.* **2020**, *79*, 7515–7541. [CrossRef]
14. Tang, M.; Zhou, F. A Robust and Secure Watermarking Algorithm Based on DWT and SVD in the Fractional Order Fourier Transform Domain. *Array* **2022**, *15*, 100230. [CrossRef]
15. Liu, J.; Li, J.; Cheng, J.; Ma, J.; Sadiq, N.; Han, B.; Geng, Q.; Ai, Y. A Novel Robust Watermarking Algorithm for Encrypted Medical Image Based on DTCWT-DCT and Chaotic Map. *Comput. Mater. Contin.* **2019**, *61*, 889–910.
16. Jose, A.; Subramaniam, K. Comparative Analysis of Reversible Data Hiding Schemes. *IET Image Process.* **2020**, *14*, 2064–2073. [CrossRef]
17. Lowe, D.G. Distinctive Image Features from Scale-Invariant Keypoints. *Int. J. Comput. Vis.* **2004**, *60*, 91–110. [CrossRef]
18. Bay, H.; Ess, A.; Tuytelaars, T.; Van Gool, L. Speeded-Up Robust Features (SURF). *Comput. Vis. Image Underst.* **2008**, *110*, 346–359. [CrossRef]
19. Alcantarilla, P.F.; Bartoli, A.; Davison, A.J. KAZE Features. In Proceedings of the Computer Vision—ECCV 2012, Florence, Italy, 7–13 October 2012; Fitzgibbon, A., Lazebnik, S., Perona, P., Sato, Y., Schmid, C., Eds.; Springer: Berlin/Heidelberg, Germany, 2012; pp. 214–227.
20. Sjöstrand, T.; Mrenna, S.; Skands, P. A Brief Introduction to PYTHIA 8.1. *Comput. Phys. Commun.* **2008**, *178*, 852–867. [CrossRef]
21. Rublee, E.; Rabaud, V.; Konolige, K.; Bradski, G. ORB: An Efficient Alternative to SIFT or SURF. In Proceedings of the 2011 International Conference on Computer Vision, Barcelona, Spain, 6–13 November 2011; pp. 2564–2571.
22. Leutenegger, S.; Chli, M.; Siegwart, R.Y. BRISK: Binary Robust Invariant Scalable Keypoints. In Proceedings of the 2011 International Conference on Computer Vision, Barcelona, Spain, 6–13 November 2011; pp. 2548–2555.
23. Hamidi, M.; El Haziti, M.; Cherifi, H.; El Hassouni, M. A Hybrid Robust Image Watermarking Method Based on Dwt-Dct and Sift for Copyright Protection. *J. Imaging* **2021**, *7*, 218. [CrossRef]
24. Soualmi, A.; Alti, A.; Laouamer, L. An Imperceptible Watermarking Scheme for Medical Image Tamper Detection. *Int. J. Inf. Secur. Priv.* **2022**, *16*, 18. [CrossRef]
25. Zeng, C.; Liu, J.; Li, J.; Cheng, J.; Zhou, J.; Nawaz, S.A.; Xiliang, X.; Bhatti, U.A. Multi-Watermarking Algorithm for Medical Image Based on KAZE-DCT. *J. Ambient. Intell. Humaniz. Comput.* **2022**, 1–9. [CrossRef]
26. Meng, R.; Cui, Q.; Yuan, C. A Survey of Image Information Hiding Algorithms Based on Deep Learning. *CMES Comput. Model. Eng. Sci.* **2018**, *117*, 425–454. [CrossRef]
27. Bao, Z.; Xue, R. Survey on Deep Learning Applications in Digital Image Security. *Opt. Eng.* **2021**, *60*, 120901. [CrossRef]
28. Chacko, A.; Chacko, S. Deep Learning-Based Robust Medical Image Watermarking Exploiting DCT and Harris Hawks Optimization. *Int. J. Intell. Syst.* **2022**, *37*, 4810–4844. [CrossRef]
29. Fan, Y.; Li, J.; Bhatti, U.A.; Shao, C.; Gong, C.; Cheng, J.; Chen, Y. A Multi-Watermarking Algorithm for Medical Images Using Inception V3 and DCT. *Comput. Mater. Contin.* **2023**, *74*, 1279–1302.
30. Zhang, W.; Li, J.; Bhatti, U.A.; Liu, J.; Zheng, J.; Chen, Y.-W. Robust Multi-Watermarking Algorithm for Medical Images Based on GoogLeNet and Henon Map. *Comput. Mater. Contin.* **2023**, *75*, 565–586. [CrossRef]
31. Zoph, B.; Vasudevan, V.; Shlens, J.; Le, Q.V. Learning Transferable Architectures for Scalable Image Recognition. In Proceedings of the 2018 IEEE/CVF Conference on Computer Vision and Pattern Recognition (CVPR), Salt Lake City, UT, USA, 18–23 June 2018; IEEE: New York, NY, USA, 2018; pp. 8697–8710.
32. Liu, Y.L.; Li, J.B. DCT and Logistic Map Based Multiple Robust Watermarks for Medical Image. *Appl. Res. Comput.* **2013**, *30*, 3430–3433.
33. Liu, Y.; Li, J. The Medical Image Watermarking Algorithm Using DWT-DCT and Logistic. In Proceedings of the 2012 7th International Conference on Computing and Convergence Technology (ICCCT), Seoul, Republic of Korea, 3–5 December 2012; pp. 599–603.
34. Fang, Y.; Liu, J.; Li, J.; Cheng, J.; Hu, J.; Yi, D.; Xiao, X.; Bhatti, U.A. Robust Zero-Watermarking Algorithm for Medical Images Based on SIFT and Bandelet-DCT. *Multimed. Tools Appl.* **2022**, *81*, 16863–16879. [CrossRef]

Disclaimer/Publisher's Note: The statements, opinions and data contained in all publications are solely those of the individual author(s) and contributor(s) and not of MDPI and/or the editor(s). MDPI and/or the editor(s) disclaim responsibility for any injury to people or property resulting from any ideas, methods, instructions or products referred to in the content.

Article

Hybrid Encrypted Watermarking Algorithm for Medical Images Based on DCT and Improved DarkNet53

Dekai Li [1], Jingbing Li [1,*], Uzair Aslam Bhatti [1], Saqib Ali Nawaz [1], Jing Liu [2], Yen-Wei Chen [3] and Lei Cao [1]

1. School of Information and Communication Engineering, Hainan University, Haikou 570228, China
2. Research Center for Healthcare Data Science, Zhejiang Laboratory, Hangzhou 311121, China
3. Graduate School of Information Science and Engineering, Ritsumeikan University, Kusatsu 525-8577, Shiga, Japan
* Correspondence: jingbingli2008@hotmail.com; Tel.: +136-37658206

Abstract: To solve the problem of robustness of encrypted medical image watermarking algorithms, a zero watermarking algorithm based on the discrete cosine transform (DCT) and an improved DarkNet53 convolutional neural network is proposed. The algorithm targets medical images in the encrypted domain. In this algorithm, DCT is performed on the encrypted medical image to extract 32-bit features as feature 1. DarkNet53, a pre-trained network, was chosen for migration learning for the network model. The network uses a fully connected layer and a regression layer instead of the original Softmax layer and classification layer, changing the original classification network into a regression network with an output of 128. With these transformations, 128-bit features can be extracted from encrypted medical images by this network, and then DCT is performed to extract 32-bit features as feature 2. The fusion of features 1 and 2 can effectively improve the robustness of the algorithm. The experimental results show that the algorithm can accurately distinguish different encrypted medical images and can effectively restore the original information from the encrypted watermarked information under traditional and geometric attacks. Compared with other algorithms, the proposed method demonstrates better robustness and invisibility.

Keywords: cryptographic medical images; convolutional neural network; DarkNet53; migration learning; DCT

1. Introduction

With the gradual digitization of current medical technology, a large amount of medical information needs to be transmitted via the internet. Watermarking technology is effective for concealing patient information in images and facilitating transmission. However, this puts the patient's information at risk of leakage. The use of digital image watermarking technology in the medical industry is steadily becoming more widespread [1,2], thanks to the rapid advancements that have been made in artificial intelligence, computer vision, image processing, and other areas of study. At this time, the vast majority of patient information, including images of patients, must be transmitted online. Researchers must devise a method to safeguard the patients' information and prevent it from being stolen. The digital watermarking technique offers a potentially useful solution to the problem described above [3]. This is because the technology is undetectable, and it also has the capacity to continually upgrade and improve upon older encryption methods. Because of this capability, sensitive patient information can be concealed within medical images.

Since the unique qualities of medical images mean that the watermark will not interfere with the doctor's ability to diagnose the original image, zero watermark technology is an excellent solution to this issue [4]. Currently, most digital picture watermarking methods are designed for use in the plaintext domain, where they can be embedded and later extracted. However, the patient's private information could be stolen if the medical image in the plaintext domain is intercepted in transit. Therefore, the original image cannot

be guaranteed to be secure using the digital watermarking process in the plaintext domain, especially when transmitting medical images. It has been shown that the digital watermarking approach in the ciphertext domain is superior at resolving the aforementioned issue [5].

By embedding and extracting the watermark in the ciphertext domain, the information carried by the carrier image will be effectively hidden, significantly improving the carrier image's security. Moreover, homomorphic encryption can safely hand over the encrypted carrier image and watermark to a third party for processing, so there is no need to worry about security risks such as information theft and alteration [6]. The zero watermarking technique is implemented by taking advantage of the vital resources of third parties. The original image needs to be encrypted first for embedding and extracting watermarks in the ciphertext domain. Researchers have provided a large number of image encryption algorithms, such as Yang et al.'s proposed image encryption algorithm based on adaptive two-dimensional compression perception and a chaotic system, which improves the visual security of encrypted images and can effectively enhance the embedding rate [7]. Musanna et al. proposed an image encryption algorithm based on fractional chaos and cellular neural networks [8]. Zhong et al. proposed a multi-image encryption algorithm based on wavelet transform and 3D shuffle scrambling by performing a wavelet transform on each layer of the reconstructed image cube and then using a 3D shuffle algorithm and heteroskedastic operation to achieve encryption, achieving high operation speed and resistance to attack [9]. Kamil et al. [10] proposed block-wise reversible watermarking technique for security of images using dynamic reversible blocks. The work of Sahu et al. [11] shows the significance of tools used for the security of data from tempering and highlights the forensic techniques to further improve data security. While previous research has focused on securing 2D mesh fog data, the work of Raghunandan et al. [12] presents an innovative method of securing 3D point fog data. Initially, the sequence produced by the chaotic behavior is used to transform the coordinates of the fog data. The expanded scope of the suggested map is then represented via bifurcation analysis. Then, the Lyapunov exponent and the approximate entropy are used to evaluate the proposed chaotic system.

There are two basic categories for watermark embedding: spatial domain and transform domain [13]. Medical image watermarking strategies are typically studied in the transform domain because it is more challenging to demonstrate improved resilience for spatial domain embedding and extraction procedures. To implement transform domain-based image watermarking, several transform techniques are applied to the carrier image to extract the transform coefficients, which are then modified to embed the watermark. Conventional transform techniques include the discrete cosine transform (DCT), the discrete wavelet transform (DWT), the singular value decomposition (SVD), etc. [14–16]. A technique for zero watermarking images using DCT and DFT was proposed by S. Xing et al. [17]. To create the zero-watermark image, we first perform a discrete Fourier transformation (DFT) on the image to obtain the coefficient matrix, then a discrete cosine transform (DCT) to select the low-frequency coefficients as the feature image of the original image, and finally, an exclusive-or (XOR) operation on the encrypted watermark data. Using 2D discrete wavelet transforms, SVDs, and chaotic maps, Wang Kunshu et al. [18] proposed a safe method of watermarking two-color images. First, a color space transformation (RGB to NTSC) is performed on the original image and the encrypted watermark, and then a multi-level 2D discrete wavelet transform (DWT) is performed. Ultimately, the encrypted watermark is embedded by altering the single values of the original image's low-frequency sub-bands.

The expanding applications of deep learning have led to its increasing popularity among researchers as the go-to method for addressing complex problems [19]. Deep learning shows excellent performance even in computer vision tasks such as pedestrian recognition, image categorization, etc. [20,21]. As one of the most popular network models, convolutional neural networks leverage their formidable processing capability to reliably extract deep information. Recently, Liu et al. [22] suggested an undetectable and robust watermarking approach employing convolutional neural networks to address the shortcomings of digital watermarking techniques in the face of geometric attacks. Zero-watermarking algorithms for medical images using the VGG-19 deep convolutional neural network were proposed by Han et al. [23]. The algorithm first extracts deep features from medical images using a pre-trained VGG19 network, then uses the Fourier transform on the extracted features, selects the transformed 64-bit low-frequency coefficients to construct the feature matrix, then uses the hash transform to generate a binary sequence, and finally uses the encrypted watermarked image and the binary sequence to perform calculations to achieve zero watermarking. When compared to conventional algorithms, this one performs better in geometric attacks.

In summary, although many watermarking algorithms have been studied, watermarking algorithms for encrypted medical images are still inadequate, and even fewer algorithms can achieve better robustness, especially against geometric attacks. Therefore, in this paper, we propose an encrypted medical image watermarking algorithm based on DCT and an improved DarkNet53 convolutional neural network, which has the primary purpose of authentication and privacy information protection [24]. Firstly, DarkNet53's pre-trained network needs to be improved and trained. The medical images are then encrypted, and the encrypted medical images are subjected to DCT to extract features 1 and 2. At the same time, the encrypted medical image is fed into the improved DarkNet53 convolutional neural network to extract feature 2. Secondly, the watermarked image is encrypted using chaos encryption. Finally, features 1 and 2 are simply fused, and an aliasing operation is performed on the encrypted watermark to achieve watermark embedding and extraction.

The main contributions of this study are as follows:

(1) It is proposed that DCT and an improved DarkNet53 convolutional neural network can be used to make a robust zero-watermarking algorithm for cryptographic medical images;
(2) Encrypting both the carrier image and the watermark information ensures that the carrier image information is safe and that the watermark information is safe and easy to see;
(3) The network's structure is changed and trained with a certain set of data so that robust features can be extracted;
(4) The algorithm has high robustness against both geometric and conventional attacks.

2. Basic Theory

2.1. DarkNet53 Convolutional Neural Network

DarkNet53 is the backbone feature extraction network used by the target detection network YOLOv3 for extracting features with 8, 16, and 32-fold downsampling, respectively [25]. The network structure of DarkNet53 is shown in Figure 1, and this network model combines the deep residual network with DarkNet19, the feature extraction network used by YOLOv2 [26]. This network partly makes extensive use of 1×1 convolution and 3×3 convolution, where 1×1 is mainly applied to the expansion and reduction of channels. The overall convolutional network uses a structural model of a convolutional layer + batch normalization (BN) layer + Leaky ReLU layer.

2.2. Tent Map

The tent map is a segmented linear mapping in mathematics with a tent-like function image, as shown in Figure 2 [27]. It is also a two-dimensional chaotic mapping, which is widely used in chaotic cryptosystems (e.g., image encryption) and is often used in the generation of chaotic spreading codes, in the construction of chaotic cryptosystems, and in the implementation of chaotic preference algorithms. The chaotic sequences generated by its mapping have good statistical properties. The formula is as follows:

$$X_n = \begin{cases} \frac{X_n}{\alpha}, 0 \leq X_n < \alpha \\ \frac{1-X_n}{1-\alpha}, \alpha \leq X_n < 1 \end{cases} \quad (1)$$

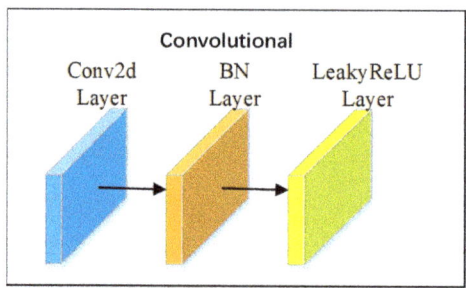

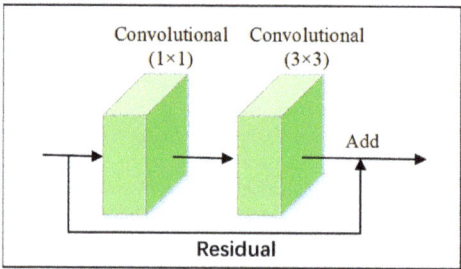

Figure 1. Structure of DarkNet53 network model.

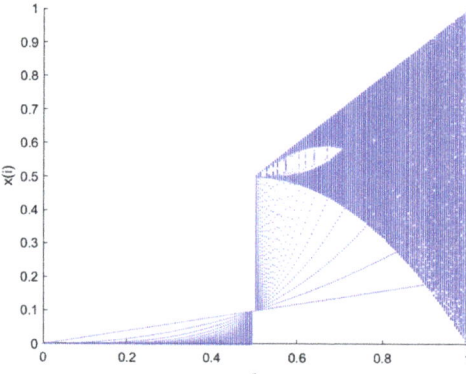

Figure 2. Tent map bifurcation diagram [28].

The mapping is in a chaotic state when $\alpha \in (0, 1)$ and has a uniform distribution function on $(0, 1)$.

2.3. Discrete Cosine Transform (DCT)

A commonly used one-dimensional DCT transformation formula is as follows:

$$F(u) = c(u) \sum_{i=0}^{N-1} f(i) \cos[\frac{(i+0.5)\pi}{N} u] \quad (2)$$

Among them, $c(u) = \begin{cases} \sqrt{\frac{1}{N}}, u = 0 \\ \sqrt{\frac{1}{N}}, u \neq 0 \end{cases}$, $c(u)$ is a coefficient and N is the total number of $f(x)$.

The two-dimensional discrete cosine transform formula is as follows:

$$F(u,v) = C(u)C(v)\sum_{x=0}^{M-1}\sum_{y=0}^{N-1} f(x,y) \cos\left[\frac{(x+0.5)u\pi}{M}\right]\cos\left[\frac{(y+0.5)v\pi}{N}\right] \quad (3)$$
$$u = 0,1,\ldots,M-1; v = 0,1,\ldots,N-1$$

Among them, $C(u) = \begin{cases} \sqrt{\frac{1}{M}}, u=0 \\ \sqrt{\frac{2}{M}}, u\neq 0 \end{cases}$, $C(v) = \begin{cases} \sqrt{\frac{1}{N}}, v=0 \\ \sqrt{\frac{2}{N}}, v\neq 0 \end{cases}$, $f(x,y)$ is the pixel value of point (x,y), and $F(u,v)$ is the 2D-DCT transform coefficient of $f(x,y)$. DCT is preferred in digital image processing as compared to other transformations, such as DFT or FFT, because signal will "lose its form" if the representation coefficients are truncated in DFT because the signal is represented periodically. Due to the continuous periodic structure in DCT, however, the signal can withstand larger amounts of coefficient truncation while still maintaining the desired shape [29].

2.4. Logistic Map

The logistic map is one of the most famous chaotic mappings, a simple dynamic nonlinear regression with chaotic behavior, as shown in Figure 3 [30]. Its mathematical definition can be expressed as follows:

$$X_{k+1} = \mu \cdot X_k \cdot (1 - X_k) \quad (4)$$

Among them, $X_k \in (0,1), 0 < \mu \leq 4$.

Experiments show that when $3.5699456 < \mu \leq 4$, the logistic mapping enters a chaotic state and the logistic chaotic sequence can be used as an ideal key sequence.

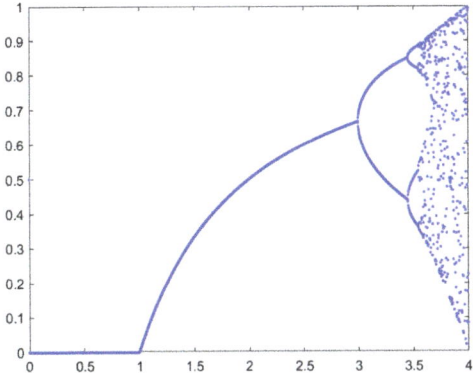

Figure 3. Logistic mapping bifurcation diagram [31].

3. The Proposed Algorithm

In this paper, we propose a robust watermarking algorithm for encrypted medical images based on DCT and an improved DarkNet53 convolutional neural network [32]. The main parts are: improvement of the network, migration learning, encryption of medical images and watermark information, feature extraction of images and embedding, and extraction of watermarks.

3.1. Medical Image Encryption

This paper opts to embed and remove the watermark in the ciphertext domain due to the unique nature of medical photographs, and the corresponding encryption method is depicted in Figure 4. Firstly, the coefficient matrix D(i, j) is obtained by DCT of the original image; secondly, the tent mapping chaotic sequence X(j) is extracted and binarized to obtain C(i, j); and finally, the dot product operation is performed on D(i, j) and C(i, j) to obtain ED'(i, j). Finally, the IDCT transform of ED'(i, j) is performed to obtain the encrypted medical image.

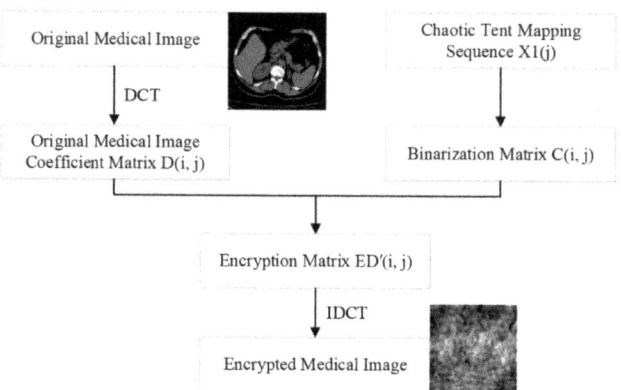

Figure 4. Image encryption process.

3.2. Improved DarkNet53 Network Model

3.2.1. Improvement of Network Structure

Since convolutional neural networks have powerful feature extraction abilities and can effectively extract stable features of images, they are of high research value for medical image watermarking algorithms. In this paper, the DarkNet53 convolutional neural network, which has been trained on more than one million natural images in the ImageNet database, is selected for its inherently good feature extraction ability. In order to achieve strong robustness in the watermarking algorithm, this paper makes a simple change to the network. First, the Softmax layer and classification layer of the DarkNet53 convolutional neural network are removed, then a fully connected layer with 128 values of output is added, and finally a regression output layer is connected after the fully connected layer so that the modified network can complete the regression task and the output of the fully connected layer is used as our extracted medical image features.

3.2.2. Data Set Creation

The medical image data selected for this paper comes from the Medical Imaging Park and American Research Institute, Inc., which contains tens of thousands of medical images. In this paper, we selected 125 medical images in each of the five major categories of brain, pelvis, bone and muscle, colon, and chest from the website as dataset 1, and encrypted these 125 medical images to obtain 125 encrypted medical images as dataset 2. Some of these 250 images are shown in Figure 5. Data sets 1 and 2 are completely disrupted, respectively, and then divided into three parts in the ratio of 3:1:1: the training set, validation set, and test set. In order to improve the robustness of the network in extracting features, in this paper, the training set and the validation set are enhanced with the data separately, as shown in Table 1. Thus, we obtained 12,850 images as the total dataset for this training. Because the input size of the DarkNet53 convolutional neural network is 2,562,563, all medical images are resized to 2,562,563 here. For the production of dataset labels, this paper first performs DCT on the images of the training and validation sets and then selects the 128-bit feature vectors of the low-frequency part as labels.

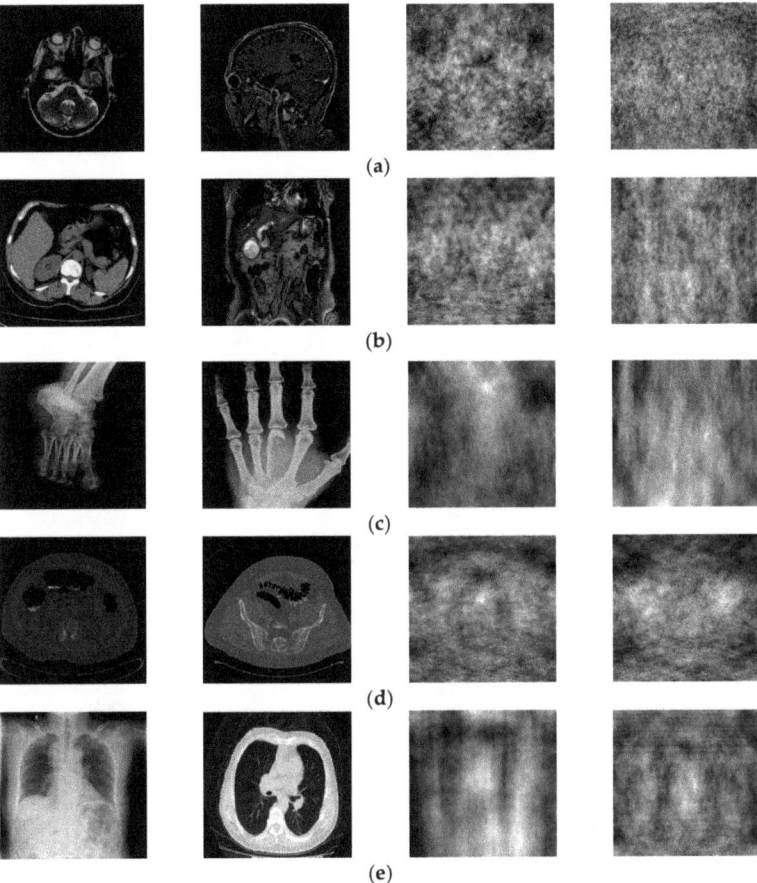

Figure 5. Two original images and corresponding encrypted images for each type of image. Brain image (**a**); abdominal pelvis image (**b**); bone muscle image (**c**); colon image (**d**); and chest image (**e**).

Table 1. Specific implementation operations for data enhancement.

Enhancement Methods	Intensity	Number of New Images
Gaussian noise (%)	3, 6, 9, 12, 15	5
JPEG compression (%)	5, 10, 15, 20, 25	5
Median filter (10 times)	$3 \times 3, 5 \times 5, 7 \times 7$	3
Clockwise rotation (°)	5, 10, 15, 20, 25, 30, 35, 40	8
Scaling	0.3, 0.6, 0.9, 1.2, 1.5, 1.8	6
Down-shift (%)	5, 10, 15, 20, 25, 30	6
Up-shift (%)	5, 10, 15, 20, 25, 30	6
Y-axis shear (%)	5, 10, 15, 20, 25, 30	6
X-axis shear (%)	5, 10, 15, 20, 25, 30	6
Left-shift (%)	5, 10, 15, 20, 25, 30	6
Right-shift (%)	5, 10, 15, 20, 25, 30	6

3.2.3. Training Network

The computer configuration used for this experiment was an NVIDIA GeForce GTX 1050Ti 4GB graphics card (Santa Clara, CA, USA) and Intel@RCoreTM i5-8300H CPU @ 2.30GHz4 (Santa Clara, CA, USA). The software uses the neural network toolbox that comes with Matlab 2022a, and the network selected was the DarkNet53 pre-trained network. In this paper, the DarkNet53 pre-trained network is trained by first setting the learning rate of 1:84 layers to 0 to "freeze" the weights of these layers, because the parameters of the frozen layers will not be updated during the whole training process. Next, the initial learning rate is set to 0.001, the MiniBatchSize is set to 30, and the Epochs are set to 8 for training. Finally, the trained network is saved as a key part of the watermarking algorithm.

3.3. Encryption of Watermarks

In this research, we make use of a chaotic system of logistic mapping to create an encrypted watermarked image through the utilization of chaotic dislocation. The watermarking process will now be more secure and resistant to interference as a result of this change. The first thing that needs to be done in order to generate the encrypted watermarked image is to enter the chaotic system by providing values for the coefficients and the initial state. This is done so that the system can begin to generate the image. To begin the process of decrypting the image, we will first need to use the chaotic system to create a chaotic sequence. After we have obtained this sequence, we will need to perform a bit-by-bit XOR operation between it and the binary image that has been watermarked with it. The intricate algorithmic structure of the watermark chaos encryption is shown in Figure 6.

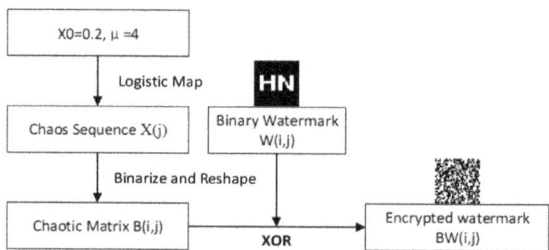

Figure 6. Watermark encryption process.

3.4. Feature Extraction of Encrypted Medical Images

Traditional watermarking algorithms mainly embed watermarks directly into medical images, which may not only change the quality of the images but also their resistance to attacks, especially geometric attacks, which often do not have good robustness. In this paper, we perform DCT on encrypted medical images and select the 32-bit feature vector of the low-frequency part for hash transform as feature 1, denoted as $V1(i, j)$ [33]. Meanwhile, the 128-bit feature matrix of the fully connected layer is extracted from the encrypted medical image using a DarkNet53 convolutional neural network after migration learning, and then DCT is performed on this 128-bit feature matrix, and the 32-bit feature vector of the low-frequency part is extracted for the hash transform as feature 2, denoted as $V2(i, j)$. Finally, the feature set $V(i, j)$ is established, which can be better combined with the zero-watermarking technique. The specific steps are shown in Figure 7.

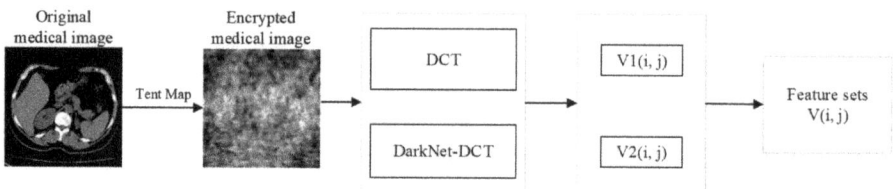

Figure 7. Extraction process of encrypted medical image features.

3.5. Encrypted Watermark Embedding

The process of watermark embedding in this paper is primarily broken down into the following steps: the feature vectors V1(i, j) and V2(i, j) in the feature set and each row of the encrypted watermark BW(i, j) are each subjected to bit-by-bit XOR operations, respectively; the watermark information can then be hidden in the medical image. Additionally, when embedding a watermark using this method, there is no change to the pixel values in the original image, achieving a zero watermark. The specific watermark embedding process is shown in Figure 8.

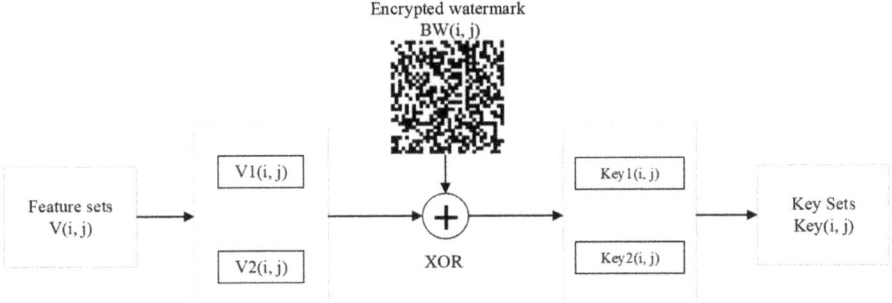

Figure 8. Flow chart of embedding watermark.

3.6. Extraction of Watermarks

The steps for watermark extraction are identical to those for the watermark embedding process, where V1′(i, j) is the feature vector extracted by DCT and V2′(i, j) is the feature vector extracted by DarkNet-DCT, and the specific operation flow is shown in Figure 9.

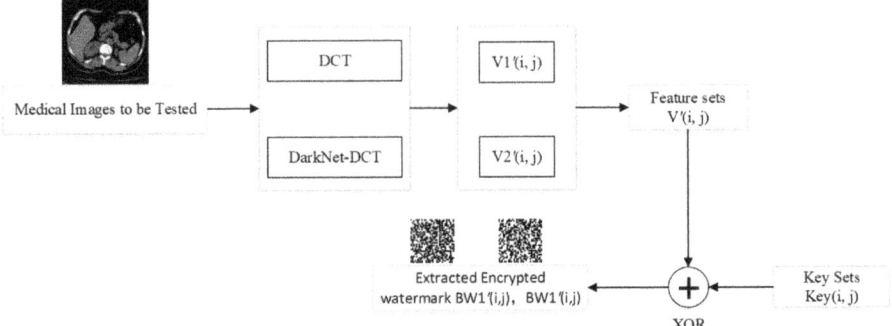

Figure 9. Flowchart of watermark extraction.

3.7. Decryption of Watermark

The decryption of the watermark is consistent with the chaotic sequence X(j) used in the encryption method of the watermark, and X(j) and the encrypted watermarks BW1′(i, j) and BW2′(i, j) are subjected to the XOR operation to obtain the decrypted watermarks W1′(i, j) and W2′(i, j), respectively. Calculate the correlation coefficients NC1 and NC2 of W(i, j) and W′(i, j), then discriminate NC1 and NC2, and output the larger correlation coefficient and the corresponding watermark image. The specific flow of watermark extraction and decryption is shown in Figure 10.

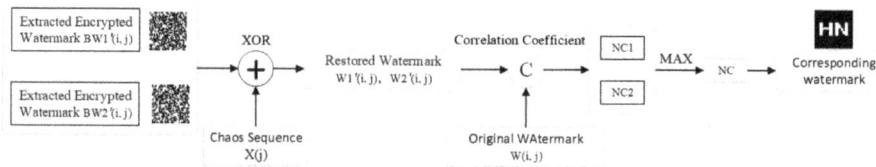

Figure 10. Decryption process of watermark.

4. Experimental Results and Analysis

In this research, a medical image and a 32 × 32 watermarked image carrying information from the test set were randomly selected for the Matlab 2022a simulation platform to study and test the robustness of the mentioned watermarking algorithm. To improve the security, we used tent chaos mapping to encrypt the medical image and logistic chaos encryption to encrypt the watermarked image, as shown in Figure 11.

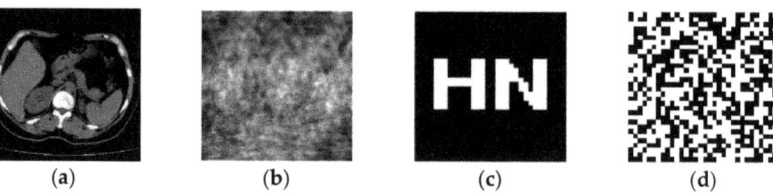

Figure 11. Medical image and watermarked image. Original medical image (**a**), encrypted medical image (**b**), original watermarked image (**c**), and encrypted watermarked image (**d**).

4.1. Performance Index

In this paper, the robustness of the algorithm is reflected by the normalized correlation coefficient (NC) and the peak signal-to-noise ratio (PSNR). Where NC indicates the similarity between the original watermark and the extracted watermark, and the closer its value is to 1, the higher the correlation between the two and the better the robustness of the algorithm. The calculation formula is shown in (5). PSNR indicates the degree of distortion of the image containing the watermark, and a smaller value means a greater degree of distortion of the original image; the calculation formula is shown in Equation (6).

$$NC = \frac{\sum_i \sum_j W_{(i,j)} W'_{(i,j)}}{\sum_i \sum_j W^2_{(i,j)}} \qquad (5)$$

$$PSNR = 10\lg\left[\frac{MN\max_{i,j}(I(i,j))^2}{\sum_i \sum_j (I(i,j) - I'(i,j))^2}\right] \qquad (6)$$

4.2. Reliability Analysis

In order to prove that the deep-learning algorithm proposed in this paper has certain reliability, eight medical images were randomly selected from the test set for testing, as shown in Figure 12. The NC is used to calculate the correlation between different images, and when the NC < 0.5, it indicates that the correlation between different image feature vectors is low, and the feature vectors extracted by this algorithm are representative. Table 2 shows the NC values between eight different cryptographic medical images. Since the absolute values of NC values of different images are less than 0.5 and the NC value of the same image is 1, the algorithm can distinguish different encrypted medical images and is reliable.

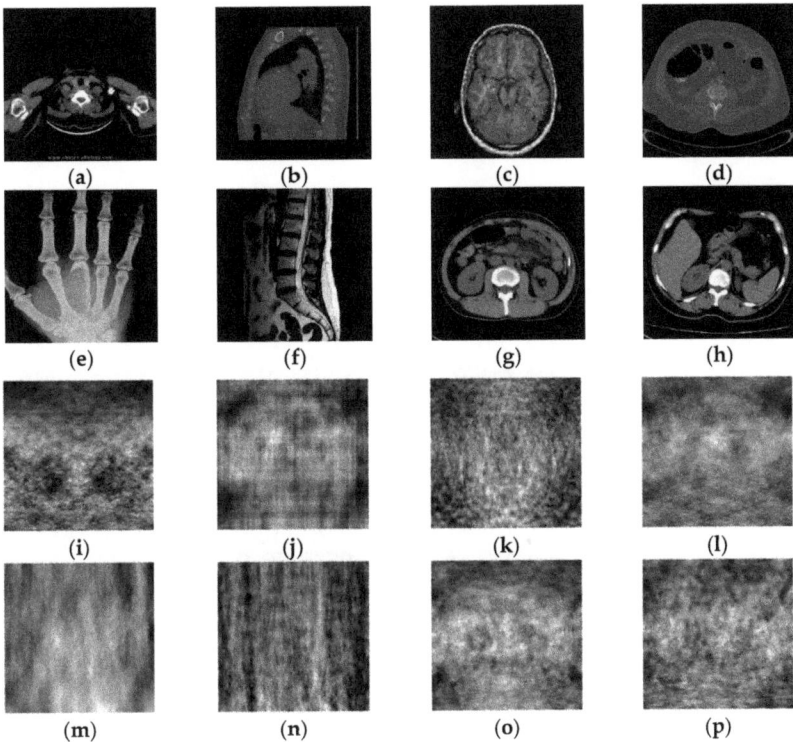

Figure 12. Different medical images within the test (**a**–**h**), related encrypted images (**i**–**p**).

Table 2. NC between different encrypted images.

Image	1	2	3	4	5	6	7	8
1	1							
2	0.32	1						
3	0.22	0.22	1					
4	0.26	0.04	0.12	1				
5	0.25	0.07	0.17	0.24	1			
6	0.01	0.16	0.01	0.22	0.49	1		
7	0.12	0.07	0.17	0.11	0.12	0.24	1	
8	0.37	0.05	0.36	0.39	0.25	0.11	0.25	1

4.3. Conventional Attacks

To test the robustness of the algorithm against conventional attacks, three conventional attacks—Gaussian noise, JPEG compression, and median filtering—were selected for testing in this paper. The NC value between the original watermark and the extracted watermark was calculated, with larger values indicating better robustness. The experimental results are shown in Table 3. It can be seen that when the Gaussian attack reaches 13%, the NC value is 1.00; when the JPEG compression quality is 5%, the NC value is 0.85; and when the median filtering [7 × 7] is 10 times, the NC value is 1.00. Figure 13 shows some of the experimental results. It shows that the watermark information can be effectively recovered with good robustness in the face of all three conventional attacks.

Table 3. Experimental data under conventional attack.

Attacks	Intensity	PSNR(dB)	NC
Gaussian noise (%)	3	15.37	0.91
	7	12.27	1.00
	9	11.47	0.94
	13	10.43	1.00
JPEG compression (%)	5	26.46	0.85
	15	31.36	0.91
	30	34.32	1.00
Median filter	[3 × 3]	31.35	1.00
	[5 × 5]	26.10	1.00
	[7 × 7]	23.95	1.00

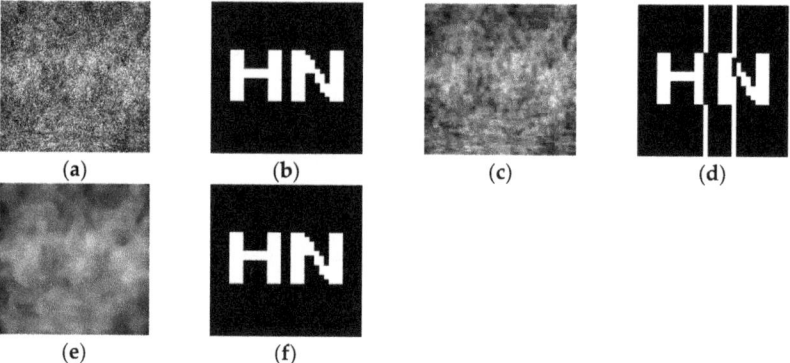

Figure 13. Encrypted medical images and extracted watermarks after some conventional attacks. Images after 13% attack of Gaussian noise and corresponding extracted watermarks (a,b), images after 5% attack of JPEG compression and corresponding extracted watermarks (c,d), and images after 10 attacks of median filtering [7 × 7] and corresponding extracted watermarks (e,f).

4.4. Geometric Attacks

As geometric attacks are a more difficult problem for existing algorithms to solve, this paper tests the robustness of the algorithm after rotation, scaling, and shear attacks. The NC value between the original watermark and the extracted watermark was calculated, with larger values indicating that the algorithm is more resistant to geometric attacks. The experimental results are shown in Table 4. It can be seen that the NC value was 0.62 when rotating 30° counterclockwise. When rotating 50° clockwise, the NC value was 0.53. When the scaling factor was between 0.1 and 2, the NC value was 1. When shifting 30% left, the NC value was 0.62. When shifting 40% right, the NC value was 0.64. When shifting 40% up, the NC value was 0.72. When shifting 40% down, the NC value was 0.58. When shearing 40% along the X-axis, the NC value was 0.55. When shearing 40% along the Y-axis, the NC value was 0.67. When shearing 40% along the X-axis direction, the NC was 0.55. When shearing 40% along the Y-axis direction, the NC was 0.67. The watermark information could be effectively recovered for all the above geometric attacks. Figure 14 shows the experimental results after partial geometric attacks.

Table 4. Experimental data under geometric attack.

Attacks	Intensity	PSNR(dB)	NC
Anticlockwise Rotation (°)	10	15.43	0.78
	20	13.90	0.62
	30	13.16	0.62
Clockwise Rotation (°)	10	15.14	0.85
	30	13.21	0.80
	50	12.73	0.53
Scaling Factor	0.1	-	1.00
	0.5	-	1.00
	2	-	1.00
Translation Left (%)	10	13.32	0.81
	20	11.01	0.63
	30	9.64	0.62
Translation Right (%)	5	16.16	0.80
	20	11.57	0.81
	40	8.90	0.64
Translation Up (%)	10	13.28	0.85
	20	10.92	0.75
	40	8.46	0.72
Translation Down (%)	5	15.94	0.86
	20	11.82	0.81
	40	8.84	0.58
X-axis Crop (%)	10	-	0.85
	20	-	0.87
	40	-	0.55
Y-axis Crop (%)	10	-	0.85
	20	-	0.76
	40	-	0.67

4.5. Comparison between Different Algorithms

In order to better verify the robustness of this algorithm, this paper compares the more classical watermarking algorithms, Inception V3-DCT, PHTs-DCT, KAZE-DCT, DWT-DCT, and Curvelet-DCT, in recent years [34–38]. During the experiments, the same medical image and watermarked image were selected for testing in order to ensure the consistency of the conclusions. The results of the comparison experiments are shown in Table 5 and Figure 15. It can be seen that DWT-DCT and Curvelet-DCT have the best results in the face of traditional attacks. Facing the geometric attack, the algorithm proposed in this paper shows strong robustness. In a comprehensive comparison, the algorithm proposed in this paper demonstrates stronger robustness in the face of different geometric attacks and conventional attacks.

Table 5. Comparison of NC values between different algorithms.

Attacks	Intensity	Inception V3-DCT [34]	PHTs-DCT [35]	KAZE-DCT [36]	DWT-DCT [37]	Curvelet-DCT [38]	Proposed
Gussian Noise	13	0.35	0.45	0.32	1.00	1.00	0.94
JPEG Compression	10	0.63	0.63	0.76	1.00	1.00	0.94
Median Filter	[7 × 7]	0.29	0.55	0.40	0.84	1.00	1.00
Rotation (°)	30	0.05	0.62	0.42	0.46	0.41	0.80
Scaling	×0.1	0.32	-	0.43	0.90	0.90	1.00
Right Translation (%)	40	0.39	0.49	0.04	0.13	0.20	0.64
Up Translation (%)	40	0.39	0.31	0.20	0.02	0.02	0.72
Cropping (X-axis)	20	0.76	0.59	0.68	0.31	0.30	0.87
Cropping (Y-axis)	15	0.68	0.45	0.62	0.65	0.74	0.81

Note: The bold part indicates that the algorithm has the best robustness compared to these three algorithms.

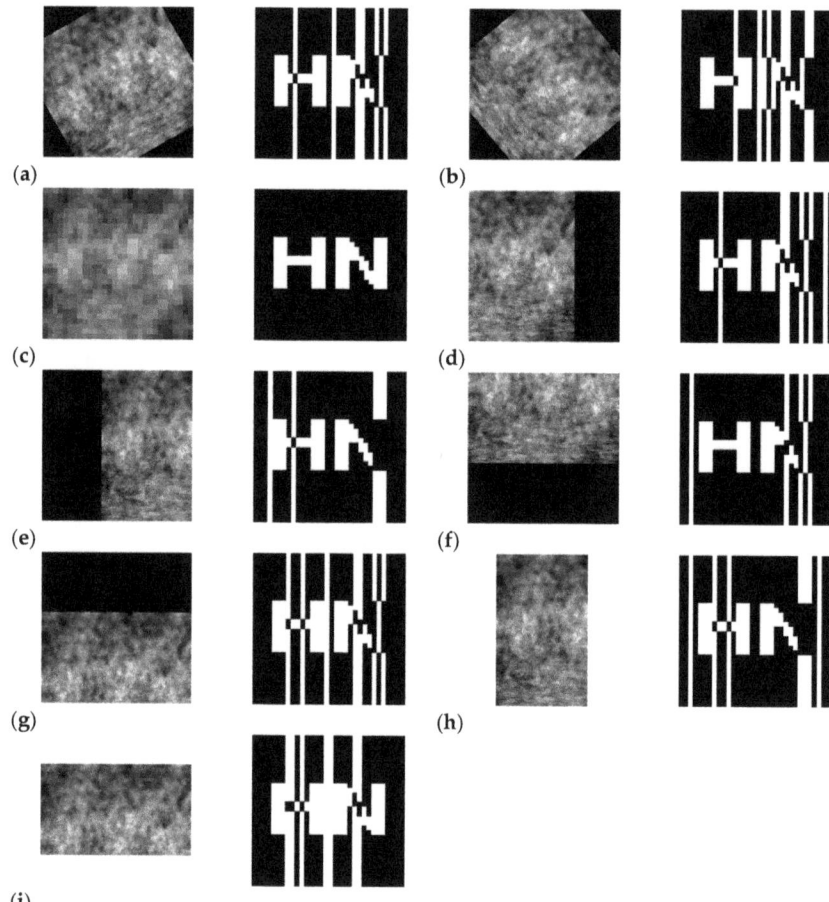

Figure 14. Encrypted medical images and extracted watermarks after some geometric attacks. Image and extracted watermark after 30° counterclockwise rotation (**a**), image and extracted watermark after 50° clockwise rotation (**b**), image and extracted watermark after 0.1 times scaling (**c**), image and extracted watermark after 30% left-shift (**d**), image and extracted watermark after 40% right-shift (**e**), image and extracted watermark after 40% up-shift (**f**), image and extracted watermark after 40% down-shift (**g**), image and extracted watermark after 40% clipping in X-axis direction (**h**), and image and extracted watermark after 40% clipping in Y-axis direction watermark (**i**).

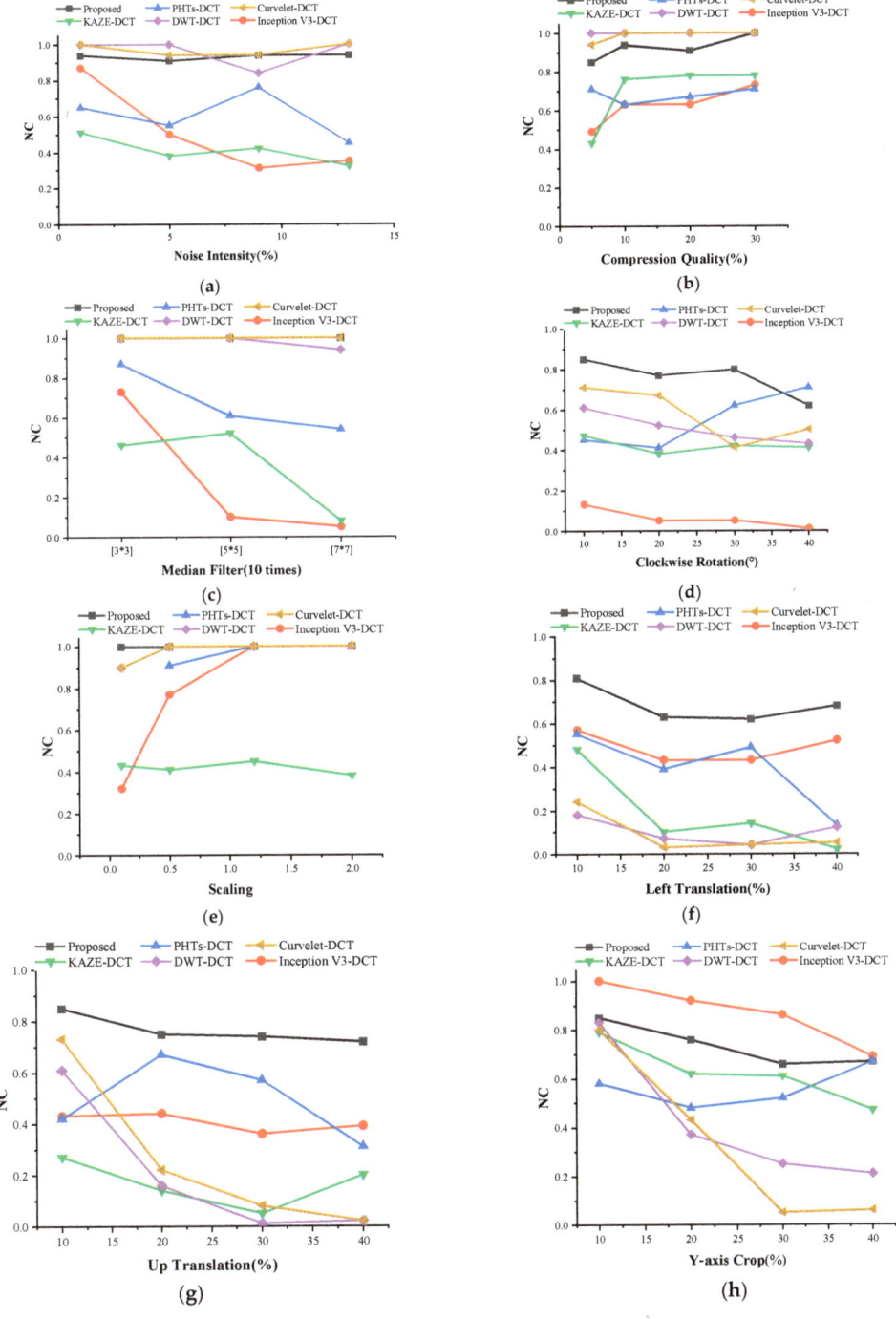

Figure 15. Comparison of NC values between different algorithms, where (**a**–**h**) indicate the results after Gaussian noise, JPEG compression, median filter, clockwise rotation, scaling, left-shift, up-shift, and Y-axis shear attacks, respectively.

5. Conclusions

In this paper, we propose an encrypted medical image watermarking algorithm that is based on DCT and Darknet53 convolutional neural networks. This algorithm combines migration learning, DCT, Tent Map, Logistic Map, hash transform, and zero watermarking techniques. The algorithm is designed to protect medical images from unauthorized use. Improving the Darknet53 pre-trained network was the first step in the experimental procedure. Next, migration learning was performed on the improved network in order to extract features from encrypted medical images. After that, the medical images and watermark information were encrypted with Tent Map and Logistic Map. Finally, the zero-watermarking technique was used to embed the watermark information and then extract it. The findings of the experiments demonstrate that the method has a high degree of robustness when subjected to both conventional and geometric attacks. As a result, the technique may prove to be superior for use with encrypted medical photos. Naturally, there is still a great deal of space for development of this method, and in order to enhance the performance of the algorithm, we will continue to tune the neural network in order to extract characteristics that are more reflective of the whole.

Author Contributions: Formal analysis, validation, data curation, and writing—original draft preparation, D.L.; funding acquisition, J.L. (Jingbing Li); visualization, S.A.N.; supervision, J.L. (Jing Liu); software, Y.-W.C.; investigation, L.C. Data curation, Supervision, Resources, Writing—original draft, U.A.B. All authors have read and agreed to the published version of the manuscript.

Funding: This research was supported, in part, by the Natural Science Foundation of China under grants 62063004, the Key Research Project of Hainan Province under grant ZDYF2021SHFZ093, the Hainan Provincial Natural Science Foundation of China under grants 2019RC018 and 619QN246, and the postdoctoral research from Zhejiang Province under grant ZJ2021028.

Data Availability Statement: Data is contained within the article.

Conflicts of Interest: The authors declare no conflict of interest.

References

1. Thomas, A.M.; Burkhart, J.M.; Nichols, C.S. On a mathematical framework for object recognition from multi-perspective remotely sensed imagery. In Proceedings of the 2011 Proceedings of IEEE Southeastcon, Nashville, TN, USA, 17–20 March 2011.
2. Sun, Q.Y.; Zhao, C.Q.; Tang, Y.; Qian, F. A survey on unsupervised domain adaptation in computer vision tasks. *Sci. Sin. Technol.* **2021**, *52*, 26–54. [CrossRef]
3. Evsutin, O.; Dzhanashia, K. Watermarking schemes for digital images: Robustness overview. *Signal Process. Image Commun.* **2022**, *100*, 116523. [CrossRef]
4. Liu, X.; Wang, Y.; Sun, Z.; Wang, L.; Zhao, R.; Zhu, Y.; Zou, B.; Zhao, Y.; Fang, H. Robust and discriminative zero-watermark scheme based on invariant features and similarity-based retrieval to protect large-scale DIBR 3D videos. *Inf. Sci.* **2021**, *542*, 263–285. [CrossRef]
5. Xiang, S.; He, J. Database authentication watermarking scheme in encrypted domain. *IET Inf. Secur.* **2018**, *12*, 42–51. [CrossRef]
6. Ma, Y.; Zhao, J.; Li, K.; Cao, Y.; Chen, H.; Zhang, Y. Research review on the application of homomorphic encryption in database privacy protection. *Int. J. Cogn. Inform. Nat. Intell.* **2021**, *15*, 1–22. [CrossRef]
7. Yang, Y.-G.; Wang, B.-P.; Yang, Y.-L.; Zhou, Y.-H.; Shi, W.-M.; Liao, X. A visually meaningful image encryption algorithm based on adaptive 2D compressive sensing and chaotic system. *Multimed. Tools Appl.* **2022**. [CrossRef]
8. Musanna, F.; Dangwal, D.; Kumar, S. Novel image encryption algorithm using fractional chaos and cellular neural network. *J. Ambient. Intell. Humaniz. Comput.* **2021**, *13*, 2205–2226. [CrossRef]
9. Zhong, H.; Li, G. Multi-image encryption algorithm based on wavelet transform and 3D shuffling scrambling. *Multimed. Tools Appl.* **2022**, *81*, 24757–24776. [CrossRef]
10. Kamil, S.; Sahu, M.; KR, R.; Sahu, A.K. Secure Reversible Data Hiding Using Block-Wise Histogram Shifting. *Electronics* **2023**, *12*, 1222. [CrossRef]
11. Sahu, A.K.; Umachandran, K.; Biradar, V.D.; Comfort, O.; Sri Vigna Hema, V.; Odimegwu, F. A Study on Content Tampering in Multimedia Watermarking. *SN Comput. Sci.* **2023**, *4*, 222. [CrossRef]
12. Raghunandan, K.R.; Dodmane, R.; Bhavya, K.; Rao, N.S.K.; Sahu, A.K. Chaotic-Map Based Encryption for 3D Point and 3D Mesh Fog Data in Edge Computing. *IEEE Access* **2023**, *11*, 3545–3554. [CrossRef]
13. Cheung, W.N. Digital Image Watermarking in spatial and transform domains. In Proceedings of the 2000 TENCON Proceedings, Intelligent Systems and Technologies for the New Millennium (Cat. No.00CH37119), Kuala Lumpur, Malaysia, 24–27 September 2000.

14. Singh, R.; Ashok, A.; Saraswat, M. Optimised robust watermarking technique using CKGSA in DCT-SVD domain. *IET Image Process.* **2020**, *14*, 2052–2063. [CrossRef]
15. Wang, X.; Liu, C.; Jiang, D. A novel triple-image encryption and hiding algorithm based on chaos, compressive sensing and 3D DCT. *Inf. Sci.* **2021**, *574*, 505–527. [CrossRef]
16. Anand, A.; Singh, A.K. An improved DWT-SVD domain watermarking for medical information security. *Comput. Commun.* **2020**, *152*, 72–80. [CrossRef]
17. Xing, S.M.; Li, T.Y.; Liang, J. A zero-watermark hybrid algorithm for remote sensing images based on DCT and DFT. *J. Phys. Conf. Ser.* **2021**, *1952*, 022049. [CrossRef]
18. Wang, K.; Gao, T.; You, D.; Wu, X.; Kan, H. A secure dual-color image watermarking scheme based 2D DWT, SVD and Chaotic Map. *Multimed. Tools Appl.* **2022**, *81*, 6159–6190. [CrossRef]
19. Le, W.T.; Maleki, F.; Romero, F.P.; Forghani, R.; Kadoury, S. Overview of Machine Learning: Part 2: Deep Learning for Medical Image Analysis. *Neuroimaging Clin. N. Am.* **2020**, *30*, 417–431. [CrossRef]
20. Bhatti, U.A.; Tang, H.; Wu, G.; Marjan, S.; Hussain, A. Deep Learning with Graph Convolutional Networks: An Overview and Latest Applications in Computational Intelligence. *Int. J. Intell. Syst.* **2023**, *2023*, 8342104. [CrossRef]
21. Bhatti, U.A.; Yu, Z.; Chanussot, J.; Zeeshan, Z.; Yuan, L.; Luo, W.; Nawaz, S.A.; Bhatti, M.A.; Ain, Q.U.; Mehmood, A. Local similarity-based spatial–spectral fusion hyperspectral image classification with deep CNN and Gabor filtering. *IEEE Trans. Geosci. Remote Sens.* **2021**, *60*, 1–15. [CrossRef]
22. Liu, G.; Xiang, R.; Liu, J.; Pan, R.; Zhang, Z. An invisible and robust watermarking scheme using convolutional neural networks. *Expert Syst. Appl.* **2022**, *210*, 118529. [CrossRef]
23. Han, B.; Du, J.; Jia, Y.; Zhu, H. Zero-watermarking algorithm for medical image based on VGG19 deep convolution neural network. *J. Healthc. Eng.* **2021**, *2021*, 5551520. [CrossRef] [PubMed]
24. Wang, H.; Zhang, F.; Wang, L. Fruit classification model based on improved Darknet53 Convolutional Neural Network. In Proceedings of the 2020 International Conference on Intelligent Transportation, Big Data & Smart City (ICITBS), Vientiane, Laos, 11–12 January 2020.
25. Yao, Z.; Song, X.; Zhao, L.; Yin, Y. Real-time method for traffic sign detection and recognition based on yolov3-tiny with multiscale feature extraction. *Proc. Inst. Mech. Eng. Part D J. Automob. Eng.* **2020**, *235*, 1978–1991. [CrossRef]
26. Abas, S.M.; Abdulazeez, A.M. Detection and classification of leukocytes in leukemia using yolov2 with CNN. *Asian J. Res. Comput. Sci.* **2021**, *8*, 64–75. [CrossRef]
27. Arora, A.; Sharma, R.K. Known-plaintext attack (KPA) on an image encryption scheme using enhanced skew tent map (ESTM) and its improvement. *Optik* **2021**, *244*, 167526. [CrossRef]
28. Liu, W.; Zhang, J.; Wei, W.; Qin, T.; Fan, Y.; Long, F.; Yang, J. A hybrid bald eagle search algorithm for time difference of arrival localization. *Appl. Sci.* **2022**, *12*, 5221. [CrossRef]
29. Khayam, S.A. The discrete cosine transform (DCT): Theory and application. *Mich. State Univ.* **2003**, *114*, 31.
30. Khokhar, B.; Dahiya, S.; Parmar, K.P.S. Load frequency control of a microgrid employing a 2D sine logistic map based chaotic sine cosine algorithm. *Appl. Soft Comput.* **2021**, *109*, 107564. [CrossRef]
31. Gong, C.; Li, J.; Bhatti, U.A.; Gong, M.; Ma, J.; Huang, M. Robust and secure zero-watermarking algorithm for medical images based on Harris-SURF-DCT and chaotic map. *Secur. Commun. Netw.* **2021**, *2021*, 3084153. [CrossRef]
32. Siar, M.; Teshnehlab, M. A combination of feature extraction methods and deep learning for Brain tumour classification. *IET Image Process.* **2021**, *16*, 416–441. [CrossRef]
33. Bi, X. A New Grading Sorting Arithmetic Based on the HASH Transform. *Comput. Eng. Appl.* **2006**, *42*, 50–51.
34. Fan, Y.; Li, J.; Aslam Bhatti, U.; Shao, C.; Gong, C.; Cheng, J.; Chen, Y. A multi-watermarking algorithm for medical images using inception v3 and dct. *Comput. Mater. Contin.* **2023**, *74*, 1279–1302.
35. Yi, D.; Li, J.; Fang, Y.; Cui, W.; Xiao, X.; Bhatti, U.A.; Han, B. A robust zero-watermarkinging algorithm based on phts-DCT for medical images in the encrypted domain. *Innov. Med. Healthc.* **2021**. [CrossRef]
36. Zeng, C.; Liu, J.; Li, J.; Cheng, J.; Zhou, J.; Nawaz, S.A.; Xiao, X.; Bhatti, U.A. Multi-watermarking algorithm for medical image based on Kaze-DCT. *J. Ambient. Intell. Humaniz. Comput.* **2022**. [CrossRef]
37. Al-Haj, A. Combined DWT-DCT digital image watermarking. *J. Comput. Sci.* **2007**, *3*, 740–746. [CrossRef]
38. Qin, F.; Li, J.; Li, H.; Liu, J.; Nawaz, S.A.; Liu, Y. A.; Liu, Y. A robust zero-watermarking algorithm for medical images using curvelet-DCT and RSA pseudo-random sequences. In *Lecture Notes in Computer Science*; Springer: Berlin/Heidelberg, Germany, 2020; pp. 179–190.

Disclaimer/Publisher's Note: The statements, opinions and data contained in all publications are solely those of the individual author(s) and contributor(s) and not of MDPI and/or the editor(s). MDPI and/or the editor(s) disclaim responsibility for any injury to people or property resulting from any ideas, methods, instructions or products referred to in the content.

Article

Modeling Noncommutative Composition of Relations for Knowledge Graph Embedding

Chao Xiang [1,*], Cong Fu [1], Deng Cai [1] and Xiaofei He [1,2]

[1] State Key Lab of CAD&CG, Zhejiang University, Hangzhou 310058, China
[2] Fabu Inc., Hangzhou 310030, China
* Correspondence: chaoxiang@zju.edu.cn

Abstract: Knowledge Graph Embedding (KGE) is a powerful way to express Knowledge Graphs (KGs), which can help machines learn patterns hidden in the KGs. Relation patterns are useful hidden patterns, and they usually assist machines to predict unseen facts. Many existing KGE approaches can model some common relation patterns like symmetry/antisymmetry, inversion, and commutative composition patterns. However, most of them are weak in modeling noncommutative composition patterns. It means these approaches can not distinguish a lot of composite relations like "father's mother" and "mother's father". In this work, we propose a new KGE method called QuatRotatScalE (QRSE) to overcome this weakness, since it utilizes rotation and scaling transformations of quaternions to design the relation embedding. Specifically, we embed the relations and entities into a quaternion vector space under the difference norm KGE framework. Since the multiplication of quaternions does not satisfy the commutative law, QRSE can model noncommutative composition patterns naturally. The experimental results on the synthetic dataset also support that QRSE has this ability. In addition, the experimental results on real-world datasets show that QRSE reaches state-of-the-art in link prediction problem.

Keywords: knowledge graph; knowledge graph embedding; link prediction; quaternion; relation pattern

Citation: Xiang, C.; Fu, C.; Cai, D.; He, X. Modeling Noncommutative Composition of Relations for Knowledge Graph Embedding. *Electronics* **2023**, *12*, 1348. https://doi.org/10.3390/electronics12061348

Academic Editor: Stefanos Kollias

Received: 7 February 2023
Revised: 6 March 2023
Accepted: 7 March 2023
Published: 12 March 2023

Copyright: © 2023 by the authors. Licensee MDPI, Basel, Switzerland. This article is an open access article distributed under the terms and conditions of the Creative Commons Attribution (CC BY) license (https://creativecommons.org/licenses/by/4.0/).

1. Introduction

Knowledge Graph (KG) is composed by structured, objective facts. The facts are usually expressed in the form of triples as (h, r, t), where h, r, and t express the head entity, the relation, and the tail entity, respectively. For example, (China, located_in, Asia). Knowledge graphs have successfully supported many applications in various fields, such as recommender systems [1], question answering [2], information retrieval [3], and natural language processing [4]. KGs have also attracted increased attention from both industry and academic communities. However, real-world knowledge graphs, such as Dbpedia [5], Freebase [6], Yago [7], and WordNet [8], are usually incomplete, which restricts their applications. Thus, knowledge graph completion has become a widely studied subject. This subject is usually formulated as a link prediction problem, i.e., predicting the missing links that should be in the knowledge graph. Generally speaking, it asks us to design an agent that takes the query as input and outputs some entities. The query may contain a head entity and a relation or a tail entity and a relation. Every outputted entity should be able to form a plausible triple together with the query.

So far, the fundamental way to deal with the link prediction problem is Knowledge Graph Embedding (KGE) in industry and academia [9–13]. In this way, the agent needs to learn a low-dimensional vector representation, also called embedding, for each entity and relation. We have to design a scorer that can grade any triple in the embedding form for its plausibility. When predicting the unknown entity, the agent only needs to grade all possible triples (composed by the query with each candidate entity) and then take the candidate entities of high score triples as the predicted result.

There are two reasons why these knowledge-graph embedding methods can tackle the link prediction problem effectively. On the one hand, there are many utilizable relation patterns in real-world KGs, such as symmetry/antisymmetry, inversion, and composition. These relation patterns are generally presented as natural redundancies in KGs, such as triple (China, located_in, Asia) and triple (Asia, includes, China) may exist in some KGs simultaneously, and they are describing the same fact. Here, located_in and includes are inverse relations for each other. On the other hand, existing KGE models have been able to model most relation patterns, i.e., evaluate the plausibility of triples by utilizing the relation patterns. For example, TransE [10] can model inversion patterns. When there are many natural redundancies relevant to located_in and includes in training KG, even if it has only seen triple (China, located_in, Asia) but not seen triple (Asia, includes, China), the TransE model can still mark a high plausibility score for triple (Asia, includes, China).

However, as far as we know, almost none of the existing KGE models can perfectly model the aforementioned relation patterns. For example, RotatE [13] declares that it can model all of the relation patterns, but it still has a fatal defect in modeling the composition patterns: *It can only model commutative composition patterns, but can not model noncommutative composition patterns.* This defect is also existing in some other KGE models which claim themselves can model composition patterns, such as TransE. Briefly speaking, a composition pattern implies the relation pattern that in the shape of $r_1 \oplus r_2 = r_3$, where $\oplus$ means the ordered composition of r_1 and r_2. If composition pattern $r_1 \oplus r_2 = r_3$ exists in some KG, it means that KG has frequent natural redundancies in the form of $[(e_1, r_1, e_2), (e_2, r_2, e_3), (e_1, r_3, e_3)]$, $e_i(i = 1, 2, 3)$ can be any entity. If $r_1 \oplus r_2 = r_3$ and $r_2 \oplus r_1 = r_3$ are both in a KG, we call $r_1 \oplus r_2 = r_3$ a commutative composition pattern, such as is_on_the_east_of $\oplus$ is_on_the_north_of = is_on_the_northeast_of and is_on_the_north_of $\oplus$ is_on_the_east_of = is_on_the_northeast_of. Otherwise, if only $r_1 \oplus r_2 = r_3$ is in the KG, it is a noncommutative composition pattern, such as is_the_husband_of $\oplus$ is_the_mother_of = is_the_father_of.

Both of RotatE and TransE model the noncommutative composition pattern as the commutative composition pattern by mistake. This mistake will bring severely ridiculous inferences. For example, they will infer (i.e., mark a high score for) triple (Mary, is_the_father_of, Barbara) based on existing triples (Mary, is_the_mother_of, James) and (James, is_the_husband_of, Barbara). The primary cause of this mistake is that they have not taken the design inspiration of their models carefully. They both expect to express a fact triple (h, r, t) through an equation relevant to the embeddings of h, r, and t (noted as boldface letters $\mathbf{h}$, $\mathbf{r}$, and $\mathbf{t}$): $\mathbf{h} \odot \mathbf{r} = \mathbf{t}$, where $\odot$ is some binary operation. Thus, they design the score function in the form of $-\|\mathbf{h} \odot \mathbf{r} - \mathbf{t}\|$, and we can see that the closer the equation is to hold, the higher the plausibility score is. TransE embeds entities and relations into the real number vector space and takes the addition in that space as $\odot$, while RotatE replaces the real numbers with the complex numbers and takes the element-wise multiplication as $\odot$. Since these two operations both satisfy the commutative law, the corresponding two models can only model commutative composition patterns.

Inspired by QuatE [14], which will be discussed in Section 2.1.2, we propose a new KGE model called QuatRotatScalE (or QRSE, for short) in this paper. The main difference from TransE and RotatE is it embeds entities and relations into the quaternion [15] vector space and takes the element-wise multiplication in that space as $\odot$. Because the quaternion multiplication generally does not satisfy the commutative law (but there are special cases where the law holds), QRSE can model both composition patterns. Furthermore, we can prove that QRSE can also model the rest relation patterns. Thus it has become one of the KGE models that can model most relation patterns up to now. We evaluated QRSE and compared it with many baselines in two well-established and widely used real-world datasets FB15k-237 [16] and WN18RR [17]. The results indicate our method has reached the state-of-the-art in link prediction problem.

2. Related Work

At present, there are two classes of methods to solve the knowledge graph completion or link prediction problem. One class of methods is the KGE methods, and the other is the path-finding methods. Both of them are introduced below:

2.1. KGE Method

Embedding methods are widely used in many fields of machine learning since the embeddings of sentences, graphs, and many other data types can be easily transferred to various downstream tasks with only a little task-specific fine-tuning. For example, studies [18,19] first learn the embeddings of sentences and then use these embeddings to perform sentiment classification. Study [20] first learns an embedding for each graph, then use these embeddings to predict the missing labels of graphs. In addition, some other studies learn an embedding vector for each object (i.e., the node in a graph) of a given Heterogeneous Information Network (HIN) in a (semi-)supervised [21] or self-supervised [22] manner. Taking advantage of the learned embeddings of objects, they can fulfill many tasks, e.g., object classification, clustering, and visualization.

In knowledge graph completion or link prediction problem, Knowledge Graph Embedding methods are also the most studied methods. Let us use $\mathcal{E}$ to represent the set of all entities and use $\mathcal{R}$ to represent the set of all relations in KG. KGE methods need to assign a vector representation to every entity $e \in \mathcal{E}$ and relation $r \in \mathcal{R}$, noted in boldface letters $\mathbf{e}$ and $\mathbf{r}$, respectively. $\mathbf{e}$ or $\mathbf{r}$ is also called the embedding of e or r. In addition to this, KGE methods still need to design a score function $f_r(\mathbf{h}, \mathbf{t})$ to mark the plausibility of the triple (h, r, t). The objective of optimization is to mark high scores for the true triples and low scores for the false triples. Based on the type of score function, we can further divide the KGE methods into two sorts, KGE based on difference norm and KGE based on semantic matching:

2.1.1. KGE Based on Difference Norm

The common motivation of this sort of method is they want to use a *triple approximate equation* $f_1(\mathbf{h}, \mathbf{r}) \approx f_2(\mathbf{t}, \mathbf{r})$ to describe any triple (h, r, t), and the strict equation should hold for fact triples. As for the unknown triples, they think the proximity of the two sides can reflect the plausibility of the triple. Thus, the score functions of these methods are always in the form of $f_r(\mathbf{h}, \mathbf{t}) = -\|f_1(\mathbf{h}, \mathbf{r}) - f_2(\mathbf{t}, \mathbf{r})\|$.

Among them, there is a kind of method that is widely studied, called translational methods. We call them "translational" because the origin of this kind of method, TransE, uses the translation transformation to design the triple approximate equation. Precisely, it chooses the real number vector space $\mathbb{R}^k$ as the embedding space and regards the relation embedding $\mathbf{r}$ as a translation transformation from head entity embedding $\mathbf{h}$ to tail entity embedding $\mathbf{t}$. So it designs the triple approximate equation as $\mathbf{h} + \mathbf{r} \approx \mathbf{t}$. Following TransE, many improvements have emerged. TransH [23] claims it is better to assign a hyperplane in embedding space for every relation (the hyperplane's normal vector noted as $\mathbf{r}_p$), and only regards $\mathbf{r}$ as a translation from the projection of $\mathbf{h}$ to the projection of $\mathbf{t}$ on that hyperplane. Hence the triple approximate equation of TransH is $(\mathbf{I} - \mathbf{r}_p \mathbf{r}_p^\top)\mathbf{h} + \mathbf{r} \approx (\mathbf{I} - \mathbf{r}_p \mathbf{r}_p^\top)\mathbf{t}$, where $\mathbf{I}$ is the identity matrix. TransR [24] generalizes TransH, it assigns a linear map to every relation r, noted as transfer matrix $\mathbf{W}_r$. This linear map maps $\mathbf{h}$ and $\mathbf{t}$ into the relation space. Then TransR utilizes the images of $\mathbf{h}$ and $\mathbf{t}$ in the relation space with $\mathbf{r}$ to design the triple approximate equation in TransE's style: $\mathbf{W}_r \mathbf{h} + \mathbf{r} \approx \mathbf{W}_r \mathbf{t}$. Further, StransE [25] assigns each relation r two different transfer matrices $\mathbf{W}_{r,1}$ and $\mathbf{W}_{r,2}$. Similarly, the triple approximate equation is designed as $\mathbf{W}_{r,1} \mathbf{h} + \mathbf{r} \approx \mathbf{W}_{r,2} \mathbf{t}$. These derivative methods of TransE are collectively known as TransX. Their score functions can be written in the form of $f_r(\mathbf{h}, \mathbf{t}) = -\|g_{r,1}(\mathbf{h}) + \mathbf{r} - g_{r,2}(\mathbf{t})\|$, where $g_{r,i}(\cdot)$ denotes a matrix multiplication concerning relation r.

Since the large number of the derivative methods of TransE, some literature uses the translational methods to refer to KGE based on difference norm in general. But this is not accurate enough. Some other methods do not turn to translation transformation to design their triple approximate equations, such as TorusE [26] and RotatE. TorusE chooses a compact Lie group as its embedding space and can be regarded as a special case of RotatE when the embedding modulus are fixed [13]. RotatE embeds entities and relations into the complex number vector space $\mathbb{C}^k$. It wants to replace the translation in $\mathbb{R}^k$ with the rotation in $\mathbb{C}^k$. Specifically, for each element r_i $(1 \leq i \leq k)$ of $\mathbf{r}$, RotatE fixes it as a unitary complex number (i.e., $|r_i| = 1$). Hence the complex multiplication between the i-th element of $\mathbf{h}$ (i.e., h_i) and r_i means h_i rotates in its complex plane with angle $Arg(r_i)$ (i.e., the argument of complex r_i). Let us use ∘ to denote the Hadamard (element-wise) product between two complex vectors, the triple approximate equation of RotatE is $\mathbf{h} \circ \mathbf{r} \approx \mathbf{t}$.

There are some KGE methods with score functions belonging to a special case of difference norm, which is in the form of $-\|\mathbf{h} \odot \mathbf{r} - \mathbf{t}\|$, where $\odot$ is some binary operation. When the ideal optimization is achieved, the triple approximate equations of these methods hold: $\mathbf{h} \odot \mathbf{r} = \mathbf{t}$. This property is useful to explain some abilities to model relation patterns. For example, TransE and RotatE are two of these methods, and because their binary operations are both associative and commutative, they can only model commutative composition patterns. For more details, please see Section 5.

2.1.2. KGE Based on Semantic Matching

The intuition of this sort of method is to measure the plausibility of a triple by inspecting the matching degree of the latent semantics of the two entities and the relation.

There is a family of methods called bilinear models that design score functions as bilinear maps of head and tail entities. RESCAL [9] may be the first bilinear model. It selects real vector space $\mathbb{R}^k$ as the embedding space of entities and assigns a $k \times k$ real matrix $\mathbf{W}_r$ to each relation r. Then it directly applies $\mathbf{W}_r$ to define a bilinear map as the score function. To reduce the complexity of $\mathbf{W}_r$, DistMult [11] restricts $\mathbf{W}_r$ to be a diagonal matrix. So DistMult can express $\mathbf{W}_r$ as a vector $\mathbf{r}$ in $\mathbb{R}^k$ and rewrite the score function in the form of the multi-linear dot product of $\mathbf{h}$, $\mathbf{r}$, and $\mathbf{t}$. To overcome DistMult's weakness in modeling antisymmetry relation pattern, ComplEx [12] extends the embedding space into the complex vector space $\mathbb{C}^k$, and modifies the score function. QuatE [14] further develops ComplEx, it extends the embedding space into the quaternion vector space to obtain better expression ability. DualE [27] uses the dual quaternion vectors to design the embeddings of entities and relations, and chooses the dual quaternion inner product as the score function. DihEdral [28] designs entity embeddings with real vectors, and designs relation embeddings with dihedral group vectors, where each dihedral group is expressed as a second-order discrete real matrix. Although its score function is a bilinear form, which belongs to the type of semantic matching, it is theoretically proven that this score function is equivalent to a difference norm function in the form of $-\|\mathbf{h} \odot \mathbf{r} - \mathbf{t}\|$ for optimizing relation embeddings. So DihEdral has the ability to model composition patterns like TransE and RotatE. Furthermore, since the multiplication of dihedral groups generally does not satisfy the commutative law, DihEdral can model noncommutative composition patterns. However, because the relation embeddings take discrete values, DihEdral has to use special treatments of the relation embeddings during the training process, and the actual performance is easily affected by special treatments. As for QuatE and DualE, their relation embeddings have the potential to model noncommutative composition patterns for the (dual) quaternion multiplication generally does not satisfy the commutative law. Nevertheless, because their score functions belong to the type of semantic matching and lack the theoretical equivalence to a difference norm function in the form of $-\|\mathbf{h} \odot \mathbf{r} - \mathbf{t}\|$ like DihEdral at present, their abilities to model the composition patterns have no strict theoretical guarantees. More precisely, their triple approximate equations, if any, do not necessarily hold when the ideal optimization is achieved, which is a crucial but easily overlooked step for a rigorous proof.

Apart from bilinear models, some models based on neural networks emerged recently. Such as ConvE [17] and ConvKB [29] take the convolutional neural networks to construct the score functions.

Some mentioned KGE methods are listed in Table 1 with their score functions. Their abilities to model the relation patterns are shown in Table 2. We can see that our QRSE can model all relation patterns, which is a rare ability.

Table 1. Score functions and embedding spaces of several KGE models. $\langle \mathbf{a}, \mathbf{b}, \mathbf{c} \rangle \doteq \sum_{i=1}^{k} a_i b_i c_i$ means the multi-linear dot product of vector $\mathbf{a}$, $\mathbf{b}$, and $\mathbf{c}$; $\bar{\cdot}$ denotes conjugate for a complex or quaternion vectors; $\mathrm{Re}(\cdot)$ denotes the real part of a complex number or quaternion; $\otimes$ indicates the Hadamard (element-wise) product between two quaternion vectors. Note that we report an equivalent formulation for QuatE to show the inheritance relationship with ComplEx.

Model	Score Function	Embedding Space
TransE	$-\|\mathbf{h} + \mathbf{r} - \mathbf{t}\|$	$\mathbf{h}, \mathbf{r}, \mathbf{t} \in \mathbb{R}^k$
TransX	$-\|g_{r,1}(\mathbf{h}) + \mathbf{r} - g_{r,2}(\mathbf{t})\|$	$\mathbf{h}, \mathbf{r}, \mathbf{t} \in \mathbb{R}^k$
RotatE	$-\|\mathbf{h} \circ \mathbf{r} - \mathbf{t}\|$	$\mathbf{h}, \mathbf{r}, \mathbf{t} \in \mathbb{C}^k, |r_i| = 1$
RESCAL	$\mathbf{h}^\top \mathbf{W}_r \mathbf{t}$	$\mathbf{h}, \mathbf{t} \in \mathbb{R}^k, \mathbf{W}_r \in \mathbb{R}^{k \times k}$
DistMult	$\langle \mathbf{h}, \mathbf{r}, \mathbf{t} \rangle$	$\mathbf{h}, \mathbf{r}, \mathbf{t} \in \mathbb{R}^k$
ComplEx	$\mathrm{Re}(\langle \mathbf{h}, \mathbf{r}, \bar{\mathbf{t}} \rangle)$	$\mathbf{h}, \mathbf{r}, \mathbf{t} \in \mathbb{C}^k$
QuatE	$\mathrm{Re}(\langle \mathbf{h}, \mathbf{r}, \bar{\mathbf{t}} \rangle)$	$\mathbf{h}, \mathbf{r}, \mathbf{t} \in \mathbb{H}^k, |r_i| = 1$
QRSE	$-\|\mathbf{h} \otimes \mathbf{r} - \mathbf{t}\|$	$\mathbf{h}, \mathbf{r}, \mathbf{t} \in \mathbb{H}^k$

Table 2. The modeling ability comparison for various relation patterns among different models (partial reference from [13]).

Model	Symmetry	Anti-Symmetry	Inversion	Commutative Composition	Noncommutative Composition
TransE	×	✓	✓	✓	×
TransX	✓	✓	×	×	×
RotatE	✓	✓	✓	✓	×
RESCAL	✓	✓	✓	×	×
DistMult	✓	×	×	×	×
ComplEx	✓	✓	✓	×	×
QuatE	✓	✓	✓	×	×
QRSE	✓	✓	✓	✓	✓

Additionally, "supervised relation composition" [30] is a method that can model composition patterns under supervision. But it is not a KGE method. Its goal is to design and train a function model that can take the embeddings of two relations as input and output the embedding of the composite relation of these two relations. The relation embeddings used are provided by an existing KGE model and are fixed once obtained. The supervisory information used for training is mined from the original KGs by another method. This method and the KGE models mentioned before belong to different research directions. The direction of KGE models studies how to directly model relation patterns (including composition patterns) by training entity and relation embeddings from the original KGs.

2.2. Path-Finding Method

This class of methods does not need score function to predict unknown entities, such as MINERVA [31], MultiHopKG [32], and DeepPath [33]. Instead, they should start from the query entity node and follow the direction implied by the query relation to search the KG for the unknown entity. Compared with KGE methods, their results are explainable to some extent since they can provide the inference paths as evidence, but the lack of precision is their weakness at present.

3. Preliminaries

Before introducing our proposed method, let us briefly explain the related concepts and geometric meaning of quaternions.

3.1. A Brief Introduction of Quaternion

As an extened number system from the complex numbers $\mathbb{C}$, quaternions $\mathbb{H}$ [15] have to import three fundamental quaternion units i, j, and k, which are not existing in the real numbers. Each quaternion q can be expressed as $q = a + bi + cj + dk$, where a, b, c, and d are all real numbers. The addition of quaternions is defined as $(a_1 + b_1 i + c_1 j + d_1 k) + (a_2 + b_2 i + c_2 j + d_2 k) \doteq (a_1 + a_2) + (b_1 + b_2)i + (c_1 + c_2)j + (d_1 + d_2)k$. The multiplication between any two fundamental quaternion units are defined as $i^2 = j^2 = k^2 = -1$ and $ij = -ji = k, jk = -kj = i, ki = -ik = j$. Obviously, this multiplication is associative but not commutative. For completeness, we also confirm the multiplication between any one in $\{i, j, k\}$, and a real number is commutative and associative. To obey the distributive law, we consequently get the multiplication between two arbitrary quaternions as:

$$
\begin{aligned}
&(a_1 + b_1 i + c_1 j + d_1 k)(a_2 + b_2 i + c_2 j + d_2 k) \\
\doteq\ & a_1 a_2 - b_1 b_2 - c_1 c_2 - d_1 d_2 \\
& + (a_1 b_2 + b_1 a_2 + c_1 d_2 - d_1 c_2)i \\
& + (a_1 c_2 + c_1 a_2 + d_1 b_2 - b_1 d_2)j \\
& + (a_1 d_2 + d_1 a_2 + b_1 c_2 - c_1 b_2)k\ .
\end{aligned}
\qquad (1)
$$

We can conclude that the multiplication of quaternions (also known as the Hamilton product) holds the associative and distributive law, but does not hold the commutative law in general. Nevertheless, there are some special cases where the commutative law holds.

Some useful concepts of quaternions are listed as follows (let $q = a + bi + cj + dk$):

Modulus: The modulus of q is written as $|q|$ and is defined as $|q| \doteq \sqrt{a^2 + b^2 + c^2 + d^2}$. Since the set of quaternions $\mathbb{H}$ is a linear space isomorphic to $\mathbb{R}^4$ with basis $(1, i, j, k)$, modulus means the length of q intuitively. In addition, if $|q| = 1$, q is called a unit quaternion.

Real and imaginary part: Similar to complex numbers, real number a is the real part of q, and real vector $\mathbf{v} \doteq (b, c, d)^\top$ is the imaginary part of q. Sometimes we would like to express q in the form of $[a, \mathbf{v}]$ for convenience. Then, the multiplication of quaternions can be written as $[a_1, \mathbf{v}_1][a_2, \mathbf{v}_2] = [a_1 a_2 - \mathbf{v}_1 \cdot \mathbf{v}_2, a_1 \mathbf{v}_2 + a_2 \mathbf{v}_1 + \mathbf{v}_1 \times \mathbf{v}_2]$, where $\cdot$ is the dot product and $\times$ is the cross product.

Conjugate: The conjugate of q is the quaternion $\bar{q} \doteq a - bi - cj - dk$. It has thses properties: (1) $\overline{q_1 q_2} = \bar{q}_2 \bar{q}_1$; (2) $q\bar{q} = \bar{q}q = |q|^2$, and from (1), (2) we get (3) $|q_1||q_2| = |q_1 q_2|$. As a corollary, the product of two unit quaternions is also a unit quaternion.

Reciprocal: If $q \neq 0$, the reciprocal of q is the quaternion q^{-1} such that $qq^{-1} = q^{-1}q = 1$, and it is equivalent to define $q^{-1} \doteq \bar{q}/|q|^2$.

3.2. The Geometric Meaning of the Multiplication of Quaternions

To see the geometric meaning of the multiplication of quaternions, we have to view the $\mathbb{H}$ as a linear space isomorphic to $\mathbb{R}^4$ with an orthonormal basis $(1, i, j, k)$. Any q in $\mathbb{H}$ can be expressed in the form as $\rho[\cos\theta, \sin\theta \mathbf{n}]$, where $\rho \geq 0$ and $\|\mathbf{n}\| = 1$. This is because if $q \neq 0$ we could set $\rho = |q|$, $\theta = \arccos(a/|q|)$, and $\mathbf{n} = \mathbf{v}/\|\mathbf{v}\|$, whereas if $q = 0$ we could set $\rho = 0$ and choose θ and $\mathbf{n}$ arbitrarily. Note that $[\cos\theta, \sin\theta\mathbf{n}]$ is a unit quaternion and implies the direction of q, while ρ implies the length of q.

Take another quaternion $p = [s, \mathbf{u}]$ from $\mathbb{H}$, then the product $pq = \rho(p[\cos\theta, \sin\theta\mathbf{n}])$ means a new quaternion reached via two steps from p: (1) changing the direction of p according to $[\cos\theta, \sin\theta\mathbf{n}]$, (2) stretching the length by ρ times. So we only have to see what is the change implied by $p[\cos\theta, \sin\theta\mathbf{n}]$.

Without loss of generality, we suppose $\mathbf{u} \neq \mathbf{0}$ and $\mathbf{u}$ is not parallel with $\mathbf{n}$. Thus we can find another orthonormal basis of $\mathbb{H}$: $([1,0], [0,\mathbf{n}], [0,\mathbf{n}_\perp], [0,\mathbf{n}_\times])$. Here, $\mathbf{n}_\perp \doteq (\mathbf{u} - (\mathbf{u}\cdot\mathbf{n})\mathbf{n})/\|\mathbf{u} - (\mathbf{u}\cdot\mathbf{n})\mathbf{n}\|$ and $\mathbf{n}_\times \doteq \mathbf{n}_\perp \times \mathbf{n}$. Besides, we confirm the coordinates of p under this basis is $(s, l, l_\perp, 0)^\top$, where $l = \mathbf{u}\cdot\mathbf{n}$ and $l_\perp = \|\mathbf{u} - (\mathbf{u}\cdot\mathbf{n})\mathbf{n}\|$. Thus we can split p into two parts: $p = p_1 + p_2$, where $p_1 = [s, l\mathbf{n}]$ and $p_2 = [0, l_\perp\mathbf{n}_\perp]$. So we only have to see what do $p_1[\cos\theta, \sin\theta\mathbf{n}]$ and $p_2[\cos\theta, \sin\theta\mathbf{n}]$ mean.

Since $p_1[\cos\theta, \sin\theta\mathbf{n}] = [s\cos\theta - l\sin\theta, (s\sin\theta + l\cos\theta)\mathbf{n}]$, this product and p_1 are both in the plane with basis $([1,0], [0,\mathbf{n}])$. And we can show the transformation from p_1 to the product by their coordinates under basis $([1,0], [0,\mathbf{n}])$ as:

$$p_1 \to p_1[\cos\theta, \sin\theta\mathbf{n}] : \begin{pmatrix} s \\ l \end{pmatrix} \longrightarrow \begin{pmatrix} s\cos\theta - l\sin\theta \\ s\sin\theta + l\cos\theta \end{pmatrix} = \begin{pmatrix} \cos\theta & -\sin\theta \\ \sin\theta & \cos\theta \end{pmatrix}\begin{pmatrix} s \\ l \end{pmatrix}. \quad (2)$$

So $p_1[\cos\theta, \sin\theta\mathbf{n}]$ means p_1 rotates with angle θ counterclockwise in plane $span([1,0], [0,\mathbf{n}])$. In the same way, since $p_2[\cos\theta, \sin\theta\mathbf{n}] = [0, l_\perp\cos\theta\mathbf{n}_\perp + l_\perp\sin\theta\mathbf{n}_\times]$, this product and p_2 are both in the plane with basis $([0,\mathbf{n}_\perp], [0,\mathbf{n}_\times])$. And we can show the transformation from p_2 to the product by their coordinates under basis $([0,\mathbf{n}_\perp], [0,\mathbf{n}_\times])$ as:

$$p_2 \to p_2[\cos\theta, \sin\theta\mathbf{n}] : \begin{pmatrix} l_\perp \\ 0 \end{pmatrix} \longrightarrow \begin{pmatrix} l_\perp\cos\theta \\ l_\perp\sin\theta \end{pmatrix} = \begin{pmatrix} \cos\theta & -\sin\theta \\ \sin\theta & \cos\theta \end{pmatrix}\begin{pmatrix} l_\perp \\ 0 \end{pmatrix}. \quad (3)$$

So $p_2[\cos\theta, \sin\theta\mathbf{n}]$ means p_2 rotates with angle θ counterclockwise in plane $span([0,\mathbf{n}_\perp], [0,\mathbf{n}_\times])$.

In a word, the change implied by $p[\cos\theta, \sin\theta\mathbf{n}]$ is: (1) Split p into two components p_1 and p_2, where p_1 is in plane $span([1,0], [0,\mathbf{n}])$ and p_2 is in plane $span([0,\mathbf{n}_\perp], [0,\mathbf{n}_\times])$; (2) Rotate p_1 and p_2 with angle θ counterclockwise in each plane simultaneously, as shown in Figure 1; (3) Add two new components together.

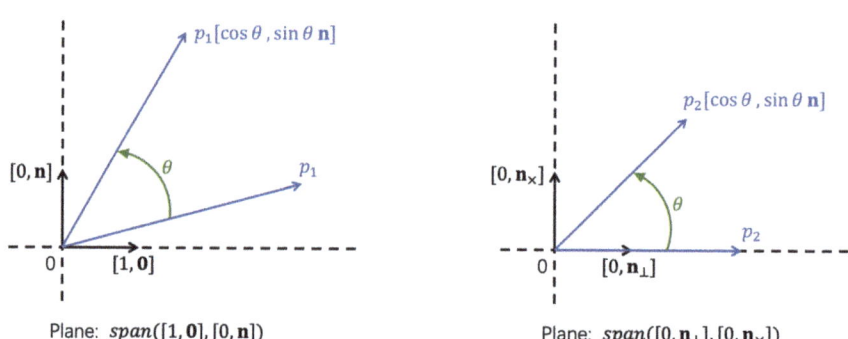

Figure 1. How do p_1 and p_2 rotate when they are multiplied by $[\cos\theta, \sin\theta\mathbf{n}]$ on the right.

As a special case, when $\mathbf{u} = \mathbf{0}$ or $\mathbf{u}$ is parallel with $\mathbf{n}$, $p = p_1$. Thus at that time, $p[\cos\theta, \sin\theta\mathbf{n}]$ only means the rotation in plane $span([1,0], [0,\mathbf{n}])$. Moreover, the geometric meaning of qp is almost the same with pq, except that the rotation for p_2 is clockwise.

4. Proposed Method

Now we start to introduce our proposed KGE model. The embedding spaces of entities $\mathcal{E}$ and relations $\mathcal{R}$ are both the quaternion vector space $\mathbb{H}^k$. For any $e \in \mathcal{E}$ and $r \in \mathcal{R}$, their embeddings are noted as **e** and **r** in lower case bold letters, respectively. The i-th elements of **e** and **r** are written as e_i ($e_i \in \mathbb{H}$) and r_i ($r_i \in \mathbb{H}$) for every integer i from 1 to k. Our model is based on difference norm, so we first define its triple approximate equation as $\mathbf{h} \otimes \mathbf{r} \approx \mathbf{t}$ for any triple (h, r, t). Here, $\otimes$ denotes the Hadamard (element-wise) product between two quaternion vectors. So this triple approximate equation is equivalent to asking for $h_i r_i \approx t_i$ for all i ($1 \leq i \leq k$). In consequence, we get our score function:

$$f_r(\mathbf{h}, \mathbf{t}) \doteq -\|\mathbf{h} \otimes \mathbf{r} - \mathbf{t}\|. \tag{4}$$

Here, $\|\mathbf{q}\|$ is the abbreviation of $\|\mathbf{q}\|_{p,1} \doteq \sum_{i=1}^{k} (|a_i|^p + |b_i|^p + |c_i|^p + |d_i|^p)^{\frac{1}{p}}$, for any quaternion vector $\mathbf{q}$ ($q_i = a_i + b_i \mathbf{i} + c_i \mathbf{j} + d_i \mathbf{k}, 1 \leq i \leq k$). p ($p \geq 1$) is a hyperparameter.

According to the geometric meaning of the quaternion multiplication, we can explain the purpose of this triple approximate equation intuitively: We treat each element of relation embedding r_i (written in the form of $\rho_i[\cos\theta_i, \sin\theta_i \mathbf{n}_i]$) as a two-step transformation from h_i to t_i: (1) Rotate h_i in two planes ($span([1,0],[0,\mathbf{n}_i])$ and $span([0,\mathbf{n}_{i,\perp}],[0,\mathbf{n}_{i,\times}])$) counterclockwise with angle θ_i; (2) Stretch h_i with scaling factor ρ_i. Thus we refer to our model as QuatRotatScalE (or QRSE, for short) due to we use Quaternions with Rotation and Scaling transformations to design the Embedding model.

Optimization

The general objective of KGE models is to return high scores for true triples and low scores for false triples. We adopt negative sampling as our training style to avoid the efficiency loss brought by the huge number of entities like most of the other KGE methods. The training KG usually only contains true triples (positive samples, noted as Ω) without false triples (negative samples). Thus we apply a common way (i.e., corrupting the positive samples) to obtain the negative samples. Suppose (h, r, t) is a positive sample, we can get two sets of negative samples by replacing the head or tail entity with other entities: $\mathcal{N}_h(r,t) \doteq \{(h', r, t) \mid h' \text{ is uniformly sampled from } \mathcal{E} \text{ s.t. } (h', r, t) \notin \Omega\}$ and $\mathcal{N}_t(h,r) \doteq \{(h, r, t') \mid t' \text{ is uniformly sampled from } \mathcal{E} \text{ s.t. } (h, r, t') \notin \Omega\}$. The size of negative samples $\mathcal{N}_h(r,t)$ and $\mathcal{N}_t(h,r)$ is fixed and much smaller than $|\mathcal{E}|$.

Following RotatE [13], we use the loss function on each triple (h, r, t) in the training KG as

$$L = -\log\sigma(\gamma + f_r(\mathbf{h}, \mathbf{t})) - \sum_{(h',r,t') \in \mathcal{N}} p(h', r, t') \log\sigma(-\gamma - f_r(\mathbf{h}', \mathbf{t}')) \tag{5}$$

where σ is the sigmoid function, γ is a fixed margin, and $\mathcal{N}$ is $\mathcal{N}_h(r,t)$ or $\mathcal{N}_t(h,r)$. In practice, $\mathcal{N}$ is regenerated in the same way ($\mathcal{N}_h(r,t)$ or $\mathcal{N}_t(h,r)$) for every positive sample in one training batch. Once it turns to the next training batch, $\mathcal{N}$ should switch the regenerating way. $p(h', r, t')$ is the distribution of self-adversarial negative sampling proposed by RotatE [13] and is defined as

$$p(h', r, t') = \frac{\exp(\alpha f_r(\mathbf{h}', \mathbf{t}'))}{\sum_{(h',r,t') \in \mathcal{N}} \exp(\alpha f_r(\mathbf{h}', \mathbf{t}'))} \tag{6}$$

where α is the temperature of sampling. The self-adversarial negative sampling can moderate the low efficiency of the uniform negative sampling. We also take Adam as our optimizer. Moreover, $p(h', r, t')$ plays a role of importance sampling ratio in L, so it need not backpropagate gradients through it.

5. Theoretic Analysis

5.1. Relation Patterns

As mentioned in introduction Section 1, modeling (i.e., identifying and utilizing) the relation patterns in KGs are the fundamental for KGE models to solve the link prediction problem. There are three types of relation patterns, which are very powerful and widely exist in various KGs [12,13,16,34,35]:

Symmetry/antisymmetry: A relation r is *symmetric (antisymmetric)* if $\forall e_1, e_2 \in \mathcal{E}$, $(e_1, r, e_2) \Rightarrow (e_2, r, e_1)$ $((e_1, r, e_2) \Rightarrow \neg(e_2, r, e_1))$.

Inversion: Relation r_1 is *inverse* to relation r_2 if $\forall e_1, e_2 \in \mathcal{E}$, $(e_1, r_2, e_2) \Rightarrow (e_2, r_1, e_1)$.

Composition: Relation r_1 is *composed* of relation r_2 and relation r_3 if $\forall e_1, e_2, e_3 \in \mathcal{E}$, $(e_1, r_2, e_2) \wedge (e_2, r_3, e_3) \Rightarrow (e_1, r_1, e_3)$. We adopt form $r_2 \oplus r_3 = r_1$ to describe this composition pattern for simplicity. Moreover, if both of $r_2 \oplus r_3 = r_1$ and $r_3 \oplus r_2 = r_1$ make sense, $r_2 \oplus r_3 = r_1$ is a commutative composition pattern. Otherwise, if only $r_2 \oplus r_3 = r_1$ holds, it is a noncommutative composition pattern.

5.2. Abilities to Model Relation Patterns

In this subsection, we prove that QRSE can model symmetry/antisymmetry, inversion, and composition patterns. Additionally, TransE and RotatE are unable to model noncommutative composition patterns. Next, if triple (h, r, t) is in the knowledge graph, we write it in the embedding space as $\mathbf{h} \otimes \mathbf{r} = \mathbf{t}$ for QRSE because its score function is a special case of difference norm $-\|\mathbf{h} \otimes \mathbf{r} - \mathbf{t}\|$ and when the ideal optimization is achieved, we can directly get $\mathbf{h} \otimes \mathbf{r} = \mathbf{t}$ (we can replace $\otimes$ with $+$ or $\circ$ for TransE or RotatE for the same reason).

- **QRSE can model symmetry/antisymmetry patterns**:
  Suppose $\mathbf{e}_2 \otimes \mathbf{r} = \mathbf{e}_1$ and $\mathbf{e}_1 \otimes \mathbf{r} = \mathbf{e}_2$. We can get $\mathbf{e}_1 \otimes \mathbf{r} \otimes \mathbf{r} = \mathbf{e}_1$. It means for any i $(1 \leq i \leq k)$, $e_{1,i} r_i r_i = e_{1,i}$. If $e_{1,i} = 0$, r_i can be any quaternion. But if $e_{1,i} \neq 0$, r_i must satisfies:

$$e_{1,i} r_i r_i = e_{1,i} \iff e_{1,i}^{-1} e_{1,i} r_i r_i = e_{1,i}^{-1} e_{1,i} \iff r_i r_i = 1 \iff r_i = r_i^{-1}. \tag{7}$$

$\because \forall q_1, q_2 \in \mathbb{H}, |q_1||q_2| = |q_1 q_2|, \therefore |r_i| = 1$. $\because \forall q \in \mathbb{H}, q^{-1} = \bar{q}/|q|^2, \therefore r_i = \bar{r}_i$. Thus r_i is 1 or -1. In a word, if $\mathbf{r}$ satisfies $r_i \in \{1, -1\}$ $(1 \leq i \leq k)$, $\mathbf{r}$ models a symmetry pattern, otherwise, it models a antisymmetry pattern.

- **QRSE can model inversion patterns**:
  Suppose $\mathbf{e}_2 \otimes \mathbf{r}_1 = \mathbf{e}_1$ and $\mathbf{e}_1 \otimes \mathbf{r}_2 = \mathbf{e}_2$. We can get $\mathbf{e}_1 \otimes \mathbf{r}_2 \otimes \mathbf{r}_1 = \mathbf{e}_1$. It means for any i $(1 \leq i \leq k)$, $e_{1,i} r_{2,i} r_{1,i} = e_{1,i}$. If $e_{1,i} = 0$, $r_{2,i}$ and $r_{1,i}$ can be any quaternions. But if $e_{1,i} \neq 0$, $r_{2,i}$ and $r_{1,i}$ must satisfy:

$$\begin{aligned} e_{1,i} r_{2,i} r_{1,i} = e_{1,i} &\iff e_{1,i}^{-1} e_{1,i} r_{2,i} r_{1,i} = e_{1,i}^{-1} e_{1,i} \\ &\iff r_{2,i} r_{1,i} = 1 \iff r_{1,i} = r_{2,i}^{-1}. \end{aligned} \tag{8}$$

Define $\mathbf{q}^{-1} \doteq (q_1^{-1}, q_2^{-1}, ..., q_k^{-1})^\top$ for all $\mathbf{q} \in \mathbb{H}^k$, $q_i \neq 0$ $(1 \leq i \leq k)$. We can conclude that if $\mathbf{r}_1 = \mathbf{r}_2^{-1}$, $\mathbf{r}_1$ and $\mathbf{r}_2$ model an inversion pattern.

- **QRSE can model composition patterns**:
  Suppose $\mathbf{e}_1 \otimes \mathbf{r}_2 = \mathbf{e}_2$, $\mathbf{e}_2 \otimes \mathbf{r}_3 = \mathbf{e}_3$, and $\mathbf{e}_1 \otimes \mathbf{r}_1 = \mathbf{e}_3$. We can get $\mathbf{e}_1 \otimes \mathbf{r}_2 \otimes \mathbf{r}_3 = \mathbf{e}_1 \otimes \mathbf{r}_1$. It means for any i $(1 \leq i \leq k)$, $e_{1,i} r_{2,i} r_{3,i} = e_{1,i} r_{1,i}$. If $e_{1,i} = 0$, $r_{2,i}$, $r_{3,i}$, and $r_{1,i}$ can be any quaternions. But if $e_{1,i} \neq 0$, $r_{2,i}$, $r_{3,i}$, and $r_{1,i}$ must satisfy:

$$e_{1,i} r_{2,i} r_{3,i} = e_{1,i} r_{1,i} \iff e_{1,i}^{-1} e_{1,i} r_{2,i} r_{3,i} = e_{1,i}^{-1} e_{1,i} r_{1,i} \iff r_{2,i} r_{3,i} = r_{1,i}. \tag{9}$$

Moreover, if we still suppose $\mathbf{e}_4 \otimes \mathbf{r}_3 = \mathbf{e}_5$, $\mathbf{e}_5 \otimes \mathbf{r}_2 = \mathbf{e}_6$, and $\mathbf{e}_4 \otimes \mathbf{r}_1 = \mathbf{e}_6$. Then if $e_{4,i} \neq 0$ for all i $(1 \leq i \leq k)$, $r_{3,i}$, $r_{2,i}$, and $r_{1,i}$ must satisfy: $r_{3,i} r_{2,i} = r_{1,i}$. This means $r_{2,i} r_{3,i} = r_{3,i} r_{2,i}$. If we note $r_{2,i} = [a_{2,i}, \mathbf{v}_{2,i}]$ and $r_{3,i} = [a_{3,i}, \mathbf{v}_{3,i}]$, then we get:

$$\begin{aligned} & [a_{2,i} a_{3,i} - \mathbf{v}_{2,i} \cdot \mathbf{v}_{3,i},\ a_{2,i} \mathbf{v}_{3,i} + a_{3,i} \mathbf{v}_{2,i} + \mathbf{v}_{2,i} \times \mathbf{v}_{3,i}] \\ =& [a_{3,i} a_{2,i} - \mathbf{v}_{3,i} \cdot \mathbf{v}_{2,i},\ a_{3,i} \mathbf{v}_{2,i} + a_{2,i} \mathbf{v}_{3,i} + \mathbf{v}_{3,i} \times \mathbf{v}_{2,i}] \\ \iff& \mathbf{v}_{2,i} \times \mathbf{v}_{3,i} = \mathbf{v}_{3,i} \times \mathbf{v}_{2,i} \\ \iff& \mathbf{v}_{2,i} = 0 \text{ or } \mathbf{v}_{3,i} = \lambda \mathbf{v}_{2,i}\ (\lambda \in \mathbb{R}). \end{aligned} \tag{10}$$

We can conclude that if $r_2 \otimes r_3 = r_1$, r_2, r_3, and r_1 model a composition pattern. Moreover, if $v_{2,i}$ is parallel with $v_{3,i}$ for all $i (1 \le i \le k)$, it is a commutative composition pattern, otherwise, it is a noncommutative composition pattern.

- **TransE and RotatE can not model noncommutative composition patterns, and they can only model commutative composition patterns:**
  For TransE, we suppose $e_1 + r_2 = e_2$, $e_2 + r_3 = e_3$, $e_1 + r_1 = e_3$, $e_4 + r_3 = e_5$, $e_5 + r_2 = e_6$, but $e_4 + r_1 \ne e_6$, which means the composition of relation r_2 and r_3 is noncommutative. From the first three equations we get $r_2 + r_3 = r_1$, and from the fourth and fifth equations we get $e_4 + r_3 + r_2 = e_6$. Because $r_2 + r_3 = r_3 + r_2$, we get $e_4 + r_1 = e_6$, which contradicts the condition. Therefore TransE can not model noncommutative composition patterns. If we replace the condition $e_4 + r_1 \ne e_6$ with $e_4 + r_1 = e_6$, then the composition of relation r_2 and r_3 becomes commutative composition. In this case the previous contradiction disappears, which means TransE can model commutative composition patterns.
  As for RotatE, we suppose $e_1 \circ r_2 = e_2$, $e_2 \circ r_3 = e_3$, $e_1 \circ r_1 = e_3$, $e_4 \circ r_3 = e_5$, $e_5 \circ r_2 = e_6$, but $e_4 \circ r_1 \ne e_6$, which means the composition of relation r_2 and r_3 is noncommutative. Since $r_2 \circ r_3 = r_3 \circ r_2$ (the multiplication of complex numbers satisfies the commutative law), we can get $e_4 \circ r_1 = e_6$ in the same way as TransE, which contradicts the condition. So RotatE can not model noncommutative composition patterns. If we replace the condition $e_4 \circ r_1 \ne e_6$ with $e_4 \circ r_1 = e_6$, then the composition of relation r_2 and r_3 becomes commutative composition. In this case the previous contradiction disappears, which means RotatE can model commutative composition patterns.

6. Experiments

In this section, we first evaluate QRSE with RotatE on a small knowledge graph made up of two families. This experiment will verify the superiority of QRSE in modeling noncommutative composition relation patterns. Then we evaluate QRSE and compare it with many baselines in two well-established and widely used real-world datasets.

6.1. Experiment on a KG about Two Families

There are 10 entities and 4 relations in the training KG. Each entity is a member of one family, and each relation is a type of kinship. Such as triple (Am1, son, Am2) means Am1 has a son called Am2. All of the triples in the training KG are shown in Figure 2, where each directed edge represents a triple, and its direction is from the head entity to the tail entity. Furthermore, the test set contains two triples: (Bm1, daughter_of_son, Bw3) and (Bm1, son_of_daughter, Bm3). We let models predict the head or tail entity for each test triple, so there are 4 queries during the test process.

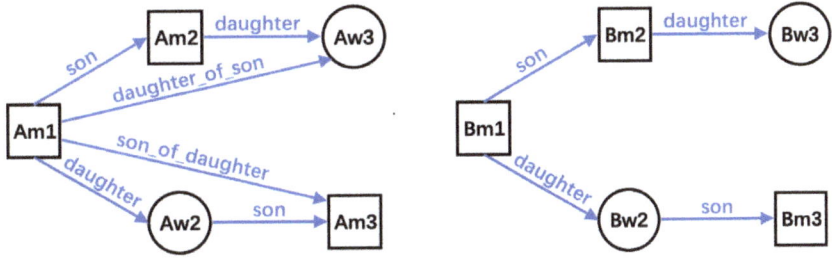

Figure 2. The structure of the training KG, where each directed edge represents a triple.

Since we need 2 and 4 real numbers to determine a complex number and a quaternion respectively, we take $\mathbb{C}^{10}$ (i.e., embedding dimension $k = 10$) and $\mathbb{H}^5$ (i.e., $k = 5$) as the entity embedding spaces for RotatE and QRSE. Thus in practice, we can express the entity embeddings of RotatE and QRSE as 20-D real vectors. Except for the embedding dimension k, we keep other hyperparameters the same for two models: batch size $b = 10$, self-adversarial sampling temperature $\alpha = 0$, fixed margin $\gamma = 0$, learning rate $\eta = 0.001$, negative sampling size $|\mathcal{N}| = 2$, and the order of norm in score function $p = 2$.

We use Hit@1 to measure the performance of models, which means the proportion of the correctly answered queries (i.e., the true answer's score is ranked first) among all test queries. The test performances of RotatE and QRSE are shown in Figure 3. We can see that QRSE gets the best Hit@1 value 1.00 quickly, and after that, it keeps this Hit@1 value all the time during the training process. RotatE also gets the best Hit@1 value quickly; however, after that, it's Hit@1 value is always fluctuating between 0.5 and 1.00 randomly. To explain this phenomenon, we inspected the detailed scores and embeddings at step 16,000, which is large enough to ensure the convergence of the two models.

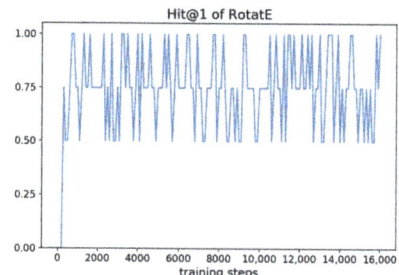 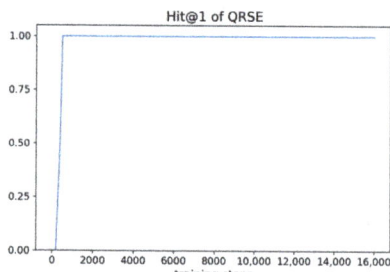

Figure 3. The Hit@1 performance of RotatE and QRSE on the test set along with the training process.

The top 3 scores for all test queries are shown in Table 3. For the two queries to predict the head entity Bm1, the scores of Bm1 are much higher than the second candidate entities for both RotatE and QRSE. However for the two queries to predict the tail entities Bm3 and Bw3, only QRSE keeps the large gap between the first and the second score, whereas RotatE gives very close scores for the top 2 candidate entities on both of the two queries. This result reveals that, for RotatE, the score ranks for the top 2 candidates are unstable and easily affected by the random noise on the two queries to predict the tail. That is why the Hit@1 of RotatE fluctuates during training. Moreover, for RotatE, the top 2 candidate entities are Bm3 and Bw3 for both of the two tail queries. Thus we guess the embeddings of these two entities are also very close.

Table 3. The detailed test results of RotatE and QRSE at training step 16000.

Model	Test Triple	Entity to Predict	Ranked Scores for Top 3 Candidate Entities
RotatE	(Bm1, son_of_daughter, Bm3)	Bm1	Bm1: -0.0224, Am2: -5.4026, Bm3: -5.6849
		Bm3	Bm3: -0.0224, Bw3: -0.0227, Bm1: -5.6840
	(Bm1, daughter_of_son, Bw3)	Bm1	Bm1: -0.0178, Am2: -5.3975, Bm3: -5.6668
		Bw3	Bw3: -0.0178, Bm3: -0.0179, Bm1: -5.6654
QRSE	(Bm1, son_of_daughter, Bm3)	Bm1	Bm1: -0.00087, Aw2: -4.8535, Aw3: -4.9947
		Bm3	Bm3: -0.00087, Aw3: -5.2716, Bw3: -5.3903
	(Bm1, daughter_of_son, Bw3)	Bm1	Bm1: -0.00094, Aw2: -4.8532, Aw3: -4.9948
		Bw3	Bw3: -0.00094, Bm3: -5.3905, Am2: -5.8095

Figure 4 shows the embeddings of Bm3 and Bw3 in RotatE and QRSE. As we guessed, the two embeddings are very close in RotatE but different in QRSE. This result verified that RotatE is unable to model noncommutative composition patterns, but QRSE can. Let us use the bold type to indicate the embeddings as before. For RotatE, along with the training process, **Bw3** will close to **Bm2** ∘ **daughter**, and **Bm2** will close to **Bm1** ∘ **son**. Hence **Bw3** will close to **Bm1** ∘ **son** ∘ **daughter**. Similarly, **Bm3** will close to **Bm1** ∘ **daughter** ∘ **son**. Because **daughter** ∘ **son** = **son** ∘ **daughter**, **Bw3** will close to **Bm3**. For QRSE, **daughter** ⊗ **son** ≠ **son** ⊗ **daughter** in general, so **Bw3** will not close to **Bm3**.

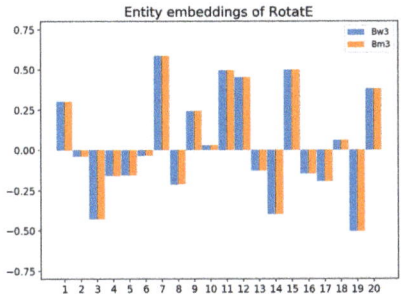
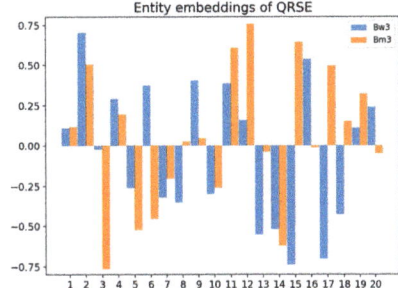

Figure 4. The entity embeddings of RotatE and QRSE on training step 16,000. The 10-D complex or 5-D quaternion vectors are expressed in the corresponding 20-D real vectors.

We can also show this fact by directly inspecting the relation embeddings of the two models in Figure 5. Note that daughter ⊕ son and son ⊕ daughter are not the relations in KG but the combinations made up of the relations in KG. Their "embeddings" are calculated from the embeddings of some relations (e.g., the "embedding" of daughter ⊕ son is **daughter** ⊗ **son** in QRSE). Obviously, the embeddings of son_of_daughter and daughter_of_son are almost the same in RotatE, since they are both approaching **daughter** ∘ **son** during training. However, they are different in QRSE since the embeddings of son_of_daughter is approaching **daughter** ⊗ **son** while the other is approaching **son** ⊗ **daughter** during training.

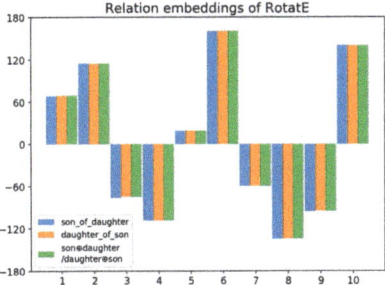
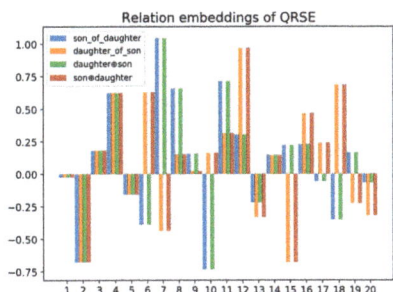

Figure 5. The relation embeddings of RotatE and QRSE on training step 16,000. A relation embedding of RotatE has 10 complex numbers with modulus 1, which are determined by their 10 arguments. Thus we express it by its 10 arguments in angle degrees. For QRSE, we continue use the corresponding 20-D real vectors for each relation embedding.

6.2. Experiment on Real-World Datasets

6.2.1. Experimental Setting

We still evaluated our method on two well-established and widely used real-world knowledge graphs, FB15k-237 [16] and WN18RR [17], with several strong baselines.

FB15k-237 is selected from FB15k [10], which is a subset of Freebase and mainly records the facts about movies, actors, and sports. Because FB15k suffers from test leakage through inverse relations: there are too many inversion patterns in KG, which are too easy to model, and even a simple rule-based model can perform well [17]. To make the results more reliable, FB15k-237 removed these inverse patterns. The statistics of FB15k-237 are 14,541 entities, 237 relations, 272,115 training triples, 17,535 validation triples, and 20,466 test triples.

WN18RR is selected from WN18 [10], which is a subset of WordNet and records lexical relations between words. WN18 also suffers from test leakage through inverse relations, so WN18RR removed its inverse patterns too. The statistics of WN18RR are 40,943 entities, 11 relations, 86,835 training triples, 3034 validation triples, and 3134 test triples.

The ranges of the hyperparameters for the grid search are following RotatE as embedding dimension $k \in \{125, 250, 500, 1000\}$, batch size $b \in \{512, 1024, 2048\}$, and fixed margin $\gamma \in \{3, 6, 9, 12, 18, 24, 30\}$. Moreover, we searched self-adversarial sampling temperature α in $\{0.5, 1.0, 1.5\}$, learning rate η in $\{0.00005, 0.0001, 0.0002\}$, negative sampling size $|\mathcal{N}|$ in $\{16, 32, 64, 128\}$, and the order p of norm in score function in $\{2, 3, 4, 5, 6, 7\}$. The embeddings are also uniformly initialized.

From each test triple (h, r, t), we generate two queries: $(?, r, t)$ and $(h, r, ?)$. Given each query, we can make a candidate triple by placing a candidate entity on the place of the entity to predict. The score of each candidate entity is just the score of its corresponding candidate triple. While ranking all the scores, we omit the scores of those candidate triples that already exist in training, validation, and test set, except the true answer for the query. This process is called "filtered" in some literature and is widely adopted in existing methods to avoid possibly flawed evaluation.

6.2.2. Results

We adopt these standard evaluation measures for both of the datasets: the mean reciprocal rank of the true answers (MRR), the proportion of queries whose true answers are ranked in the top k (Hit@k).

The link prediction results on real-world datasets are shown in Table 4. The result of TransE is taken from [29]. The results of DistMult, ComplEx, and ConvE are taken from [17]. The results of RotatE and DualE are taken from [13,27], respectively. The results of DihEdral(STE) and DihEdral(Gumbel) are taken from [28], where STE and Gumbel are two special treatments of the discrete relation embeddings. The results of QuatE and QuatE(TC) are taken from [14], where TC indicates the corresponding model using type constraints [36]. From this table, we can see that QRSE outperforms RotatE largely on all datasets and evaluation measures. This result supports our analysis of the modeling ability of the composition patterns. Compared with DihEdral(STE) and DihEdral(Gumbel), we find QRSE outperforms both of them on the two real-world datasets, whereas DihEdral(STE) is better than DihEdral(Gumbel) on FB15k-237 and just the opposite on WN18RR. This means the performance of DihEdral is easily affected by special treatments, and DihEdral can not perform well on the two real-world datasets simultaneously. Compared with DualE and QuatE, we find QRSE outperforms both of them too. This means that among all methods using (dual) quaternions so far, QRSE has explored the greatest potential of the (dual) quaternion space in the implementation of knowledge graph embedding. Because type constraints [36] can integrate prior knowledge into various KGE models and can significantly improve their performance in link prediction tasks, QRSE and most baselines display the results without it for fairness except QuatE(TC). Surprisingly, we can even see that QRSE is superior to QuatE with type constraints overall slightly. The success on this unfair comparison further demonstrates the excellence of QRSE. Overall, our QRSE has reached the state-of-the-art in link prediction problem on real-world datasets.

Table 4. Link prediction results on the FB15k-237 and WN18RR datasets. Numbers in boldface are the best, and underlined numbers are the second best.

Model	FB15k-237				WN18RR			
	MRR	Hit@1	Hit@3	Hit@10	MRR	Hit@1	Hit@3	Hit@10
TransE	0.294	-	-	0.465	0.226	-	-	0.501
DistMult	0.241	0.155	0.263	0.419	0.43	0.39	0.44	0.49
ComplEx	0.247	0.158	0.275	0.428	0.44	0.41	0.46	0.51
ConvE	0.325	0.237	0.356	0.501	0.43	0.40	0.44	0.52
RotatE	0.338	0.241	0.375	0.533	0.476	0.428	0.492	0.571
DualE	0.330	0.237	0.363	0.518	0.482	0.440	0.500	0.561
DihEdral(STE)	0.320	0.230	0.353	0.502	0.480	**0.452**	0.491	0.536
DihEdral(Gumbel)	0.300	0.204	0.332	0.496	0.486	0.442	0.505	0.557
QuatE	0.311	0.221	0.342	0.495	0.481	0.436	0.500	0.564
QuatE(TC)	0.348	0.248	0.382	**0.550**	0.488	0.438	**0.508**	**0.582**
QRSE	**0.350**	**0.252**	**0.390**	0.548	**0.491**	0.443	**0.508**	0.581

7. Conclusions and Future Work

We proposed a novel knowledge graph embedding model QRSE based on quaternions. QRSE is a KGE model that can model the noncommutative composition patterns. Besides, it can also model many other relation patterns, such as symmetry/antisymmetry, inversion, and commutative composition patterns. We varified these properties by theoretical proofs and experiments. From the definition of the triple approximate equation of QRSE, we can easily see that QRSE is a generalization of RotatE. Conversely, in some special cases, QRSE will degenerate to RotatE. For example, the case when the coefficients of j and k are fixed as 0 for all quaternions in all embeddings, and the modulus of all quaternions in relation embeddings are fixed as 1. Before QRSE, QuatE has already generalized ComplEx through replacing the complex numbers with quaternions. However, QuatE only takes advantage of that quaternions are more expressive than complex numbers. While our method not only leverages the expression advantage but also exploits the noncommutative property of quaternion multiplication to model the noncommutative composition patterns. The results of experiments on real-world datasets show that QRSE reaches the state-of-the-art on the link prediction problem. For future work, our plan is to combine QRSE with deep models for natural language processing. With its help, we expect deep models to achieve higher accuracy on question answering tasks and make the model's answers more interpretable.

Author Contributions: Conceptualization, C.X., C.F., D.C. and X.H.; methodology, C.X.; software, C.X.; validation, C.X. and C.F.; formal analysis, C.X.; investigation, C.X.; resources, D.C. and X.H.; data curation, C.X.; writing—original draft preparation, C.X.; writing—review and editing, C.X., C.F., D.C. and X.H.; visualization, C.X.; supervision, D.C. and X.H.; project administration, D.C. and X.H.; funding acquisition, D.C. and X.H. All authors have read and agreed to the published version of the manuscript.

Funding: This work was supported in part by The National Nature Science Foundation of China (Grant Nos. 62273302, 62036009, U1909203, 61936006), in part by Innovation Capability Support Program of Shaanxi (Program No. 2021TD-05).

Institutional Review Board Statement: Not applicable.

Informed Consent Statement: Not applicable.

Data Availability Statement: The data presented in this study and the code are available on request from the corresponding author.

Conflicts of Interest: The authors declare no conflict of interest. The funders had no role in the design of the study; in the collection, analyses, or interpretation of data; in the writing of the manuscript; or in the decision to publish the results.

References

1. Zhang, F.; Yuan, N.J.; Lian, D.; Xie, X.; Ma, W. Collaborative Knowledge Base Embedding for Recommender Systems. In Proceedings of the 22nd ACM SIGKDD International Conference on Knowledge Discovery and Data Mining, San Francisco, CA, USA, 13–17 August 2016; pp. 353–362. [CrossRef]
2. Hao, Y.; Zhang, Y.; Liu, K.; He, S.; Liu, Z.; Wu, H.; Zhao, J. An End-to-End Model for Question Answering over Knowledge Base with Cross-Attention Combining Global Knowledge. In Proceedings of the 55th Annual Meeting of the Association for Computational Linguistics, ACL 2017, Vancouver, BC, Canada, 30 July–4 August 2017; Volume 1, pp. 221–231. [CrossRef]
3. Xiong, C.; Power, R.; Callan, J. Explicit Semantic Ranking for Academic Search via Knowledge Graph Embedding. In Proceedings of the 26th International Conference on World Wide Web, WWW 2017, Perth, Australia, 3–7 April 2017; pp. 1271–1279. [CrossRef]
4. Yang, B.; Mitchell, T.M. Leveraging Knowledge Bases in LSTMs for Improving Machine Reading. In Proceedings of the 55th Annual Meeting of the Association for Computational Linguistics, ACL 2017, Vancouver, BC, Canada, 30 July–4 August 2017; Volume 1, pp. 1436–1446. [CrossRef]
5. Auer, S.; Bizer, C.; Kobilarov, G.; Lehmann, J.; Cyganiak, R.; Ives, Z.G. DBpedia: A Nucleus for a Web of Open Data. In Proceedings of the The Semantic Web, 6th International Semantic Web Conference, 2nd Asian Semantic Web Conference, ISWC 2007 + ASWC 2007, Busan, Republic of Korea, 11–15 November 2007; pp. 722–735. [CrossRef]
6. Bollacker, K.D.; Evans, C.; Paritosh, P.; Sturge, T.; Taylor, J. Freebase: A collaboratively created graph database for structuring human knowledge. In Proceedings of the ACM SIGMOD International Conference on Management of Data, SIGMOD 2008, Vancouver, BC, Canada, 10–12 June 2008; pp. 1247–1250. [CrossRef]
7. Suchanek, F.M.; Kasneci, G.; Weikum, G. Yago: A core of semantic knowledge. In Proceedings of the 16th International Conference on World Wide Web, WWW 2007, Banff, AB, Canada, 8–12 May 2007; pp. 697–706. [CrossRef]
8. Miller, G.A. WordNet: A Lexical Database for English. *Commun. ACM* **1995**, *38*, 39–41. [CrossRef]
9. Nickel, M.; Tresp, V.; Kriegel, H. A Three-Way Model for Collective Learning on Multi-Relational Data. In Proceedings of the 28th International Conference on Machine Learning, ICML 2011, Bellevue, Washington, DC, USA, 28 June–2 July 2011; pp. 809–816.
10. Bordes, A.; Usunier, N.; García-Durán, A.; Weston, J.; Yakhnenko, O. Translating Embeddings for Modeling Multi-relational Data. In Proceedings of the Advances in Neural Information Processing Systems 26: 27th Annual Conference on Neural Information Processing Systems 2013, Lake Tahoe, NV, USA, 5–8 December 2013; pp. 2787–2795.
11. Yang, B.; Yih, W.; He, X.; Gao, J.; Deng, L. Embedding Entities and Relations for Learning and Inference in Knowledge Bases. In Proceedings of the 3rd International Conference on Learning Representations, ICLR 2015, San Diego, CA, USA, 7–9 May 2015.
12. Trouillon, T.; Welbl, J.; Riedel, S.; Gaussier, É.; Bouchard, G. Complex Embeddings for Simple Link Prediction. In Proceedings of the 33nd International Conference on Machine Learning, ICML 2016, New York, NY, USA, 19–24 June 2016; pp. 2071–2080.
13. Sun, Z.; Deng, Z.; Nie, J.; Tang, J. RotatE: Knowledge Graph Embedding by Relational Rotation in Complex Space. In Proceedings of the 7th International Conference on Learning Representations, ICLR 2019, New Orleans, LA, USA, 6–9 May 2019.
14. Zhang, S.; Tay, Y.; Yao, L.; Liu, Q. Quaternion Knowledge Graph Embeddings. In Proceedings of the Advances in Neural Information Processing Systems 32: Annual Conference on Neural Information Processing Systems 2019, NeurIPS 2019, Vancouver, BC, Canada, 8–14 December 2019; pp. 2731–2741.
15. Hamilton, W.R. LXXVIII. On quaternions; or on a new system of imaginaries in Algebra: To the editors of the Philosophical Magazine and Journal. *Philos. Mag. J. Sci.* **1844**, *25*, 489–495. [CrossRef]
16. Toutanova, K.; Chen, D. Observed versus latent features for knowledge base and text inference. In Proceedings of the 3rd Workshop on Continuous Vector Space Models and their Compositionality, Beijing, China, 31 July 2015; pp. 57–66.
17. Dettmers, T.; Minervini, P.; Stenetorp, P.; Riedel, S. Convolutional 2D Knowledge Graph Embeddings. In Proceedings of the Thirty-Second AAAI Conference on Artificial Intelligence, (AAAI-18), the 30th innovative Applications of Artificial Intelligence (IAAI-18), and the 8th AAAI Symposium on Educational Advances in Artificial Intelligence (EAAI-18), New Orleans, LA, USA, 2–7 February 2018; pp. 1811–1818.
18. Chen, L.; Wang, F.; Yang, R.; Xie, F.; Wang, W.; Xu, C.; Zhao, W.; Guan, Z. Representation learning from noisy user-tagged data for sentiment classification. *Int. J. Mach. Learn. Cybern.* **2022**, *13*, 3727–3742. [CrossRef]
19. Zhao, W.; Guan, Z.; Chen, L.; He, X.; Cai, D.; Wang, B.; Wang, Q. Weakly-Supervised Deep Embedding for Product Review Sentiment Analysis. *IEEE Trans. Knowl. Data Eng.* **2018**, *30*, 185–197. [CrossRef]
20. Yang, Y.; Guan, Z.; Zhao, W.; Weigang, L.; Zong, B. Graph Substructure Assembling Network with Soft Sequence and Context Attention. *IEEE Trans. Knowl. Data Eng.* **2022**, 1. [CrossRef]
21. Yang, Y.; Guan, Z.; Li, J.; Zhao, W.; Cui, J.; Wang, Q. Interpretable and Efficient Heterogeneous Graph Convolutional Network. *IEEE Trans. Knowl. Data Eng.* **2023**, *35*, 1637–1650. [CrossRef]
22. Yang, Y.; Guan, Z.; Wang, Z.; Zhao, W.; Xu, C.; Lu, W.; Huang, J. Self-supervised Heterogeneous Graph Pre-training Based on Structural Clustering. In Proceedings of the Advances in Neural Information Processing Systems, New Orleans, LA, USA, 16–19 May 2022; Oh, A.H., Agarwal, A., Belgrave, D., Cho, K., Eds.; 2022.

23. Wang, Z.; Zhang, J.; Feng, J.; Chen, Z. Knowledge Graph Embedding by Translating on Hyperplanes. In Proceedings of the 28th AAAI Conference on Artificial Intelligence, Québec City, QC, Canada, 27–31 July 2014; pp. 1112–1119.
24. Lin, Y.; Liu, Z.; Sun, M.; Liu, Y.; Zhu, X. Learning Entity and Relation Embeddings for Knowledge Graph Completion. In Proceedings of the 29thh AAAI Conference on Artificial Intelligence, Austin, TX, USA, 25–30 January 2015; pp. 2181–2187.
25. Nguyen, D.Q.; Sirts, K.; Qu, L.; Johnson, M. STransE: A novel embedding model of entities and relationships in knowledge bases. In Proceedings of the NAACL HLT 2016, The 2016 Conference of the North American Chapter of the Association for Computational Linguistics: Human Language Technologies, San Diego, CA, USA, 12–17 June 2016; pp. 460–466.
26. Ebisu, T.; Ichise, R. TorusE: Knowledge Graph Embedding on a Lie Group. In Proceedings of the Thirty-Second AAAI Conference on Artificial Intelligence, (AAAI-18), the 30th innovative Applications of Artificial Intelligence (IAAI-18), and the 8th AAAI Symposium on Educational Advances in Artificial Intelligence (EAAI-18), New Orleans, LA, USA, 2–7 February 2018; pp. 1819–1826.
27. Cao, Z.; Xu, Q.; Yang, Z.; Cao, X.; Huang, Q. Dual quaternion knowledge graph embeddings. In Proceedings of the AAAI Conference on Artificial Intelligence, Virtual Event, 2–9 February 2021; Volume 35, pp. 6894–6902.
28. Xu, C.; Li, R. Relation Embedding with Dihedral Group in Knowledge Graph. In Proceedings of the 57th Annual Meeting of the Association for Computational Linguistics, Florence, Italy, 28 July–2 August 2019; pp. 263–272.
29. Nguyen, D.Q.; Nguyen, T.D.; Nguyen, D.Q.; Phung, D.Q. A Novel Embedding Model for Knowledge Base Completion Based on Convolutional Neural Network. In Proceedings of the 2018 Conference of the North American Chapter of the Association for Computational Linguistics: Human Language Technologies, NAACL-HLT, New Orleans, LA, USA, 1–6 June 2018; Volume 2, pp. 327–333.
30. Chen, W.; Hakami, H.; Bollegala, D. Learning to compose relational embeddings in knowledge graphs. In Proceedings of the Computational Linguistics: 16th International Conference of the Pacific Association for Computational Linguistics, PACLING 2019, Hanoi, Vietnam, 11–13 October 2019; Revised Selected Papers 16; Springer: Berlin/Heidelberg, Germany, 2020; pp. 56–66.
31. Das, R.; Dhuliawala, S.; Zaheer, M.; Vilnis, L.; Durugkar, I.; Krishnamurthy, A.; Smola, A.; McCallum, A. Go for a Walk and Arrive at the Answer: Reasoning Over Paths in Knowledge Bases using Reinforcement Learning. In Proceedings of the 6th International Conference on Learning Representations, ICLR 2018, Vancouver, BC, Canada, 30 April–3 May 2018.
32. Lin, X.V.; Socher, R.; Xiong, C. Multi-Hop Knowledge Graph Reasoning with Reward Shaping. In Proceedings of the 2018 Conference on Empirical Methods in Natural Language Processing, Brussels, Belgium, 31 October–4 November 2018; pp. 3243–3253.
33. Xiong, W.; Hoang, T.; Wang, W.Y. DeepPath: A Reinforcement Learning Method for Knowledge Graph Reasoning. In Proceedings of the 2017 Conference on Empirical Methods in Natural Language Processing, EMNLP 2017, Copenhagen, Denmark, 9–11 September 2017; pp. 564–573.
34. Guu, K.; Miller, J.; Liang, P. Traversing Knowledge Graphs in Vector Space. In Proceedings of the 2015 Conference on Empirical Methods in Natural Language Processing, EMNLP 2015, Lisbon, Portugal, 17–21 September 2015; pp. 318–327.
35. Lin, Y.; Liu, Z.; Luan, H.; Sun, M.; Rao, S.; Liu, S. Modeling Relation Paths for Representation Learning of Knowledge Bases. In Proceedings of the 2015 Conference on Empirical Methods in Natural Language Processing, EMNLP 2015, Lisbon, Portugal, 17–21 September 2015; pp. 705–714.
36. Krompaß, D.; Baier, S.; Tresp, V. Type-constrained representation learning in knowledge graphs. In Proceedings of the The Semantic Web-ISWC 2015: 14th International Semantic Web Conference, Bethlehem, PA, USA, 11–15 October 2015; Proceedings, Part I 14; Springer: Berlin/Heidelberg, Germany, 2015; pp. 640–655.

Disclaimer/Publisher's Note: The statements, opinions and data contained in all publications are solely those of the individual author(s) and contributor(s) and not of MDPI and/or the editor(s). MDPI and/or the editor(s) disclaim responsibility for any injury to people or property resulting from any ideas, methods, instructions or products referred to in the content.

MDPI AG
Grosspeteranlage 5
4052 Basel
Switzerland
Tel.: +41 61 683 77 34

Electronics Editorial Office
E-mail: electronics@mdpi.com
www.mdpi.com/journal/electronics

Disclaimer/Publisher's Note: The title and front matter of this reprint are at the discretion of the Guest Editors. The publisher is not responsible for their content or any associated concerns. The statements, opinions and data contained in all individual articles are solely those of the individual Editors and contributors and not of MDPI. MDPI disclaims responsibility for any injury to people or property resulting from any ideas, methods, instructions or products referred to in the content.

www.ingramcontent.com/pod-product-compliance
Lightning Source LLC
LaVergne TN
LVHW070736100526
838202LV00013B/1247